PRAISE FOR
Admission Matters: What Students and Parents Need to Know About Getting into College

Fourth Edition

"If you are looking for a book where you can get the best possible advice from authors who have the ability to anticipate and answer your questions with a marvelous combination of experience and insight, then this is the book you need to buy . . . quickly!"

Gary L. Ross, vice president and dean of admission, Colgate University

"Written by deeply experienced and respected professionals, *Admission Matters* aims to 'empower students and their families to make good choices . . . and retain their balance and sanity at the same time.' Bullseye!"

Philip Ballinger, associate vice provost for enrollment and undergraduate admissions, University of Washington

"You can't ask for a better introduction into college admissions. From exploring colleges, to applying, and deciding, *Admission Matters* continues to be an essential, comprehensive book for high school students and families."

Art D. Rodriguez, dean of admission and financial aid, Vassar College

"*Admission Matters* demystifies college admissions like no other book has, with the most current information on testing, paying for college, and finding the right college."

Robert Massa, senior vice president for enrollment and institutional planning, Drew University, and former vice president, Dickinson College and dean of enrollment, Johns Hopkins University

"I absolutely love this book and highly recommend it as a must-read resource for students and parents going through the college admission search and application process. It's easy to understand, current, and contains spot on advice."

Bob Bardwell, school counselor and director of school counseling, Monson High School (MA)

"A thoughtful, thorough tour of the college selection process. *Admission Matters* goes well beyond the basics, and invites the student to personalize the college process as few books do."

Patrick O'Connor, associate dean, college counseling, Cranbrook Kingswood Upper School (MI)

"Clear, comprehensive, and sane advice from trusted experts. This updated guide provides a road map to what is often a bewildering and anxious process for students and families."

Debra Shaver, dean of admission, Smith College

"Comprehensive, insightful, based on current research and insider expertise. A straightforward guide to today's complex college admission process that is anything but straightforward."

Bruce Reed, co-founder, Compass Education Group

"I wish I had this book when my daughters were applying to college. *Admission Matters* somehow finds clarity amidst the complicated set of confusing, even contradictory college admission practices."

Kirk Brennan, director of undergraduate admission, University of Southern California

"An enormously useful and easy-to-read guide to getting into college. While others may claim to be the 'gold standard,' this one is the real deal."

Nancy Griesemer, independent educational consultant and long-time blogger on colleges and the admissions process

"All readers of *Admission Matters*—whether students, parents, or counselors—will benefit from the deep insights and expertise of the authors. Accessible and a good read, the book provides much needed guidance for the college admissions process."

Sam Carpenter, senior assistant director of admissions, Duke University

"This book is a 'must read' for all families going through the college admissions process. If you are looking for a guide to help you approach the college search in a meaningful way, this is the book for you."

Angel Perez, vice president for enrollment and student success, Trinity College

"*Admission Matters* provides a straightforward, no nonsense blueprint to navigate the complex college admissions process."

Jon Westover, senior associate director of undergraduate admissions, University of Massachusetts, Amherst

"As an experienced counselor and the parent of a high school junior, I found this book packed with so many helpful and informative ideas to share with both my students and my own children. A must-have for every college-bound student's household."

Kathi Moody, school counselor, Lynnfield High School (MA)

"This brand new edition of *Admission Matters* is just what the doctor ordered. It is filled with wise, up-to-date information and insider knowledge. Families will love it."

Marjorie Hansen Shaevitz, author and founder, adMISSIONPOSSIBLE

"This is a must-have resource for students and families navigating the college admissions process. The authors are respected, long-time professionals and get it right from the search to enrollment."

Jeff Rickey, vice president and dean, admissions and financial aid, St. Lawrence University

ADMISSION MATTERS

What Students and Parents Need to Know About Getting into College

FOURTH EDITION

Sally P. Springer

Jon Reider

Joyce Vining Morgan

JB JOSSEY-BASS™

A Wiley Brand

Published by Jossey-Bass
A Wiley Brand
One Montgomery Street, Suite 1000, San Francisco, CA 94104-4594—www.josseybass.com

Jossey-Bass books and products are available through most bookstores. To contact Jossey-Bass directly call our Customer Care Department within the U.S. at 800-956-7739, outside the U.S. at 317-572-3986, or fax 317-572-4002.

Wiley publishes in a variety of print and electronic formats and by print-on-demand. Some material included with standard print versions of this book may not be included in e-books or in print-on-demand. If this book refers to media such as a CD or DVD that is not included in the version you purchased, you may download this material at http://booksupport.wiley.com. For more information about Wiley products, visit www.wiley.com.

Library of Congress Cataloging-in-Publication Data is Available

ISBN 9781119328391 (Paper)
ISBN 9781119329909 (ePDF)
ISBN 9781119329893 (ePUB)

Cover design: Wiley
Cover image: © FatCamera/Getty Images, Inc.

Printed in the United States of America
FOURTH EDITION
PB Printing   10 9 8 7 6 5 4 3 2 1

Contents

Acknowledgments   xi

Introduction   xiii

Part 1   What You Need to Know Before You Begin   1

  1   Why Has College Admissions Become So Competitive?   3
  2   What Do Colleges Look for in an Applicant?   20
  3   How Do Colleges Make Their Decisions?   45
  4   How Colleges (and Students) Differ: Finding What Fits   62

Part 2   Making the Right Choices for You   99

  5   Where Should You Apply?   101
  6   The Big Tests   127
  7   Deciding About Early Decision and Other Early Options   150
  8   Paying the Bill   164

Part 3   Tackling Your Applications   197

  9   Applying Well, Part I: The Application and the Essay   199
 10   Applying Well, Part II: Recommendations, Interviews, and Activities   219
 11   Making the Most of Your Special Talents   242
 12   Students with Special Circumstances   266
 13   Advice for International Students   289

Part 4 Bringing the Process to a Close   **311**

  14 Making *Your* Decision After the Colleges Make Theirs   **313**
  15 What Matters Most: Advice to Parents and Students   **336**

Appendixes

  A. College Research Worksheet   347
  B. Essay Prompts, 2017–2018   351
  C. Financial Aid Shopping Sheet   353
  D. Cost of Attendance Worksheet   355

College Preparation Time Line   357

Resources   367

Notes   375

About the Authors   383

Index   385

To our children

Acknowledgments

Many colleagues have shared our goal of improving the college admissions process for students and parents and have helped us, in ways large and small, in the writing of the fourth edition of *Admission Matters*. We are grateful to all of them: Jed Applerouth, Terry Axe, Carolyn Barr, Bonnie Burks Becker, Jeffrey Corton, Jeffrey Durso-Finley, Frances Fee, Duffy Grant, Vicki Kleinman, Douglas Long, Marybeth Kravets, Nancy Hargrave Meislahn, Bruce Poch, John H. Provost Jr., John Raftrey, Bruce Reed, Zita Riedlová, Gary Ross, Pam Schachter, Beatrice Schultz, Catherine Sinclair, Leanne Stillman, Ken Suratt, Marilyn van Loben Sels, Sue Wilbur, and Kim Zwitserloot.

We are indebted as well to the Jossey-Bass editorial team for the fourth edition—Kate Bradford, senior editor; Connor O'Brien, project editor; and Sharmila Boominathan, production editor—for guiding us so capably through the publication process.

Three people who have made lasting contributions to *Admission Matters* through all four editions deserve special acknowledgment and recognition. The insights and wisdom of Marian Franck, coauthor of the first edition, remain an integral part of the book. Lesley Iura, then education editor at Jossey-Bass, saw the value and potential of *Admission Matters* when it first arrived on her desk more than 13 years ago. Later, as publisher at Jossey-Bass, she continued to support *Admission Matters* as a valued part of the Jossey-Bass list. Professor emeritus Håkon Hope has contributed encouragement, insights, and support from the earliest stages of planning for the first edition through the final stages of reviewing page proofs for the fourth edition. His dedication to his students and their academic and personal development has been an inspiration throughout.

Finally, we want to thank the thousands of high school and college students whose lives we have touched over the course of our careers, both in the classroom and as counselors. Their dreams and aspirations have encouraged us to try to ease the path for others yet to undertake the college admissions journey.

Introduction

It is easy to understand why the college admissions process has become such a challenge, and even an ordeal, for many students and their families. Everywhere they look, families are barraged by evidence of "college mania." Online and print media regularly regale readers with horror stories about the competition involved in gaining admission to selective colleges as application numbers rise and admissions rates fall, sometimes dramatically in a given year. Classmates, neighbors, coworkers, and even virtual strangers are all too eager to share tales about terrific kids with great academic and extracurricular records who were denied admission by the colleges of their choice.

As likelihood of admission becomes harder to predict at many schools, students find themselves applying to an increasing number of colleges to protect themselves. Of course, one major consequence of such behavior is an overall increase in application numbers and corresponding declines in admissions rates at those schools, feeding the very problem students are hoping to address by submitting more applications.

Adding to the challenge is the continuing rise in the cost of college, with the sticker price at some private four-year colleges now approaching $70,000 per year. Recent changes in the standardized testing policies of many schools, as well as changes in the tests themselves, have also contributed to the uncertainty surrounding college admission.

The result of all of this is that families often find themselves caught up in a high-stakes competition in which they are uncertain about the rules and even more uncertain about the outcome. Parents feel uncomfortable trying to support their children in a process that they do not completely understand and are not sure they can afford. Even those who consider themselves knowledgeable may quickly find that much of what they know is out-of-date or based on unverifiable hearsay.

Frank Bruni, author of a widely acclaimed book entitled *Where You Go Is Not Who You'll Be: An Antidote to the College Admissions Mania,* dedicated his book as follows: "To all the high school kids in this country who are dreading the crossroads of college admissions and to all the young adults who felt ravaged by it. We owe you and the whole country a better, more constructive way."[1] We fully agree.

College admissions does not have to be, and should not be, an ordeal. A clear understanding of the process can empower students and their families to make good choices for themselves and allow them to retain their balance and sanity at the same time. That has always been the goal of *Admission Matters,* from its first edition in 2005 through this fourth edition today.

We have written this book to demystify the college admissions process by explaining how it works and to level the playing field for those without access to extensive assistance from knowledgeable high school counselors or sometimes any counselors at all. It will also help those who have access to good counseling but would still like some extra support. Our advice is designed for students planning to apply to any four-year college, whether highly selective or not.

Admission Matters explains

- How rankings motivated by profits contribute to the application frenzy
- How the admissions process really works, and what you can, and cannot, control
- The ways in which colleges differ that really matter
- How you can build a list of colleges that are a good fit for you and submit strong, competitive applications to gain admission to them
- How and why many colleges use standardized tests and how you can best prepare for them

- What recent changes in standardized tests as well as testing policies at many schools mean for you

- When an early application makes sense, when it can be a mistake, and how to tell the difference

- How financial aid works, what you can expect from it, and how you can increase your chances of receiving more

- How to prepare strong applications that can help you distinguish yourself from other applicants

- What you—student and parent—can do to work together in appropriate and respectful ways throughout the admissions process to achieve a happy outcome

And much more. In this thoroughly revised fourth edition of *Admission Matters,* we have worked hard to address the many changes that have occurred in the world of college admissions since our last edition. We want you, our student and parent readers, to begin the college admissions journey confidently with the latest and most complete information available. As before, students with disabilities, international students, and transfer students will find much needed guidance to address their special circumstances, as will athletes, artists, and homeschoolers. Information for first-generation college students and undocumented students is included as well. We want *Admission Matters* to continue to be the most up-to-date, clear, insightful, supportive, and practical book on college admissions anywhere.

We recognize, however, that you may want more information on certain topics than space allows us to include. To help you access that additional information easily, we have provided a list of resources, many of them on the web, that give detailed information on topics such as financial aid and athletic recruiting to supplement our own coverage. To keep *Admission Matters* as up-to-date as possible, we are maintaining a website with free updates and additional materials. You can find it at www.admissionmatters.com. We welcome your feedback.

We feel we are especially well qualified to be your guides. Among the three of us, we have more than 100 years of experience in secondary and higher education in the roles of high school teacher and college counselor, college admissions officer, college professor and administrator, and independent educational consultant. Collectively we have worked with thousands of students across the United States and abroad. We are also proud parents of successful college graduates, so we have experienced the admissions process firsthand from the parent perspective as well. We are delighted that our readers in the general public have found *Admission Matters* enjoyable and easy to read, and we are honored that professional colleagues use it widely as a text in courses on college admissions for those studying to be counselors themselves.

We hope *Admission Matters* will serve as your trusted road map through the college admissions journey.

PART 1

What You Need to Know Before You Begin

Chapter 1   Why Has College Admissions Become So Competitive?

Chapter 2   What Do Colleges Look for in an Applicant?

Chapter 3   How Do Colleges Make Their Decisions?

Chapter 4   How Colleges (and Students) Differ: Finding What Fits

Why Has College Admissions Become So Competitive?

For members of the baby boom generation born between 1946 and 1964, applying to college was a pretty simple process. Those bound for a four-year college usually planned to go to a school in their home state or one fairly close by; many considered a college even 300 miles from home to be far away. Few students felt the need to apply to more than two or three colleges, and many applied to just one. They chose their colleges based on location, program offerings, cost, and difficulty of admission, with a parental alma mater sometimes thrown in for good measure. For the most part, the whole process was fairly low key. If students did their homework carefully before deciding where to apply, the outcome was usually predictable. Of course, there were surprises—some pleasant and some disappointing—but nothing that would raise the issue of college as to the level of a national obsession.

IT USED TO BE SIMPLE . . . BUT NOT ANYMORE

Fast-forward 50 to 60 years when headlines tell a very different story for students applying to college now: "Why Is College Admissions Such a Mess,"[1] "Applied to Stanford or Harvard? You Probably Didn't Get In. Admit Rates Drop, Again,"[2] "New SAT Brings New Challenges, Same Old Pressure,"[3] "Best, Brightest and

Rejected: Elite Colleges Turn Away up to 95%,"[4] "How College Admissions Has Turned into Something Akin to 'The Hunger Games,'"[5] "Why Colleges Aggressively Recruit Applicants Just to Turn Them Down,"[6] and "The Absurdity of College Admissions."[7]

Colleges themselves make equally jarring announcements. In spring 2003, Harvard announced that for the first time it had accepted just under 10 percent of the students who applied for freshman admission for the class of 2007, or about 2,000 out of 21,000 applicants. This was a new low not only for Harvard but also for colleges nationwide. But much more was to come. By spring 2016, the admissions rate at Harvard had fallen to 5.2 percent out of an applicant pool of over 39,000 for the class of 2020, and at least nine other colleges had joined Harvard in the "under 10 percent" club. Among them was the University of Chicago, reporting an admissions rate of less than 9 percent for the class of 2020, down from a little less than 16 percent five years earlier and just over 38 percent a decade before.

Many public universities, particularly state flagship campuses, have also experienced dramatic growth in applications as well as falling admission rates. For example, UC Berkeley received 82,000 applications for the freshman class of 2020 and admitted 17.5 percent. Ten years prior, the campus received fewer than 42,000 applications and admitted 23.8 percent.

These are just a few of the many colleges reporting record-breaking numbers of applications and record-low rates of admission, continuing a trend that began two decades earlier. What has happened to change the college admissions picture so dramatically in such a relatively short time?

POPULATION GROWTH

The simple explanation seems to be supply and demand: more high school graduates than ever are now competing for seats in the freshman class. After declining somewhat in the late 1980s and early 1990s, the number of students graduating from high school in the United States has risen steadily. In 1997 there were 2.6 million graduates; by 2013, the number had grown to almost 3.5 million. Although the numbers are now declining slightly, they are projected to stay at or above 3.4 million until 2028.[8]

> I don't think anyone is complacent about getting a high-quality applicant pool.
>
> HARVARD UNIVERSITY
> ADMISSIONS OFFICER

SOCIAL CHANGES

But it turns out that the increase in applications is not just because of population growth. Application numbers have risen much faster than the age cohort because of important social changes. Not only are more students graduating from high school each year but also a greater percentage of them are interested in going to college. Studies confirm that a college diploma increases lifetime earnings, and many desirable careers require education beyond the bachelor's degree. As a result, more students are seeking to attend four year colleges, including students from underrepresented minority groups who previously attended college at much lower rates.

At the same time, colleges themselves have increased their efforts to attract large, diverse pools of applicants. Many have mounted aggressive programs to spread the word about their offerings nationally and internationally. Through colorful brochures mailed directly to students, e-mail blitzes and social media activity, visits to high schools by admissions officers, college nights at local hotels, and information booths at college fairs, colleges are reaching out to prospective freshmen in the United States and abroad with unprecedented energy and at great expense.

Sophisticated marketing techniques are used not only by colleges that may have problems filling their freshman class but also by colleges with an overabundance of qualified applicants. And it works! As a result, more and more college-bound students have become aware of and are willing to seriously consider colleges far away from home. Rising standards of living across the globe are also contributing to the number of students from abroad, particularly Asia, choosing to study in the United States.

THE ROLE OF THE INTERNET

In addition, the Internet has played a major role in how students approach college admissions. Although printed material and in-person presentations still help students learn about different colleges, the web has become the primary source of information for students. Students can visit campuses through sophisticated online virtual tours and videos and find answers to many of their questions from college Facebook pages, FAQs posted on their websites, and by tracking college-sponsored blogs and Twitter, Instagram, and Snapchat feeds. Colleges have invested heavily in technology to showcase themselves.

The Internet has also made it easier than ever to apply to college. Applications can be completed and submitted online, saving a lot of the time and effort that traditional paper applications once required. Simplifying things even more, more than 700 colleges now accept the Common Application, a standardized application in which a student can put in his or her basic information just once and then submit it online to up to 20 of those colleges.

With admission harder to predict, students are now submitting more applications than ever before. Ten to 12 applications are now the norm at many private schools and high-performing public high schools; 15 or more applications are not uncommon. Through technology students can apply to an ever-larger number of colleges.

All of these factors taken together—growth in the population of 18 year olds, greater interest in college, sophisticated marketing efforts, ready access to information, and ease of applying made possible by the Internet—explain why it is harder to get into college now than ever before.

But even that is not the whole answer.

> As word spreads about the competition for college admission, students respond by applying to even more colleges to increase their chances of acceptance. In so doing, they end up unwittingly contributing to the very problem they are trying to solve for themselves.
>
> HIGH SCHOOL COUNSELOR CONCERNED ABOUT THE TREND

WHERE THE REAL CRUNCH LIES

Many people are quite surprised to learn that with relatively few exceptions, most four-year colleges in the United States still accept well over half of their applicants. In fact, each May, the National Association for College Admission Counseling posts on its website a list of hundreds of colleges still seeking applicants for the fall. Many of these have vacancies well into the summer. How can this fact be reconciled with the newspaper headlines (not to mention firsthand reports from students and parents) about a crisis of hyper-selectivity in college admissions?

It turns out that the real crunch in admissions—the crunch that drives the newspaper headlines and the anxiety that afflicts many families at college application time—applies to only about 150 of the most selective colleges that attract applicants from all over the country and the world. What's wrong with all the rest? Nothing, of course, except that they aren't in that list of 150. Bill Mayher, a college advisor, summarizes the problem succinctly: "It's hard for kids to get into colleges because they only want to get into colleges that are hard to get into."[9]

WHAT IS SELECTIVITY ALL ABOUT?

The percentage of students offered admission to a college is a major factor in determining its selectivity. As the number of applications to a college increases, its admissions rate decreases. Another key factor affecting selectivity is the academic strength of the applicant pool because strong applicants tend to self-select when applying to certain colleges, especially some smaller ones, well-known for their academic rigor. Both of these factors—admissions rate and strength of the applicant pool—help determine the selectivity of a particular school. Complicating matters even more is that some schools have different admissions processes for different programs, with some programs, such as engineering or business, more selective than others within the same school.

Our Definition of Selectivity

To simplify our discussion here, we define *selectivity* only in terms of admissions rate and define a *selective* college as one with an overall admissions rate of less than 50 percent. We further divide selective colleges into four categories: ultra-selective colleges (those admitting less than 10 percent of their applicants), super-selective colleges (those admitting less than 20 percent of their applicants), highly selective colleges (those admitting less than 35 percent of applicants), and very selective colleges (those admitting less than 50 percent of applicants). In the following box we include colleges that offer a broad array of programs and not those that have a highly specialized mission such as military academies, conservatories, or those offering instruction in only one academic area such as business. We will discuss these specialized programs further on in *Admission Matters*, but for now we are not including them in the data presented here.

Our selectivity classifications are arbitrary, of course, and they don't consider the self-selection factor we previously noted. Nevertheless, they provide a general idea of the relative difficulty of gaining admission to various schools. Although

⚏ Colleges by Admissions Rate for the Class of 2020

Ultra-selective (less than 10 percent of applicants admitted)

- Brown University
- Caltech
- University of Chicago
- Claremont McKenna College
- Columbia University
- Harvard University
- MIT
- University of Pennsylvania
- Pomona College
- Princeton University
- Stanford University
- Yale University

Super-selective (less than 20 percent of applicants admitted)

- Amherst College
- Barnard College
- University of California, Berkeley
- Bowdoin College
- Colby College
- Colorado College
- Cornell University
- Dartmouth College
- Duke University
- Georgetown University
- Grinnell College
- Harvey Mudd College
- Johns Hopkins University
- University of California, Los Angeles
- Middlebury College
- Northwestern University

- University of Notre Dame
- Pitzer College
- Rice University
- University of Southern California
- Swarthmore College
- Tufts University
- Vanderbilt University
- Washington University, St. Louis
- Wesleyan University
- Williams College

Highly Selective (less than 35 percent of applicants admitted)

- American University
- Bard College
- Bates College
- Boston College
- Boston University
- Bucknell College
- Carleton College
- Carnegie Mellon University
- Colgate University
- Davidson College
- Emory University
- Franklin and Marshall College
- Georgia Tech
- Hamilton College
- Haverford College
- Kenyon College
- Lafayette College
- Lehigh University
- University of Michigan, Ann Arbor

- New York University
- University of North Carolina
- Northeastern University
- Oberlin College
- Reed College
- University of Richmond
- Scripps College
- Skidmore College
- Trinity College (Connecticut)
- Tulane University
- University of Rochester
- Vassar College
- University of Virginia
- Wake Forest University
- Washington and Lee College
- Wellesley College

Very Selective Colleges (less than 50 percent of applicants admitted)

- Baylor University
- Binghamton University
- Brandeis University
- Bryn Mawr College
- Case Western Reserve University
- University of Connecticut
- Connecticut College
- University of California, Davis
- Denison University
- Dickinson College
- University of Florida
- Fordham University

- George Washington University
- Gettysburg College
- College of the Holy Cross
- University of California, Irvine
- University of LaVerne
- Macalester College
- University of Maryland
- University of Miami
- University of Minnesota, Twin Cities
- Muhlenberg College
- North Carolina State University, Raleigh
- Occidental College
- Ohio State University

- Pepperdine University
- Rensselaer Polytechnic Institute
- St. Lawrence University
- University of California, San Diego
- University of California, Santa Barbara
- Sarah Lawrence College
- Smith College
- University of South Florida
- Southern Methodist University
- Southwestern University
- Spelman College
- Stony Brook University
- Syracuse University

- Texas Christian University
- Trinity University
- University of Tulsa
- Union College
- Villanova University
- Washington and Jefferson College
- College of William and Mary
- University of Wisconsin, Madison
- Worcester Polytechnic Institute

Note: This list is not all-inclusive and omits schools with a highly specialized focus.

over 2,000 nonprofit four-year institutions of higher education in the United States admit 50 percent or more of their applicants (and many admit at least 75 percent), many students focus their attention on the colleges that fall into the four groups we have just defined as selective.

The students applying to these colleges (and especially those in the super-selective and ultra-selective tiers) are the ones experiencing the "crisis" in college admissions. The crisis does not affect those applying to community colleges or seeking admission to the many colleges that accept most or all of their applicants. Nevertheless, it is very real to those who are applying to selective colleges in the next few years. You (or your child) may be one of them. In fact, that may be why you are reading this book. We will help you understand all aspects of the college admissions process, build a college list that is right for you, and submit strong applications.

But you don't have to plan to apply to schools we define as selective for this book to be valuable reading. If you'll be applying to some of the many schools that admit at least half of their applicants, this book will help you, too. All students need to understand the admissions process, and all face the challenges of identifying colleges that will be a good fit and then submitting strong applications. We wrote *Admission Matters* to help all students take the college admissions journey successfully.

WHY IS THERE SO MUCH INTEREST IN A SMALL GROUP OF COLLEGES?

What is behind the intense interest in the small group of colleges and universities that is driving the headlines about a crisis in college admissions, and, in particular, why is there a mystique surrounding the colleges in the Ivy League and a few others accorded similar status? Just what benefits do these elite colleges bestow (or do people believe they bestow) on their graduates?

Prestige, of course, is one obvious answer. The more selective a college, the more difficult it is to get into and usually the greater the prestige associated with being admitted. The student enjoys the prestige directly, and parents do so also by association. Parents are often the primary driver of the push toward prestige, but students also report similar pressures from peers in high school. And, of course, some students seek prestige themselves. Over the last generation, going to a highly ranked college has become a status symbol of greater value than almost any other consumer good, in part because, unlike an expensive car, it cannot simply be purchased if you have enough money.

Although some people openly acknowledge considering prestige in college choice, many more cite the assumed quality of the educational experience as the basis for their interest in an elite college. But this rationale often depends on the unstated and untested assumption that a good indicator of the quality of something is how much others seek it. People assume that selective colleges offer a better education: the more selective, the higher the quality. But is this really true?

Take the eight colleges in the Ivy League, for example: Brown University, Columbia University, Cornell University, Dartmouth College, Harvard University, Princeton University, University of Pennsylvania, and Yale University. One counselor we know refers to them as the "climbing vine" schools to take away some of the glamour attached to the common brand. The Ivy League originally referred only to a football league. (At first, only seven colleges belonged. Brown eventually joined as the eighth member, although several other colleges were considered possibilities at the time.)

> Lots of times it's kids, I think, trying to define themselves by their school choice, not so much choosing the school that's right for them, but trying to look good through it. I'm not sure if they get it from parents or from other kids or from teachers. But they get it from somewhere.
>
> VOLUNTEER IN COUNSELING OFFICE AT PRIVATE HIGH SCHOOL

Over time, though, the term *Ivy League* became synonymous with prestige and a very strong academic reputation rather than an athletic league. The admissions rate of each Ivy places it in the ultra-selective or super-selective category. Certainly, each has fine students and faculty members renowned for their research. Everyone agrees that they are excellent schools, but do the Ivies automatically offer undergraduates a better educational experience than many other institutions? The answer, commonplace to those in academic circles but surprising to much of the public, is assuredly no.

THE RANKINGS GAME

A major contributor to the mystique of selective colleges has been the annual rankings of colleges published since 1983 by *U.S. News and World Report*. Over time, the rankings became so popular that they outgrew the magazine itself and became a separate annual guidebook simply called *Best Colleges*. A number of other rankings have emerged as competitors, but the *U.S. News* rankings are the best known and most influential.

> Harvard is perhaps the most overrated institution of higher learning in America. This is not to imply that Harvard isn't a good school—on the contrary, Harvard is an excellent school. But its reputation creates an unattainable standard; no school could ever be as good as most people think Harvard is.
>
> COMMENT BY A HARVARD STUDENT

Although *U.S. News* no longer exists as a print magazine, the rankings continue through the guidebook and an accompanying website published every year in August that feature extensive information and advice about applying to college, as well as rankings based on reputational and complex statistical formulas. The yearly rankings drive the sales of *Best Colleges* and generate considerable media attention and controversy among those, including us, who believe the ranking process is fundamentally flawed.

Concern about the rankings is not new. More than 20 years ago, Gerhard Casper, the president of Stanford University, expressed his concern about the rankings to the editor of *U.S. News* as follows: "As the president of a university that is among the top-ranked universities, I hope I have the standing to persuade you that much about these rankings—particularly their specious formulas and spurious precision—is utterly misleading."[10]

WHAT GOES INTO THE *U.S. NEWS* RANKINGS?

For the 2016 rankings, a little less than one quarter—22.5 percent to be exact—of a college's ranking is based on reputational ratings it receives in the poll that *U.S. News* conducts annually of college presidents, provosts, admissions deans, and a small group of high school counselors. The administrators are asked to rate the academic quality of undergraduate programs at schools with the same mission as their own (for example, liberal arts colleges or research universities) on a scale of 1 to 5 from "marginal" to "distinguished," with an option to respond "don't know." The counselors are asked to rate both liberal arts colleges and research universities. Many of the recipients of the questionnaire acknowledge that they lack the kind of detailed knowledge of other colleges that they would need to respond meaningfully. Why would the president of George Washington University be familiar with the undergraduate program at Georgia Tech? The response rate is usually fairly low: less than 50 percent for college administrators and less than 10 percent for the high school counselors.

The remaining 77.5 percent of a college's ranking is based on data collected in five categories, each weighted in the final calculation as follows: retention and graduation rate (22.5 percent), faculty resources (20 percent), student selectivity (12.5 percent), financial resources (10 percent), alumni giving (5 percent), and graduation rate performance (7.5 percent).[11]

U.S. News collects all of these measures annually for each college, puts them into a formula that weights them differentially, and then computes an overall "ranking." To avoid comparing apples with oranges, *U.S. News* ranks campuses of the same type, so that research universities and liberal arts colleges, for example, are ranked separately. (We'll discuss the differences between these two kinds of institutions, as well as others, in chapter 4 when we look at factors to consider in choosing colleges.) Every few years, *U.S. News* slightly modifies its formula, ostensibly to demonstrate its precision and respond to criticism.

Overall, the rankings don't change much from year to year, although a school's position may bounce up or down a few notches because of a change in the formula or some aberration in a statistic reported for a given year. Does its quality relative to its peers really change significantly in one or two years? We think not. Critics of the rankings argue that meaningful changes in college quality cannot be measured in the short term and that *U.S. News* changes the formula primarily to appear fresh and up-to-date—and to sell more guidebooks.

MORE CONCERNS ABOUT RANKINGS

Critics have pointed out that although the *U.S. News* variables may contribute indirectly to educational quality (perhaps higher salaries lead to more motivated faculty members, and smaller classes mean more personal attention), educators do not agree on how those variables can be used to measure the quality of a college. To make things worse, colleges can manipulate directly or indirectly some of the factors in the *U.S. News* formula to raise their standing. Alumni, boards of trustees, and even bond-rating agencies on Wall Street pay close attention to the rankings and expect to see "improvement." As much as college leaders disparage rankings, they are too high profile and too influential to be ignored.

Under pressure, some colleges have actively worked to look better in ways that have little to do with educational quality but will boost the school's ranking. One common but harmless approach that has been used for many years is the production of elegant, full-color booklets that typically highlight a college's new programs and facilities, as well as its ambitious plans for the future. In addition to distributing them for fundraising and other purposes, some college presidents send them to their colleagues at other campuses in the hope that the booklets will raise awareness of their college and possibly lead to a higher reputation rating when the *U.S. News* questionnaire arrives the following year. No one knows if this actually works, but some colleges expend considerable effort in the

> Now more than ever, people believe that the ranking—or the presumed hierarchy of "quality" or "prestige"—of the college or university one attends matters, and matters enormously. More than ever before, education is being viewed as a commodity . . . The large and fundamental problem is that we are at risk of it all seeming and becoming increasingly a game. What matters is less the education and more the brand.[12]
>
> LEE BOLLINGER, PRESIDENT OF COLUMBIA UNIVERSITY

> While rankings such as this should always be taken with a grain of salt, it is certainly a clear sign that we are a top university and recognized as such.[13]
>
> COLLEGE PRESIDENT COMMENTING ON JUST-RELEASED RANKINGS SHOWING AN IMPROVEMENT FOR HIS SCHOOL

hope that it does. Much more troubling are recent disclosures by several well-known colleges that admissions staff members misrepresented data used in the rankings in an apparent effort to enhance their school's position.

WHY ARE RANKINGS SO POPULAR?

It is not surprising that students and parents turn to rankings such as those published by *U.S. News* when they think about colleges. Deciding where to apply isn't easy, and having supposed experts do the evaluating is an attractive alternative to trying to figure things out on your own, especially if you have no experience. We accept ratings that assess washing machines, restaurants, football teams, hospitals, and movies, so why not colleges, too?

College rankings, though, are very different. Although they offer the illusion of precision, the rankings simply don't measure what most people think they measure: the educational experience for an individual student. Doing that requires a personal look at a college through the eyes of that student. No standardized ranking can hope to evaluate how you as an individual might fare at a certain college.

There is no easy substitute for investing the time and effort to determine which colleges will be a good fit for you. Merely knowing which ones are the most selective or enjoy the highest reputations among college administrators (which, as we have said, is essentially what the *U.S. News* rankings are telling you) doesn't get you very far toward finding a place where you will thrive and learn.

ADMISSIONS RATE AND YIELD AND HOW THEY CONTRIBUTE TO COLLEGE FRENZY

Rankings aside, a college's admissions rate or selectivity is the one figure that captures the public's attention and the most headlines. A decline in the admit rate from the previous year is often interpreted as a reflection of a college's increased quality, not just the result of successful marketing. Sample headline: "College *X* Admits Record Low Percentage of Applicants." This is news.

FACTORS THAT AFFECT ADMISSIONS RATE

Aggressive outreach to students to encourage them to apply, although the college knows that they will admit only a fraction of those applying, is the easiest way for a college to become more selective. Although most colleges engage in outreach

---

I overheard a conversation at a reception for the parents of newly admitted students. A mom was chatting with a young admissions officer who was mingling with parents on the lawn of the president's house. "I have a question I'd like to ask you," she said. "Since Elite U takes less than 15 percent of those who apply, why does the university work so hard to encourage more applications?" The admissions officer was silent for a moment. "I'm afraid you'll have to ask the dean of admissions that question," she said.

PARENT OF PROSPECTIVE FRESHMAN

---

with more noble goals, such as increasing diversity, the result is the same. Rachel Toor, a former Duke University admissions officer, vividly describes her own experience: "I travel around the country whipping kids (and their parents) into a frenzy so that they will apply. I tell them how great a school Duke is academically and how much fun they will have socially. Then, come April, we reject most of them."[14]

Colleges can also lower their admissions percentage by offering admission to those students who are most likely to enroll. Yield—the percentage of admitted students who decide to enroll—varies greatly from college to college, from about 80 percent at Stanford and Harvard to less than 20 percent at many others. A college with a high yield can admit fewer students and still fill its classes. If it has a low yield, it has to admit more to meet enrollment targets.

WAYS COLLEGES CAN INCREASE THEIR YIELD

High yields are prized as a symbol of a college's attractiveness to potential freshmen. There are several admissions practices that will increase yield.

Accepting More Early Decision Applicants

A college can raise its yield by admitting a larger percentage of the incoming class by early decision, often referred to as ED. Through an ED application, students submit a completed application by November 1 or November 15 rather than the traditional January 1 deadline, in exchange for receiving an admission decision by mid-December rather than in the spring. The catch is that an ED application is binding on the student, meaning that the student is obligated to attend if admitted, subject to the availability of adequate financial aid. So a student admitted by ED is a sure thing for a college. The yield is close to 100 percent. We'll talk much more about ED and its cousin, early action, in chapter 7, but we mention it now because it indirectly increases a college's overall yield and thereby reduces its overall admit rate. Some colleges admit from a third to more than half of their incoming freshman class under ED.

Wait-Listing the "Overqualified"

A college may also increase its yield and lower its admit rate by rejecting or, more likely, wait-listing students they consider "overqualified" because the college believes the student won't accept the college's offer of admission and will go elsewhere. The dean of admissions at one such college realistically defended the practice at his institution as follows: "We know our place in the food chain of higher education. We're not a community college. And we're not Harvard." This practice is not common, but it is not rare either.[15]

Considering Demonstrated Interest

Finally, a college may increase its yield by preferentially admitting students who have shown that they are strongly interested in that school in some way beyond simply submitting an application. Colleges know from experience that students who connect with a college in different ways beyond submitting an application are more likely to enroll if offered admission than students who do not make such a connection. Some colleges, but not all, take this into account when they make their decisions. We'll talk more about "demonstrated interest" and its role in admissions in chapter 10.

"I'LL MAKE MORE MONEY IF I GRADUATE FROM AN ELITE COLLEGE": A MYTH

Let's return now to the basic question of why there is so much interest in the most selective colleges. Okay, you say, you now see that name recognition and rankings do not necessarily equal educational quality. But maybe that is irrelevant to you. Isn't the value of an elite college education the contacts you make while there? Everyone knows that the rich, the famous, and the well-connected attended these colleges. Wouldn't attending one of them increase your chances of getting to know the right people, getting into a prestigious graduate school, or getting an important career-enhancing break—all eventually leading to fortune if not fame?

The Association Between Income and College Selectivity

Several studies have been interpreted as supporting this conclusion. Years after graduation, graduates of elite institutions on average earn more than graduates of less well-known colleges, just as the income of college graduates is higher those with a high school education. The simple interpretation is that attending a selective college is responsible for the income difference. But economists Stacy Dale and Alan Krueger investigated another possibility in two studies conducted a decade apart. Perhaps, they hypothesized, the students who apply to elite colleges have personal qualities to begin with that lead in some way to later income differences.

The Characteristics of the Student, and Not the College, Are Key

When Dale and Krueger controlled for a student's grade point average and test scores on entering college, they found no difference years later in the income of students who attended elite colleges versus those who had applied, were denied, and subsequently attended less selective schools. Students of similar academic ability who had the self-confidence and motivation to envision themselves attending a selective college showed the economic benefit usually ascribed to those who actually attended such a college. However, some subgroups of students—African American and Hispanic

Students may have a better sense of their potential ability than college admissions committees. To cite one prominent example, Steven Spielberg was rejected by the University of Southern California and UCLA film schools.[16]

STACEY DALE AND ALAN KRUEGER, RESEARCHERS WHO STUDIED THE LONG-TERM EFFECTS OF ATTENDING DIFFERENT TYPES OF COLLEGES

My advice to students: Don't believe that the only school worth attending is one that would not admit you. That you go to college is more important than where you go. Find a school whose academic strengths match your interests and that devotes resources to instruction in those fields. Recognize that your own motivation, ambition, and talents will determine your success more than the college name on your diploma.[17]

ALAN KRUEGER, PROFESSOR OF ECONOMICS, PRINCETON UNIVERSITY

students as well as those from less-educated or low-income families—did show significantly increased future earnings associated with attending a selective college. Overall, with these exceptions, Dale and Krueger's research suggests that the kind of college that students attend is less important than their inherent ability, motivation, and ambition.

Getting into Graduate School

What about admission to graduate school? Does attending a selective college affect your chances of getting into a highly regarded law, business, medical, or other graduate program? A disproportionate number of graduates of selective colleges attend prestigious graduate and professional schools. But here, too, perhaps students admitted to selective colleges bring personal qualities with them that make their subsequent success in gaining admission to these schools after graduation more likely. Those same students may have done just as well if they had gone to a less selective college.

Dale and Krueger found that people who went to a selective college were no more likely to obtain an advanced degree than those who were admitted to a selective college but chose to attend a less selective school. In addition, they found no evidence to suggest that the selectivity of a student's undergraduate college was related to the quality of the graduate school the student attended. Students admitted to a selective college but who chose to attend a less selective one seemed to fare just as well in graduate or professional school admissions as those who actually attended a more selective college.

Do not choose a college by the numbers. Most of those numbers are about resources and reputation and not actual quality or performance. Base your choice on your own needs and aspirations and which colleges can best meet them. As Albert Einstein reminded us, "Not everything that counts can be counted, and not everything that can be counted counts."[18]

DAVID DAVENPORT, FORMER PRESIDENT OF PEPPERDINE UNIVERSITY

THE IMPORTANCE OF FIT

We believe that the college selection process should be about finding colleges that are a good fit for you. A number of factors contribute to fit—academic, extracurricular, social, and geographical, and just feeling comfortable there, among others—and the determination of fit will be different for different people. Assessing fit takes time and effort and is much harder to do than simply looking at a ranked list. It is not a shoe that you slip on once and decide if it fits well.

This book does not try to dissuade you from selecting a college based on prestige—you would have lots of company if you choose this route. However, in chapter 4, we discuss many other important dimensions to consider in selecting colleges and encourage you to think carefully about them. Nor does finding a good fit mean that you must find just one perfect school for you. Rather, it means exploring many factors that can lead to your academic and personal success.

In the end, you may make the same choices as you would have before, but your choices will be more informed. You may also seriously consider other options that you had previously overlooked. Either outcome is fine. We simply want to help you understand as much as possible about yourself, the college admissions process, and colleges themselves so that you can make the best choices for you.

Stephen Lewis, former president of Carleton College, stated it well: "The question should not be, what are the best colleges? The real question should be, best for whom?"[19]

CHAPTER 2

What Do Colleges Look for in an Applicant?

One often hears that college admissions decisions are just not predictable. Everyone knows that it is harder to get into some colleges than ever before, but the criteria for admission seem to be getting murkier and murkier. For example, a student may be admitted to a super-selective college yet find herself placed on the wait list at a less selective one. Or a student is admitted to three colleges but denied by three others, all about the same in terms of selectivity. Why aren't decisions more consistent?

Even more puzzling are cases involving students from the same high school who apply to the same college. One student may have a significantly stronger academic record than his classmate, yet be denied by a college while the classmate receives an acceptance. Why wasn't the student with the stronger record accepted also? And although many colleges claim to use exactly the same admissions criteria for early decision applications as they use for regular decision applications, anecdotal as well as documented evidence strongly argues that early applicants often have an edge in the admissions process. Why should when you apply make so much difference?

This chapter will help you understand the many factors colleges consider in reviewing applications. Knowing what colleges look for as they sort through thousands of applications will demystify the admissions process and help you approach it with confidence. We have no magic bullet or formula that will guarantee you acceptance to a college that does not admit students by the numbers alone. But the more you know about how colleges select their freshman class, the wiser you will be in undertaking the tasks before you—from choosing colleges, to preparing your applications, to dealing with the successes and, yes, even the disappointments you may encounter along the way.

HOW COLLEGE ADMISSIONS HAS CHANGED

Before we begin, we'll share a little history that dramatically illustrates how college admissions have changed over the years. About 85 years ago, colleges that are now considered among the most selective filled their classes in ways that reflected the times. Yale University, for example, filled its class of 1936 by accepting 72 percent of those who applied.

YALE THEN

Almost 30 percent of those who enrolled in the class of 1936 were the sons of Yale University alumni, known as legacies. Many of those admitted were students from feeder schools—elite prep schools with headmasters whose close relationships with college admissions officers virtually ensured the admission of their graduates to the school of their choice. Less than 20 percent of the freshman class graduated from a public high school.[1] Women were not eligible then to apply to Yale; they had separate elite colleges, known as the Seven Sisters, which had similar admissions practices. Also excluded were young men who, no matter how bright and accomplished, did not fit the mold of privilege and wealth, to say nothing of race, religion, and ethnicity. But few of the latter even considered applying. Everyone understood the criteria for admission, even if they weren't stated.

YALE NOW

Today, of course, institutions like Yale University pride themselves on the diversity of their student body and actively recruit high-achieving men and women from all backgrounds. The men and women invited to join the Yale University class of 2020 were selected from an applicant pool about 23 times the size of the pool for the class of 1936, and just 6.3 percent were offered admission. Even more significantly, the class is very different compared to 84 years before. The percentage of enrolled legacies has dropped to just 13 percent, and over 60 percent of the class now comes from public high schools. This example is typical of the current admissions picture at similar colleges. Those who in a prior era would have been easily assured of admission by virtue of birth or circumstance no longer are. The rules have changed.

CHANGING TIMES AT YALE UNIVERSITY

	Class of 1936	Class of 2020
Number of applicants	1,330	31,455
Accepted (%)	72%	6.3%
Size of freshman class	884	1,373
From public high schools (%)	Less than 20%	60.4%
Legacies (%)	30%	13%

WHAT MATTERS NOW

The admissions web pages of most colleges provide general information about the characteristics they are seeking in their prospective freshmen. You will frequently see listed things such as academic excellence, strong evidence of engagement and leadership, a sense of social responsibility, and intellectual curiosity. Colleges also note the factors they consider to assess these characteristics. Grades and rigor of academic program, test scores, recommendations, extracurricular activities, essays, and interviews are often mentioned. Context can also play an important role in the process—colleges evaluate students in the context of the opportunities they have had and the challenges they have faced.

All this information is surprisingly consistent from school to school. It's as if they had all attended the same admissions training program. But information on the web page is the public version of the admissions story. It is vague on purpose, though not intended to mislead. This is just all they can legitimately disclose. The private version is what actually goes on behind closed doors as admissions officers read through many thousands of applications to select a freshman class that may have just a few hundred places. We don't mean to suggest an atmosphere of smoke-filled rooms and sneaky deals being made. It is just that the process can be enormously complex and subtle, and it may vary somewhat for each college and for different applicants. In this chapter, we will discuss the many criteria that colleges may consider in their evaluations. In chapter 3, we will explore the review process itself.

Students and parents are often surprised to learn about the full range of criteria that admissions officers at many colleges consider. Although some are well-known and predictable (for example, grades and test scores), others are not, and not all schools use all criteria. The level of competition for admission to the most selective colleges can also come as a big surprise to those without recent firsthand experience with college admissions.

THE ACADEMIC RECORD

The heart of a college application is the student's academic record: the courses taken and the grades achieved in those courses during the high school career. Colleges almost uniformly state that they are looking for students who show convincing evidence of being able to do well in a demanding academic program and that they place the greatest weight in admissions decisions on that record.

How Challenging Is Your Academic Program?

Many colleges provide students with guidelines about the preparation they expect successful applicants to have in high school—the number of years of English, mathematics, foreign language, and so forth.

> Students and parents sometimes ask if it is better to get an A in a regular course or a B in an AP course. My answer is that it is best to get an A in the AP course.
>
> COMMENT BY A HARVARD ADMISSIONS OFFICER AT A GROUP INFORMATION SESSION, FOLLOWED BY NERVOUS LAUGHTER FROM THE AUDIENCE

What Kinds of Courses Should You Take?

Trinity University, for example, a selective college in San Antonio, Texas, provides the following guidelines to prospective students:

> Trinity seeks students who have made the most of their academic opportunities and who challenge themselves intellectually. A student's grade point average, the rigor of their courses, class rank (when applicable), and the diversity of their curriculum are all important considerations for admission.
>
> The Office of Admissions recalculates each applicant's GPA using a standardized un-weighted scale in order to compensate for discrepancies in grading scales among different high schools.

Academic Record
- Grades
- Class rank
- Rigor of curriculum

Standardized Test Scores
- SAT
- ACT
- SAT Subject Tests

Engagement Outside the Classroom
- Extracurricular activities
- Community service
- Work experience

Personal Qualities
- Letters of recommendation
- Essays
- Interview report

Hooks and Institutional Priorities
- Legacy connection
- Donation potential
- Underrepresented race or ethnicity
- Recruited athlete status
- Socioeconomic and geographical background
- Exceptional talent

Rigor of curriculum is an important part of the application review. Particular notice is given to those who take honors, Advanced Placement, or International Baccalaureate courses, if their school offers them. We also take into consideration the breadth and depth of coursework taken.[2]

The guidelines at Trinity University are like those at many colleges. The differences among schools will be in the details, such as the number of years of mathematics or foreign language that are recommended as well as in what a typical successful applicant's record actually looks like. Regardless of specific details, however, most schools strongly emphasize the importance of the academic preparation needed to gain admission.

Why Colleges Like a Challenging Curriculum

Many colleges, especially selective ones, expect students to take advantage of opportunities their school may offer to challenge themselves academically. This includes taking honors or Advanced Placement (AP) courses or participating in the International Baccalaureate (IB) program that is offered at some high schools. Strong performance indicates that a student can do college-level work. As a general rule, if you can take challenging high school classes, whatever their titles, a selective college will expect you to have taken some of them. In some communities with high-performing high schools, juniors and seniors may also take classes at a local community college, a nearby four-year college, or online in subjects in which they have exhausted their high school's offerings. Admissions officers also favorably note these classes in reviewing applications.

Course Load and Grades Are Both Important

Many high schools acknowledge the extra demands of a challenging course by providing weighted grade. If an A in a regular course is worth four points, for example, an A in an AP or honors class may be worth five points. Grade weighting sometimes extends to the pluses and minuses that a student may receive as well, so that an A+ in an AP course might be assigned 5.25 points, while an A– in such a course might be worth 4.75 points. The weighting of honors, IB, and AP classes can result in some very high grade point averages (for example, a GPA of 4.6) for students who take heavy loads of such courses and do exceptionally well in them. Such students represent a very small fraction of high school students overall, but they are disproportionately represented in the applicant pools of the most selective colleges. If your high school doesn't weight grades, that is fine. Colleges will know this and adjust: a 4.6 from a school that weights is not necessarily better than a 4.0 from a school that does not.

Colleges May Recalculate Your GPA

Many colleges recompute each applicant's GPA in unweighted form, from ninth grade on including only the classes (usually academic "solids" such as English, foreign language, math, science, and social studies) they consider truly academic. Religion, debate, PE, and journalism courses, among others, are usually excluded. This creates a common standard for evaluating applicants from different high schools. But despite any recalculation, these colleges will look carefully at the quality of the courses you are taking, within the context of your opportunities. Other colleges will simply take the GPA off your transcript without recalculating it. In any event, a high GPA in a less challenging curriculum will definitely be less well received by a selective college than a more mixed record in a challenging one.

Be Reasonable and Stay Sane

But what exactly is expected? When students return from visits to selective colleges over spring break or the summer, they frequently report to their counselors that they heard that colleges expect students to take the "most demanding" program available. What is the "most demanding" program? Is it three, four, or five APs a year, or would six be even better if you can squeeze another one in? What if your school doesn't offer as many APs as the other high school across town, or what if it doesn't offer any at all? Are you at a disadvantage? (No, as we will discuss shortly, because colleges learn about this from information that your high school sends along with your transcript, and they evaluate you in the context of the opportunities available at your school.)

Many students ask, and we admit it is hard to answer: "Just how many 'challenging' courses should I take if they are available?" Our answer is a highly qualified, "it all depends." Are you interested in them? Are they well taught? Are they courses you are likely to do well in? What other, unweighted courses do you really want to take and need room for in your schedule? What are you doing with the rest of your time: activities, family responsibilities, just living a daily life? Each student will have a different answer. Unfortunately, colleges often don't add a few simple words to their advice: "Be reasonable and stay sane. Take what you can manage and do well in, and what makes sense for you." This would go a long way toward relieving some of the pressure some students feel to take every honors or AP course in sight. Too much of a good thing can be just that: too much.

> What admission officers almost always say . . . is focus on what lights your fire and take advantage of the most challenging offerings in those areas. That's a very different message from "Take all the AP classes."[3]
>
> DAVID HAWKINS, EXECUTIVE DIRECTOR FOR EDUCATIONAL CONTENT AND POLICY, NATIONAL ASSOCIATION FOR COLLEGE ADMISSION COUNSELING

PUTTING THE GPA IN CONTEXT

Although colleges strongly emphasize grades and courses, they recognize that grades can be hard to evaluate in isolation. Admissions officers know, just as you do, that some high schools (and some teachers) are generous with top marks, and others have more rigorous standards. Grade inflation has become widespread at many high schools, public and private. According to the College Board, 48 percent of students in the high school graduating class of 2015 who took the SAT reported GPAs of at least A–. Twenty years earlier that figure was just 35 percent. High grades alone are less impressive than they once were.

The Role of Class Rank

Some high schools, mostly public, assign a class rank to students on the basis of GPA. Class rank provides information about a student's grades relative to his or her classmates, and colleges have found it makes the task of evaluating grades easier, especially at large high schools. But fewer and fewer high schools now compute class rank. Private schools in particular are reluctant to rank their students, because they believe it promotes a more competitive school environment and magnifies small differences in achievement so that students below the very top are disadvantaged. Increasingly, public high schools are recognizing these same drawbacks and have stopped ranking their students as well.

The absence of explicit class rank makes the job of admissions officers more challenging, but colleges adapt to it and use any available information about school grading practices to get a sense of where students stand in their class. Even if they don't have class rank from a high school, they can compare the GPAs of the different students applying from the same high school or to previous years, because these standards change only slightly from year to year.

An Upward Trend Is a Good Thing

In addition, colleges consider improvement and decline over time. Two students may have identical GPAs in comparable courses, but one has improved over time while the other's grades have declined. The evaluation of these two students' academic records will be very different; admissions staff members will view the improving student much more favorably, unless extenuating circumstances such as an extended illness can explain the decline. The central point is that the evaluation process considers an applicant's record in context.

> There is simply too much variance between schools, their grading policies, and individual grading by teachers for GPAs as a raw number to have much meaning by themselves.
>
> HIGH SCHOOL COUNSELOR COMMENTING ON VARIABILITY IN GPAS

The School Profile

High schools usually include a school profile with each transcript sent as part of a college application. The profile summarizes the school's curriculum and grading policies so that a college can get a general idea of how students have performed relative to their peers. A profile may show the grade range for each decile or quintile of the senior class and list the AP, IB, and honors courses offered, as well as the percentage of students who go on to four-year colleges directly from that high school and a list of colleges its recent graduates have attended. It may also include items such as the SAT and ACT distributions in the class and the number of students taking and passing AP tests. The profile provides important context about the student's high school and the opportunities that are available, and it is valuable information regardless of whether or not the school ranks its students.

Colleges also require students to have a school official, usually a counselor, complete a recommendation form, called the *school report*. The form includes an evaluation of the rigor of a student's academic program relative to the offerings at the high school. This information helps colleges calibrate a student's grades while ensuring that students from schools that do not offer many advanced classes are not penalized.

Part of the college mania we noted in the introduction to this book is the frequently quoted tidbit that Harvard denies over 75 percent of the high school valedictorians who apply each year. Several other ultra-selective and super-selective colleges also deny a majority of their valedictorian applicants. But if you reflect on this for a minute, it is not really that surprising.

There are over 27,000 high schools, public and private, in the United States that prepare students for college, with more charter schools being founded every year. Each of them has a student (or often several) who achieved the highest possible grades. Clearly, grades can't be the whole story in college admissions. Too many students have very high grades, with those grades varying too much in what they really mean for grades alone to determine who is admitted to a selective college. So the common parental complaint, "My child had perfect grades but still didn't get into College Q," is no surprise to the admissions officer at the other end of the phone the day after students receive their decisions.

STANDARDIZED TESTS

Most colleges require a standardized test—the SAT or the ACT. Colleges do not have a preference and either test will satisfy the requirement. The question students ask most often is how much the tests count in admissions decisions. David Erdmann, the late dean of admissions at Rollins College, has given the most candid answer of all: "At most institutions, standardized test scores count less than students think and more than colleges are willing to admit."[4] Chapter 6 discusses these tests in detail, including information about how to choose between them and how best to prepare.

Both colleges and students see these tests as more "objective" than grades because they are independent of the varying grading standards of high schools. They can also help colleges distinguish students with similar grades from each other.

But the tests have many critics, and most colleges are wary of relying too heavily on them because of doubts about what they really measure and lingering concerns that they may be biased in some way. Of special concern is the growth of the test prep industry that often "guarantees" significant score improvements for students who take special courses that can cost a thousand dollars or more. Clearly, the only ones who can benefit from this assistance are those who can afford to pay for it.

> There is a socioeconomic bias in standardized testing, and test optional may be eliminating that.[5]
>
> WILLIAM BLACK, SENIOR VICE PRESIDENT FOR ENROLLMENT MANAGEMENT, TEMPLE UNIVERSITY

In response to these concerns, a growing number of colleges have made standardized tests optional for many or all of their applicants—the decision whether to submit scores is left to the student. These colleges find that other information in a student's record helps them select their freshman class with confidence. Other colleges still want to see some standardized testing, but they let the student decide which tests to submit from several choices, including SAT Subject Tests and APs or IBs. We talk about test-optional and test-flexible schools and how to find them in chapter 6.

Despite calls to eliminate standardized tests entirely from college admissions or to move to a test-optional process, most colleges will probably continue to use them for the foreseeable future. With grades difficult to interpret, they are unwilling to give up the additional information, however imperfect, that these tests provide.

ENGAGEMENT BEYOND THE CLASSROOM

Many colleges not only expect students to be strong academically but also to be interesting, engaged, and contributing members of the school community and the community at large. Admissions officers used to talk about the importance of being well-rounded and showing evidence of leadership in extracurricular activities. Today they more often speak about having a "well-rounded class" composed of students who each have exceptional talent or commitment in one or two areas.

This summons up the ubiquitous buzzword *passion:* that elusive quality that all teenagers are supposed to have discovered in themselves by the time they apply to college.

This shift in language reflects the realization that there are just so many hours in the day for any adolescent and that achieving excellence in a given area can take up most of those hours. As David Gould, former dean of admissions at Brandeis, has said, "The embodiment at age seventeen of a Renaissance person is difficult to find. We realized we could accomplish the same thing [for our freshman class] with lots of different people."[6] Colleges examine whether a student has made a sustained commitment to an activity over a number of years in high school, so involvement in one activity over time can be more helpful than involvement in several more briefly. We think *commitment* is a better term than *passion*, and it is the one we choose to use.

EXTRACURRICULAR ACTIVITIES

But just what does *exceptional talent* or *commitment* mean? In general, the more selective the college, the higher the bar in evaluating extracurricular activities and leadership. Involvement in debate, for example, can range from participating on a high school team to winning occasional local tournaments, to having a winning record at the regional, state, or national level. More selective colleges look for higher levels of achievement and recognition. Being a dedicated member of the high school orchestra is good, but being first violinist and concertmaster is better. Better still is winning regional, state, national, or even international competitions as a soloist. We'll address the special case of athletic talent further on in this chapter under the topic of hooks.

Colleges like to see evidence of leadership in an applicant as well. Serving as president of an active high school club, a student body officer, or an editor of the high school newspaper or yearbook are all common examples of high school leadership roles colleges see. Again, the more selective the college, the greater the expectation that applicants will hold leadership positions and that they will be at the highest levels, possibly extending beyond the high school to local, regional, state, or national organizations, when applicable. Certainly, participation at the higher levels is quite rare.

Students often ask what activities will "look good" on a college application. Admissions officers repeatedly say that they do not give preference to one kind of activity over another—what matters is the student's commitment to an activity and level of involvement and achievement in it. Having an impact and taking initiative in whatever you do, in a leadership role or not, and then articulating it on your application is far more important than the nature of the activity or your formal title.

COMMUNITY SERVICE AND SERVICE TO OTHERS

Colleges like to see that a student has been willing to contribute time and effort to help others, even when required at a high school, although it is not formally required for admission any more than involvement in sports, the arts, or student government is. Students can contribute in many ways, including tutoring other students; volunteering at a soup kitchen, hospital, or homeless shelter; volunteer coaching or refereeing for children's sports teams; and fundraising for a worthy cause. Informal ways, such as caring for a sibling or an aging relative, are also valuable ways to contribute to others.

Just as with extracurricular activities, sustained involvement over time is the key, and a major time commitment will have a greater effect on an application than a minor one would. A leadership role in a community service activity that requires a major time commitment will reflect the student's altruism, energy level, and ability to work effectively with others.

Service trips over the summer to other parts of the world to experience another culture as well as contribute time and effort to teaching or helping construct much-need facilities in impoverished countries are popular with many students. Although these can be valuable experiences for the participants (as well as the locals who benefit), admissions officers do not see these as more valuable than efforts to serve a community much closer to home. You do not have to travel to an exotic location to take initiative and have impact. Creating your own opportunities to serve can be added evidence of your commitment to helping others as well as your initiative.

WORK EXPERIENCE

Most college applications give students an opportunity to list their work experience. Depending on its nature, paid work can nicely complement a student's special interests (for example, designing web pages or working with developmentally disabled children). Work can also demonstrate personal responsibility and leadership ability if the student's work involves supervising others. Finally, an extensive work commitment, regardless of the nature of the work, can reflect a student's modest socioeconomic background and indicate that her income is important to her and her family. Admissions officers know that such work responsibilities can limit the amount of time a student can devote to other activities, so work can compensate for an otherwise limited extracurricular record and be highly valued in its own right.

INVOLVEMENT IN RESEARCH, INTERNSHIPS, AND SPECIAL PROGRAMS

Some students choose to devote significant amounts of time to research activities, perhaps working with a faculty member at a local university or a researcher at a company engaged in research and development work. Depending on the nature and extent of involvement, these can be very valuable experiences for a student and be something viewed quite favorably in an admissions review. In a small number of cases, the student's work can lead to local, regional, or even national recognition.

A wide variety of summer programs, research and otherwise, designed specifically for high school students is offered by universities and organizations using university facilities. These can be enriching experiences, but unless the program is highly selective itself, participation alone will not be something a selective college will weigh in its review. That doesn't mean the program isn't valuable for the student; it simply means that the program's value is intrinsic to what it offers, not in how it will be viewed by colleges in the admissions process.

FOLLOW YOUR INTERESTS

In chapter 10, we will discuss how you can share information about your extracurricular, community service, and work experiences as part of your application. Students sometimes try to join activities solely because they think will look good to college admissions officers, such as community service. In reality, admissions officers want to see students who have sustained their involvement in one or more activities; have shown initiative, creativity, and impact; and have grown from them. As we noted previously, it doesn't much matter what those activities are. A long list filled with activities that require little time or devotion is not helpful. Here, again, less is more.

Second-guessing what activities colleges are seeking is usually futile. Just do what you love and what excites you. It makes much more sense to get involved in what really interests you than to try to fit your interests to some preconceived (and likely inaccurate) idea about what colleges want to see.

PERSONAL QUALITIES: THE PERSON BEHIND THE PAPER

You know that your written record—test scores, transcript, and even a list of extracurricular activities—doesn't tell the whole story of what kind of person you are right now, much less what kind of person you might become.

> Students who do activities out of their own interests and passions and who create activities for themselves stand out—even if the activities were done down the street and not in an exotic locale. Students who do activities because their parents pay for them and they need résumé dressing are a dime a dozen and blend into the overall pool.
>
> PARENT WITH EXPERIENCE IN THE ADMISSIONS PROCESS

For that reason, many colleges request qualitative information as well: letters from people who know you especially in an academic context, essays, and in some cases an interview.

LETTERS

As you'll see in chapter 10, many schools, including almost all selective private colleges, require or recommend a letter of recommendation from a student's high school counselor and one or two letters from teachers. Admissions officers look at letters for evidence that a student has, for want of a better word, "sparkle." They are looking for a smart, intellectually curious, good-hearted, talented, and energetic student, but most of all, they are looking for insight into how you learn. They also hope that a counselor letter will help place the student in the context of his or her high school.

Some Letters Are More Useful Than Others

Letters of recommendation can vary widely in their usefulness. One admissions reader described her experience as follows:

> I had to take into account that the harried guidance counselors at a large urban school, writing hundreds of recommendations, often did not know the applicant well—this letter would be short and vague. The applicants attending private schools, where the rate of college acceptances is an important recruiting tool, received four-page tomes from their counselors. . . . Fairness demanded that I factor in the inequity, but invariably I was told more—though in hyperbolic terms—about the private school student than I ever learned about the public school one.[7]

Although four-page letters are very rare from any counselor, private or public, the lesson here is clear: regardless of where you go to high school, try to get to know your counselor, even if takes extra effort. Some students go to schools with low student-to-counselor ratios and can get to know a counselor easily. Others have to work harder at it. It's not always easy, and it isn't fair, but it is definitely worth the effort.

Get to Know Your Teachers

It also helps to get to know several teachers well because you may have to ask one or two of them to write on your behalf. Being memorable (in a positive way) and actively participating in your classes are the best ways to ensure that your teachers will have something helpful to say. Hold on to your best papers and projects from your classes. At letter-writing time, you may want to remind a teacher about the work you did in his or her class. Some colleges encourage applicants to submit a graded academic paper, and a few require them if you do not submit test scores, so you may have additional uses for work that you have saved. In reading such a paper, the college is trying to evaluate your analytical and writing skills as well as your high school's academic standards.

THE ESSAY

Perhaps no other part of the application process besides standardized tests is as dreaded as the essay. Many colleges have supplementary essays as well (see chapter 9), but for now we will include them all together as "the essay." The essay asks students to expose themselves to a stranger who will be judging them as a person, not just their grades and scores. It is also a new kind of writing for many students; they know colleges want good grades and scores, but what exactly does a college want in an essay? They say they want authenticity and for you to be yourself, but just what does it mean to "be yourself" in an essay?

How Do Colleges Use the Essays?

The essay enables a student to show how she writes and, more important, how she thinks and how she has been able to learn from her experiences. It can also convey important information that isn't included elsewhere in the application. The essay is also the only part of the application over which you exercise substantial control, and if you have something valuable to say, it can make an impact.

College admissions officers see the essay as an important way to gain insight into who the student is. With so many applicants with similar grades, GPAs, and activities, through the essay students can present their own individuality. So look at the essay as an opportunity to be thoughtful about yourself, not as a dreaded ordeal. An effective essay leaves the reader feeling that he has gotten to know the student and likes what he sees.

> Save for the few instances in which candidates write essays so completely lacking in taste as to make us marvel at the fact that they even bothered to apply, in my experience no one is ever admitted solely on the basis of a great essay and no one was ever denied admission solely on the basis of a poor essay.[8]
>
> FRED HARGADON, FORMER DEAN OF ADMISSIONS AT PRINCETON UNIVERSITY AND STANFORD UNIVERSITY

How Much Do Essays Count?

How much do essays count in admissions decisions? A survey posing this question found that students and parents rated the essay as more important than admissions officers said it was. This is not surprising, considering the time and energy students put into writing it, but admissions officers must read them quickly. Nevertheless, the results confirmed that the essay can still make a difference in the admissions decision.[9]

A good essay can strengthen an application to a selective school, especially if your grades and test scores are strong. A weak essay, however, can spoil your chances at a college with many strong candidates. An essay that falls in the middle—neither strong nor weak but simply flat—doesn't give the reader a reason to accept you beyond what is in the rest of your file. A wise student tries to have as many factors in the plus column as possible—including the essay, which can be a positive experience if you start early. We'll talk more about writing your essays in chapter 9.

INTERVIEWS

Interviews are perhaps the most misunderstood part of the college admissions process. At some colleges, they can be helpful in the overall evaluation of candidates, and at the same time students can learn more about a college through an interview. The importance of interviews varies from school to school: many offer no interviews at all.

In a small percentage of cases, an interview can produce new information about a student, but usually an interview confirms what is already available in the application. Students who act boorishly or immaturely in an interview could damage their chances, but short of such exceptionally negative (and rare) behavior, an interview will rarely harm the outcome of an admissions decision.

An interview can also help a college assess how interested you really are in enrolling. As we will see in chapter 10, demonstrating interest may be part of the decision-making process at some colleges, especially in close cases. We'll also talk more in chapter 10 about the different kinds of interviews, what you can expect, and how you can make a good impression.

HOOKS AND HOW THEY HELP

Most applicants compete not with the whole applicant pool but within specific categories, where the applicant-to-available-space ratio may be more, or less, favorable than in the pool at large. . . . Students in the selected categories, which vary from institution to institution, have a "hook" because they help meet institutional needs.[10]

PAUL MARTHERS, FORMER DEAN
OF ADMISSIONS AT REED COLLEGE,
REFLECTING ON ADMISSIONS PRACTICES
AT SELECTIVE INSTITUTIONS

In admissions parlance, a "hook" is a special characteristic a college deems desirable over and above the qualities it is seeking in its students in general. These institutional priorities can be powerful factors, tipping the outcome in favor of the applicant at a selective college. Hooks, sometimes also called *tags*, can be controversial, and they can vary greatly from college to college and even from year to year at a given college. In our discussion of hooks, we simply want you to understand the different factors that may go into crafting a freshman class. If you have a hook, it can help, but most students don't have one.

LEGACY STATUS

A legacy is a child of an alumnus or alumna who received an undergraduate degree (and the alum doesn't have to be a donor). Some colleges, such as Bucknell University and the University of Pennsylvania, even count grandchildren of alumni as legacies. Still others, such as Stanford University and Princeton University, consider children to be legacies if a parent received a graduate degree there.

How Big Is the Legacy Advantage?

At many private colleges with low admissions rates, legacies tend to be admitted at up to two or three times the overall rate of admission. Colleges sometimes defend the difference in admissions rate by claiming that the legacy pool overall is somewhat stronger than the general applicant pool and that many legacies apply early, which by itself can boost the chances of admission. But clearly a separate, distinct boost comes with legacy status at many institutions. Being a legacy by no means ensures admission, however, especially at colleges that have low admissions rates to begin with.

Why Do Colleges Give Legacies Preference?

Colleges are usually eager to enroll legacy children. They believe that legacies are more likely to have a strong commitment to their parent's college and then to accept an offer of admission and become enthusiastic, contributing students. In short, they are good for school morale. Parents, in turn, like the idea of a child following in their footsteps. Also, colleges like to present themselves as a humane, caring community, even a family of sorts. In a sense, a legacy child is joining the college family. The bottom line plays a major role as well. Giving special admissions preference to legacies can be a wise financial decision for colleges because they regularly solicit alumni for donations.

Although legacy status may factor in admissions at a few public institutions, such as the University of Virginia and University of Michigan, it plays a more important role in admissions at most private ones. Some private colleges, in fact, have special information sessions for legacy applicants, special legacy-only interviews, and staff members assigned to deal specifically with legacy concerns. Legacy preference is a double-edged sword because a college becomes more selective and has to deny admission to many legacy applicants. A spurned legacy parent will remember the rejection. The college has to walk a fine line between upholding its standards and looking after its "family."

The Legacy Admissions Controversy

The practice of legacy admissions has come under fire from time to time as inconsistent with the values of equal opportunity. Critics claim that because most alumni of selective colleges are well-off and white, the use of

> We take a look at the level of loyalty— contributions, alumni interviewing, etc.— that graduates have maintained over the years. If alumni have been engaged in the community since they left, supporting them in return just makes sense.[11]
>
> CHARLES DEACON, DEAN OF ADMISSIONS AT GEORGETOWN UNIVERSITY

> If it weren't for the generosity of alumni, we would not be able to provide the education we do. So yes, we do give preference.[12]
>
> THOMAS PARKER, FORMER DEAN OF ADMISSIONS AND FINANCIAL AID AT AMHERST COLLEGE

legacy status as an admissions factor amounts to affirmative action for upper-middle-class white students. Colleges, however, assert that the legacy preference is small and the benefit to the institution is potentially great. For now, legacy status continues to be a hook, and an important one, at most private colleges.

DEVELOPMENT ADMITS

Many selective colleges have a small number of so-called development admits each year—students who would be unlikely to be admitted if not for their potential to bring significant donations to the college. The children of alumni who are major donors to a college get a double hook when they apply: as legacies and as development cases.

How big a donation does it have to be? This varies from college to college, and, not surprisingly, colleges do not advertise what those amounts might be. Colleges justify development admits because of the institution's need for additional funding to support the school. The development office may or may not be actively involved in recruiting such students, but they are certainly gracious and welcoming to these families. Once they apply, development prospects are usually flagged for special admissions consideration. In these cases, admissions staff members evaluate whether the student can "do the work" that will enable them to graduate from the institution.

Development admits don't significantly affect the admission of other students because they are very few. Nevertheless, the practice is kept low profile to avoid uncomfortable publicity. The publication in 2006 of *The Price of Admission* by Daniel Golden, a *Wall Street Journal* reporter, threw new light on these often controversial practices.[13] The colleges were generally not pleased with the publicity, but the continuing pressures of financing colleges meant that nothing changed.

RECRUITED ATHLETES

Outstanding athletic ability is yet another important institutional priority or hook. Most colleges have active athletics programs that they see as integral to the college experience. The student body and alumni, even the faculty, want their teams to win. So does the development office, whose fundraising success may reflect their teams' win-loss record. Most colleges allow coaches to identify a limited number of athletes whom they can strongly support for admission.

Who Is a Recruited Athlete?

We define a recruited athlete as one who earns a spot on the coach's final list for admissions purposes. The more important the sport at a college, the greater the weight of a coach's recommendations for admission. For basketball and football, the two highest-profile sports on most campuses because they can produce significant revenue for the school, the coach's recommendation usually counts for a lot. Although some recruited athletes have academic records that would earn them admission independent of their special talent, some do not.

> The kids who get in on sports, they're good enough students to go there and hang in there, but they're not always students who were good enough to have gotten there on academics alone.
>
> HIGH SCHOOL SENIOR WHO UNDERSTANDS THE ATHLETIC HOOK

What Is the Admissions Advantage for Athletes?

William Bowen, former president of Princeton University, and his research associate, Sarah Levin, investigated what they call the "admissions advantage" for athletes at Ivy League colleges—the difference between the average admissions probability for a recruited athlete and the average admissions probability for any other applicant after controlling for differences in their academic records.[14] Their analysis of an extensive database of student records led them to conclude that the average male recruited athlete had four times the chance of being admitted to an Ivy League college than a male student with a comparable academic record and no other hooks who was not a recruited athlete.

Although Bowen and Levin based their conclusions on data that are now over 20 years old, we believe that they generally hold today and may even underestimate the size of the athletics hook because overall admissions rates at these schools have decreased so much over time. The same hook applies to non-Ivy colleges as well.

Exceptional athletic ability may be the strongest college admissions hook of all aside, perhaps, from development, in which the data are not public and the numbers are small. We'll talk at greater length about athletes and college admissions in chapter 11.

DIVERSITY

Most colleges believe that a diverse student body is an essential part of a high-quality educational experience for all students, and many applicants list diversity as an attribute they are seeking in a college. Diversity can take many forms: ethnic and racial, socioeconomic, and geographic, among others.

Underrepresented Students

> Were we to have only 440 applicants, which is how many we're hoping to enroll in the fall, . . . we wouldn't have very many choices and we'd just simply have to accept the composition as it is. But we have a lot of goals that are aligned with our institutional mission . . .[15]
>
> JOE BAGNOLI, VICE PRESIDENT FOR ENROLLMENT, GRINNELL COLLEGE

Being a member of a traditionally underrepresented group (African American, Native American, or Hispanic) can be a hook at colleges eager to diversify their student bodies. Asian Americans are occasionally included in this group, especially at colleges in parts of the country with low Asian American populations, such as the rural Midwest, South, and Northeast, but usually they are not.

Colleges are becoming increasingly proactive in seeking out and supporting underrepresented students in the admissions process because they may have less access to information about college, especially financial aid, and may not even consider applying beyond their local public university. Some colleges fly in groups of minority and first-generation-to-go-to-college applicants in the fall of their senior year so the students can get a taste of their college. Students can apply for some of these programs directly, but other schools require a transcript, test scores, an essay, and a counselor's endorsement before issuing a formal invitation. A Google search for "multicultural fly-in programs" or "diversity fly-in programs" will help you identify these opportunities. A good list can also be found on Get Me To College at http://getmetocollege.org under the College Readiness tab.

The diversity hook in college admissions is formally known as race-sensitive admissions or, more commonly, affirmative action. Eight states currently do not allow race to be used in the admission process at their public colleges. These states are Arizona, California, Florida, Michigan, Nebraska, New Hampshire, Oklahoma, and Washington. Private colleges in those states as well as public and private colleges elsewhere are able to consider race when deciding which students to admit in an effort to diversify their student body.

Socioeconomic and Geographical Diversity

Many colleges want to assemble a freshman class with students from a wide variety of backgrounds because of the contributions they can make in the classroom and in the campus community. Colleges are particularly interested in identifying students who are the first in their families to attend college, often called "first-gen" students, and have succeeded against the odds. High school students from disadvantaged backgrounds who do well in school despite their socioeconomic challenges are likely to be highly motivated and successful in college.

Geographical diversity is another variable that many colleges consider in selecting their freshman class, because geographical diversity is often correlated with diversity of life experience. Students from underrepresented parts of the country can benefit when it comes to admission to a selective college. But the definition of "underrepresented region" is relative; it depends on the college. Although few students from Nevada may apply to Colby College in Maine, Pitzer College in California will probably have an ample supply to choose from. Talented students from sparsely populated Wyoming or rural Mississippi are in short supply everywhere, except in their home states.

Major exceptions to the geographical diversity advantage are selective public institutions such as the University of Texas at Austin, the University of North Carolina at Chapel Hill, and the University of Virginia, which have higher academic standards for out-of-state students because they have many more highly qualified applicants than they can accept. Until recently, we would have included the University of California system in this list, but funding needs have led UC campuses to actively recruit and even favor out-of-state and international students because they pay substantially higher out-of-state tuition. And although many private colleges seek geographical diversity in their student body, they may also give a small preference to students from their own local area in an effort to maintain goodwill with the immediate community. Tufts University, Duke University, and Northeastern University are among those that acknowledge this kind of preference.

SPECIAL TALENTS

Still other hooks include exceptional talent—as a musician, dancer, actress, or ice skater; as a visual artist or published writer; or as a scientist, among others— that a college wants to have represented in its student body. An Olympic ice skater, an actress who has appeared in commercial films, the author of a published novel, and the winner of a major Intel science award—all of these applicants have hooks based on exceptional talent that will catch the attention of admissions committees. A diverse class with a wide range of exceptional talents is an interesting class. Some of these talents (e.g., the science award winner or the published author) may support the educational mission of the school. Others may just add some glamour. Although the majority of students admitted even to the most selective colleges do not have a special talent at this level, some do. If you are fortunate enough to have a talent, it will be a definite plus in admissions. In chapters 10 and 11, we'll explore how students with special talents can present these to colleges.

ARE HOOKS FAIR?

Are hooks fair? This is a tough question. If you have one, you are likely to be glad you do; few students would willingly give up an advantage, real or imagined. If you don't have a hook you may feel that the system is structured against you. Unfortunately, this contributes to the widely held idea that college admissions is an intricate game, and you have to exploit the fine points to win. If you find yourself feeling this way, just remember that most students admitted to every college do not have a hook and that many students are admitted on the basis of the normal mixture of criteria: grades, test scores, activities, essays, and recommendations, even at highly selective schools.

FITTING IT ALL TOGETHER

We hope this chapter has given you a good sense of the many factors that play a role in selective college admissions. Two other considerations—the timing of a student's application and demonstrated interest—are covered in chapters 7 and 10, respectively. In chapter 3, we consider how admissions offices actually make decisions. We present all of this in general terms, because there is no single answer to how college admissions offices weigh all of these factors and what process they use to make their decisions. Each college shapes its own admissions policies and practices based on institutional priorities, tradition, and, sometimes, the previous experience of a newly hired admissions dean.

Many parents and students react to learning about all of this for the first time by asking, "Does getting into college really have to be this complicated and ultimately so stressful?" Counselors, admissions officers, and higher education leaders have asked themselves the same question. Of course, the admissions process is much simpler and more predictable at colleges that make their decisions primarily or solely on the basis of grades and test scores or that admit most of those who apply. But for those applying to many other schools, the process can seem daunting.

Periodically recommendations come forward to fundamentally change the college admissions process. One such recommendation that surfaces frequently, only partially in jest, is that college admissions at many selective schools should be conducted by lottery. All applicants who meet certain criteria for admission would be included in the pool, with the freshman class selected randomly from that group. As satisfying a thought as that may be to some who complain about the "lottery" quality of current admissions outcomes, there is little enthusiasm for such an approach.

The most recent challenge to the status quo is a report entitled "Turning the Tide: Inspiring Concern for Others and the Common Good Through College Admissions" from the School of Education at Harvard University. More than 100 colleges have endorsed the report and its recommendations, making it potentially the most far-reaching effort at admissions reform ever. The executive summary of the report may be found at www.mcc.gse.harvard.edu.

The report criticizes how the current approach to college admissions overemphasizes individual achievement at the expense of concern for others and the common good. Its recommendations challenge its member colleges to fundamentally reshape the existing admissions process and "reward those who demonstrate true citizenship, deflate undue academic performance pressure, and redefine achievement to create greater equity and access for economically diverse students." A key recommendation is that "the admissions process should both clearly signal that concern for others and the common good are highly valued in admissions and describe what kinds of service, contributions, and engagement are most likely to lead to responsible work, caring relationships, and ethical citizenship."

The spirit of the report can be seen in the supplementary application essay prompts that some colleges are using. These prompts ask students to reflect on their engagement with and contribution to their family, community, or the public good. The extent of the report's eventual impact on student behavior and on the admissions review process itself, however, is yet to be determined. A key recommendation is the one saved for last in the report: that admissions officers, guidance counselors, and parents should challenge the misconception that there are only a handful of excellent colleges and that only a handful create networks vital to job success. We couldn't agree more. It is a recommendation that few would disagree with and one that you can vigorously act on right now.

CHAPTER 3

How Do Colleges Make Their Decisions?

For most students and their parents, the college admissions process is shrouded in mystery. Hundreds of thousands of students apply every year to colleges across the spectrum of selectivity. Each application presents the academic and personal accomplishments of a teenager hoping for admission. After a period ranging from a few weeks to several months, the college's verdict arrives: the student is accepted, denied, wait-listed, or, in the case of some early applicants, deferred until a later round of decision making.

This chapter will focus on what goes on behind the scenes between the time a student submits an application and the time she learns of the college's decision. We end the chapter with a discussion of the roles that high school counselors, college access programs, and parents can play in helping ensure a happy outcome. We also include a short section on independent educational consultants because more families are seeking their services.

WHO WORKS IN ADMISSIONS?

College admissions officers have varied backgrounds. Some make college admissions their careers and may have many years of experience; others are generally younger, spending a few years in admissions before embarking on graduate school or other careers. The latter are often recent graduates of the college where they work and display the energy, maturity, and dedication to do a good job in a very demanding position.

Colleges consciously want an ethnically diverse staff with members who have varied personal interests and backgrounds. Every college will now have one or several Asian, Hispanic, and African American staff members. In addition, colleges want different sets of life perspectives to be heard at the table at decision time. Larger schools with many thousands of applications also hire seasonal readers to help read applicant files, although they do not usually participate in making the final decisions.

Helping Build the Applicant Pool

Evaluating applications is only part of an admissions officer's job, however. Admissions officers typically do more than read applications and make decisions. They work with the dean of admissions, who develops the strategy for marketing the college. This includes planning all the brochures, letters, e-mail, and other outreach that come from the admissions office, as well as the website and perhaps the blog where students and parents easily find information about a college. The staff members decide who will get which mailings, print and electronic, and when they will get them. Special unsolicited mailings from some colleges target selected students as early as the sophomore year of high school. We'll talk more about these unsolicited communications in chapter 5.

Ambassadors and Gatekeepers

Because outreach to prospective students involves much more than e-mail and letters, admissions officers also serve as ambassadors, personally spreading the word about their college. Each fall, they spend up to six to eight weeks on the road visiting high schools and hosting events to meet with students and counselors. Typically, they visit four high schools a day.

Colleges usually assign their staff members to specific regions of the country (and increasingly to other countries). These visits help officers learn more about the high schools in those areas; later they will read the applications of students from those schools. Officers also participate in college nights at hotels or other venues (schools, libraries, private homes of alumni) in their assigned region. These events, sometimes hosted by a single college but often by several together, familiarize parents and students with a college and help the college reach more students than just those at the high schools they can arrange to visit. Some schools hold events in the spring to reach juniors before the following year's application cycle begins. We will discuss these at greater length in chapter 5.

Back on campus, admissions officers conduct group information sessions for college visitors. Spring, summer, and fall bring a steady stream of high school students and their parents to visit colleges. These one-hour information sessions, along with a student-led campus tour, attempt to present the special qualities of the college to prospective families. Admissions staff members also respond to an enormous volume of e-mail and phone calls, answering questions on every conceivable topic and forwarding questions to other college offices and faculty. It is an intense, busy job.

Once the fruits of the admissions officers' outreach efforts arrive—the large pool of applications from eager, well-prepared high school seniors—the primary focus of their work shifts. Formerly ambassadors (one former admissions dean called them "missionaries" for their dedication), admissions officers now become gatekeepers, determining who is admitted and who is denied. From gregarious greeters and public speakers, they become more solitary, reading applications in their offices and homes for much of the winter. Then they may huddle with their colleagues in conference rooms for committee discussions, emerging later once the decisions have been made to greet the hordes of accepted students in the spring.

WHAT HAPPENS TO YOUR APPLICATION?

Once a paper-based process, college applications are now primarily submitted and reviewed online. Most high schools submit counselor and teacher recommendations and transcripts electronically as well. SAT and ACT scores are also transmitted electronically once a student has designated the schools that should receive them. Any material that arrives at the admissions office by regular mail is usually scanned so that it can become part of a student's electronic file. Once a file is complete, with all parts accounted for, it is ready for review.

The review process itself will vary depending on the school. A college that admits students on the basis of grades and test scores alone can use a straightforward, automated process. By contrast, schools that practice "holistic" admissions carefully read and evaluate each individual application, often multiple times.

Trained readers consider many different aspects of a student's record and background to determine whether to offer a given student admission. The process outlined in the following sections is similar to the holistic review used at many private colleges. Specific details will vary from college to college, of course, and will depend to some extent on its selectivity. Some of the specifics we describe are based on the process used by Wesleyan University, a highly selective liberal arts college in Connecticut.[1]

Further on in this section, we will describe the process used at UCLA, a highly selective public university. UCLA conducts its reviews in a manner that is broadly similar to Wesleyan's, although the scale of the process is clearly different. While Wesleyan received about 12,000 applications for the class of 2020 and offered admission to 2,100, UCLA received 97,100 freshman applications and admitted 17,500.

Who Will Be Reading Your File?

A typical private college may have two people read an application, and sometimes more than that, depending on the file itself. Of the two readers, one is frequently the admissions officer assigned to the region where an applicant attends school. Sometimes this same officer may have visited the student's high school earlier in the fall and may also have conducted a formal regional presentation at a local hotel or other public setting. The other evaluator is often randomly selected from among the remaining admissions officers or readers. The admissions office may want one reader with specific expertise and one with a broader view of the entire pool. Sometimes both evaluators are randomly selected. Many colleges assign an admissions officer the task of recruiting applicants from a specific minority group. This officer may read the file of students of color as a third reader. At a few colleges (Caltech, Wellesley College, and Georgetown University are examples), faculty members may also read files, but many more use faculty members as occasional evaluators of special talents—mathematical, musical, and artistic—when a professional assessment is needed.

What Are the First Steps?

Each of the two readers assigned to a file reads it thoroughly. The first reader usually extracts key information and enters it into an electronic snapshot. Grades, class rank, SAT scores, notations about the strength of the student's curriculum, codes for extracurricular activities—all get entered for an at-a-glance objective view of the application. Other factors are noted as well—any special interest in the applicant by coaches or the development office, minority background, or exceptional talent, for example.

Both readers then prepare written summary comments highlighting what is most significant in the candidate's essay, letters of recommendation, and personal qualities that convey a sense of the student beyond a list of grades and activities. The first reader, whether an admissions officer or seasonal reader, usually makes more detailed notes than the second reader. Those notes generally will then be read out loud if the file ends up being discussed in committee. A straightforward application might take only 10 to 15 minutes to read and work up. A complex file could take 30 minutes to digest fully.

Admissions staff members typically have to read 30 files a day during peak reading season, which usually runs from early January through mid-March. Long days and weekends are the norm once reading begins. An admissions officer may read a thousand files or more over the application cycle.

How Is an Application Evaluated?

Usually each evaluator assigns a numerical rating along at least two dimensions—academic qualifications and personal qualities—as well as an overall judgment or recommendation that combines the two in some way. The scale used by colleges can vary—from 1 to 5 at one, from 1 to 9 at another. Some have a separate rating for athletics, others for intellectual curiosity. But the idea is the same: to reduce the complex and often incommensurable data (such as GPAs from different high schools) in a file to a standardized format.

Evaluators may have a list of specific qualities to rate as a key to guide them in assigning ratings on the broader dimensions. At Wesleyan, for example, the academic rating is a rough average of the ratings, from 1 to 9, with 9 the highest possible, in three academic categories: academic achievement, intellectual curiosity, and commitment. This can also include SAT or ACT scores if the student submits them. Wesleyan has a test-optional admissions policy so test scores are not required.

At Wesleyan, a rating of 4 in academic achievement is used for those with "fair to good recommendations" with "some weaknesses apparent in application." A rating of 5 is reserved for students with a "solid academic" load, and a rating of

6 or 7 is used for "an excellent academic record in a demanding curriculum." The top ratings of 8 or 9 go to those with a "flawless academic record in the most demanding curriculum." A rating of 5 in intellectual curiosity would go to a student described as "conscientious," and "strong interest and activity" in "research, independent projects, competitions, etc." would receive a rating of 6 or 7. A student with a "sophisticated grasp of world events and technical information" and "passionate interest in numerous disciplines" would receive 8 or 9 for intellectual curiosity. Personal qualities, or extracurricular strengths, are rated similarly, with each reader assigning an overall "personal" rating or scores based on different aspects of the record, such as evidence of unusual commitment to community service, leadership, or engagement in activities. Wesleyan has two nonacademic categories, personal and extracurricular, each having a 1–9 scale.

Rating systems such as Wesleyan's are based on your overall record through high school. Although you will never know the ratings assigned to you by a college, we describe it to show you how your high school years can be sifted, analyzed, and reduced to numbers so that applicants can be roughly compared to each other. The committee may still want to discuss the application after it has been rated, but, not surprisingly, the higher the ratings, the more likely the student is to be admitted.

TENTATIVE DECISIONS

Once a reader completes the ratings and notes for a given applicant, it is the moment of decision—his or her call on the applicant's status: admit, deny, wait-list, or perhaps something less definitive such as admit-minus or deny-plus, which will lead to further discussion. This call can be a very difficult, even subjective one, though the reader is always expected to use professional judgment and provide a reason for the decision. In reality, most applicants to most colleges can do well enough to graduate within four years, so the question becomes not who is qualified, but who should receive that opportunity.

COLLEGE PRIORITIES

At this point, the full range of a college's priorities plays out, along with, to some extent, the personal preferences and inclinations of the readers. Colleges are complex academic communities that seek to create a rich, stimulating environment academically, culturally, athletically, and socially. As we discussed in the previous chapter, this means crafting a class that includes not only academic superstars but also winning athletes, talented performers and musicians, students from all parts of the country and diverse ethnic and socioeconomic backgrounds, the children of alums, as well as some whose parents are willing and able to make exceptionally generous donations.

These categories are not necessarily mutually exclusive, but realistically few, if any, students can excel in everything. Thus the admissions office makes decisions about individual students so that the class as a whole embodies the priorities of the campus. Here the hooks we described in chapter 2 come into play. With lots of applicants to choose from with similar grades and test scores, the admissions staff members have considerable leeway in exactly who the accepted students will be. Institutional priorities can play a big role in the outcome.

> I went to a college reunion. Some guy got up and said, "You all need to know that 65 percent of you sitting here would not get into this college if you applied today." Parents don't understand that. In our day, if you were a really bright kid, got good grades, did well on your SAT, and could afford it, you could go. Today kids are playing, not just on a different field, but on a different planet.
>
> MOM WHO VOLUNTEERS IN THE COUNSELING OFFICE AT A PRIVATE HIGH SCHOOL

CLEAR-CUT ADMIT OR DENY?

Sometimes the decision is clear-cut. Some applicants are so outstanding in ways important to the college that the decision is obvious to both reviewers of a file: admit. In some cases, the first reader may send a file right to the dean with a recommendation to admit. Colleges may automatically admit students who score at or above a very high rating threshold without further review.

Similarly, at the other end of the continuum, readers prescreen files to identify applicants who fall far short of a college's standards. Identifying these before they are thoroughly read saves readers their time for the stronger files that require careful consideration. They can make these decisions on the basis of grades, test scores, or some other easily detected major weakness, relative to the rest of the pool, that cannot be offset by other factors. It may sound harsh to learn that some files get a decision after only five minutes of evaluation, but that can be the case. The number of applications is increasingly just too large for every file to receive the same level of analysis.

In other cases, two readers may independently recommend denial even though the student's record is academically competitive. At highly selective colleges with many more applicants than spots in the freshman class, some applicants do not distinguish themselves in any way. You don't have to have done anything wrong or have a serious flaw. You just are not distinguished enough from the rest of the pool. To use the lingo of admission officers, you "DSO" (don't stand out) or you are "LMO" (like many others). Here, too, this can end the decision process, or the dean or another senior staff member may review the file briefly to confirm the decision others have made. Colleges may also establish a threshold at the low end: students who score below the threshold will be denied without further review.

THE GRAY ZONE

The most difficult decisions are for those in the middle of the pack—the deny-plus or admit-minus applicants whose ratings total falls between the obvious deny and admit thresholds or the ones referred to committee for additional review. A good number of applicants fall into this gray zone. These applicants have a lot that makes them attractive to the two reviewers, but so do many other applicants. Here the decisions get tougher—more personal and more human—and, as a consequence, more unpredictable and, to some extent, mysterious, at least as seen from the outside.

HOW THE FINAL DECISION IS MADE

The final round is often review by committee.

COMMITTEE DISCUSSION

Consisting of all or a subset of the senior admissions officers (or subcommittee chairs), the committee typically hears an oral overview of each applicant who is referred to it. The admissions officer from the applicant's geographical region usually serves as the student's advocate in the discussion. One young admissions officer, when asked what he had learned in his first year that he could apply in his second, replied, "I learned who it was worth bringing to committee. You can't bring them all." Questions go back and forth, thoughts are exchanged and debated, and then a final, usually decisive, vote is taken: admit, deny, or wait-list (or defer, in the case of early action or early decision). The Tina Fey movie *Admission* pokes satirical fun at this process. (The movie also includes, very briefly, a view of the second edition of this book!) At smaller colleges, the committee may review and act on all decisions, even the easiest ones; some larger colleges do not use committees at all.

DIFFICULT CHOICES

Regardless of how the process unfolds, clearly many of the final decisions are difficult ones that might have turned out differently on another day and with another set of reviewers. The qualitative nature of admissions reviews, along with all the dimensions that a college may consider in crafting its class, creates a lot of uncertainty. Two equally wonderful students apply to a college, and one is admitted, but the other is not. Why?

Unfortunately, this question may not have a clear answer, or the answer may make you uncomfortable. As Shawn Abbott, assistant vice president and dean of admissions at New York University, has stated, "Most of the highly selective institutions in the country could easily fill their classes twice over with candidates possessing similar academic credentials."[3] The colleges cannot always easily explain or defend their decisions, and they almost never explain their decisions to applicants, and only rarely even to school counselors beyond a few generalities. They prefer to talk about the "tremendous quality and size of the applicant pool" and "what a tough year it was."

> I don't know what colleges want. My daughter has the curriculum, extracurriculars (two state championships), high class rank and SATs, and still got deferred from Elite U. She is one of those amazing kids who parents and teachers think is so unique that of course they would want her. I guess we should have had her practice walking on water at birth.
>
> FRUSTRATED PARENT WHO DIDN'T UNDERSTAND HOW COMPETITIVE THE APPLICANT POOL ACTUALLY WAS

I applied early to Yale and was rejected. I had great grades, high SATs, lots of extracurriculars, blah, blah, blah. Everyone thought I was a shoo-in—my parents, my teachers, my relatives, my friends. Then I was rejected. Just plain rejected. I was bummed out for a few days but got over it. But my mom couldn't understand how this could happen. She sent a nice e-mail to the admissions office asking for reasons. This is what they wrote back:

> Realize the personalities on Yale's committee are distinctive to Yale, as are the personalities on admission committees at other schools. And even within a given school, there are sometimes multiple committees that have different constellations of personalities presiding and voting as they see fit. Also within a single committee, three people may like an essay, recommendation, extracurricular activity, etc., but four or even three others on the committee may feel very differently. Such a divided sensibility would result in an unfavorable outcome. Frequently committee members do not agree, which leads to some tough arguments and split votes. This does not mean that the applicant is not extraordinary; it just means that not enough people voted favorably.

I'm not sure this made her feel any better.

HIGH SCHOOL SENIOR

⋈

A LOOK INSIDE THE UCLA ADMISSIONS PROCESS

The admissions process at UCLA gives us additional insight into how difficult admissions decisions are made, this time at the campus that now receives the largest number of freshman applications in the country, with more than 100,000 students applying for fall 2017.

UCLA admissions readers evaluate each application along a set of 14 published criteria, used by all the University of California campuses, that include traditional academic factors such as grades, rigor of curriculum, and standardized test scores, as well as other factors such as special talents, achievements and awards, and "experiences that demonstrate unusual promise for leadership." All accomplishments are viewed in the context of the applicants' "academic and personal circumstances and the overall strength of the UCLA applicant pool." Context is key throughout the review process.

In addition to the application itself, readers have access to detailed information that places each applicant in context, such as where an applicant's GPA, curriculum, and test scores fall percentile-wise among peers at the student's high school and within the overall UCLA applicant pool. Readers also have information about the academic strength of the applicant's high school, the average test scores of all test-takers within a given school and the availability of and student performance in honors-level courses, and factors that may have limited an applicant's opportunities, such as location of the school in a socioeconomically disadvantaged neighborhood. Legacy status is not considered, and state law prohibits consideration of race, gender, or ethnicity. Each application is read and rated independently at least twice, with each reader assigning a single overall "holistic score" from 1 to 5 based on the reader's overall assessment of the student's application. The scores of multiple readers are then averaged, with 1 the highest possible score and 5 the lowest. The average is known as the "read score."

A score of 1 is given to the most outstanding applicants—typically those in the top 5 percent of the applicant pool—across the full range of selection criteria. A score of 1 can also be given to applicants who are academically strong, but whose level of achievement in other areas, such as leadership or service, the strength of their personal qualities, or their likely contributions to the campus, are judged to be extraordinary. A score of 2.5 is given to applicants who have demonstrated high, but not outstanding, levels of achievement across the full range of selection criteria. Applicants receiving scores of 1 to 2.5 constitute roughly the top 25 percent of UCLA's applicant pool and are the most competitive for admission. Approximately half of UCLA's applicant pool earns a score of 4. These applicants are qualified academically for admission, but their overall level of achievement does not stand out.

Freshman applicants to UCLA's College of Letters and Science are reviewed without regard for major, and selection is determined by the read score and available space. Admission to other schools is based on a combination of a student's read score as well as other considerations, such as preparation in mathematics and science for engineering and a portfolio review for an arts program.

THE SPECIAL CASE OF THE MOST SELECTIVE COLLEGES

Parents and students need to realize how complex and fundamentally messy college admissions decisions at selective colleges can be. The purpose of sharing this information is not to discourage you but to help you approach college admissions with a flexible mind-set and encourage you to develop a list of good-fit colleges that includes some where your admission is largely assured.

THE OUTCOME CAN BE UNPREDICTABLE

Almost no one's record will guarantee him or her admission to the most selective colleges in the country. Too many variables, including institutional priorities that are not under your control, may factor into the admissions equation. No one can predict the outcome with absolute certainty. Knowing this may be disillusioning initially, but it also can be liberating. It can help you understand, in your head and heart, that the admit or deny decision made in the admissions office of a selective college is not an evaluation of your worth as a student and as a person. Equally, it does not measure the success of a parent's child-rearing efforts.

Nevertheless, appreciating what goes on behind the scenes in the college admissions process can help explain some of the puzzling situations with which we began this chapter. A student with a terrific record may receive serious consideration at several highly selective schools. But because of the judgments involved, the differing needs of each college, and the qualitative nature of the review process, some schools may admit her and others may end up waitlisting or even denying her: same application, similar schools, different outcomes.

> It looks to the family that this is a perfect student, but most of the students look like that. We're making hairline decisions.[4]
>
> ANN WRIGHT, FORMER VICE PRESIDENT FOR ENROLLMENT, RICE UNIVERSITY

BUT IT IS NOT RANDOM

Although the result of an admissions review may be unpredictable, it is not random. A super-selective college may have a 15 percent admissions rate, but that does not mean that all applicants to that college have the same 15 percent chance of admission. The overall admissions rate for a college is just that—an overall rate that does not consider the factors that make an individual applicant more or less likely to be accepted.

If a college collected and shared more information about its admissions process, in principle you could know the probability of acceptance for a male legacy applying early decision with a midrange (for that school) ACT score and 3.9 unweighted grade point average in a demanding curriculum. Maybe the chances of acceptance for a student with that profile are 70 percent, not the 15 percent figure for the overall applicant pool.

But even then, a fair amount of uncertainty about the outcome would remain. A 70 percent chance of admission means that on average, seven out of ten applicants with that profile will be admitted, but three will not. What may seem like a fair outcome to one of the chosen seven may still seem capricious to the unlucky three. Although the same chance of admission applies to all ten, the outcome for a given individual can be very different.

> I have seen some kids get into selective schools with unlikely stats, and some with very high stats get turned down. As a rule, though, the better the kid's stats, the better the chances. Every applicant does not have the same odds.
>
> EXPERIENCED PRIVATE COUNSELOR

THE ROLE OF YOUR HIGH SCHOOL COUNSELOR

Ideally, your counselor will know you well and have the knowledge and time to help you identify a list of good-fit colleges, as well as help with the application process itself. The more background work you do on your own, researching colleges and learning about the college admissions process, however, the more productive your time with your counselor will be. As we will discuss in chapter 10, your counselor will also prepare the school report that many colleges require. The report recommends you to the college and fleshes out your academic and extra-curricular record in the context of your high school.

At many schools, heavy workloads with hundreds of counselees make it impossible for many counselors, even the most dedicated and hardworking, to do all they would like to do. The college admissions process is certainly easier for students who have extensive, high-quality assistance from their high school counseling office. If help from your school is limited, the best approach is to take advantage of what is available and be prepared to fill in the gaps yourself. Rest assured that you are in good company. If you are willing to make the effort and continue reading this book carefully, you will do just fine.

HOW COLLEGE ACCESS PROGRAMS CAN HELP

If you are the first in your family to attend college, come from a low-income background, or attend a high school without a strong college-going culture, you may find that you need more focused help than your teachers, counselors, parents, and this book alone can provide. Fortunately, many community-based organizations, known commonly as CBOs, as well as federally funded college access programs exist to support you and students like you across the country.

These programs vary in exactly what they do and how they do it, but most offer one-on-one counseling for college, test prep, tutoring, assistance with applying for financial aid, college trips, and more. They usually don't advertise their services but work through schools and other organizations in the community to let students know about their work and how to get involved. One such program is College Summit, the largest nonprofit organization in the United States dedicated to helping low-income students achieve their college and career aspirations. College access programs can supplement other resources, such as those we describe in chapter 5, that are open to all students. Most are local without a national presence. Your high school counselor may know about programs in your area, or you can search for them online.

> Students who don't have a family history of higher education need support and encouragement from home, school, and their community. But the important message is that the opportunity for college is there for any student who wants it.[5]
>
> MATT RUBINOFF, CHIEF STRATEGY OFFICER, STRIVE FOR COLLEGE

Another valuable resource is TRIO, a set of federally funded college opportunity programs designed to help students from disadvantaged backgrounds pursue a college degree. Upward Bound and Educational Talent Search are the best known of the TRIO precollege programs, serving hundreds of thousands of students each year through participating colleges around the country. You can find a directory of all TRIO programs by state and region at the Council for Opportunity in Education website at www.coenet.us.

Online resources can also help. Websites designed primarily for first-generation students include College Greenlight at www.collegegreenlight.com and Strive for College at http://striveforcollege.org. Both offer support, advice, and encouragement on the road to college and provide a wide range of resources to help you research and connect with colleges that are especially welcoming to first-generation students. In addition to college search and planning resources, Strive for College provides free one-on-one online mentoring provided by trained volunteers to help with specific tasks such as college essay writing and applying for financial aid.

At relevant points throughout *Admission Matters* we will highlight specific programs that help first-generation and disadvantaged students gain admission and then succeed in college.

SHOULD YOU CONSIDER HIRING AN INDEPENDENT COLLEGE COUNSELOR?

In many areas of the country, independent, fee-based counselors have become much more popular than they were just a few years ago. Such services can range from a few hours of help with college selection and applications to multiyear "platinum packages" that provide extensive guidance, costing $40,000 or more, geared to preparing students as young as the eighth grade for admission to selective colleges. The platinum package approach is quite rare, however, with the vast majority of independent counselors charging much more modest fees. Sometimes they reduce their fees for less-affluent families and offer pro-bono services through local college-access organizations.

Although we believe that the services of an independent counselor are never absolutely necessary, under some conditions they can be quite helpful. When parents and students have limited access to good counseling at school for any reason, an independent counselor can help a student do an honest self-analysis and develop a balanced list of colleges, as well as help him highlight his strengths in his application essays. Independent counselors can often help with the financial aid side of the application, answering questions and helping families understand a process they may find challenging. Finally, an independent counselor can act as a gentle buffer between parent and child when it comes to deadlines—the counselor, not the parent, becomes the taskmaster.

All of this is light-years away from the platinum package approach to college counseling that involves retaining an expensive, multiyear personal trainer who essentially makes admission to an elite college the center of every life decision her teenage client makes. We think that is an unwise and an unnecessary investment of the few remaining years of childhood, and it puts too much emphasis on getting into the "right" college. Nor is it good training for college and adulthood when a young person will have to make his or her own way in the world.

If you decide to hire an independent counselor, remember that you need your high school counselor to know you as well as possible so he or she can write an effective recommendation for you. You cannot substitute an independent counselor for your high school counselor. Professional independent counselors should be willing to discuss the advice they give you with your school counselor if you ask them to. Information about working with an independent counselor can be found on the websites of the Independent Educational Consultants Association (IECA), www.iecaonline.org, and the Higher Education Consultants Association (HECA), www.hecaonline.org. IECA and HECA set standards for membership and have a searchable directory of member consultants on their sites.

THE PARENTS' ROLE

Parents of course play an important role in their child's college admissions process long before an application is even filed. A loving home where education is valued is the most lasting gift a parent can give a child. When it comes time to seriously begin thinking about college, however, you can take some specific steps to help your child deal with an unfamiliar and sometimes overwhelming process.

Teens differ in the kind and amount of help they will need and are willing to accept, however, so you will have to see what works for both of you. We provide specific suggestions in the following chapters for ways to support your child. For now, we offer a word of caution about over-involvement. Marilee Jones, former dean of admissions at MIT, has vividly described what can happen at the extremes when parents lose perspective:

> More and more, today's parents are getting too involved in their child's college admissions process, and in many cases, their actions and attitudes are getting out of hand. At MIT we've been asked to return an application already in process so that the parent can double-check his/her child's spelling. We've been sent daily faxes by parents with updates on their child's life. We've been asked by

parents whether they should use their official letterhead when writing a letter of recommendation for their own child. Parents write their kids' essays and even attempt to attend their interviews. They make excuses for their child's bad grades and threaten to sue high school personnel who reveal any information perceived to be potentially harmful to their child's chances of admission.[6]

Fortunately, antics like these are exceptional, but many behaviors that might seem less extreme are still worth avoiding. One counselor gives this advice: "It seems very important, at the moment, to get everything just right. The temptation to micromanage is strong. You have experience, and you are probably correct. They are young and have no experience. But they will be your children for the rest of your lives. Don't do anything between now and May 1 of the senior year (or even after that) that might hurt your long-term relationship with your child. Whatever the short-term benefit, it isn't worth it." This same counselor steamed open his daughter's SAT scores when they arrived in the mail so that he could see them while she was away at camp. Sometimes it is hard to take your own advice. Over-involvement sends a clear signal to the child and the college that he can't make it on his own.

CHAPTER 4

How Colleges (and Students) Differ

Finding What Fits

Everyone knows some students who have known exactly where they want to go to college since sixth grade. It may be mom's alma mater on the other side of the country, or the well-regarded state university they have heard about all their lives, or a school whose football team they often seen on TV on New Year's Day. But scratch beneath the surface and ask those same students why that particular college is their first choice; you might not get much of an answer. When you ask them what other colleges they are considering if, heaven forbid, they are not accepted at their top choice, you may find they can't even imagine such an impossible outcome.

At the other extreme, we know many students who have a hard time even beginning to think about a list of potential colleges. Not only do they not have a first choice but also they don't have any well-defined choices at all—nor even a clear idea of where to begin.

Most students, of course, fall somewhere in between. They have some ideas about college choices but no good way to determine whether those choices are really the best ones for them.

SO MANY CHOICES: HOW DO YOU BEGIN?

For all students—even those who think they know what they want—the first step in developing a good college list is an honest self-assessment. You need to look inward before you look outward. A bit further on in this chapter, we'll discuss what should go into that assessment. We'll then spend much of this chapter showing the important differences among colleges. In chapter 5, we'll show you how to take all of this information and use it to identify schools for your own personal college list.

> My original criteria for choosing a college were (1) it had to have cute squirrels, (2) it had to be bigger than my high school, and (3) PE should not be required. But my school does have PE, the squirrels are vicious, and it's about the same size as my high school. So I violated all three of my criteria. I'm sure I could have found my own niche somewhere else, too, but I absolutely love it here.
>
> College sophomore happy with her choice

No Colleges Are Perfect

At the outset, we want to emphasize that as much as the websites and campus tour guides would have you believe otherwise, no college is perfect. The college application process is all about fit—finding colleges that are a good match for you based on your interests, abilities, values, aspirations, and preferences, social and academic. The more you know about yourself and the more you know about colleges, the better that fit can be. Although no perfect college exists, you can find many where you will be perfectly happy. That is a key point to accept. Even if you eventually apply early decision to a college you are sure is *the* college for you, you actually could have chosen many others where you would be happy.

You Are in Control

You have full control over where you apply. You create your own list of colleges, based on your research. The colleges do not decide for you, even though they are marketing themselves to you like crazy. So make the most of the opportunity and select carefully. Later in the college admissions process, control will shift from you to the admissions offices, where the colleges decide whom to accept. At that point, you simply wait patiently for the review process to play out. Finally, at the end of the process, control shifts back to you as you decide which offer of admission to accept, ideally from among two or more fine choices that you are happy with.

DOING YOUR HOMEWORK

But let's not get ahead of ourselves. We are still near the beginning, laying the foundation for building a list of good-fit colleges. Thoughtfully considering your own preferences as well as how colleges differ and then narrowing the list carefully to the right choices for you are critical parts of the admissions process. College rankings certainly can't do this for you. They only tell you what someone else thinks. Doing your homework to identify a group of good-fit colleges is easily half the battle.

SOME QUESTIONS TO ASK YOURSELF

Be honest with yourself as you try to answer the questions that follow. Most students find some of these questions easy to answer and others much more difficult. You may have strong preferences or weak ones. Perhaps you have never thought about your preferences before, and maybe you just plain don't know. That's okay. You have lots of company regardless of which description fits you.

- **What are your academic interests?** Do you have a strong interest in a particular profession, such as nursing or engineering, and plan to work in that field right after college? Do you think you would like to study psychology (or biology or French) but are unsure of your final career path? How specialized is your field of interest? Are you undecided about a major and want to explore different options before making a commitment? Are you somewhere in between?

- **What kind of student are you?** Are you strongly self-motivated to achieve, or are you somewhat less ambitious academically (although you may have done very well)? Do you thrive on intellectual engagement with bright and talented peers, or is that less of a priority? Do you need to be at or near the top of your class to feel good about yourself, or is lower down okay if the competition is stiff? Are you willing to actively seek out help or resources if you need them, or do you want them to be easily available with little effort on your part? Do you want to be independent or looked after to some degree?

- **How do you learn best?** Does the format of your classes matter to you? Do you prefer large classes with no pressure to participate actively, or small classes where you can contribute to the discussion and you always have to be prepared? Do you want a mix of both?

- **What activities outside class matter most to you?** Do you enjoy being involved in a number of different activities at once, or do you prefer to focus on one or two? Do you want to participate in athletics in college, either competitively or just for fun? How specialized is your sport, and how good are you at it? Is your sport relatively unusual, such as squash or fencing, and therefore available on only some campuses? Do you want to be active in community service and on a campus with many like-minded students? Do you strive to be a leader in all your activities, or is just being a contributor okay?

- **How important is prestige to you?** Do you want people to be visibly impressed when they hear where you are going to college? Would you be disappointed if they have never heard of your school or don't know much about it? Even if this is true, why is this important to you when balanced against other factors? Because the allure of aiming for a prestigious college may be so attractive, we caution you to balance this factor against others because the most prestigious schools are also the most selective.

- **Do you want a diverse college?** Do you want a campus that is highly diverse in gender, race, ethnicity, or sexual and religious preferences? Or would you prefer a more homogeneous campus, or does it not matter to you one way or the other? How important to you are campus programs that openly welcome and celebrate diversity?

- **What kind of social and cultural environment would you like best?** Would you like to join a fraternity or sorority? How do you feel about a campus with, or without, a strong Greek presence? Do you want a campus known for its sense of community, or would you prefer to "do your own thing"? Do you like the feeling of knowing almost everyone, or are you comfortable with a large campus where you will never know most of the students? Do you prefer an artsy environment, a politically active one (liberal or conservative), or something else? Preppy or not? Do you want lots of options on how to spend a Friday night, or will a smaller list of possibilities work for you?

- **Where do you want to live for the next four years?** Do you want or need to stay close to home, or are you interested in experiencing a new part of the country? Do you like big cities, or do you prefer a small town or suburban setting? Are you open to all options? Do you want guaranteed on-campus housing for four years, or are you happy or at least willing to live off campus, maybe as soon as sophomore year? Do you want to be near skiing, surfing, lots of bookstores, restaurants, a shopping mall? What kind of weather do you really like, and what kind can you tolerate?

Keep these questions in mind as you research colleges. As your list develops, you may be surprised by changes in your preferences and by just how flexible you really are (or aren't). The purpose of self-assessment is to help you identify your preferences so you can consider colleges systematically. At the end of this chapter, you'll find a questionnaire to help you record all of your preferences for later use in evaluating specific colleges. You can also download it at www .admissionmatters.com.

You also need to know how colleges vary. Institutional mission—the goals a college sets for itself—is key to understanding how one type of college differs from another.

COMMUNITY COLLEGES

One experienced high school counselor we know likes to tell all her junior year students at the assembly welcoming them back in the fall that they have already been accepted to college. She always gets lots of puzzled looks until she explains that community colleges have an open door admissions policy and admit anyone with a high school diploma or its equivalent. Although we have written *Admission Matters* primarily for students seeking to enter a four-year college directly, it is important to briefly note another college option that can lead to that four-year degree. Students choose a community college for many reasons: financial, personal, or because they need to demonstrate that they can succeed in college-level work to gain admission to a four-year college of their choosing.

Community colleges offer two-year associate of science or associate of arts degrees designed to prepare students to transfer to other colleges to complete their work for a bachelor's degree. Community college tuition and fees are generally much lower than those of public universities, and they are known for small classes and flexible schedules. They can be a good, cost-effective alternative for the first two years of a student's college education. Some community colleges have school-affiliated housing, although most do not, and a few even offer four-year degrees themselves.

Most community colleges have articulation agreements with public universities in their states to ease the transition to a state university on completion of the associate's degree, and some have agreements with selected private colleges. But you can also transfer to schools without an articulation agreement. We will talk more about the transfer process in chapter 12.

We turn now to a discussion of the different types of colleges that offer bachelors degrees.

LIBERAL ARTS COLLEGES

Undergraduate education is the primary, and often the only, mission of a liberal arts college. Swarthmore College, Beloit College, Davidson College, Knox College, and College of Wooster are examples of liberal arts colleges. They award most of their degrees to undergraduates in the liberal arts and sciences disciplines, which include the social sciences such as economics and political science, sciences such as physics and biology as well as mathematics, and humanities and arts fields such as English, music, and history.

The focus that liberal arts colleges place on these academic fields distinguishes them from colleges that also offer more practical programs, such as engineering, education, or business—although some liberal arts colleges do both to some extent. Lafayette College and Union College, for example, are liberal arts colleges that offer engineering; Skidmore College has education and business majors. Harvey Mudd College and Bucknell University, both especially well-known for their strong engineering programs, are classified as liberal arts colleges because they award a high percentage of degrees in fields other than engineering.

Most liberal arts colleges enroll only undergraduates, but some have very small graduate programs as well. The key to classifying a school as a liberal arts college is how much it focuses on educating undergraduates in liberal

> A liberal arts college has a special quality. You see your friends all over campus; the president actually knows your name. Professors have their class to dinner. You feel like you belong.
>
> PARENT OF STUDENT AT A LIBERAL ARTS COLLEGE

arts and sciences disciplines. Almost all liberal arts colleges in the United States are private and charge higher tuition fees than public universities.

The Academic Program

As we noted, a liberal arts college provides students with a sound foundation in core areas such as English, philosophy, history, psychology, music, physics, and mathematics. Perhaps a better term for them would be liberal arts and sciences colleges to reflect the breadth of their academic programs. They also often offer interdisciplinary programs that draw from several different fields, such as women's studies, philosophy of science, and international relations. Liberal arts programs are not directly career focused, although virtually all can connect students with internships to help them explore careers loosely related to their subject of study.

Classes at liberal arts colleges are usually taught exclusively by faculty members, without the help of graduate student teaching assistants, also known at TAs. Except for introductory courses in popular fields, they are generally small and frequently conducted in seminar format when the professor and students explore a subject together and when everyone takes an active part in the conversation. Small classes generally mean many opportunities to write, contribute to class discussion, and receive individualized feedback on your academic progress.

Obviously, a smaller school cannot offer as many courses in a subject as are offered at larger institutions, but undergraduates take only a dozen or so courses in their major anyway, so you will always have enough courses to satisfy your desire for depth. At some colleges, cross-registration with nearby colleges expands the options beyond one campus. Consortiums such as the Claremont Colleges (Pomona College, Claremont McKenna College, Scripps College, Pitzer College, and Harvey Mudd College) and the Five College Consortium (University of Massachusetts at Amherst, Smith College, Hampshire College, Amherst College, and Mt. Holyoke College) are good examples.

Students also have ample opportunities to participate in faculty research as well as to design independent research projects, although the variety and intensity will be less than that found at research universities that we discuss further on. Liberal arts colleges believe that a broad, non-vocationally oriented education that emphasizes critical thinking and analysis is excellent preparation for any later career choice, as well as for graduate and professional school. Graduates of liberal arts colleges succeed in all walks of life.

CAMPUS SIZE AND COMMUNITY FEEL

Enrollment at liberal arts colleges typically ranges from about 1,000 to 2,500 undergraduates, although a small number, such as Bucknell University, the University of Richmond, and Wesleyan University, have more. Because most liberal arts colleges are located in small towns and in suburbs, student life tends to center on the college and its rich array of extracurricular clubs and activities. Students generally live on campus all four years and know many of their classmates well. It is also generally easy to get to know your professors, inside and outside of the classroom. Most keep generous office hours. These relationships create the strong sense of community that is the signature of a liberal arts college.

For those who like the idea of a liberal arts college but also want a big city at their doorstep, a small number of schools meet both criteria. Among them are Barnard College in New York City, Macalester College in St. Paul, Trinity College in Hartford, and Rhodes College in Memphis.

ATHLETICS AND ACTIVITIES

Many liberal arts colleges have athletic programs at the National Collegiate Athletic Association (NCAA) Division III level. As we will discuss in chapter 11, the NCAA divides its member teams into three categories, Divisions I, II, and III, in descending order of athletic competitiveness. With fewer students and a less intense level of competition than that found at Division I or II schools, liberal arts colleges usually have a higher percentage of their students playing varsity sports than other types of schools.

This same general principle applies to other extracurricular activities. With fewer students vying for a newspaper job or a seat in the violin section of the orchestra, a greater percentage of students can get involved. But the scale of the activity may be smaller. The campus newspaper at a liberal arts college may come out just once a week, whereas a larger school is likely to have a daily (and bigger) paper. You may have fewer organized activities to choose from at a liberal arts college compared to a larger school, but regardless of the absolute number, you will always find many options for involvement. Students can start new activities if they want to. You'll keep bumping into your friends, acquaintances, and professors even in diverse activities, because the community is small. At Hendrix College in Arkansas, the servers in the campus dining hall know all the students by name.

RESEARCH UNIVERSITIES

In contrast to liberal arts colleges, research universities have three interconnected missions: teaching undergraduate and graduate students, research, and public service (especially at public universities). Research generates new knowledge, and through public service, the knowledge generated is shared with society at large.

> My mother kept talking about the small class size at the great liberal arts college we visited, but I didn't care about that. I liked the idea of having just about every possible option open to me.
>
> Freshman happy at a large research university

Columbia University, Rice University, Duke University, Oklahoma State University, the University of Michigan, and the University of Nebraska are examples of research universities. An institution is classified as a research university based on the number of doctoral degrees it awards each year across a number of fields. About two-thirds of research universities are public and one-third private.

Academic Programs

Research universities offer undergraduate degrees in a wide range of academic subjects, from the traditional liberal arts fields, to interdisciplinary programs that cut across two or more areas of inquiry, to programs that are applied or professional in their focus. At the University of California, Davis, for example, a student can major in fields as diverse as Russian, cognitive science, chemical physics, civil engineering, or animal science, among many others.

Research universities are often organized into "colleges" that focus on a group of disciplines. At UC Davis, Russian, cognitive science, and chemical physics are offered by the College of Letters and Science, civil engineering is offered by the College of Engineering, and animal science is in the College of Agricultural and Environmental Sciences. Although all students can participate in all aspects of campus life, the college that offers the major determines the kind of academic experience a student will have.

Students with a major that is offered within a letters and science college will have a liberal arts education in a research university setting. They will take courses across a wide range of subject areas, as well as in-depth work in their major.

Students in other colleges, such as engineering, will typically have a more specialized education with fewer opportunities to branch out beyond the major—you can't fit in everything if you want to graduate in four years.

Classes at research universities, particularly at the introductory level, may be quite large, with several hundred students each. These large lecture classes are usually accompanied by small discussion or lab sections, often taught by graduate students serving as TAs. Research university faculty members generally teach fewer classes per term because of their other responsibilities, and thus they may be less accessible to undergraduate students than faculty members at liberal arts colleges.

How you feel about all of this will depend on how much contact you want with professors and how much you care about the relative anonymity of large classes. Research universities also vary greatly in how much they use TAs for undergraduate instruction. Although often enthusiastic and committed teachers, TAs have less teaching experience than faculty members, and they may be hard to find when you need letters of recommendation for a job or graduate school.

THE ROLE OF RESEARCH

More so than at liberal arts colleges, faculty members at research universities are evaluated, promoted, and given raises on the quality and quantity of their research as well as the quality of their teaching. At the strongest and best-known research universities, faculty members do research at the frontiers of their fields using well-equipped research laboratories and libraries.

This does not mean, however, that these schools ignore undergraduates. You are still important, but you are not the center of the enterprise as you are in high school or at a liberal arts college. In fact, learning from professors who are very active in research is a valuable opportunity for undergraduates, particularly those majoring in the sciences or social sciences, where new research can rapidly change a field. It is exciting to learn from teachers whose research will appear in tomorrow's headlines and next year's textbooks and who can convey firsthand what discovery and scholarship are all about.

Research universities offer many opportunities for undergraduates, not just graduate students, to become involved in faculty research projects, but you have to be energetic in seeking them out. Motivated, prepared students can almost always find a faculty member happy to welcome them as a junior colleague in their research activities.

CAMPUS SIZE AND COMMUNITY FEEL

Research universities come in all sizes. They range from quite small (Caltech, for example, has about 1,000 undergraduate students and about 1,250 graduate students) to medium (Johns Hopkins University has about 6,000 undergraduates and 8,200 graduate students) to very large (Texas A&M University in College Station has almost 49,000 undergraduates and about 14,500 graduate students). Most research universities enroll about 20,000 to 30,000 students, graduate and undergraduate combined, so that overall they are more than 10 times the size of a typical liberal arts college. Research universities are located everywhere—in cities, suburbs, and rural areas.

Because of the size of most research universities, you will need to be more deliberate about seeking out friends. Because many students may live off campus after freshman year, the community may have less of a feeling of belonging unless you make an effort to build your own by joining clubs and groups and generally getting involved in campus life outside the classroom.

ATHLETICS AND ACTIVITIES

Research universities and their Division I teams dominate media coverage of college football and basketball. Homecoming on many research university campuses is often scheduled around a home football game, and returning alums join current students in rooting for their alma mater. School spirit surrounding athletics can be an important part of campus life on large campuses, with the local stadium filling to capacity with students cheering wildly for the home team.

Of course, life outside of class at a research university is not limited to spectator sports. Research universities generally host hundreds of activities and clubs, plus club and intramural sports teams. They also often have major performing arts halls on campus that serve as cultural hubs not only for the campus but also for the community. These facilities tend to attract big name performers and speakers. The array of options for involvement is generally vast and sometimes overwhelming. Choosing wisely among them is important.

> There is so much to do here—it's like putting your head in front of an open fire hydrant to get a drink.
>
> STUDENT COMMENTING ABOUT ACTIVITIES AT A RESEARCH UNIVERSITY

HONORS PROGRAMS

Research universities, especially public ones, often have honors programs or other special opportunities for their most academically motivated and able students. These programs offer small discussion-based seminars, honors housing, and special advising and mentoring opportunities, among other features. Good examples can be found at the University of Michigan; University of Texas, Austin; Pennsylvania State University; Arizona State University; UCLA; and a number of others. In these programs highly qualified students can learn in some smaller classes and receive the personal attention of a liberal arts college in a setting that also provides the advantages of a large research university, potentially at a much lower cost. At some schools, students have to apply separately for the honors program when they apply for admission; other schools simply invite students to participate based on their strong academic credentials.

WHAT'S IN A NAME?

Don't let the name of an institution mislead you. Bucknell University, Colgate University, and the University of Richmond, for example, are liberal arts colleges, and Dartmouth College and the College of William and Mary are medium-sized research universities. You'll need to look deeper than the word *college* or *university* in its name to determine a school's actual mission and the kind of education it provides. In this book, we use the terms pretty much interchangeably, although we probably use the term *college* more often for simplicity. Much more important than the name is the actual undergraduate experience.

It pays, however, to watch out for similar names that can be easily confused. As examples, Trinity College and Wesleyan University are both in Connecticut, but Trinity University and Wesleyan College are in Texas and Georgia, respectively. Miami University is located in Ohio, but the University of Miami is in— you guessed it—Miami, Florida. We could offer more examples, but you get the idea.

MASTER'S UNIVERSITIES AND BACCALAUREATE COLLEGES

Despite all the attention they get, research universities and liberal arts colleges make up a little less than 25 percent of all four-year colleges and universities in the United States. The remaining schools, with the exception of specialized colleges that we discuss further on, fall into two additional categories: master's universities and general baccalaureate colleges with diverse programs.

MASTER'S UNIVERSITIES

Master's universities, public and private, typically offer undergraduate degrees in the liberal arts and in some applied fields such as business, engineering, education, or nursing, but they award more than half of their degrees to students enrolled in graduate programs leading to the master's degree. Master's universities generally draw most of their students from their own area of the country.

As a rule—but again with major exceptions in the private sector such as Villanova University, Elon University, and Providence College—a significant percentage of students at master's universities commute from home or live off campus. Master's universities are about evenly divided between public and private control. San Francisco State University, Morehead State University (Kentucky), and Jacksonville State University (Alabama) are examples of public master's universities. The size of master's universities varies widely. Average class size varies, too, although in general, classes tend to be somewhere between those of a liberal arts college and a research university.

Most master's universities have Division II athletic programs, although some are members of the National Association of Intercollegiate Athletics (NAIA), another collegiate athletics–governing organization. Campuses with a higher percentage of undergraduate students living on campus generally have a rich array of extracurricular activities available. Less-residential campuses may have many activities available as well, but fewer students tend to be involved in them.

Because master's universities vary so widely along so many different dimensions, you will need to pay particularly close attention to the college attributes you are looking for when you consider them. Some have the feel and offerings of a liberal arts college—Saint Mary's College of California and Rollins College are examples—whereas others, such as San Jose State University and Creighton University, are more like smaller-scale research universities.

BACCALAUREATE COLLEGES WITH DIVERSE PROGRAMS

Baccalaureate is simply another word for *undergraduate*. Baccalaureate colleges with diverse programs primarily emphasize undergraduate education just like liberal arts colleges, but they award more than half of their degrees in applied fields such as business, nursing, and education and so do not meet the formal criteria for classification as a liberal arts college. Some of these campuses enroll significant numbers of older students returning to college and part-time students, as well as traditional-age full-time undergraduates. About 85 percent of schools in this category are private. Examples are Elizabethtown College (Pennsylvania), Asbury College (Kentucky), Carroll College (Montana), and High Point University (North Carolina). The majority enroll under 2,000 students, although some are larger. Baccalaureate colleges tend to be regionally focused like master's universities, but they are generally more residential than the average master's university.

Baccalaureate colleges with diverse programs with a high percentage of students living on campus for freshman year and beyond generally offer a full array of on-campus activities, including intercollegiate and intramural athletics, and share many features with liberal arts colleges. Athletics at these schools tend to be Division III, with some campuses belonging instead to the NAIA.

CONSIDERING ALL THE OPTIONS

Master's universities and baccalaureate colleges with diverse programs vary widely in selectivity, but only a few would be considered selective using our definition of a school that accepts fewer than half its applicants. They can be affordable and accessible alternatives to liberal arts colleges or research universities and can be a wonderful choice for many students. Baccalaureate colleges can be especially attractive to students who would like the benefits of a smaller residential school while pursuing an undergraduate degree in an applied field such as nursing, sports management, or criminal justice.

The approach to finding the good fit that we will describe further on works just as well for colleges in these categories as it does for research universities and liberal arts colleges. The most important thing is to understand the mission of each school you are considering and what the undergraduate experience will be like. Once you understand that, how a school is officially classified really shouldn't matter to you at all.

SPECIALIZED PROGRAMS

Yet another kind of college is the highly specialized school, such as a music conservatory (for example, the Juilliard School or the New England Conservatory), art institute (for example, California Institute of the Arts or the Rhode Island School of Design), or undergraduate business (for example, Babson College or

Bentley College, both in the Boston area) or engineering school (for example, Cooper Union in New York, Rose-Hulman Institute of Technology in Indiana, and Colorado School of Mines). With their focus on military training and a career in the military, the service academies such as West Point and the Air Force Academy fall into this category as well. Some specialized schools, such as the Juilliard School and the service academies, are highly selective in admissions.

SHOULD YOU CONSIDER A SPECIALIZED COLLEGE?

Specialized schools are appropriate for students with highly focused, well-developed interests and clear career goals. A student who wants to be a professional musician and is committed to a career as a performer, for example, may decide that a conservatory is the best fit. A student planning to study civil engineering may opt for a school that prepares only engineers. And so forth.

Other students who want to study these same subjects may find that one of the many colleges that are not specialized will allow them greater educational breadth in addition to courses in their special area of interest. It is much easier to explore other fields if the courses are readily available. If your interests change later, even though you don't expect them to, it is almost always simpler to switch majors within a given college than it is to switch colleges.

LEARNING MORE ABOUT THE OPTIONS

Which way to go depends a lot on your level of commitment to your field of interest: for specialized schools, you need to be very sure about what you want to study and do after college. Doing in-depth research into career choices as well as a careful assessment of your level of commitment to a specific career is critical. Specialized programs usually have detailed requirements for admission that require demonstrating your particular talent or skill at a high level, and students often have to start assembling the different pieces during their junior year. So find out early what is needed. We'll discuss specialized options for artists and performers in chapter 11.

COLLEGES WITH SPECIAL AFFILIATIONS

Some colleges have historical affiliations with an appealing and distinctive environment.

RELIGIOUS AFFILIATIONS

Many colleges have a religious affiliation that goes back to their founding and that varies widely in terms of how much it affects the daily life of students. Perhaps the best known of these are the Catholic colleges, such as Georgetown University, University of Notre Dame, and Boston College. Davidson College was founded by Presbyterians and Wesleyan University by Methodists; Swarthmore College and Haverford College still retain echoes of their Quaker origins; Brigham Young University remains a formal part of the Mormon Church; St. Olaf College is Lutheran; and Brandeis University has its roots in Judaism. There are hundreds more. Most colleges with religious origins, whether still active or historical, welcome students of all backgrounds.

The extent to which the founding religion is a visible part of everyday campus life varies greatly from school to school. At some, it may be readily accessible to those who seek involvement but pretty much in the background for everyone else. At other schools, it is much more prominent, with mandatory chapel attendance, faith-based declarations, and other religion-based requirements. Some web-based research will help you sort this out fairly easily and help you determine where you would feel most comfortable.

HISTORICALLY BLACK COLLEGES

Established at a time when may American universities were closed to African Americans, the 100 Historically Black Colleges and Universities (HBCUs) in existence today have the principal mission of educating African Americans, although they are open to all. Located primarily in the South, the HBCUs enroll almost 8 percent of all African American college students yet award about 15 percent of bachelor's degrees earned by them. Most, such as Howard University, are coeducational, but a few, such as Spelman College and Morehouse College, enroll only women or men, respectively. These colleges provide a highly supportive environment and successfully launch their students on careers of distinction. A link to more information about HBCUs can be found in the Resources section at the back of this book.

WOMEN'S COLLEGES

Until the last third of the twentieth century, some of the best-known private colleges in the United States were single sex. A number of high-profile women's colleges have elected to remain open to women only. As a group they are an academically strong and attractive option for students who would welcome the kind of empowering environment that an all-female student body provides. Women-only colleges include Stephens College, Wellesley College, Mount Holyoke College, Agnes Scott College, Smith College, and about 35 others as of this writing.

A few women's colleges are part of a formal consortium whose member colleges share resources and facilities. Scripps College, for example, is a member of the Claremont Colleges in Southern California. Scripps students can take courses, use the libraries, and eat in the dining halls at the other four member campuses of the consortium and vice versa. They also share sports teams with Claremont McKenna College and Harvey Mudd College, two of the consortium members. Other colleges have arrangements with individual colleges; Barnard College, for example, has a cooperative arrangement with Columbia University. These arrangements provide students with coeducational experiences while still retaining the ambience of a women's college. Research has documented that alumnae of women's colleges are more positive about their experiences than alumnae of coed schools. Some major figures in contemporary American life such as former Secretary of State Hillary Clinton and journalists Gwen Ifill and Diane Sawyer are graduates of women's colleges. More information about women's colleges can be found at www.womenscolleges.org.

EARNING YOUR DEGREE ABROAD, IN ENGLISH

The combination of quality education and immersion in a different culture can entice some to earn a degree, in English, at a wide range of programs abroad, such as those at the American Universities of Paris, Rome, Cairo, and Beirut or the bachelor's programs at Utrecht University in Holland or Sophia University in Japan. An increasing number of US universities also have campuses abroad, in places as disparate as China and the Middle East, central Europe and central Asia.

To date, most American students who decide to study abroad full-time look to universities in the English-speaking world, particularly in Canada and the United Kingdom (UK). In this section we will preview some of those popular programs. At the same time, the internationalization of education worldwide has led to a proliferation of English-taught degrees in non-English-speaking countries, with low or even no tuition cost. We will introduce you to examples of those in one

European country as well. More detailed information about a broader range of options can be found in the *Guide to International University Admission* on the International page of the Knowledge Center at www.nacacnet.org.

CANADA

For Americans, Canadian universities offer the advantage of proximity. Almost all of them are located within a hundred miles of the US border. Although Canada has fewer universities than the United States, you can find world-class specialized programs and liberal arts degrees, with campus environments like those in the United States. Because one of every six Canadians was born outside Canada, Canadian campuses are extraordinarily multicultural. They also have broadly available co-op programs that offer paid work experience as part of their educational programs, and the cost of tuition is half to two-thirds that of comparable US colleges.

All but a couple of Canadian universities are public, and their quality of teaching and research is continually assessed, sometimes by provincial or regional authorities as well as by university overseers. Most undergraduate degrees are four years, but some provinces offer a three-year bachelor's degree with an optional fourth year "honours" degree for those who wish to go on to a graduate program. Because Canada has two official languages, you can also study in French or in a bilingual university program, especially in the eastern provinces.

As in most American universities, you do not have to have a specific major in mind when you apply, but you usually apply to a broad school, such as natural sciences, social sciences, arts (including the humanities), or business. The general model is like most US public universities. Most Canadian schools are medium-sized to large, like American state schools.

THE UNITED KINGDOM AND IRELAND

Farther away and culturally diverse in a different way, the universities of England, Wales, and Northern Ireland have special appeal if you are ready to concentrate on one academic subject or, in the case of Scotland and the Irish Republic, an initial three or four subjects within a given field of study, such as science

> While there are many similarities between living in the States and Canada, the multitude of cultures I have found up here is amazing. You see so many people from so many different nations live, work, and study together. It really opens your eyes to the world.
>
> AMERICAN STUDENT ATTENDING COLLEGE IN CANADA

or business. We go into much more detail in chapter 10, but here are some basics you should know as you do your research.

Choosing a Major and Time to Degree

For most British universities you apply to an individual major rather than the university as a whole, so you have to have a very solid idea of what you want to study. In many majors, which are called "courses" there, you will take few, if any, courses (in the American sense) outside your major. It is also very difficult to switch majors once you have enrolled. Because you were admitted to a particular major, there is probably no room for you in another one if you change your mind. The approach is very different from the American philosophy of a liberal arts education, which asks students in all majors to take courses across the curriculum. So before applying to these universities, you have to know for sure what your primary academic interest is.

As in Canada, tuition is much lower than at comparable universities in the United States, but it can vary according to the subject studied, with sciences being more expensive than the humanities. Degrees typically take three years, occasionally four years (mostly in Scotland), depending on the program and university, with degrees in the professions taking up to seven years. Through the Erasmus Programme, you may be able to study or work abroad for a semester or a year to teach or train in any of 33 European countries as part of your degree. At most Irish universities, a year of study abroad or participation in the Erasmus Programme would entail four years of study rather than the usual three; the UK refers to this year away for work or study as the "sandwich year," and it would also require an extra year at university.

Language is worth mentioning here: both island nations use familiar words in a very unfamiliar way, as we saw previously when we mentioned the different meanings of the term "courses." A "catalog" is called a "prospectus," "faculty" is what we call "department," residence halls are called "accommodations," and teachers may be called "staff," "lecturers," or "tutors." North American English speakers might want a glossary to translate their native tongue into British English.

Campus Life

Campus life is rich and lively, but not quite like North American universities. For example, though sports are just as competitive, varied, and spirited as sports in North America, students train and compete in clubs sponsored by student unions (student governments) rather than by the universities themselves. Many universities have traditions, both solemn and silly, that have endured, sometimes for centuries. Continental Europe is accessible and close, making vacations unsurpassed opportunities to travel affordably. The best all-around online resource for research about schools is UCAS at www.ucas.ac.uk for the UK and the Irish Universities Association at www.iua.ie for the Irish Republic. The British Council also has a useful website covering many aspects of studying in the UK and applying to its universities at www.educationuk.org/global.

UK Rankings

Several national rankings of universities in the UK are published annually using official data collected by Higher Education Statistics Agency and the National Student Survey. Each ranks UK universities overall based on a variety of criteria including student satisfaction (including teaching quality), career placement, and research quality, and also by individual subjects. The specific criteria used and their weightings vary depending on the ranking system. Although somewhat controversial in the UK, the rankings are generally more highly respected than their American counterparts and can help in learning about UK universities from afar.

The most popular publication presenting rankings information is the *Good University Guide*, published by the *London Times* and available through Amazon .com. You can access interactive tables through an online subscription to the *London Times*. *The Guardian*, another major British newspaper, publishes *The Guardian University Guide*, with the data available at no cost at www.theguardian .com/education/universityguide. A third set of rankings, the *Complete University Guide*, is also available free of charge at www.thecompleteuniversityguide.co.uk. Finally, an official website for comparing UK higher education data on programs and outcomes at all UK universities can be found at http://unistats.direct.gov.uk.

STUDYING IN ENGLISH-TAUGHT DEGREE PROGRAMS IN A NON-ENGLISH-SPEAKING COUNTRY: THE DUTCH EXAMPLE

Many countries in Europe, as well as in other parts of the world, have undergraduate degree programs taught in English. Each national university system is different, with differing admission requirements, procedures, terminology, and costs, including a few that are tuition-free for all. (Bear in mind that "tuition" is the cost of instruction only and does not include living expenses, books, and so on.) You can research each easily on the Internet by searching English-taught undergraduate degrees in the country you are interested in. Most European universities are public.

Holland, where 60 percent of undergraduate programs are taught in English, offers a good case study of one such option. There are well over 100 undergraduate degree programs taught in English in Holland's research universities—with a free course in Dutch to help international students feel more at home (although English speakers will find virtually no language barriers in Holland). These three-year programs focus on a broad spectrum of subjects from a research perspective. Another 200 undergraduate programs are taught in English at Dutch universities of applied science, with a focus on professional preparation and practical experience—these degrees take four years. The Dutch undergraduate system also includes eight university colleges—small residential learning communities affiliated with larger research universities and usually located there—that offer a three-year liberal arts education, in English. All of these institutions have access to the Erasmus Programme.

The Dutch approach to teaching is interactive and student-centered, with a focus on teamwork and instructors who facilitate and guide the learning process. As in Canada and the UK, the quality of higher education is assured by a national system of regulation and quality assurance. Tuition for a US student would generally be somewhat less than in the UK or Canada. If you are a dual citizen with an EU or EEA passport, you would pay the same very low tuition as a Dutch citizen.

WHICH KIND OF COLLEGE IS BEST FOR YOU?

Which kind of college is best for you? Well, as with most things in life generally and in college admissions, it depends. It depends on your personality, your learning style, and your academic interests. After doing some research and introspection, do your preferences align better with one type of college than another? If so, you have taken a major step forward. You may also find, though, that you do not have a clear preference. Many students feel comfortable in different kinds of settings, and their final choice depends on where they are admitted as well as the other factors that they discovered as part of their self-assessment. In this section, we'll look at some characteristics of colleges that we've touched on in our previous discussion of types of colleges. We think it will help to revisit them, one by one, as you reflect on what is important to you.

LOCATION, LOCATION, LOCATION

When you close your eyes and try to imagine yourself in your ideal college environment, what do you see? Do you envision a bustling city, with the excitement, anonymity, and diversity of a large population? Or do you envision a more bucolic setting, perhaps near a small town, with expansive lawns and a slower pace? Or something in between? Despite the trend for students to think more nationally rather than locally when considering colleges, most students still go to college in their home part of the country. Some students, however, see college as an opportunity to explore a different part of the country and factor this into their college search plans accordingly.

> I was really surprised by my son's reaction to certain colleges. The original Birkenstock-wearing California kid, he fell in love with a small liberal arts college in rural Massachusetts (enrollment 2,000) as well as a large research university in New York City (enrollment 23,000). Go figure.
>
> OBSERVATION OF A SURPRISED PARENT

Weather and Culture

Each area of the country has its own weather and, more important, elements of its own culture. Try to keep your mind and options open, and don't automatically rule out a part of the country without carefully considering why. Be aware, though, that a campus in rural Maine or the Upper Midwest that is gorgeous when you visit in the fall could be less appealing in winter if you don't care for snow. Cultural differences can also pose a challenge for some. We know a young woman from the East who was determined to go to the most prestigious college that accepted her, no matter what. She chose to attend an ultra-selective college on the West Coast for that reason and ended up miserable because she thought it rained too much and that everyone was too laid back. Few people would describe Stanford University that way, but she did. The fit, for her, was a poor one.

Be Sure to Do Your Homework

If you are drawn to colleges in other parts of the country, be sure to do your homework about what life would actually be like if you were to spend four years there. Consider possible differences in food, politics, weather, and life in general. In addition, it can sometimes be a little harder to get home for the holidays from more remote colleges. Some parents want a "one-plane-ride" school for their child. However, living in a different part of the country can be wonderful if you are open to change.

> My son grew up in a town with a big university, and that's what he's used to. When we toured small schools, he would say, "This is their union? This is their athletic facility?"
>
> MOTHER OF A COLLEGE FRESHMAN HAPPY AT A LARGE UNIVERSITY

SIZE

As we have previously described, colleges vary greatly in size. Some have fewer than 1,000 undergraduate students, and a handful of them have 40,000 or more, with the rest somewhere in between. Private liberal arts colleges tend to be among the smallest; the largest campuses are research universities, usually public.

How Size Affects the Feel of a Campus

Size can play a major role in how a campus feels. Michael Tamada, former director of institutional research at Occidental College and now at Reed College, has reflected on the differences: "A small college is like a small town; simply walking through the quad, you will pass by familiar faces of people whom you know. A large university is more like a city; as you walk through the quad or hallways, you'll mainly see faces of strangers, with an occasional encounter with someone who you know. These experiences can be comforting, stifling, liberating, or alienating depending on your personality."[1]

> At UC Santa Cruz, I thought, "This is so neat," but my son said, "This is the boonies." At UCLA, I thought, "He'll get lost in a place like this," but he came back beaming.
>
> CALIFORNIA PARENT

Size and the Educational Experience

Size affects not only the ambience of a campus but also often the educational experience as well. For one thing, a larger campus usually has a broader choice of programs and courses. You will find majors in symbolic systems, botany, public policy, and many foreign languages. But the downside is that the larger the campus, the larger the classes, at least at the introductory level and possibly beyond. Exceptions to this, as we mentioned, are the honors programs within a college or university. If you care about class size, you'll want to find out about the size of specific classes in your likely major. They will probably be smaller in philosophy or history than in economics or biology, which are among the most popular majors on many campuses. The low student-faculty ratios that colleges often cite may mislead you about the size of actual classes, because they include all faculty members, even those who do little or no undergraduate teaching.

There is no right or wrong when it comes to size. Preferences vary from person to person. Some students find it helpful to visit different-sized colleges near home, even if they are not interested in attending them, just to compare schools of different sizes.

THE INTANGIBLES

Size, location, and curriculum: all of these are readily observable and easily described and compared. More difficult to assess and compare are the many factors that contribute to the feel of a campus—the ambience—academically and socially. Just as with size, there is no right or wrong ambience—each person will have his or her own set of preferences and needs. What is important is finding a set of colleges that feels right for you.

Where Do Students Live?

Most colleges with residence halls require or strongly recommend that freshmen live on campus but are more flexible after that. Big public universities may simply not have enough on-campus housing for all four years. So you should ask, "Where do most students live after freshman year? On or off campus? How far away do students live if they are off campus? Do they seem generally satisfied with their housing options?" Campuses where most students live on or near campus tend to feel more like a community than those with many commuters, but living off campus is usually cheaper, in part because you are not required to eat on an expensive meal plan.

Campus safety can be an issue for some. Is the campus well lit at night? Is an escort service available for a student who is working late at night in a library or lab and would prefer not to walk back to the residence hall alone? Is access to residence halls secure? Unfortunately, no campus is immune from crime, but a campus can take steps to reduce it.

Federal law requires every college to publish an annual Clery Report providing statistics about crime on campus. Entering "Clery Report" on a college's home page will take you to that institution's report. A visit to the campus security office can also provide helpful information if safety is an issue of particular concern to you or your family.

What Is the Campus Social Life Like?

Do fraternities and sororities play a big role on campus? What percentage of students affiliate with a Greek organization, and how many live in a fraternity or sorority house? Do the answers fit with what you are looking for? Campuses also differ in their ethnic, racial, and geographical diversity. Some are very diverse, others less so, and some are quite homogeneous. Colleges readily provide information about the gender and racial mix of their student body, as well as their geographical diversity. These numbers can help give you a sense of their diversity. But if you are interested, you can go further than this: Are there special housing arrangements for minority students who want them? How do the different groups get along? Do they integrate or self-segregate? You need to ask.

Other factors contribute to the social atmosphere as well. How big a role does athletics play on campus? Is there a lot of school spirit, and does social life tend to revolve around home football Saturdays or other big events? Does this appeal to you? Finally, some campuses are known for their liberal, eclectic student bodies, and others have a reputation for attracting more conservative students. These labels develop and stick because people like to put colleges into categories. The labels may not be accurate, or they may be out of date because the campus has changed. Each school probably has more variety inside it than is usually ascribed to it from the outside. Think about what you want to experience, but be cautious about the labels just as you should be about the rankings. They may serve the marketing purposes of the college more than your own.

What Is the Intellectual Atmosphere of the Campus?

Campuses differ in their reputations for academic intensity. Although some students work harder than others at any college, some colleges seem to have greater expectations for intellectual engagement among their students. And at some campuses, students seem to place greater demands on themselves. Campuses known for intellectual rigor and the work ethos of the student body, such as Swarthmore College, Reed College, and the University of Chicago, can be exciting places to live and study. They can be a perfect match for one student—and a poor one for another. Ultimately, however, academic intensity is subjective. We encourage you to do some thoughtful research about colleges and yourself. Your own assessment of a campus is, after all, the only one that really counts in the end.

How Do Students Spend Their Time Outside Class?

A typical full-time student takes three or four courses each term, and classes rarely meet every day as they usually do in high school. That leaves lots of time outside class, not all of which is needed for studying. How do students spend their free time? Do they belong to a wide range of student groups? More important, are there activities in your areas of interest, including new interests that your high school didn't have? Are the recreational facilities attractive and accessible? What do students do on Saturday night? If you visit a campus, ask your tour guide how she and her friends spent last weekend.

Campuses also vary somewhat in their tolerance for alcohol use by underage students. Excessive and abusive use of alcohol among college students is a serious national problem and at all types of colleges, except the most religiously observant. Although no college encourages underage students to drink alcohol, they differ in how strictly they enforce their own rules and state law, which influences how much drinking occurs on campus. So you should find out: Do students feel pressured to drink by their classmates, or can you be comfortable in abstaining? Are alcohol- and substance-free residence halls available for those who want them?

MAJORS, CAREERS, AND CURRICULUM

What is a college major? A student majoring in a particular field must take a certain number of credits in that field and in related fields to help build knowledge and skills in that subject. The major will require some specific courses for everyone, say, statistics for psychology or organic chemistry for chemistry majors, whereas other courses are electives, so you can choose which courses to take from a large array. At many schools, you can also declare a minor in another field that still gives you in-depth knowledge of a second area but requires fewer credits. Double majors and occasionally triple majors, for the very energetic, are sometimes available, and some schools allow students to design their own custom majors with the help of an academic advisor. Some programs in the health fields or engineering, for example, have requirements that begin in freshman year.

Selecting a Major

Students often feel pressure to pick a major while applying to college. Some schools, especially some public ones, admit students to different majors at different rates. The most popular majors may have additional requirements for admission and may be more selective than less popular majors. If you are admitted to the school but not to the specific major you hoped for, it may be difficult, and maybe even impossible, to switch later. Find this out before you specify a major on your application.

Most schools, though, simply ask students about potential interests, but don't hold them to it. In fact, "undecided" is offered as an option at many colleges and is the most popular initial "major." Although some students enter college with a clearly defined plan of study that they pursue until graduation, others are completely undecided or change their minds at least once before they receive their degree.

As educators, we like the model that lets students explore their interests for the first two years of college before they have to commit to a major. That gives you time to take courses in different areas to see what really excites you and captures your interest. How are you supposed to know you would like to study psychology or philosophy until you take a course in college? Although we prefer this approach, we know that some schools require students to declare a major earlier in certain fields.

The Relationship Between Major and Career

Excellent information about college majors and the careers they can lead to can be found on the free BigFuture website of the College Board at www.bigfuture.org. Colorful and easy to use, the career planning tools on the website describe many college majors and the careers these majors prepare students for, as well as the job prospects for each career. The site's search engine helps you identify colleges offering a particular major.

Especially interesting are the wide range of career opportunities open to students who major in humanities subjects such as English or history or French, despite the common misconception that these fields do not prepare students for the world of work. People in these majors work in all walks of life. The BigFuture website can reassure students who want to study a subject they love but aren't sure how it might translate into a job after graduation.

College websites and printed admissions material will help you sort out specifics of the major or majors you are interested in at a given school as well as school policy toward selection and changing majors. If you still have questions about flexibility in choosing majors and when they must be declared after reading those materials, ask for help from the colleges you are considering. A quick e-mail or phone call to the admissions office should answer any remaining questions.

Majors and Choosing a College

As we noted, some students enter college with a clearly defined plan of study, and others are completely undecided. How should this play into your thinking about colleges? If you are interested in special programs (for example, engineering, dance, business, sports management), whether a school has such a program *can* be important.

There's More Flexibility Than You May Think

But notice that we said "can be important" rather than "is important." Things may be more flexible than you think, at least in some fields. Say, for example, that you want to study engineering. Although you will certainly want to look at schools that offer engineering degrees, many schools without engineering programs partner with engineering schools to offer what is known as a 3/2 program. The student spends three years at the first school, usually majoring in physics or mathematics and receiving specialized advising for 3/2 students, and then transfers to a school with an engineering program for the final two years. At the end of five years, the student receives two degrees: a bachelor's degree in math or physics from the first college and a bachelor's degree in engineering from the second one. As a bonus, the student has had a broad-based liberal arts education that may set him or her apart from other engineering graduates on the job market. We have never met a graduate of a 3/2 program who regretted having a liberal arts background in addition to his or her engineering degree.

Different Paths to the Same Destination

As another example, a student may want to become a marine biologist. Most jobs for marine biologists require a graduate degree, and it turns out that the best preparation for graduate study in marine biology is a solid foundation in biology and chemistry, something that just about any college's major in biology or biochemistry would readily provide. So, in looking at colleges, prospective marine biologists don't have to limit themselves to the relatively few schools that offer an actual major in that subject.

The same general principle applies to students who are interested in business as a career. The natural tendency for such a student is to look for a school with a business major. But a recent survey of employers showed that many actually prefer to recruit students who majored in something other than business—perhaps economics or international relations—because they value students with a broader background and different analytic skills than a business major typically provides. A banker we know majored in history and says he likes to hire English majors because much of banking involves writing and speaking.

Both of these examples, and there are many others, illustrate that the seemingly obvious path to a given career may not be the only one, and it may not even be the best one in some cases. If you have a career in mind when you are applying to college, be sure to do some research into the various paths and majors that will lead to that career. You may find some surprising options.

Remember also that the average student switches major at least once before graduation. Ideally, look for colleges that offer the kinds of programs that fit your interests as well as the flexibility to switch fields if your interests change.

Dual-Degree Programs

Some schools offer special dual-degree programs that enable students to obtain a bachelor's degree and a graduate degree, often in less time than it would take if the two were pursued separately. These programs can appeal to students with focused career objectives. In some dual BS-MD programs, for example, a student receives both degrees at the end of seven years, dual BA-JD programs can be completed in six years, and dual BA-MBA programs take five years. These programs generally save a year of time and thus a year of tuition. Similar programs exist for BA-MA programs in some fields at some schools, as well as in other professional fields such as pharmacy (BS-PharmD), physical therapy (BS-DPT), and dentistry (BS-DDS). Smaller schools offering these programs usually have cooperative arrangements with a university that offers graduate degrees, and large universities may offer both parts themselves. In either case, being accepted to a dual program means that if you do well, you won't have to go through a second admissions process to achieve your educational goals. The downside is that many of these programs, especially the dual BS-MD programs, are highly selective.

GENERAL EDUCATION REQUIREMENTS

Another important aspect of undergraduate education is how a college organizes its general education (GE) or distribution requirements. Students tend to focus on majors when looking at colleges and overlook this important part of the curriculum.

What Is General Education?

General education requirements try to ensure that every student, regardless of major, will emerge from college with the background to be an educated person. This means exposing the student majoring in the humanities to the social sciences and sciences and the engineering student to the humanities and social sciences. College is often the last chance students have to encounter such a broad range of knowledge, and the benefits can be lifelong.

Different Types of General Education

General education means different things at different schools. Some schools have what is known as distribution requirements—a Chinese-menu-style approach in which a student must select a number of courses in the sciences, humanities, and social sciences from a long list. Another approach is the core curriculum—a small set of specially designed courses that all students must take. Sometimes the two approaches are combined. Some colleges no longer require courses identified with different disciplines, such as humanities, social sciences, and natural science, and instead expose students to different skills, such as quantitative reasoning, moral reasoning, and global citizenship, through an array of courses.

Some schools have limited GE or no formal requirements at all. Brown University, Amherst College, Hamilton College, and Wesleyan University, for example, have no GE requirement. Despite the lack of requirements, these schools hope that their students will not overspecialize and that they will still take a broad range of courses but of their own free will. Naturally, these schools are very popular with students who want a lot of freedom.

Be sure to find out how GE is handled by the colleges you are exploring so you won't be surprised or disappointed once you enroll. In the end, you may not have to take more than one or two extra courses because of GE than you would have anyway, and you might enjoy the requirements once you see how much choice you actually have.

HOW EASILY CAN YOU GET ADVICE AND HELP?

Almost all students need advice at various points in their college career, whether it involves help in selecting courses, deciding on a major, securing an internship, or applying for jobs or graduate school. A recent study showed that students at public colleges ranked access to good academic advising as the most important aspect of their educational experience; students at private colleges ranked it second, after good teaching. Both groups ranked financial aid, campus climate, and campus life much lower in importance.[2]

ACADEMIC ADVISING AND HELP

Despite the importance of advising, families pay surprisingly little attention to it when exploring colleges. Colleges vary widely in the quality and accessibility of their advising services. College websites can provide some information. How does advising at the school work for freshmen and more advanced students? How does the college assist students in identifying and securing internships? What kinds of pre-professional advising are available, and how extensive is it? You also want to learn about support services to assist students with writing papers and study skills, as well as tutoring help in specific subject areas.

First-generation students should inquire about advising and other services specifically designed for them. At each of the University of California campuses, for example, the Educational Opportunity Program, or EOP, provides services including special orientation, academic and personal advising, peer advising, special tutoring assistance in specific subject areas, and help preparing for graduate and professional school.

Descriptions, though, are just a beginning. You should try to find out how effective advising actually is by talking with current and former students. Schools are usually happy to provide the names of students willing to answer questions by e-mail, and if you visit a campus, you can talk directly with students you meet. You want to hear that advisors are available when needed, informed and able to provide useful information about requirements and courses, able to direct students to sources of help when they have academic difficulty, and able to provide guidance about special opportunities, career interests, and post-graduation plans.

Pre-Professional Advising

For students interested in professional degrees such as law, medicine, or other health professions, good advising about course work, extracurricular activities, and the application process itself, including interviews, can be crucial. Colleges often have offices or specific faculty members who do such advising. Find out what kind of help is provided and the record of students gaining admission to the kind of professional program you are interested in.

Internship opportunities—a chance to tackle a real job, whether paid or not, while still a student—can be very helpful not only in exploring careers but also in obtaining a first job. Most engineering programs offer co-ops for their students, but Northeastern University and Drexel University have gone further and offer co-ops for all students, alternating semesters of academic study with an occasional semester of full-time employment. Colleges usually have offices or staff members specifically devoted to matching students with internship opportunities. What kind of internship and career advising do the schools you are interested in have? How helpful is it in finding internships for students? Are résumé and interviewing help provided? Can the services be used even after graduation?

How many recruiters and what kind visit campus each year? All of these are legitimate questions to ask as you explore how colleges differ.

HEALTH AND COUNSELING SERVICES

Students occasionally get sick or injured and need to go to the campus health center. Some students have chronic medical conditions that require ongoing management. Others have ongoing mental health challenges. Still others experience psychological difficulties and need counseling or psychiatric care for the first time while in college. And some just get lonely or homesick. What kinds of services assist students facing these challenges? Are support services available in residence halls to help students adjust smoothly and to provide help when they hit a bump in the road? Is the campus health center well staffed, or do students use other nearby resources? How are referrals made?

ADVANCE PLANNING

Overall, you want to know how well the campus takes care of its students. It is well worth asking these questions, probing more deeply into the areas of special interest to you. In particular, we strongly encourage parents of students with prior mental health problems or learning disabilities to contact the appropriate campus offices to discuss the available support services. We'll talk more about this in chapter 12. Parents of students with chronic health problems should consider contacting the student health center to inquire about services that are offered. You want to be sure that appropriate help will be there if you need it.

DETERMINING YOUR PRIORITIES

This chapter was designed to help you learn more about colleges and more about yourself. You may still be trying to figure out what is really important to you, and it certainly takes time to learn about different colleges. But while everything is still fresh in your mind, we encourage you to fill out the "Determining Your Priorities" questionnaire. Your answers—even tentative ones—will help you begin to identify the best colleges for you. Chapter 5 will show you how to get information about specific colleges that match your priorities.

Determining Your Priorities

This questionnaire will help you identify what is most important to you as you think about choosing colleges. Questions are divided into three categories: physical environment, academic environment, and extracurricular and social environment. Answer each question as accurately as you can. For each one, note whether your preference is very important (V), somewhat important (S), or not important (N) to you.

Physical Environment	Your Preference	Importance		
		V	S	N
1. How far from home would you like to live? Close by? Easy or longer drive? Accessible by plane?				
2. Do you prefer a large city, small city or town, suburb, or country environment?				
3. Does weather matter to you? Is there an area of the country where you do not want to live?				
4. What size college do you prefer: small (fewer than 2, 500), medium (fewer than 10, 000), large (fewer than 20, 000), or very large (more than 20, 000)?				
5. Do you want to live on or off campus after freshman year?				
Other:				
Other:				

(continued)

Academic Environment	Your Preference	Importance		
		V	S	N
1. Do you prefer a liberal arts college or a research university?				
2. Are there specific majors or courses that you want a college to offer?				
3. Do you prefer small classes, large classes, or a mix?				
4. Are you interested in a specific major?				
5. Are there any special curricular features that you want (core curriculum, honors program, and so forth)?				
6. What kind of intellectual environment do you prefer: exceptionally rigorous, midrange, less intense?				
7. Do you want a "name brand" or prestigious college?				
8. Do you need special support services (e.g., learning disabilities, health issues)?				
Other:				
Other:				

Extracurricular and Social Environment	Your Preference	Importance		
		V	S	N
1. Are there particular extracurricular activities or special facilities that you would like to have available?				
2. Do you want to participate in certain sports at the varsity level? At the club sport or intramural level?				
3. How big a role should athletics play on campus?				
4. Do you want fraternities and sororities to be available and an important part of campus life?				
5. How diverse a campus do you want? What kinds of diversity are you seeking?				
6. Do you want a campus with a special focus such as religious affiliation or women only? Are you open to considering them even if you are not actively seeking such a focus?				
7. Do you seek a particular kind of atmosphere: artsy, politically active, cohesive community, other?				
Other:				
Other:				

(continued)

Miscellaneous	Their Preference	Importance		
		V	S	N
1. Do your parents have any requirements?				
Other:				
Other:				

List the preferences you have identified as very important or somewhat important in the spaces provided next. Then rank them in order of importance to you within each group. This list will guide you in identifying colleges before you apply and will help you make a final decision once you receive your acceptances.

Priorities Summary

The following preferences are very important to me:

_____

_____

_____

_____

The following preferences are somewhat important to me:

_____

_____

_____

_____

PART 2

Making the Right Choices for You

Chapter 5   Where Should You Apply?

Chapter 6   The Big Tests

Chapter 7   Deciding About Early Decision and Other Early Options

Chapter 8   Paying the Bill

Where Should You Apply?

In chapter 4, you began to build your college list by considering how colleges differ and identifying your personal preferences. This was an important first step because you need to have at least a rough idea of what you are looking for in order to find it. Your ideas about what you want may change along the way, but with more than 2,200 non-profit four-year colleges in the United States alone, you can't start by looking at them one by one.

By doing your self-assessment, you now have some specific criteria in mind to guide your search. But how do you go about identifying the colleges that fit your criteria and that may, in turn, be a good fit for you? In this chapter, we will take you through those next steps. There is no one right way to build a college list, but we are going to suggest some ways that we hope you'll find helpful.

START AT YOUR COUNSELING OFFICE

Your high school counseling office can be a good place to begin your college search. Some well-funded public high schools and most private schools have counselors whose sole job is to work with students on all aspects of the college admissions process. Other schools fold college counseling duties into the generic job description of school counselors, who may have other duties besides college advising. Still others have an arrangement that bridges these two: a college specialist provides general college guidance for students, but a student's regular school counselor provides support as well.

We know that schools vary greatly in what college planning help they offer students and that massive student-to-counselor ratios can make it very hard to get help even if it is in principle provided. Whatever the arrangement at your school, take full advantage of the available resources. You can make up for what is missing, or augment what is provided, by carefully reading and using the information in this book. We wrote *Admission Matters* so that all students can have access to the help they need.

Use Naviance If You Have It

More and more schools are providing web-based tools to assist their students with the college admissions process. One of the most popular is Naviance, a program purchased by high schools that lets you search for colleges that meet criteria you specify. Doing a college search using the SuperMatch college search engine on Naviance and then posting the schools that look promising to you on your Naviance account will help you keep track of schools as well as share them with your counselor, who can see what you post. Similar search engines are readily available, so if your school doesn't have Naviance, you can still achieve the same good results, as we will discuss shortly.

Input from Your Counselor

Junior year is a good time to start building a relationship with your counselor if you haven't already done so. Remember that she will be preparing your school report, including writing a letter on your behalf, if your colleges require one. Helping your counselor know you will serve you well. Wait until after winter break of your junior year, when your counselor is finished advising the seniors, and make an appointment to introduce yourself if you haven't already been invited to do so. You want to give a face to your name even before you start to seek your counselor's advice about college. Continue this contact as needed throughout the admissions process. In a big public school, you will probably have to be more proactive in getting to know your counselor.

Your counselor may be able to combine her knowledge about colleges with knowledge of your academic record and personal preferences to help you expand and revise the list you generate using a college search tool or other resources. The more specific your criteria, the more your counselor can help you. Counselors may know more about some colleges than others, but a preliminary list of schools generated with help from your counselor can get you going. If you can't get one, don't worry; you can develop a fine list using the tools we will be sharing with you.

In chapter 10 we will talk about how you can ensure that your counselor has the information about you that she will need even if you don't meet her for the first time until senior year. This can sometimes happen despite your best planning if the staff members change at the start of a new school year or if counselor caseloads are very large.

YOUR LIST IS JUST BEGINNING

The initial list you may get from talking with your counselor is just that: a beginning. You'll also want to talk with your parents, other family members, friends, classmates, and others who know you well and may have suggestions. Don't worry if your list is long at this point. You can narrow it down later. Your list should eventually look like an inverted pyramid: very broad at the top (beginning) and narrow down at the bottom (end).

USE A COLLEGE SEARCH TOOL

Online search engines are powerful tools that can help zero in on schools that may be an excellent match for you. Fortunately, good college search engines are available to anyone with access to a computer and Internet connection. We encourage you to try several of them because they might turn up different results. You can use them to augment a list that you have already started or even to build one from scratch. We've already mentioned SuperMatch, a search tool that you can access if your high school subscribes to Naviance.

BIGFUTURE

The BigFuture website at www.bigfuture.org that we discussed briefly in chapter 4 can help you identify colleges using criteria that you value, such as size, location, majors, sports, activities, average net price, and the academic record of a recent incoming class. It also lets you rate how important each criterion is to you: don't care, nice to have, or must have. This "fuzzy" approach helps build a list of schools that meet your criteria to varying extents.

BigFuture then presents a set of schools that meet your criteria, starting with those that satisfy them 100 percent. It is colorful, easy, and fun to use. The top of the list shows the number of schools returned in the search. You can save the schools you are interested in and instantly see how changing one or more of your criteria can expand or contract your list. Another useful feature of BigFuture is the See Similar Schools link. Located on the left-hand side of a college's main profile page, this link will display a list of additional schools viewed by other students who viewed that school's profile.

College Navigator

The US Department of Education has a search tool, College Navigator, which works much like the BigFuture search feature. You can find it through the College Affordability and Transparency Center at www.collegecost.ed.gov. College Navigator is less colorful than BigFuture or SuperMatch on Naviance, and it doesn't let you distinguish the importance of different criteria, but it has an extensive list of majors to choose from and lets you specify SAT or ACT ranges for your search. The College Navigator site also contains links to the online *Occupational Outlook Handbook*, where you can explore job prospects in different occupations.

The College Affordability and Transparency Center site includes a link that will take you immediately to the net price calculator of any college. (We will go into more detail about net price calculators, a tool that can help you estimate your actual out-of-pocket cost at different colleges, in chapter 8 when we discuss financial aid and the cost of college.) It also links to the College Scorecard that lets you compare colleges along affordability and other financial criteria using data unique to this site.

More About College Search Tools

You can find additional college search tools by looking for them on the web. We recommend starting with BigFuture, College Navigator, and SuperMatch, if available, and then going beyond those if you wish. Various search tools are usually easy and fun to use. You probably won't get exactly the same results with different search engines, but that's just what you want at this point. You will likely be able to expand your list by using several different ones.

Pay special attention to colleges that appear on different lists because they may be particularly good matches. With all search engines, if you get hundreds of results, you will need to narrow down your search criteria, and if you get very few hits, you will have to broaden them. Be especially careful of the major(s) you specify in the search. If you are very specific (or if the wording is unusual) your search may yield very few results. Each search engine makes it easy to add or drop criteria used in a search, so you can work with each one to see how changing your criteria affects the results.

COLLEGEXPRESS

Another helpful resource in building a college list is CollegeXpress (www .collegexpress.com). CollegeXpress includes a search engine along with an extensive set of lists of schools known for their strength in different majors—from international relations to business to marine science. It also includes lists of schools on topics such as sports and various aspects of college life. Generated primarily through recommendations from college counselors, the lists are not exhaustive or infallible, but they help you narrow down what might otherwise be a bewildering number of possibilities.

MEETING COLLEGE REPRESENTATIVES

Up to this point, you have been adding schools to your list. We are not yet done suggesting ways you can find additional schools, but we would like to shift our attention to ways to simultaneously add to your list and possibly narrow it down.

THE COLLEGE FAIR

Usually held in the fall or spring in cities around the country and abroad, a college fair enables you to meet with admissions representatives from many colleges all assembled in one place, often a high school gym. At college fairs, many college representatives, either admissions officers or alumni volunteers, stand at individual tables arranged alphabetically. It's an efficient way to gather information and get some questions answered. You can learn about unfamiliar colleges, as well as gather information about colleges already on your list. We encourage you to attend a college fair in your junior year if one is offered near you and use it to learn more.

My daughter found the college fair to be very helpful but she went in prepared. She went through the list of colleges and targeted out-of-area schools that she knew she might not be able to visit as a way to show interest. She had a list of good questions and engaged in some long conversations with the reps.

MOM OF A STUDENT WHO MADE THE MOST OF A COLLEGE FAIR

How to Approach a College Fair

Sometimes, though, a fair can be a free-for-all, with students and parents crowding the tables of the most popular colleges. In this case, the best you can usually hope to do is to pick up some marketing literature and add your name to the mailing lists of colleges that interest you. It is worth registering in advance if given the chance to do so, although fairs are open to non-registrants as well. Students who pre-register may get a bar code that participating colleges can scan to place a student on their mailing list. If no bar code is available, consider bringing a sheet of labels with your name and e-mail and postal addresses pre-printed so that you don't spend time writing out this information over and over at the fair.

Less well-known colleges will be much more accessible at the fairs. Go right up, introduce yourself to the rep, and ask anything you want. Be active! They are there to serve you. It can help if you already know something about the college and ask informed questions. "Can you tell me about your neuroscience program [or field hockey team]?" is better than "Do you have a neuroscience major?"

In addition to having representatives from many colleges, college fairs often feature presentations on different aspects of the college admissions process, and you can ask questions. They are free and open to everyone, including parents. Your high school counseling office will have information about dates and locations of fairs in your local area. The National Association for College Admission Counseling also posts an up-to-date list of its large, national college fairs on its website, www.nacacnet.org. Although most college fairs invite many kinds of colleges, specialized fairs are becoming more common, including fairs for students interested in STEM (science, technology, engineering, and mathematics) fields, study at colleges outside the United States, and the visual and performing arts.

Try a Virtual College Fair

At a virtual college fair you can get many of the benefits of an in-person fair without leaving your home. Several times a year, dozens of colleges participate in College Week Live, a day-long event during which students and parents can engage in live chat with students and admissions officers at colleges that interest them. These virtual fairs also feature keynote talks on different aspects of the college admissions process, such as financial aid. Individual colleges also schedule live chat events on days when a fair is not being held. You can check the schedule for the next virtual fair and other special events, as well as view the archived presentations at www.collegeweeklive.com.

MEET WITH THE COLLEGE REPRESENTATIVES WHO VISIT YOUR HIGH SCHOOL

Between Labor Day and mid-November, admissions staff members travel to selected high schools across the country to speak with interested students. There are far too many high schools, however, for them to visit every school, and they tend to visit schools where they have a history of attracting strong applicants.

Watch for Announcements

If reps do visit your school, try to attend at least a few of the visits. Watch for announcements of visits by your counseling office, and attend those that most interest you if you can take the time from class. It is fine to come even if you are just curious and know nothing previously about the college; this can be a great way to learn about a new school. But, again, it makes a better impression and is a better use of your time and theirs if you already know at least the basics.

Usually lasting about 30 to 60 minutes, visits include a short presentation and question-and-answer period with the college admissions representative. They typically visit four or even five schools a day, so they cannot spend a lot of time at one school. If you attend, they will ask you to fill out a card, so you will get on a list of students who have shown interest in the college and you will receive paper and electronic mailings. With small groups, the admissions officer may even jot down brief notes about the students he or she has met for later reference.

> I have a friend who is an admissions rep who visits high schools. He will make notes if a kid impresses him. He remembers them when their application comes in.
>
> PARENT REFLECTING ON THE VALUE OF MEETING WITH VISITING REPS

How Attending Can Help

Coming to a high school visit is an easy way to show interest in a school, which may play a role in the college's eventual admissions decision, as we discuss further on in this chapter. More important, the visit can help you decide if you want to apply. Prepare some questions in advance based on your interests. The visiting rep may be the first reader of your file, so making a favorable impression, even just showing your face, can be helpful later. In fact, if you can't meet with a rep because of a significant school conflict—that oral report in English or a physics exam—leave a note with the visit coordinator to give to the rep expressing your regret and your interest in the college. Another option is to send an e-mail to the rep with the same information.

Occasionally admissions representatives conduct individual student interviews as part of the school visit or perhaps on the nearest weekend. If you are already on the school's mailing list, the college should notify you of this in advance. But don't hesitate to contact the admissions office of a college to see if a representative will be coming to your area because interview slots can fill up quickly. We'll talk more about interviews and what to expect during them in chapter 10.

The Visiting Road Show

A number of colleges sponsor regional events intended for parents and students in addition to, or in lieu of, high school visits. This enables them to reach more students than they can by just visiting high schools. These events may include a presentation by an admissions officer and young alums, a slide show, and the opportunity to get printed materials and ask questions. Students who have previously requested material from the college may get a special invitation, but the events are always open to all students and parents. Colleges notify high schools in advance and post their travel schedules on their websites. These events are usually held in the evening or on a weekend afternoon in a large meeting room at a hotel or other public place.

Some colleges combine their efforts and offer a joint session. For example, Harvard University, Duke University, Georgetown University, Stanford University, and the University of Pennsylvania travel together across the country every spring and fall and hold a program called "Exploring College Options" in over 50 cities. Five smaller schools in the Pacific Northwest—Lewis and Clark College, Reed College, University of Puget Sound, Whitman College, and Willamette University—travel together as the Pacific Northwest College Consortium over the summer. There are many other groups, with tour schedules and membership sometimes shifting somewhat from year to year.

READ WHAT THEY SEND YOU (BUT DON'T LET IT GO TO YOUR HEAD)

If you've already taken the PreACT, PSAT, ACT, or SAT and checked the box saying you would like to receive information directly from colleges, you are probably finding your mailbox and e-mail in-box filling with glossy mailers and enthusiastic e-mails from colleges. Colleges buy the names and e-mail and postal addresses of students who meet certain criteria (for example, geography, scores above a certain point, interest in a specific major, or religious affiliation) from the testing agency. They then develop a targeted mailing list of students who might be interested in their institution. Read the literature you receive and then check out the colleges that seem interesting. Then file those so that you can retrieve them later should you need them.

My mom and I got really excited when the letter from Flite Liberal Arts College arrived. It was personally signed by the dean of admission himself and really encouraged me to apply. I did pretty well on the PSAT, so that's probably how they got my name. I had visited the college and liked it, and my mom said a personal letter meant they were very interested in me, too. I decided to apply. In May I got my decision—rejected. We both read too much into that "personal" letter.

COLLEGE FRESHMAN

Sometimes colleges send personalized letters rather than e-mail or brochures to encourage students to seek more information and then apply. Be wary of reading too much into a personalized "search" letter from a college, particularly one from a highly selective college. These colleges send out tens of thousands of letters to students who score well on standardized tests or have other desirable demographic characteristics. This helps them build a strong pool of candidates, but they know they can accept only a small percentage of them. Colleges justify this on the grounds of greater diversity and spreading the word about their college more widely. Unfortunately, these warm and flattering letters can lead a student and family to believe that the student has an inside edge on admission.

The following phrases come from actual search letters:

- "I hope that this is the beginning of a long-term relationship between you and Williams and that you will be interested enough to keep us in mind as you apply to schools in the fall."
- "We are writing to offer our congratulations on your academic achievements and to encourage you to consider the opportunities available at Harvard as you plan your academic future."
- "As you continue to explore a wide variety of colleges and universities, I am eager to share with you the enclosed snapshot of the University of Chicago."
- "We recently learned of your exceptional testing performance and think you may find NYU to be a great fit for you."

In the vast majority of cases, search letters simply mean you might be a viable candidate—no more and no less. They are certainly nice to receive, but remember that you are just receiving sophisticated marketing from the colleges.

HOW TO NARROW THINGS DOWN

If you have followed our advice up to this point, you probably have a long list of colleges—colleges that may be a good fit but that you need to learn more about before deciding for sure. We are going to turn our attention now to some of the many available tools that will help you do that effectively. Our list is not exhaustive, but these are our personal favorites and the ones we have found most helpful.

USING BIGFUTURE FOR ANOTHER PURPOSE

One of the tools we think is especially helpful we have already mentioned: the BigFuture website at www.bigfuture.org. It is not just a search engine to help you identify colleges that meet certain criteria but also a rich source of factual information about the academic programs, sports, extracurriculars, tuition, and admissions practices at each of them. It is a great way to get an overview of a school. Clicking on any college on your search list takes you to a quick summary of information as well as in-depth information about the college. Be sure to click through the various links to Majors and Learning Environment, Campus Life, Applying, and Paying, as well as the sublinks for each of those, to get information specific to a given school. Schools can also easily be compared to one another using the comparison tool on the site.

COLLEGE GUIDEBOOKS

Another useful tool for narrowing your list is a "big book" that provides anecdotal and statistical information about a wide range of colleges. These include *The Best 381 Colleges* (the number of "best" colleges changes with each edition) and *The Fiske Guide to Colleges*.[1] Updated annually and containing basic factual information about colleges like what you would find on BigFuture, they feature descriptive information about the academic and social life on campus based on student interviews. The commentaries in these books can give you a feel for the campus beyond the numbers. Plus, these books are free of direct college marketing efforts. We have found the descriptions, at least of the colleges we are very familiar with, to be quite accurate, although much of the information is anecdotal and does not fully reflect the complexity of the colleges being described.

One major drawback of such books is their limited coverage. They only report on fewer than 400 of the best-known colleges. Don't worry if some or even all of the colleges on your list are not in one of these books—you can get the information you would find there in other ways.

COLLEGE WEBSITES

College websites are perhaps the single most valuable source of information about a college. True, a college is not going to tell you that the dining hall food is tasteless or that faculty members are hard to reach outside of class (you'll have to discover this in other ways) but clicking on Admissions or Prospective Students from a college home page will lead you to much useful information. You'll usually find recent campus news and sports results, statistics about the most recent freshman class, a description of the entrance requirements, and the academic programs and majors available. Links to academic departments give you detailed information about faculty members and their specializations, as well as a list of courses offered.

Check Out Deadlines, Requirements, and Special Features

The website will also likely highlight special features of the college's undergraduate experience, including study abroad, community service, and involvement in athletics at all levels.

Information about application deadlines, testing requirements, and other application information is prominently featured on most sites, along with a link to the application or applications used by the college. Some colleges offer students a choice of application formats, as we will see in chapter 9. You can also usually complete a form to be added to a college's mailing list. You'll generally receive a packet with lots of information and pictures of the college, information about financial aid, and follow-up mailings—sometimes lots of them. If you provide an e-mail address, you'll receive e-mail from the college as well. The admissions web page will also give recommendations for visiting the college, including listings of nearby hotels and airport shuttle companies and how to set up an interview if offered.

Ways to Get a Good Feel for a Campus

Increasingly common are admissions chat rooms that enable prospective students to talk with admissions officers and current students. Admissions websites post the details of these chat sessions, which anyone can join. Some colleges have admissions blogs where admissions officers and others post useful information and comments. Social media are also widely used. You can follow a college on Twitter, Instagram, and Snapchat, and "like" it on Facebook to get additional information. Finally, you can read most student newspapers online. They can give you a feel for the hot issues on campus.

Reading a Catalog

Prospective students typically don't spend much time reading college catalogs, also known as college bulletins, but they should. Designed primarily as an official reference for current or newly admitted students, a catalog is usually a no-nonsense document free of the influence of glitzy marketing efforts but overflowing with a wealth of information about the academic offerings on a campus.

The catalog usually begins with a statement of the college's mission and a brief history, and lists the faculty members in each department as well as the courses and requirements for each major and minor. It also explains college graduation requirements such as general education courses and a senior thesis, and it includes information about dual-degree and honors programs, the academic calendar, and the honor code if the school has one. The catalog may also contain information about study abroad, internship programs, and other features of the campus.

A search for "college catalog" or "college bulletin" on a college's website will take you to a web-friendly or PDF version of the school's catalog.

ADDITIONAL SOURCES OF INFORMATION ON THE WEB

Several websites offer prospective students access to comments about a school provided by current or former students. These sites give you a sense of the culture and atmosphere on a campus from those who have actually experienced it. They are far from scientifically conducted surveys of opinions, but they can be useful if you keep their limitations in mind.

Niche (www.niche.com) and Unigo (www.unigo.com) provide student comments on academics, athletics, campus housing, diversity, social life, local atmosphere, and other facets of many colleges. Students have told us that they find Niche and Unigo especially helpful once they have narrowed their list of schools based on objective criteria such as programs, size, selectivity, and other factors. The sites give them insights into the feel of a campus that helps them narrow their list even more. Remember, though, any student can post a comment; those who take the time to do so are generally either very happy with their school or very unhappy. You generally don't hear from the middle of the pack.

THE COLLEGE VISIT

Once you have learned as much as you can about your preliminary list of colleges from indirect sources, you may find campus visits to be helpful in narrowing your list further. Some students take a college tour to look at several colleges, usually with parents or an organized group, during spring break in their junior year. A tour at that time enables you to see schools while classes are in session and the campuses are fully alive. A visit usually includes an hour-long group information session led by an admissions officer, sometimes with a student participant as well, and a group tour led by a student tour guide. Both give you a quick overview of a college and answer any questions you may have.

GO BEYOND THE FORMAL VISIT PROGRAMS

Don't limit your visit to the formal tour and information session, however. Try to spend some time on your own exploring the campus. Have lunch in the student union or school dining commons and get a feel not only for the food but also for the pace of the campus. Sit down at a table with some students and ask them what they like about the school and what they would like to see improved. Keep your list of questions handy—the ones that are important to you and are not answered in written materials or on the website. Everyone has an opinion if you are willing to listen. Of course, they will be just a sample, but most students enjoy talking about their college, and you will get honest responses.

Read the notices posted on the bulletin boards. What is being advertised? What are the upcoming events on campus? Walk through the library and see how the students are studying. Are they studying at all, and if so, are they mostly working alone, or are they interacting in small groups in separate soundproof study rooms? Does the library have lots of comfortable places to sit with good lighting?

Most important, look around at the students and try to imagine yourself among them. Take notes about what you see. If you visit several colleges in a row, the details begin to run together, so your notes can keep everything straight in your mind. Taking photos can also help. One experienced counselor we know suggests that her students take a picture of the tallest building on campus—she has found that it helps them remember other things as well. Depending on your interests, you may also want to try to speak with a coach in your sport or a professor in your major field of interest as part of your visit. The admissions office can help you arrange such meetings, which you should set up well ahead of time.

⊠ Things to Do on a College Visit

Items marked with an asterisk must usually be arranged in advance.

- ☐ Take a campus tour led by a current student.
- ☐ Attend a group information session.
- ☐ Fill out a visitor card at the admissions office and pick up printed material about the college.
- ☐ Have lunch in the student union or dining hall. While there, scan the postings on the bulletin boards and pick up a copy of the student newspaper. Browse in the bookstore, especially among the textbooks, not just the college gear.
- ☐ Walk through the library. Does it look like a comfortable place to study?
- ☐ Check out the recreational facilities that interest you.
- ☐ Sit in on a class.*
- ☐ Stay overnight in a dorm with a student.*
- ☐ Have a formal interview.*
- ☐ Meet with a coach or faculty member in your area of interest.*
- ☐ Ask students you meet what they like best about the campus and what they would change if they could.
- ☐ Explore the nearest town and transportation options.
- ☐ Sit on a bench and watch students walk by. Can you imagine yourself happily among them?

We suggest you check out a wonderful brochure, "A Pocket Guide to Choosing a College: Questions to Ask on Your College Visits" published by the National Survey of Student Engagement (NSSE) at Indiana University. The NSSE guide provides a series of questions you might consider asking about the level of student engagement at a college: for example, how much contact students have with professors, how good the advising system is, and how students can arrange to do research. You can download it for free under the Students and Parents link at www.nsse@indiana.edu.

When you visit a college, it is a good idea to stand in the busiest part of the campus with a map in hand and try to look confused. Then wait to see how many people come to your aid. Although this is not a scientific sample, it will give you a sense of the campus environment in terms of friendliness and willingness to help.[2]

JOSEPH GREENBERG, PROFESSOR EMERITUS AND FORMER REGIONAL DIRECTOR OF ADMISSIONS, GEORGE WASHINGTON UNIVERSITY

Timing Your Visit

We generally don't recommend seriously visiting colleges before the second half of the junior year. You may be an exception, but most students aren't ready to focus on specific colleges before then. They haven't had time to do the preliminary reflective thinking about themselves, and all they see are the buildings and how the students are dressed. In one case we know, a father told his daughter that her upcoming visits in the spring of her senior year to make a final choice would be especially useful because she had seen all the colleges the summer before her junior year. She said, "Oh, I don't remember anything from that trip, Dad. That was your trip."

Summer, Spring, or Fall?

The summer is a popular time to visit campuses, because it fits well with vacations. All colleges offer tours and information sessions in the summer even if classes are not in session. However, depending on the location, especially if the school is not urban, things may be pretty quiet without classes or many students around.

Visits in the fall of senior year can be a good way to see a campus after your thinking about colleges has progressed. You may also be able to schedule an overnight stay in a dorm with a student host through the admissions office. (This is not available at all colleges and may be hard to arrange at larger or more popular colleges. You can usually do this on your own if you know someone there.) Staying overnight can help you get a better feel for the campus culture, to see, for example, what students talk about at 10:00 p.m. in the dorm. Students who visit during the school year can also often sit in on a class in an area that interests them. It is best to attend a lecture class where a visitor is not intruding or even noticed. Although you don't want to draw general conclusions from just one class, notice whether the professor is well organized and clear in the presentation and if students are attentive and engaged—not texting their friends on their phone or surfing the Internet during the lecture.

The disadvantage of a fall visit is missing some school back home in the crucial first part of your senior year. If you can schedule fall visits with minimal disruption to your academic schedule, then consider them; otherwise, plan ahead and visit in the spring of your junior year and over the summer.

Look Beyond the Superficial

Remember, though, that many factors can affect your initial impression of a campus, including the personality of the tour guide and the weather that day. Colleges know that students relate best to other students, so they hire as tour guides energetic, enthusiastic students who enjoy their college and eagerly present it in the best light. Sometimes, though, a guide may be poorly trained, or just new at it, and thus less than an ideal ambassador for a campus. In this case, try to keep an eye on the bigger picture. The guide is not the entire school. Similarly, a campus you see on a beautiful day has a big leg up on one seen in the pouring rain. Try to keep this in mind as you compare your impressions of different colleges. No matter how long you spend on campus, you are seeing only a tiny slice of its life, good or bad.

My first-choice school invited me to a weekend program even before I was formally accepted. I had visited the campus once before, but now I was going to stay overnight. I didn't know what to expect, but I was excited about going. I was put in with this pretty crazy girl, and she and her friends were doing all this drinking and stuff. I was really scared because I wasn't expecting that. I had no experience with alcohol. I think the workshop leaders knew what was going on, but they just said things like, "Be careful at night." I came home and thought, "I don't really fit in at that campus." Later I learned I was in the part of the campus known for party dorms. I wonder if I had had a different roommate, if I would have had a different feeling. Anyway I chose another school, and I like it so much here that I didn't want to come home for Christmas.

COLLEGE FRESHMAN

How Can Parents Help?

Although some students visit colleges on their own or with organized tour groups, most visit with their parents. Whether the trip is part of a vacation or scheduled specifically to look at colleges, the parent perspective can be a valuable lens for viewing colleges. This can be quality time with your child, but remember that ultimately it is the student who must want to go to the college, regardless of the parents' views. As a parent, your extra set of eyes and ears on the visit serves as a sounding board for reactions. It may be helpful for you and your child to develop a game plan for your visits. You can take on tasks such as keeping track of details like meal plan options and how laundry is done, leaving your child free to focus on the feel of the campus and its academic and extracurricular offerings.

> We're just starting the search all over again. If I had known it would be this exhausting, I would have had my children further apart.
>
> MOM OF TWO

Virtually all campuses invite parents to join their children on the formal tours, but be sure to give your child plenty of freedom to look at what interests him and to ask the questions he wants to ask. If financial aid is a concern, this is a good time for parents to visit the financial aid office.

WHAT IF YOU CAN'T VISIT?

What if scheduling or cost prevents you from seeing a campus firsthand? Fortunately, campuses help you fill that gap through a range of resources including virtual tours, videos, and slide shows so that you can "visit" the campus over the Internet. These are offered directly on college admissions websites.

Another resource is YouniversityTV at www.youniversitytv.com. It has over 550 short videos to give you quick visual overviews of participating campuses. They are fun to watch, all in a uniform format, and you get a feel for campuses you can't see in person.

Consider e-mailing short questions about campus life (including, "What do you like best?" and, "What would you most like to change about your campus?") to current students willing to respond to such queries. Admissions officers can usually provide a list of names and e-mail addresses (often called "student ambassadors"). Use these opportunities to fill in the gaps in your knowledge. Your high school counselor may also have the names of graduates of your high school who attend different colleges. Once you have some names, you can often find contact information through college online directories. We have found that current students, especially from your home town, are always willing to share their experiences with you.

SELECTIVITY AND YOUR COLLEGE LIST

We mentioned previously in this chapter that the admissions profile of current students is one of the factors that you can put into the hopper when running college searches on the BigFuture website. Even if you don't make it a factor initially in your college search, as you finalize your list, the likelihood of being admitted to a given college should influence your decision to apply.

LIKELIES, POSSIBLES, AND LONG SHOTS

A wise student distributes college choices among three categories based on the likelihood of admission. The first category, which we call "likely" colleges, includes those where you are almost certain to be admitted given your record and the recent admissions profile of the schools. The next category, "possible" colleges, involves chances that can range from "pretty likely" to "50–50" to "not too likely." It is the broadest of the categories and, in an ideal list, should have the most colleges. The final category, which we call "long-shot" colleges, includes those whose acceptance rate by itself (under 10 percent or 20 percent) or in conjunction with your own record makes admission very unlikely. These three categories correspond to popular terminology with which you may be more familiar: "safety, target, and reach" colleges. We feel that our terms—likely, possible, and long shot—more accurately capture the objective reality of college admissions and the likelihood of admission rather than the scale of your hopes. Whatever the language used, the issue is selectivity, not quality. The problem is that many people confuse the two. Just because a school is a long shot doesn't mean it is desirable for you. It is just popular and therefore hard to get into.

The most common and ultimately most painful mistake is to think that if you apply to a large number of long-shot schools, your chance of being admitted to at least one of them increases. We call this the lottery principle: the more lottery tickets you buy, the better your chances of winning, even if only slightly. The lottery metaphor does not apply to selective college admissions, no matter how frequently you hear it used. Even if schools do vary somewhat in their admission practices, by and large they are looking at the same information and looking for the same qualities in applicants. There is no more depressing scene than to get bad news from 10 highly selective colleges in one week. Ten long-shot schools, one possible, and one likely is not a good list.

DETERMINING YOUR CHANCES

How can you tell what your chances of admission are at different colleges? The BigFuture website can help here, at least to give you a ballpark estimate. The admissions tab for each college will take you to data from the previous year showing the SAT and ACT range for the middle 50 percent of freshmen, as well as the percentage of freshmen ranking in the top 10, 25, and 50 percent of their high school classes for students whose high schools reported class rank. If your high school has Naviance, the scattergrams can give you a more precise idea based on past applicants from your high school. We'll talk about how to use them a little further on in this chapter.

How to Identify Likelies

The middle 50 percent of SAT and ACT scores helps you place your own scores in a better context than the average score. The data also include the percentage of applicants accepted. If you significantly exceed the midrange of standardized test scores of incoming freshmen and have a GPA that places you at the high end of the previous freshman class, the college can be considered a likely for you if its overall acceptance rate is at least 50 percent. The higher the acceptance rate, the lower your test scores or GPA can be relative to the midrange of freshmen for the college to be considered a likely.

What Makes a College a Possible

A possible college takes many forms. It can be one where your grades and test scores place you in the middle range of the freshman class and the admissions rate is 50 percent or higher. At another possible college, your scores might significantly exceed the midrange of freshmen, but the admissions rate is 35 percent or even somewhat less. The higher your scores compared to the average freshman's, the lower the admit rate can be for a school to be a possible one for you. But at schools with lower admit rates, objective data such as test scores and GPA count less heavily in the end, as long as they are in the ballpark for recently admitted students. When the admit rate is very low, nonacademic factors such as essays, recommendations, and special talents and other hooks often make the difference between the admits and the denies. At these schools no one is admitted on numbers alone.

The Long Shots

For almost all students, colleges falling in the ultra- and super-selective categories (those with admissions rates under 20 percent) should be considered long shots. The many factors that affect the admissions decision make it a challenge to predict a successful outcome at such schools, even for students with perfect or almost perfect "stats." It is much easier to predict when a student will not be admitted because of lower grades and scores.

For schools with somewhat higher admit rates, we define long shots as those where given your profile, you have less than a 35 percent chance of admission. This means that, once again, everything is relative. A school that would be a long shot for a student with a modest record can be a possible for a stronger one, and perhaps even a likely for one at the top of the class. You can never reach perfect precision about this. All you can hope for is an educated guess. That is why you need a balanced list, with several options in each category. You want to have choices in April.

> A few years ago I had a student—#3 in his class—who was bringing in his applications one by one for review. I saved them up for a while without looking at them, then took them home over the weekend. As I read them I thought to myself, "Oh, no, he isn't applying to seven schools, he's applying to the same school seven times."
>
> HIGH SCHOOL COUNSELOR

CHECK OUT THE DATA

With growing numbers of college applicants, the explosion of test preparation services, and a national trend of grade inflation, average GPA and test scores at selective colleges have been increasing every year, along with the number of applications. The websites of the colleges themselves have the most up-to-date numbers. Most colleges put the statistics for their entering class on the web by the fall. The previous spring, they issue press releases, also found on websites, that give data about the students who were just offered admission. These numbers are often more impressive than the numbers for enrolled students that will appear in the fall, because some top applicants will choose to go somewhere else. Just be sure you know what data are being presented: Are they for admitted students (those who received offers of admission) or enrolled students (freshmen who actually accepted offers of admission the previous spring)?

THE COMMON DATA SET

The Common Data Set is a collaborative project among colleges and a number of publishers. The colleges agree to provide standardized statistical data each year, including detailed information about the composition of the freshman class, along with admission and wait-list numbers and test score midranges. The participating publishers, including *U.S. News* and the College Board, present parts of the data through their websites. Some colleges make their entire report public. You can usually find the report, if available, by checking the college's institutional research office web page or by entering "Common Data Set" as a search term on the campus website. Reports usually appear in January for the class that entered the previous fall, making the data more current than the annually published guidebooks. Part C of each report gives the information about freshman admissions. The Common Data Set can provide a fascinating glimpse into admissions results if a school chooses to share it.

> My son seemed to narrow down his list very quickly. Columbia, NYU, UCLA. Five other top schools. Just one likely would have been a good idea. I wasn't as engaged as I should have been.
>
> FATHER OF SON DENIED EVERYWHERE WHO IS NOW "COMPLETELY HAPPY" AT A SCHOOL THAT WASN'T ON HIS LIST BUT SHOULD HAVE BEEN

SCATTERGRAMS CAN HELP

A scattergram is a graph that plots the GPA against the SAT or ACT score of students at your high school who were accepted, denied, or wait-listed at a college over a period of several years. In an appealing visual way you can determine where your own credentials fall compared to other students at your school who recently applied to that college. A scattergram needs at least five data points (meaning that at least five students applied and reported their results) to be really useful. Some high schools prepare their own scattergrams, but many generate scattergrams through Naviance in a standard format with their own data. If your statistics for a college are way out of the range of students who have been accepted recently from your school, you should take that as a caution, barring some exceptional hook. However, you can also determine likely schools through scattergrams.

Keep in mind, though, that a scattergram displays just those two dimensions: standardized tests and GPA. The other factors—extracurricular activities, letters of recommendation, essays, and special talents, for example—may be critical to the outcome and help explain why, when two students have identical GPAs and test scores, one was admitted and the other was not. One counselor asks students what they make of this, and when they shake their head in bewilderment, she says, "The colleges read the files. Something else is in the file that makes a difference." At best, scattergrams provide estimates, not definitive answers.

Even if your school does not use scattergrams, your counselor may be able to tell you about the recent admissions experience of students from your high school who applied to specific colleges.

HOW LONG SHOULD YOUR COLLEGE LIST BE?

One of the first questions students have when they think about developing a college list is how many schools it should have. There is no one-size-fits-all answer to this question, but here are some guidelines to consider.

A BALANCE OF LIKELIES, POSSIBLES, AND LONG SHOTS

Most students start with the long-shot schools, the ones they have heard a lot about. We recommend the opposite. Start at the other end. Develop a college list with one to three likely colleges that you would be happy to attend. This is important: these have to be schools that you like, not just ones you can get into. If you can't find such schools, you are not looking hard enough or you are being too picky about prestige. It is critical to spend significant time and energy selecting these colleges. Too often students select them as an afterthought, which can be painful, if, at the end of the admissions process, you must choose one of them. A good list of likely colleges is a crucial cushion in what can otherwise be a very uncertain process. Two to four possible colleges and two to three long shots can round out the final list

THE NUMBERS WILL VARY

These guidelines lead to college lists ranging in length from five to ten. But some successful students apply to fewer than 5 colleges and others to 12, 15, or even more if they are especially eager for acceptance at possible or long-shot colleges or want to compare many different offers of financial aid. Shorter lists are fine as long as they include at least one or two likelies that a student would be happy to attend and that are affordable. Longer lists add to the time and expense of applying and make it harder to prepare strong applications to all of your schools. So whittle the list down to a reasonable number. Some high schools limit the number of applications a student can file by restricting the number of counselor recommendations and transcripts they are willing to submit for a single student. By limiting the number of colleges, a high school is telling students to research their choices carefully and to make each one count. Even if they don't formally limit the number of schools you can apply to, most counselors will advise against an overly long and often unrealistic list.

EARLY DECISION AND YOUR COLLEGE LIST

In chapter 7, we discuss the early decision option that enables you to identify one college as your top choice and submit an application to that college by an early deadline in exchange for early review and an early, binding decision. Under the right circumstances and at the right schools, you can reap a significant advantage in submitting an early decision application, but it doesn't eliminate the need to develop your full college list carefully. If you are not admitted early to your first-choice college, you will have your carefully researched list of alternatives ready to go. Always have a plan B.

THE KEY TO A GOOD COLLEGE LIST

The key to developing an appropriate list is to be sure that you can actually see yourself happily attending any college on it. We expect you to prefer some more than others, but because the outcome of the admissions process can be so unpredictable, you need a balanced list. We would like to propose a more radical thought experiment: consider all the colleges on your final list "first choices." In other words, aside from a possible early decision school, don't rank your schools by preference too early. Enjoy the idea of any of them.

> We went to Harvard. I didn't want to apply. But Dad said, "No, you're going to apply just to apply."
>
> STUDENT WHO SAYS, "HARVARD HAD A REALLY NICE REJECTION LETTER."

Developing a college list can be an exciting and demanding process for you and your family. We encourage you to begin with a careful self-assessment using the "Determining Your Priorities" questionnaire at the end of chapter 4. Note special characteristics that are very important or somewhat important to you. Then use the results of your assessment to develop a list of possibilities, narrowing that list as you learn more about the schools themselves and their degree of selectivity in relation to your own record. A good college list comes from thoughtful introspection, as well as thorough research about colleges. The College Research Worksheet in Appendix A will help you organize the results of your research. The worksheet can also be found and easily duplicated at www.admissionmatters.com.

A WORD ABOUT FINANCES

Here, we would like to introduce another factor in the equation as you consider colleges: finances. Although some students can cover the cost of their education from family resources, many more need financial aid to cover all or part of the cost. A great deal of financial aid is available, with the largest amounts going to those with the lowest incomes and thus the greatest need. Middle-class and upper-middle-class families eligible for aid must often assume loans for part of their college expenses, although a small number of schools with large endowments have eliminated loans as part of their financial aid packages for all students. In addition, a strong academic record or outstanding talent may result in merit aid—scholarships that don't depend on demonstrated need. How much is your family willing and able to contribute to your education? How much are they comfortable borrowing? Finances alone shouldn't dictate your college list, but they can't be ignored either.

Chapter 8 will give you some important information about financing a college education and direct you to online calculators—called "net price calculators"—that can estimate your out-of-pocket cost at different colleges. If you enter the information into the net price calculators at the colleges that interest you, you will avoid surprises later.

Colleges determine financial aid using complex formulae to try to be fair and equitable. But you may not receive as much aid as you feel you need because of the great demand for financial aid. In this case, you should have at least one college that you know you can afford, probably a public university in your home state where you can pay in-state tuition *and* where you are very likely to be admitted—in other words, a likely that is also low cost. We call this a "financial likely." Regardless of the admissions and financial aid decisions you receive from your other colleges, you want to be able to afford going to one that is likely to admit you.

CHAPTER 6

The Big Tests

Standardized tests—what they actually measure, how you can prepare for them, and the role they play in getting accepted to college—probably comprise the most anxiety-provoking part of the college admissions process. Each year millions of high school students get up early on a Saturday and spend the morning filling in little ovals on a test grid, certain that their dreams for college hang in the balance.

This chapter will help you understand how standardized tests fit into the college admissions picture and how you can approach them with confidence. It will explain the similarities and differences between the two main tests: the SAT and the ACT. We'll discuss why and how colleges use standardized tests in the first place, help you determine whether one of the two tests is better for you, and consider how to best prepare for it. We'll also discuss how more and more schools are making these tests optional, giving you the choice to decide whether to submit them or not.

WHAT ARE THE SAT AND ACT?

The SAT and the ACT are widely and interchangeably used in the college admissions process. Both have long, often controversial histories behind them. A version of the SAT was first offered in 1926, and the ACT debuted in 1959. The SAT has long been known as a tricky and puzzle-like test compared to the ACT, which has been seen as a straightforward test of what a student has learned in high school. That changed in March 2016 when the College Board, the administrator of the SAT, unveiled a completely overhauled SAT that adopted many of the features of the ACT while adding distinctive features of its own.

Although their origins and evolution are different, both the SAT and the ACT are now designed to measure what students have learned in high school and to assess their readiness for college. This can be very valuable information for admissions offices evaluating students who come from schools with widely varying grading standards. A standardized test is the same for everyone, so it is independent of how strict or lenient school grading standards may be.

> No longer will it be good enough to focus on tricks and trying to eliminate answer choices. We are not interested in students just picking an answer, but justifying their answer.[1]
>
> DAVID COLEMAN, PRESIDENT OF THE COLLEGE BOARD COMMENTING ON THE REDESIGNED SAT

Because the tests focus on high school achievement, a growing number of states use the SAT or ACT to measure how well schools and districts are meeting state or federal standards. In these states, high school juniors are required to take the test, free of charge, during a special school-day administration, whether or not they plan to go to college. North Carolina, Minnesota, Wisconsin, and Missouri are among the schools that require the ACT. Connecticut, Delaware, Michigan, and New Hampshire are a few of those that require the SAT. Students can use their scores on these state-mandated tests for college admissions purposes, although many students also test on a national test date of their choosing.

In their current forms, the SAT and ACT have much in common. A student who does well on one is very likely to do well on the other and vice versa. This shouldn't be surprising because the tests are supposed to measure the same skills. But they are not identical, and their differences may matter for you.

THE STRUCTURE OF THE SAT AND ACT

Both tests consist of several sections of multiple choice questions, with the sections appearing in a predictable order, followed by an optional essay. With the exception of math questions on the ACT, which have five answer choices, the multiple choice questions on both tests have four possible answers, with no penalty for guessing. With the essay, each test runs roughly four hours, including breaks. A complete test administration is nearly five hours, from arrival at the testing center to dismissal at the end.

The tests currently administered on the national testing dates use a paper question booklet and answer sheet, with students bubbling in their answers using a pencil, just as previous generations have done. Both test companies give states and school districts across the country the option of administering online versions of the test, and the ACT began administering a computer-adaptive online version of the ACT in 2017 at its international test centers. Computer-adaptive tests adjust to each test-taker's ability level while he or she is taking the test and avoid asking too many questions that are too easy or too difficult for a given student. Known as CAT, computer adaptive testing is efficient and more secure and will likely be how all students test at some point in the future. For now, however, most students take the SAT or ACT the old-fashioned way.

The SAT and ACT differ from each other structurally in a few ways. The SAT consists of three subtests (Reading, Writing and Language, and Math) plus the optional essay. One of the two sections of math questions does not permit the use of a calculator. The SAT also includes some fill-in math questions where the student must generate the answer, rather than select it from among several given alternatives. The ACT is composed of four tests (English, Math, Reading, and Science), each consisting solely of multiple choice questions, plus the optional essay, and it allows the use of a calculator on all math questions.

CONTENT TESTED BY THE SAT AND ACT

The SAT and ACT are designed to measure what a student has learned in high school, and so the content matter they test is similar. They differ in the relative emphasis they place on certain types of questions and how the test is paced.

WHAT DO THE SAT AND ACT HAVE IN COMMON CONTENT-WISE?

Reading

- Both the SAT and ACT test your ability to comprehend what you read using reading passages followed by a series of questions that draw on your understanding of the paragraph.

- Neither test has a separate vocabulary section, although the reading passages test your knowledge of the meaning of words.

English or Writing and Language

- Both test a variety of grammar rules dealing with use, structure, tense, agreement, and punctuation.
- Both ask questions about full sentences within a paragraph to test knowledge of style, development, organization, and expression of ideas.
- The test is called English on the ACT and Writing and Language on the SAT.

Math

- Both test your knowledge of arithmetic, algebra 1 and algebra 2, geometry, and trigonometry.
- Both emphasize your ability to apply math concepts.

Essay

- Both the ACT and SAT have an optional essay that is scored separately from the rest of the test and that comes at the end.
- The essay score is not included in either your overall SAT score or in the ACT composite score.

SOME IMPORTANT WAYS THAT THE TESTS DIFFER

Reading

- Although vocabulary is not a large part of either test, the SAT has about twice as many vocabulary questions as the ACT.
- The SAT Reading section has five reading passages, two of which include graphs or charts. The ACT Reading section has four reading passages, with no graphs or charts.
- The average grade level of reading passages on the SAT, both in the Reading test and Writing and Language test, is about two grades higher than the average grade level of corresponding ACT passages—that is, the SAT passages are more challenging to read and understand.

Math

- The ACT places greater emphasis on geometry than the SAT—about 25 percent of its math questions are geometry-based compared with only about 5 percent of math questions on the SAT.

- The SAT places greater emphasis on algebra, word problems, and data analysis questions using tables and charts.

- The ACT Math test includes a small number of questions that require knowledge of some advanced topics in mathematics.

- The SAT provides a table with common formulas for reference; the ACT does not.

- Roughly 75 percent of SAT Math questions are multiple choice, and 25 percent are "fill in." All ACT Math questions are multiple choice.

- You can use a calculator on all ACT Math questions. The SAT has a calculator-allowed section and a no-calculator section.

Science

- The ACT contains a Science section; the SAT does not.

- The ACT Science section tests your ability to analyze charts and graphs and draw conclusions about scientific information.

- This section is not a test of scientific knowledge as such, but instead focuses on logic and scientific thinking. A few questions, however, do require knowledge of some scientific concepts. Typically there is one question per science passage that assesses outside knowledge.

Essay

- The SAT essay asks you to analyze a passage by discussing how the author uses evidence and develops the argument in the passage.

- The ACT essay asks you to write a persuasive argument in response to a passage dealing with a specific, contemporary issue. The passage includes three viewpoints from different sides of the debate, and you have to analyze and incorporate these viewpoints into an essay presenting your own perspective on the issue.

PACING OF THE SAT AND ACT

Both tests require you to move quickly through the test, although the SAT allows more time per question. On average, the SAT allows 75 seconds per Reading question, about 50 seconds per Writing question, and about 85 seconds per Math question. You have 50 minutes for the optional SAT essay.

By contrast, the ACT allows about 55 seconds per Reading question, about 35 seconds per English question, and 60 seconds per Math question. Test takers get a little over 50 seconds for each question in the science section, and 40 minutes for the optional essay.

As we noted, the reading level of SAT passages is generally higher. You will have more time per question on the SAT, but you will usually need it because the passages will be more challenging. Basically, with some exceptions, the difference comes down to more complexity with more time for the SAT, or less complexity with less time for the ACT.

HOW ARE THE TESTS SCORED?

The SAT and ACT are similar in overall content but are scored differently.

SCORING FOR THE SAT

The SAT score report contains two section scores, each on a 200- to 800-point scale: Evidence-Based Reading and Writing, and Math, for a total possible score on the SAT ranging from 400 to 1600. This scoring will be familiar to parents who took the SAT in their youth, although as we will discuss further on, the scores themselves are not directly comparable.

The Evidence-Based Reading and Writing section score combines the results for the Reading and the Writing and Language tests. The Math section score reflects performance on both the calculator and non-calculator questions on the Math test. The SAT score report also shows a number of cross-test subscores as well as other subscores, but colleges do not typically use them.

The SAT essay is scored differently. Two independent readers assign each essay a score of 1 to 4 along three "dimensions"—reading, analysis, and writing. The two scores for each dimension are then added together, yielding three scores, one for each dimension, ranging from 2 to 8. Scores for the essay are reported separately from the Evidence-Based Reading and Writing and the Math section scores.

Scoring for the ACT

The ACT score report contains four section scores, each ranging from 1 to 36. The four sections scores—English, Math, Reading, and Science—are averaged to provide a composite score ranging from 1 to 36. The composite is rounded up or down to the nearest whole number. A variety of subtest scores are also generated, but like the SAT, they play little role in the college admissions process.

The ACT essay is scored by two different readers on a scale of 1 to 6 across four different "domains" for a total score of 2 to 12 for each domain. The four domain totals are then averaged, producing a Writing score that ranges from 2 to 12. The graded domains are ideas and analysis, development and support, organization, and language use. An English language arts (ELA) score that combines results on English, Reading, and Writing is also reported and is used by a few schools. It is not included in the composite. If a student does not write the essay, the ELA score is not reported.

THE SAT AND ACT AT A GLANCE

	SAT	ACT
Tests	Reading Writing and Language Math Optional Essay	English Math Reading Science Optional Essay (Writing)
Scoring	Two scores, each 200–800 Maximum total 1600 Essay scored 2–8 on each of three dimensions	Four scores, each 1–36 Maximum composite 36 Essay (Writing) scored 2–12
Test length	Approximately three hours without essay	Approximately three hours without essay

(continued)

	SAT	ACT
Essay details	Optional essay at end of test is 50 minutes total	Optional essay at end of test is 40 minutes total
Format	Multiple choice and fill-in (for some math questions only); calculator and non-calculator math questions	Multiple choice only; calculator may be used on all math questions
Scoring basis	No penalty for random guessing	No penalty for random guessing
Website	www.collegeboard.org	www.act.org

HOW MUCH DO STANDARDIZED TESTS COUNT?

How important are standardized tests in the college admissions process? In chapter 2, we quoted David Erdmann, the late admissions dean at Rollins College, as saying, "At most institutions, standardized test scores count less than students think and more than colleges are willing to admit." This is a fairly accurate statement about the importance of standardized tests.

At many selective colleges, standardized test scores count significantly in the evaluation of a student's academic strengths but less than GPA, class rank (if available, but increasingly rarely reported by high schools), and the rigor of the student's course work. At some other colleges, particularly public ones with specific GPA requirements for admission, higher test scores can offset lower grades. Some schools, such as those in the California State University system, have published formulas showing how this trade-off works. So test scores can indeed be important, depending on the school's philosophy and your other credentials. At the same time, more colleges are becoming test optional, so a student can choose not to submit scores to those schools. We will talk more about test-optional schools further on in this chapter.

Scores Are Evaluated in Context

At most colleges that are not formula driven, admissions officers evaluate applications holistically and consider many factors when making their admissions decisions. Your test scores, for example, will be evaluated in context and relative to your opportunities and life circumstances. Colleges know that higher levels of parental education and family income correlate strongly with higher standardized test scores, so admissions officers expect to see higher scores from the prep school–educated son of two professional parents than from the inner city–educated son of working-class, immigrant parents. The same score can mean something quite different for two different applicants.

THE MIDDLE 50 PERCENT OF SCORES

Colleges usually report scores for the middle 50 percent of their class rather than averages. This is how they appear in the "big books" such as the *Fiske Guide* and in the *U.S. News* rankings. In general, the more selective a college, the higher the scores falling in the middle 50 percent of its freshman class. For example, College A may report that its middle 50 percent had SAT math scores ranging from 500 to 620. This means that 25 percent of freshmen had a math SAT score below 500, 25 percent had a score above 620, and the remaining 50 percent fell in between. Knowing that the math midrange for the freshman class was 500 to 620, for example, tells you more than simply knowing that the average score was 560. It also reminds you that many students were admitted with a score below 560, information that is lost when you have only the average.

College B may report that the middle 50 percent of its freshman class had SAT math scores of 620 to 730. Comparing the two sets of numbers, we can see that 75 percent of the freshmen at College B had a math score of 620 or above, and only 25 percent of the students at College A reached that level. A 500 would place you right at the 25th percentile for College A but at a much lower percentile at College B.

PERCENTILE AND LIKELIHOOD OF ADMISSION

Of course, many factors other than standardized test scores influence admission to a college that evaluates applications holistically. Scores are just one part of your complex profile. To put them in a broader context, if your test scores fall roughly in the middle 50 percent range of a selective college's freshman class SAT or ACT distribution, they won't hurt or help your chances for admission much. For most applicants, the greater you diverge from the middle, up or down, the more they will help or hurt your chances.

In the example just discussed, a math score of 740 or greater would fall in the top 25 percent of the freshman class at College B and would probably help your case for admission. Just how much a higher score will help depends on the actual score, the weight the college places on it, the rest of your record, and the college's selectivity.

Scores falling in the lowest 25 percent of the freshman class for a selective college (620 or less in this example) would usually need to be offset by some compelling factors for you to be a viable candidate at that college, especially if the college is quite selective. Scores in the bottom 25 percent of a school's freshman class will not by themselves automatically disqualify you. By definition, 25 percent of the students in the class must have scores at or below the 25th percentile. But realistically, scores in the lower end of a college's freshman class will reduce your chances of being admitted if the college does not accept a large percentage of its applicants. Some of the students admitted in the bottom quartile may have had a special admissions hook, such as athletics, first-generation background, or some other compelling factor that offset their scores.

In reality, as an applicant to a college that requires or recommends the SAT or ACT, you have no sure way of knowing how important your scores will be in the admissions decision. Given all this uncertainty, the smart approach is to try to obtain the highest scores you can with reasonable preparation, with an emphasis on *reasonable*.

College A—Math Midrange of 500 to 620

25 PERCENT OF STUDENTS SCORED	50 PERCENT OF STUDENTS	25 PERCENT OF STUDENTS
less than 500	scored 500 to 620	scored more than 620

College B—Math Midrange of 620 to 730

25 PERCENT OF STUDENTS SCORED	50 PERCENT OF STUDENTS	25 PERCENT OF STUDENTS
less than 620	scored 620 to 730	scored more than 730

HOW DO THE PSAT AND PREACT FIT INTO THE PICTURE?

The SAT and ACT come in shorter, less-expensive versions that you may be able to take at your school before you tackle the full-length test. The PSAT (or Preliminary SAT), the short version of the SAT, is traditionally offered in October to high school juniors, although at some schools, sophomores can take it. The College Board offers a special PSAT in the spring, known as the PSAT10, that your school may offer sophomores in lieu of having them take the regular PSAT in the fall along with the juniors. A version of the PSAT for even younger students is available as well from the College Board.

The PreACT, the short version of the ACT, is offered to high school sophomores from September to May, with the date at the discretion of the school. A suite of ACT-related tests for younger students, known as Aspire, is also offered by some schools. Unlike the full-length versions of the tests, registration for the PSAT and PreACT is handled by the high school, not the testing agencies. Neither the PSAT nor the PreACT has an essay.

The PSAT and PreACT give students experience taking a standardized college test and provide detailed reports along with the test results that give students valuable information about their strengths and weaknesses so that they can better prepare for the "real thing." The maximum score on each section of the PSAT is 760 (rather than 800 on SAT) and 36 on the PreACT (just like the ACT) and are designed to give you, directly or indirectly, an estimate of how you would perform on the real thing if you were to test on that same day. Because the maximum possible on the PSAT is 1520, a student who scored that high would be expected to do at least that well, and possibly higher, on the real SAT. The SAT and ACT also include unscored sections on career interests that may prove useful to you.

Some high schools offer the PSAT only, some the PreACT only, and some offer both. Check with your school counselor to find out which tests are offered and when. If a test is not offered at your school, you may be able to make arrangements to take it through a nearby school that does offer it. Planning in advance is important. Neither test will appear on your high school transcript, and colleges do not receive score reports. With one exception treated further on in this chapter, the test results are basically for your and your counselor's use, so we encourage you to take advantage of the opportunity to take one or both.

WHICH TEST SHOULD YOU TAKE?

Previously in this chapter we reviewed how the SAT and ACT are similar and how they differ. It would be great if you could easily predict if you will do better on one than the other, but you can't. In reality, most students will do about the same on the two tests if taken at roughly the same time, but some will do better on one than the other. It can be hard to predict which category you will fit in, with one exception.

Students who read slowly but are not eligible for extended time accommodations may find the ACT to be exceptionally challenging because of its faster pace. The SAT may be a better choice for those students. In general, though, we recommend that all students take timed practice tests of both types and compare the results using a concordance table. You can find full-length practice tests in PDF form for the SAT and the ACT on the College Board and ACT websites. The PreACT and PSAT can also be used for this purpose, although full-length practice tests will more accurately predict your performance.

⊠ What Is a Concordance Table?

A concordance table shows how a given SAT or ACT score compares to a score on the other test. The tables are developed by studying students who have taken both exams. A 75th percentile score on the SAT would correspond (concord) to a score on the ACT that was also at the 75th percentile. These percentiles are unique to the concordance study and should not be confused with the percentiles reported on an individual score report. Most colleges use concordance tables to assist in comparing students across tests. It is important that students use the most recent tables, because they have been reworked for the new SAT introduced in March 2016. Scores on the new test run somewhat higher than on the old SAT. Interim tables have been released by College Board, but the final SAT-ACT study results are not expected until 2018. You can find the most recent SAT-ACT concordance table at www.admissionmatters.com.

If your results indicate a clear advantage for one test over the other, we recommend preparing for that test. If the difference is small, choose the test you like best (or dislike least) and prepare for that one. Because all schools accept either test, there is no advantage to prepping for and taking both "for real."

HOW IMPORTANT IS THE ESSAY?

As we discussed, the essay on the SAT and ACT is an optional add-on at the end of each test. Relatively few schools currently require it. Most of those are selective, although they represent just a small percentage of selective schools overall. Although we are tempted to mention a few schools that do require the essay, the list would probably be outdated, and smaller, by the time you are reading this. The trend is definitely against requiring or considering the essay.

The problem, of course, is that if even if just one of the schools on your college list requires the essay, you will have to take it. And you may be testing, at least for the first time, before your list is finalized. The safest plan is to take the ACT or SAT with the essay as insurance, unless you know for sure that all of the schools you are considering do not require it.

HOW DOES TEST PREP WORK?

Testing experts know that a person's score on the ACT or SAT is based on at least three factors. First, and most important, how much do you know about the subject matter being tested? If a question requires a certain kind of calculation, for example, you probably won't get it right if you don't know how to do it. The second factor involves test-taking skills: How comfortable are you taking such tests in general, and how familiar and comfortable are you with the types of questions and the pacing? Finally, and most disconcerting, each test score has a random component—the luck of the draw—on the day of the test. No exam can exhaustively test your knowledge. It can sample it only at a certain moment. The specific questions on a given test may or may not reflect your broader knowledge. And you might not be feeling your best that day. There is no box to check if you aren't feeling well, although you can cancel your scores within a few days of taking the test.

An SAT score report shows a score for each part, as well as a score range. A math score of 570, for example, has a score range from 540 to 600. By reporting a score range, the College Board is suggesting that if you took different editions of the test within a short period of time, your performance might vary a bit but would probably fall within this 60-point spread. This variation would occur independent of any attempts to improve your score through studying or familiarizing yourself with the format of the test. The same is true for the ACT. The test makers advise that the composite score should be viewed as plus or minus one point, with scores on the subtests ranging from plus or minus two points. Colleges ignore the score range and count the actual score, just as students do.

> In certain cases, private tutors make total sense but in many others self-studying makes sense. Motivated kids with an aggressive approach to learning should definitely consider self-studying.
>
> Senior reflecting on what works best

Forms of Test Prep

Test preparation comes in many forms. You can successfully prepare with a book, an online course, an in-person class, or with a one-on-one tutor, either in person or virtual. Some options are free or low cost, whereas private tutoring may cost up to several thousand dollars. What should you do?

Any method of preparation will work if you are motivated and willing to invest the time and energy to prepare. At elite private schools and high-performing public schools, many students do significant test preparation, often with their own in-school classes or private tutors. Most other students, including low-income students or those attending under-resourced schools, do not usually have these options available. Responding to the realities of income disparities, the College Board and the ACT have developed free or low-cost study preparation tools that any student can use.

The College Board, for example, has partnered with Khan Academy (www.khanacademy.com) to offer online SAT prep that is personalized for each student based on a diagnostic test or performance on the PSAT. Specific practice is based on your results, so that you can focus on what you need to work on, rather than on what you already know. Full-length, official SAT practice tests are a part of the preparation.

The ACT offers free or low-cost test-prep options through a partnership with Kaplan test prep. Called "Online Prep Live," the program includes interactive online live-streaming instruction, access to previously recorded sessions, and official test content from the ACT. The program is available free of cost to students eligible for ACT fee waivers, and for $179 for others. The same content, but without access to the live or recorded instruction, is also available for $39.95.

What You Will Be Studying

Good preparation for the SAT or ACT should focus on subject matter and test-taking skills. You need to be motivated, you need enough time to absorb the lessons, and you need to study relatively close to the date of the test. It is not a good idea to study over winter break, do nothing afterward, and then take a test in the spring. You need to keep your preparation going.

But for many good students with strong reading and math skills, the most valuable part of standardized test preparation deals with test-taking skills, including pacing and developing the stamina to stay focused through a long test. Practicing tests under timed conditions is very important, as is learning how to approach different types of questions.

Questions tend to fall into predictable categories, and being familiar with the types of questions that appear most frequently can help a good deal. In addition, test developers know the kinds of careless mistakes that students often make and include some easy wrong answers—known as distractors—among the multiple choice options. Identifying these repeated, careless errors can raise scores significantly just by itself. You can also learn to be more astute at eliminating answers that are obviously wrong when you are unsure of the correct answer and have to guess.

All of this is independent of the type of test prep you use. You need to assess yourself honestly. If you are motivated to work consistently and diligently from a book or free or low-cost online resource in a timely manner, you can save your family a lot of money and get results like those you would have obtained from an in-person course or tutor. But the key is applying yourself regardless of how you choose to prepare.

My son got a 35 with self-administered testing. I can't stress this enough: don't cheat on the practice tests. But the most important thing is to review every single wrong answer and figure out WHY you got it wrong. Did you understand the concept? If not, study it. Timing? Do more practice. Stupid mistakes? Pay attention and skip hard ones to the end.

Mom commenting on her son's test prep experience

How can you maximize your chances of doing well on the ACT or SAT? Preparation and serious practice in any form will help most students. And for some, it may help a lot.

Remember also that the outcome will be hard to predict. Your scores may go up very little (or even decline a bit because of the random error inherent in any test), or they may improve a lot if they were on the low side to begin with. (They won't go up much if your scores were already very high, because there just isn't much room for them to increase.) The best approach to test preparation is a reasonable one that doesn't disrupt your schoolwork and extracurricular activities. Preparation that takes over your life is going too far. As with all other aspects of college admissions, stay balanced and keep the whole process in perspective.

WHEN SHOULD YOU TEST?

The SAT is offered seven times during the school year: August, October, November, December, March, May, and June; the ACT is offered seven times in September, October, December, February (except in New York State), April, June, and July (July date starts in 2018).

Taking the Test for the First Time

A good time to take the test for the first time is the second half of the junior year, although some students take the test in the previous fall. You gain little by taking it any earlier. Students do better as they get older, with more school, more reading, more math. You can register for the SAT at www.collegeboard.org or the ACT at www.act.org by using a credit card. The fees are currently $45 for the SAT without the essay and $57 with the essay. The ACT charges $42.50 without the essay and $58.50 with it. Fee waivers are available through high school counseling offices for low-income students who qualify. The test is offered at many sites, mostly at large high schools, but the sites vary on different dates. Details are available online on the websites and in printed materials in high school counseling offices. Because some test sites fill up quickly, it is good to plan ahead and register early to get the site of your choice so you don't have to drive a long distance to take the test. You generally need to register about five weeks before the test to avoid a late fee. You must submit a current photo with your online or paper registration request, and you must bring a picture ID to the test.

OBTAINING MORE THAN YOUR SCORES

Scores on both tests are mailed a few weeks after the test date or are available online (or by phone for a fee) about two weeks after the test. The same website where you register for the test will release your scores through your password-protected account. For the August, May, and October SAT test dates, you can pay a small fee, currently $18, for the Question-and-Answer Service and get a copy of the actual test you took along with an answer key and your answers. The ACT offers a similar service, known as Test Information Release, for the December, April, and June tests for $20. Getting the actual questions and answers can be a good idea for students who may want to retest. It can be a very helpful test-preparation tool for the next round, although it will take as many as five or six weeks after the test to receive your materials. You can sign up for the service when you register for a test or within five months of taking an eligible SAT test or within three months of taking an eligible ACT test.

HOW OFTEN SHOULD YOU TAKE THE TEST?

Once you receive your first set of standardized test scores, you can decide whether you want to take the test again. A lot will depend on how competitive your scores are for the schools you are considering applying to and whether you are willing to put in more time in test preparation. Students applying to more selective colleges tend to take the SAT or the ACT more than once. You can take a test as many times as you want, but actually only a small percentage of students take them even twice, and an even smaller percentage more often than that. Three times is a reasonable practical maximum. Taking it more than that is probably not the best use of your time and is unlikely to produce significant further improvement. If you decide to retest, you can take the test later in the spring of your junior year or in the fall of your senior year.

CHOOSING THE SCORES TO SEND

The College Board and the ACT keep track of all of your scores and allow you to decide which test scores you wish to submit to a college if you have taken a test more than once. All parts of a given test administration are reported, but students can choose which test dates they want to report. The College Board will automatically send all your SAT and SAT Subject Test scores to colleges, unless you elect Score Choice when ordering score reports and specify which scores you want to send to a particular school. There is no extra charge for Score Choice. The ACT, by contrast, will send results from only one test date at a time. If you want to send the results of two different ACT administrations to a college, you will have to pay a separate fee for each one.

SUPERSCORING YOUR RESULTS

Many colleges will "superscore" results on the SAT, and frequently on the ACT, which means that they will count your highest scores on the different parts of a standardized test regardless of when you obtained those scores (for example, your highest score on Evidence-Based Reading and Writing and your highest Math score obtained across two different SAT test dates). So if you took the SAT twice and did better on Math the first time and Evidence-Based Reading and Writing the second time, you should send results from both dates. Using Score Choice to send just one would actually hurt you. A major exception to the practice of superscoring are all campuses of the University of California, as well as a number of other public universities, which count the highest overall score on a single test date. The ACT is superscored less frequently than the SAT, but it is becoming more common. Some schools that currently superscore the ACT are Middlebury College, Millsaps College, New York University, and the University of Georgia.

A handful of selective colleges currently require students to submit all their SAT or ACT scores, although they too superscore in most cases. We recommend checking the testing policy of each school on its website to get the latest information on Score Choice and superscoring because policies can change. Although we always advise double-checking directly on the website of each college, a helpful, up-to-date summary of both policies at many colleges may be found on the website of Compass Test Prep at www.compassprep.org.

For schools that do not require you to submit all scores, you are free to choose the scores you wish to submit, remembering that in most cases the schools will superscore from among the test results that you send. However, we have asked dozens of college admissions officers if it could ever hurt a student to submit all scores, even if not required, and they *all* said no. They know that students take test prep, have good test days and bad ones, and might get different scores on different days.

THE NATIONAL MERIT SCHOLARSHIP COMPETITION

In September of their senior year, about 16,000 students who score high on PSAT (which is formally known as the PSAT-NMSQT) are notified that they have been selected as National Merit Scholarship semifinalists. The National Merit program uses a simple formula to calculate a "selection score" on which they base this recognition. The formula doubles the Evidence-Based Reading and Writing section score, adds in the Math section score, and then divides the total by 10. The top-scoring students from each state earn semifinalist status, with the selection score varying by state to ensure that the number of semifinalists is proportional to the population of high school students in each state. For the high school class of 2017, the selection score ranged from a low of 209 in Wyoming, West Virginia, South Dakota, and North Dakota to a high of 222 in New Jersey, District of Columbia, and Massachusetts out of a possible maximum score of 228. Boarding schools that enroll many out-of-state students have their own selection score based on the region where they are located. You can call the National Merit Scholarship Corporation's offices at (847) 866–5100 to get the most recent selection score for your state or location if you are curious, because they vary from year to year. Roughly an additional 34,000 students are named "commended students" and receive a certificate.

WHO WINS A SCHOLARSHIP?

Semifinalists are invited to submit an essay, transcript, SAT scores from a full-length test taken no later than December of senior year, and a school recommendation to be considered for finalist status. The ACT cannot be substituted for the SAT, so a semifinalist will need to take the SAT and receive a "confirming score" to advance to finalist status. If practice tests showed higher performance on the ACT, a qualified student might want to take both tests—the SAT for National Merit purposes and the ACT for the admissions process itself. About 95 percent of semifinalists become finalists, and about half of those subsequently receive a one-time monetary award directly from the National Merit Corporation itself or a participating corporation, if a parent is an employee, or from a college. Details can be found at www.nationalmerit.org.

Although the majority of National Merit awards are small and one-time, some public universities such as Iowa State University, University of Oklahoma, University of New Mexico, and Arizona State University seek to attract high-performing students and actively court National Merit finalists with automatic half- or full-tuition scholarships. A few private schools offer generous awards as well. Recognition through the National Hispanic Recognition Program, sponsored by the College Board, can also lead to generous awards at some schools. Details about this program can be found on the College Board website, www.collegeboard.org.

Should You Prepare for the PSAT?

If you are likely to do well on the PSAT, it may be worth taking the test seriously and doing some modest test prep in advance to take potential advantage of these scholarship opportunities. Except in this narrow way, though, the PSAT has no bearing on the college admissions process. Too many students are recognized through the National Merit program, either as commended students or finalists, for it to carry much weight at selective colleges. For most students, the PSAT is simply what it was originally intended to be: a practice test to identify their strengths and weaknesses early in their junior year so that they can prepare for the SAT itself. There is no reason at all to be anxious about it.

THE CASE OF SPECIAL ACCOMMODATIONS

The College Board and the ACT know that some students require special accommodations to overcome challenges that would otherwise impair their performance. Blind or visually impaired students are the most obvious example, but students with other kinds of physical impairments that make it difficult or impossible to complete the test in the standard way can also receive accommodations.

With appropriate documentation submitted in advance to either testing agency, they will approve special arrangements to address the student's needs.

Physical impairments represent just a small percentage of cases seeking such accommodations, however. Most special accommodation requests are for extra time to compensate for learning disabilities. Here, too, satisfactory documentation of the learning disability must be submitted well in advance of the test. Accommodations can range from time and a half (the most common) to untimed testing, depending on the severity of the learning disability. Just as an exam in larger typeface may help a student with visual problems, extra time accommodations for learning disabilities attempt to level the playing field for otherwise able students.

In chapter 12, we will discuss in detail the process of obtaining testing accommodations.

THE SAT SUBJECT TESTS

As we noted previously in this chapter, the College Board offers one-hour, multiple-choice subject matter tests in addition to the SAT ranging from physics to US history. Like the two parts of the SAT, the SAT Subject Tests are scored from 200 to 800, with the average score varying widely from test to test. Fewer than 35 colleges require or recommend that students submit scores from one or more of these tests and some of these allow students to submit ACT scores in lieu of both the SAT and any required SAT Subject Tests. The number of schools requiring or recommending Subject Tests for most students has been shrinking every year. Check specific college websites for the latest information. You can also find an up-to-date list in the *Compass Guide to College Admission Testing* that can be downloaded for free at www.compassprep.com.

The colleges requiring or recommending Subject Tests ask students to submit scores from two different tests; only Georgetown University currently recommends three, and even that is a recommendation, not a requirement. A science-oriented school such as MIT or the engineering major at a large school may require or recommend a specific test, such as Math II and/or a science test. Most give students complete flexibility to choose which tests to take.

Students should choose their Subject Tests carefully and plan to take appropriate tests when the subjects are freshest in their minds. Most students take the

Subject Tests at the end of their junior year. However, depending on your high school curriculum, you may want to take one or more a year earlier if you have the right preparation. For example, if you do well in World History as a sophomore, it makes sense to take the SAT World History Subject Test at the end of your sophomore year rather than wait. You can learn a great deal about the Subject Tests, including sample questions and information about the content covered on each test and in preparation books, on the College Board website. Read all of this carefully and decide which tests would be the best ones for you, keeping in mind the requirements of specific colleges in which you have an interest. As discussed in chapter 12, homeschooled students are often encouraged to submit Subject Test scores even if they are not required or recommended for traditional high school applicant.

On any given test date, except March when SAT Subject Tests are not offered, students can take the SAT by itself or up to three Subject Tests, although three tests on one day can make for a tough morning. You cannot take both the SAT and Subject Tests on the same day, and not all Subject Tests are offered on each test date. Currently, the basic registration fee for the Subject Tests is $26, plus $20 for each individual test. The fee is $26 per test for language with listening, offered only in November, and students must bring their own portable CD player and earphones to the test center. As usual, fee waivers are also available for these tests. If you have been approved for accommodations on the SAT by the College Board, the approval extends to the SAT Subject Tests as well.

TEST-OPTIONAL SCHOOLS

A rapidly growing number of schools no longer require any standardized tests, either the SAT or the ACT, for some or all of their applicants. Some schools exempt students who meet certain GPA criteria, and others require SAT or ACT scores but use them only for placement or research purposes. Still others offer students the option of submitting SAT Subject Test, Advanced Placement, or International Baccalaureate test scores in lieu of the SAT or ACT or of submitting a writing portfolio as an alternative.

These schools find that they can make sound admissions decisions based on other information in a student's record. Schools that have gone test optional report that non-submitters and submitters generally perform equally in college.

You may still benefit from submitting your scores if they are higher than average for a particular school, but the schools promise not to discriminate against you if you don't submit and will not assume you have low test scores. In fact, they feel that having a test-optional policy is attractive to students and gives their college a marketing advantage.

Some schools that are test optional for everyone include Smith College, Wake Forest University, DePaul University, College of the Holy Cross, and Lawrence University. Other schools are test optional for most applicants; among them are University of Delaware and Muhlenberg College.

Unless you are philosophically opposed to taking standardized tests or know that you are just a poor test taker, it is unlikely that you will apply only to test-optional colleges, though there are enough of them to make it a feasible strategy. So you will probably end up taking tests like everyone else, wait to see what your scores are, and then decide where to submit them. A current list of test-optional and test-flexible colleges can be found at www.fairtest.org. Be sure to check individual colleges' websites to confirm specific details and to check for updates. In this area changes happen quickly.

A WORD TO PARENTS ABOUT STANDARDIZED TESTS

There is a lot of anxiety surrounding the SAT and ACT. Some students dread receiving their scores for fear of disappointing their parents or, at the other end of the continuum, providing their parents with a reason to brag or embarrass them. Many feel that their future and their self-esteem depend on the outcome of a four-hour test taken on a Saturday morning. This is not healthy for them, and it is certainly not true.

Please help your children understand that the SAT and ACT are just tests and far from perfect indicators of potential. Even colleges that require them know this. Encourage your children to prepare thoroughly and reasonably for the tests and to do their best, but try to keep standardized tests from becoming an obsession either for you or for them.

CHAPTER 7

Deciding About Early Decision and Other Early Options

Although most students apply to college by January 1 of their senior year and choose from among their options once they receive their decisions the following spring, more and more are taking advantage of early acceptance programs. "Early admission" is an umbrella term for options that require applying to a college early in the school year, typically by November 1 or November 15, in exchange for an early response from that college, usually by December 15.

AN OVERVIEW OF EARLY ACCEPTANCE PROGRAMS

The programs offered by different colleges vary in important ways. Some, known as early decision (ED), commit you to attending if you are admitted. You can apply ED to only one college because acceptance is binding. Another approach, early action (EA), allows you to receive the college's decision by mid-December, just as with ED, but you still have until May 1 to make your final decision among all the colleges that have admitted you. Most EA programs permit you to apply EA to more than one college as well and even submit one ED application. A third type, used by a small number of schools, is generically known as restrictive early action (REA). It does not commit you to attend if accepted but it does restrict you from applying ED and sometimes EA to other colleges, depending on the college's particular form of REA. If you feel you need a scorecard to keep all of this straight, you are not alone. And the rules can change from year to year.

Almost 500 colleges currently offer at least one of these options. About 90 colleges have both EA and ED programs: University of Miami, Earlham College, Ursinus College, Spelman College, and Clark University are examples. About 70 colleges, including Smith College, Rollins College, University of Puget Sound, Vanderbilt University, Gettysburg College, and Tufts University, offer only ED but have two different dates: ED I, with an application date about November 15, and ED II, with an application date about January 1 or January 15, often the same as their regular decision application deadlines. And about 25 of the schools that have both EA and ED offer all three options: Dickinson College, University of Chicago, Colorado College, Case Western University, and Southern Methodist University, for example, offer two ED dates as well as an EA option. The specifics may change from year to year as colleges revise their EA or ED programs and as more and more schools come on board with an early option.

Early admission programs, and ED in particular, have engendered a good deal of discussion and controversy. In this chapter, we tell you what the debate is all about, guide you in sorting out the options, and help you decide whether an early acceptance program is right for you.

> There are so many early options to keep straight and choose from. I think the whole thing should be called "early confusion."
>
> PARENT OF A HIGH SCHOOL JUNIOR

THE PROS AND CONS OF EARLY DECISION

On the surface, the rationale for ED admissions programs is simple: if you have a clear first-choice college, you can express that preference by applying early and committing to attend if admitted. If accepted, you can bypass much of the drawn-out anxiety lasting into the spring that can accompany regular decision applications. If the college says "no" (a denial) or "we are not sure" (a deferral of the decision until the regular application cycle), you can still apply to other colleges by the regular cycle deadline, though it helps if you are prepared to submit those applications before you receive the news. Although some colleges have had early programs for decades, they have become much more popular in the past 15 years.

THE ADVANTAGES OF EARLY DECISION FOR THE COLLEGE AND THE STUDENT

Bluntly stated, early decision is part of the marketing plan for a college. Although it may look as if it mainly helps students (and it does indeed help those who are successful), the advantages are mostly on the side of the college, and more and more so as early programs become more popular and more competitive.

Why Colleges Offer Early Decision

From a college's perspective, ED enrolls students who are exceptionally eager to attend. The college also knows that each student who is accepted ED will indeed enroll in the fall. Unlike regular decision, they know that the yield from the pool of ED acceptances will be 100 percent, unless a student must decline because of insufficient financial aid or some other unforeseen difficulty. It can help a college minimize the likelihood of either over-enrollment or under-enrollment. This also gives a college a head start on planning to round out the rest of the class in regular decision: they can better predict their needs for geographical and ethnic diversity, athletics and other special talents, and legacies after the early round.

⊠

There is an advantage in the admissions process to applying Early Decision. In 2015–2016 we admitted 24% of students who applied Early Decision and 9% of students who applied Regular Decision. There is no financial aid advantage or disadvantage in applying Early Decision and we meet full demonstrated need, but students who wish to compare different schools' financial aid packages should apply Regular Decision.[1]

DUKE UNIVERSITY ADMISSIONS WEBSITE

⊠

Advantages for the Student

It is not news that the percentage of students accepted through ED is usually higher, sometimes much higher, than the percentage accepted during the regular round. Classmates with equivalent records sometimes have very different outcomes in the admissions process depending on when they applied. As a result, the number of ED applications has gone up dramatically over the past 20 years, increasing at a faster rate than the number of applications overall. As more and more apply early, the acceptance differential is shrinking, but it can still be considerable depending on the college.

An ED acceptance can mean admission to a student's first-choice college and an end to the anxiety and uncertainty of the college admissions process by mid-December of senior year. The process appears to efficiently match students who want a given college with a college that wants them, so everyone wins. But as with everything else in college admissions, the situation is not that simple.

⊠

"I just want to go to sleep until December 15th."

"I've taken up praying. I don't even believe in God."

"I'd sell my soul—if I still had one."

"Either the best moment in life, probably better than sex, or the worst moment, even worse than death."

STUDENT COMMENTS ABOUT EARLY DECISION AND EARLY ACTION
POSTED ON AN INTERNET BULLETIN BOARD

⊠

THE MAJOR PROBLEMS WITH EARLY DECISION

Critics of ED argue that it has become more than it was intended to be: an admissions strategy that appears to increase the chances of being accepted to a selective college for those who are savvy enough to make use of it. Some colleges have admissions rates two or three times higher for ED applicants compared with regular decision applicants, and they fill from a third to over a half of their freshman classes from the early pool. As a result, the much larger pool of regular decision applicants ends up competing for fewer slots after the much smaller group of early applicants has secured their place.

A few examples of ED admission rates compared to regular decision admission rates are found in the following table. Note that the regular decision rates shown are lower than the overall admission rate that is most often reported. The regular decision versus ED admission rate difference is what really matters, because a student must apply one way or the other. The "overall" rate simply combines data from the two.

CLASS OF 2020 ADMISSION RATES BY PERCENTAGE

College	Regular Decision	ED	Overall
Amherst	12.2	39.6	13.7
Bowdoin	11.6	33.7	14.3
Johns Hopkins	10.1	30.3	11.5
Middlebury	12.7	53.1	16.0
Northwestern	8.4	35.0	10.7
Williams	15.0	42.0	17.3

Some colleges, including Johns Hopkins University and the University of Pennsylvania, have also been open in telling legacy applicants that their legacy hook will count most if they apply early, reinforcing the message that you should use ED as a strategy. As we'll see in chapter 11, the same situation sometimes applies for recruited athletes: they may be told that they will lose their hook, even their place on the team, if they don't apply early.

> An applicant's affiliation with Penn either by being children or grandchildren of alumni, is given the most consideration through Early Decision.[2]
>
> UNIVERSITY OF PENNSYLVANIA INSTRUCTIONS TO UNDERGRADUATE APPLICANTS FOR THE CLASS OF 2021

Critics also argue that ED favors students who do not need financial aid and have access to a support system (counselors, well-informed parents) that will assist them in understanding the rules of ED and how to take best advantage of it. Students of limited financial means, who disproportionately attend poorly funded and overcrowded public schools, are much less likely to have these advantages than students from private schools or high-performing public high schools.

Students who are accepted ED may be limiting their financial aid options. Although they can be released from an ED commitment if the accompanying financial aid package is inadequate, ED admits cannot compare financial aid offers from several schools. It may also prevent them from perhaps obtaining a more desirable package at one school based on the offer from another. By contrast, students who can pay the full cost of enrollment generally don't have this concern.

MORE THOUGHTS ABOUT EARLY DECISION

Counselors cringe when they hear students say, "I want to apply early—I just don't know where." It reflects the pressure that students feel to make a choice—any choice—to maximize their chances of admission to a selective college without serious thought about the qualities of the college, except perhaps its prestige. Once students do pick a school and apply, the pressure builds, often intensely, up through mid-December. Students tend to think, often correctly, that an ED application is their best shot at their dream school if they are a competitive applicant to begin with. They greet acceptance with great joy, and they absorb denial and deferral, which are far more common outcomes, all too often with great sadness.

You should be absolutely sure of your first-choice college before applying ED because it is binding: you can't change your mind after being accepted unless the financial aid package you are offered does not meet your family's need (we discuss this at greater length in chapter 8 and chapter 14). The best way to be sure, of course, is to learn as much as possible about colleges and visit them in person, ideally when they are in session and well before the ED deadline. To be a good ED candidate, you should begin early, preferably by the spring of junior year, learning about ED options and deadlines and visiting several schools to see whether one emerges as a clear front-runner.

You should also have all your standardized testing done by October of your senior year. November SAT (the ACT is not offered in November) scores may or may not arrive in time—you have to ask each school. (If testing in October or November, be sure to arrange to have your scores sent directly to your ED school, even before you see them.) And you should have a solid first quarter (or first half of the first semester) in your senior year. Colleges often want to see how you are doing as a senior, presumably in your most challenging academic program yet. If your school doesn't automatically send first-quarter grades, some colleges may request them from your counselor before making a decision. This may be equally true for other forms of early admission (EA and rolling admissions), which we will discuss further on in this chapter.

I didn't really know about early decision until I started hearing other kids talking about it in late October. They were moaning about all the admissions stuff they had to do. I didn't see the point of all that drama, until someone explained to me that I might have a better chance if I applied early admission . . . like maybe if the college knew I wanted them, they would want me. So I started to feel pressure to "want" some place. Anyway, I didn't apply early decision anywhere, now it's March, and I'm getting awfully antsy because I don't know yet where I will be going in the fall. But that is better than picking a school for the wrong reason, getting in, and then having to go there because you applied early decision. I just wish I had gotten started earlier on the whole thing.

HIGH SCHOOL SENIOR

⋈

EARLY ACTION IN DETAIL

In contrast to early decision, early action appears to offer a student the best of both worlds: no binding commitment but still an early response from a desired college. Early action has also been offered for many years.

> I wish I would have known how early early applications were due. It seemed as though the year had just begun and I was already applying for college.
>
> COMMENT MADE IN THE SPRING OF SENIOR YEAR

HOW DOES EA DIFFER FROM ED?

The major difference between EA and ED is that students accepted through EA can wait until May 1 to decide whether to attend; the acceptance is not binding. In the meantime, students are free to apply to other colleges through the regular process and can compare financial aid packages before making a final choice. Early action colleges have traditionally also allowed students to apply to other early programs—and even one ED college as well as other EA schools.

EARLY ACTION WITH RESTRICTIONS

Some EA colleges do place restrictions, however, on applying to other schools. The most limiting are restrictive early action and single-choice early action (the term used depends on the school) employed by Harvard University, Stanford University, Princeton University, and Yale University. Under these plans, you may not apply EA *or* ED to any other college (with a few exceptions, such as schools with nonbinding rolling admissions, discussed further on in this chapter, or state universities with EA plans, such as the University of Michigan and the University of Virginia). Another form of restrictive early action, used by Boston College, University of Notre Dame, and Georgetown University, allows students to apply to other EA schools, but not to an ED school. It can get confusing pretty quickly so it is important to be clear about the restrictions that may apply.

KEEPING YOUR COMMITMENT

Students who apply ED or EA with restrictions must honor the commitments of those application choices. Colleges typically ask students to sign a statement in their application attesting that they understand and agree to the terms of that program. Some require a parent's and the high school counselor's signatures as well.

COMPARING EARLY APPLICATION OPTIONS

	Early Decision	Early Action	Restrictive Early Action
Binding?	Yes (except if financial aid is not adequate)	No	No
Allows comparison of aid packages?	No	Yes	Yes
Allows other early applications	Yes (EA applications only)	Yes (EA applications and one ED)	Varies by college
Allows regular decision applications?	Yes (these must be withdrawn if the student is admitted ED)	Yes	Yes

Note: Always check the instructions for specific colleges.

SHOULD YOU APPLY EARLY DECISION OR EARLY ACTION?

Early decision programs can work to your advantage if you (1) have a clear first-choice college that emerges after careful research, (2) don't need grades from the full first semester of your senior year to bolster your academic record, (3) have the organizational skills and time to prepare a strong early application, and (4) don't need to compare financial aid offers. If you can satisfy all of these conditions and are accepted come December 15, your college admissions process can conclude happily months before it otherwise would. Add the bonus of an increased chance of acceptance, and ED becomes an attractive option.

Early action, restrictive or otherwise, is more flexible because an acceptance is not binding. An EA application is a good way to show "demonstrated interest" to a college. The admissions boost from an EA application will likely be much smaller than you might receive from a comparable ED application, but you retain more flexibility in your final decision making if you are accepted. You may still decide to apply to a few other colleges you prefer more, but you can do so knowing that you have an acceptance in hand.

But an early application of either sort has a downside that we haven't yet discussed. You end up thinking that only one college is a "perfect fit" for you and you must pursue it vigorously. As early applications increase, however, more students will be disappointed by denials or deferrals. For some, the buildup has been so great and so much seems to be at stake that even a deferral can be a major blow. Some students face, often for the first time in their lives, what they perceive as significant failure. By contrast, at regular decision time, if you have a balanced list, being denied or wait-listed will be buffered by some good news as well.

> It's not like the 5,000 students at Ivy U are the only ones who are happy with their college and will go on to success in life. While I eagerly hope for my deferral to turn into an acceptance, I know that I have to look at my other options as a definite possibility so I am not haunted in college by the ghost of Ivy U.
>
> COMMENT MADE ON DECEMBER 16 BY STUDENT DEFERRED AT AN IVY LEAGUE COLLEGE

So where does this leave you? Well, it depends. If you have a first-choice college and satisfy the criteria for ED or EA we have noted, perhaps you should apply early. If you would be a competitive applicant, there are clear advantages to doing so.

But please remember what we said about the downside of early applications: don't let your enthusiasm for a college induce "early acceptance syndrome"—the belief that you can truly be happy at one, and only one, college. That is rarely, if ever, the case.

⌧ Is Early Decision Right for You?

☐ I have a clear first-choice college and am completely confident that it is a very good fit for me.

☐ I have done careful research about the college that supports my choice, including most of the following: visited in-person or on the web; studied the catalog, view book, and other material in detail; reviewed the college's profile in a big college guide; and talked with current or former students in person, through online chat, or e-mail.

☐ I have used the college's net price calculator and am comfortable with the financial aid that they will likely offer me. I won't need to compare financial aid offers.

☐ My grades from first-semester senior year will not be significantly better than my earlier record, and my first-quarter grades will be consistent or better than my previous work.

☐ I will have taken my standardized tests by October (or early November in some cases) so that the scores will reach my early decision college in time for November review.

☐ My overall record places me within the admissible range for this college.

☐ I will be able to prepare and submit my application by the ED deadline, including asking for letters of recommendation from my teachers and counselor.

☐ I know that ED candidates appear to get a boost in acceptance from this college.

☐ I would like to know for sure where I will be going to college as early as possible.

☐ I will do careful research on the rest of my college list and prepare applications to them in case I am deferred or denied in early decision.

☐ Although my early decision college is my clear first choice, I realize that I may not be accepted, and I know I will also be very happy and get a fine education at other colleges.

Have Plan B in Place

In theory, ED can eliminate or significantly reduce the need to complete additional applications. But this just doesn't hold up in reality for a lot of students. Some state universities have deadlines in the fall, and some consider applications on a first-come, first-served basis. You will have to submit these applications well before you will hear back from your ED school. Many other regular decision applications are due January 1 or soon after. Although you would get your ED decision before these deadlines, starting new applications during the holiday season right after receiving a disappointing decision from a first-choice college is a pretty unappealing prospect.

Many students apply regular decision to their full array of college choices although they have an early application pending. If an ED application is successful, they must withdraw those additional applications. The extra effort and expense are written off as the cost of "insurance." Others complete their additional applications but wait to actually submit them until they have heard back from their ED school. Either approach can work as long as you plan well.

How to Handle Denial or Deferral

If you are denied early, you are done with that college. You cannot reapply in the regular round or ED II to a school where you have been denied. They have decided that they know enough about you to make a final decision. If you are deferred from ED, however, you are released from your binding commitment. Then you are held in limbo while the admissions staff reads all the regular applications. Finally, in late winter, you are reconsidered with the regular applicants. We talk more about different ED outcomes in chapter 14.

Schools with Two Early Rounds

As we noted previously, a number of schools have two rounds of early decision: ED I and ED II. The date for ED II often coincides with the date for regular decision applications, but of course the ED II applicants get their decisions earlier, usually by mid-February, and are committed to attending if they are accepted, just as in ED I. Colleges offering two rounds of ED say that they do this to give students more time to decide on a first choice. Although this no doubt helps many students, a college may offer ED II to receive applications from students denied or deferred in December by another college. This approach gives both colleges and students two shots at making an early match. The ED II school will not know you applied early somewhere else.

LIKELY LETTERS AND EARLY NOTIFICATION

I am writing to let you know how much the Cornell Engineering Admissions Committee enjoyed reading your application. Your academic and personal achievements are outstanding and, although the Ivy League schools will not officially notify students of their admission decisions until the end of the month, I am pleased to inform you that you are very likely to be admitted to Cornell.

FROM A CORNELL UNIVERSITY LIKELY LETTER FOR THE CLASS OF 2020

Although notification dates vary from college to college, many colleges notify students in the regular round sometime in March to give you several weeks until May 1 to make your final choice.

A small percentage of students who apply regular decision get letters early, however—sometimes very early—that tell them that they are very likely to be accepted, even though it is not a formal letter of admission. Known in admissions circles as "likely letters," these early notifications allow a college to adhere to its official notification date while signaling to a select group of students that the college is especially interested in them.

These colleges, which include the Ivy League as well as a range of other schools, hope that a likely letter will encourage the student receiving it to accept the later, official offer of admission. Likely letters go to those the college is especially eager to recruit: athletes, outstanding members of underrepresented groups, and those with truly distinctive academic credentials. If you receive a likely letter, and only a very small percentage of accepted students do, you will be admitted unless you later commit a very serious infraction, such as cheating or using drugs. It is tantamount to admission. The problem with likely letters is that those who don't receive them begin to worry and get demoralized when they learn that others have.

We're going to get a start on some students who are going to have a number of options.[3]

ERIC FURDA, DEAN OF ADMISSIONS AT THE UNIVERSITY OF PENNSYLVANIA, COMMENTING ON LIKELY LETTERS

Remember, the vast majority of admitted students even at the most selective colleges do not receive a likely letter.

Other colleges may give a wink to their strongest regular decision applicants by inviting them to a special reception on campus a few weeks before decisions are announced or by sending them campus swag. One college we know sent selected students a nylon bag with the college's name on it several weeks before decisions came out along with a letter encouraging them to carry the bag around to the gym, and so on. That was a pretty clear signal that an acceptance letter would follow in due time. In all these cases, the idea is to get students excited before the formal acceptance arrives.

THE ADVANTAGE OF THINKING EARLY EVEN IF YOU DECIDE AGAINST APPLYING EARLY

Many students habitually procrastinate, and they extend that habit to the college application process. But even if you do not plan to apply EA or ED to a college, it may help to avoid procrastination and get your application in well before any deadline.

ROLLING ADMISSIONS AND PRIORITY DEADLINES

The greatest advantage to submitting an application early is at a school that uses rolling admissions, where applications are read as they arrive rather than waiting until after a fixed deadline. Some rolling admissions schools may not even have a formal deadline. Colleges that use rolling admissions may promise a decision for most applicants within a few weeks of submitting an application.

In some ways, rolling admission is like a continuous form of early action. Used at many public universities and some private colleges, rolling admissions colleges accept qualified students until the freshman class is full. Michigan State University, Stony Brook University, and Indiana University-Bloomington are a few of the well-known state universities that admit students via a rolling process. Some of the private colleges that use rolling admissions include Saint Louis University, Hendrix College, Maryville University, and Stetson University.

Some schools begin actively reviewing files right after their application goes live in the summer. You don't have to apply that early to be admitted, but getting your material together early in the fall will ensure that your application will be considered while there is plenty of room and while financial aid is plentiful. You will still have until May 1 to make your final decision.

Sometimes rolling admissions schools will have a "priority deadline" to encourage early submission, although they continue to accept applications as long as space is available. Meeting a priority deadline may mean a greater likelihood of acceptance to the major of your choice, earlier notification of your admissions decision, or eligibility for scholarship programs. Sometimes a priority deadline can mean not just one, but two or all three of these advantages. Here, too, you will have until May 1 to make your final decision. It is clearly to your advantage to submit your application by the priority deadline if you can. The term "priority deadline" is also used by some non-rolling admission schools; you need to check what each one means by that term because it varies from school to school.

Getting It Done Early

There are also other advantages to getting your application in well before the deadline for any college. Of course, the college will not read it until your transcript, recommendations, and test scores have arrived, but getting your part of the application in early, even for regular round review, means that it will arrive earlier than the deadline crunch and be processed and acknowledged earlier. Once you submit your application, you will usually be able to check online to see if other parts of your application have arrived, although it may show something as missing when it simply hasn't been recorded yet. If something really does end up missing, you'll have plenty of time to get a replacement sent.

Because admissions committees start reading complete files soon after the closing date, your application will be read by staff members who are fresh, not yet fatigued by the many hundreds of files they will read during the winter months. It's impossible to know, of course, if that will make any difference in the final decision, but it can't hurt. Getting applications in early also means that you can enjoy the holiday season with your family rather than spend it worrying about applications. We think you (and your family) will be glad you took this path.

CHAPTER 8

Paying the Bill

Most families would probably agree that one of their biggest concerns during the college admissions process is the cost. This chapter is devoted to helping you pay that bill. The good news is that for many students, the cost of tuition, fees, room, and board posted on the college website is not what the student actually pays. Although no one pays more than the "sticker price," many students pay less, sometimes much less, depending on the family's financial situation and the campus's financial aid policies. The not-so-good news is that financial aid can be complex and confusing to those unfamiliar with how it works, and in some cases the result can be disappointing.

In this chapter, we will help you understand the two major types of financial aid and when they are awarded. We'll show you how you can calculate roughly how much aid you might expect to receive and how it may be packaged, and we'll explain why the actual amount may vary depending on a college's financial aid policies and resources. We'll also discuss the role of financial considerations in developing a college list and making a final decision. If your family can easily cover the cost of your education and you are not

> Financial aid allowed us to send our daughter where she wanted to go, a private school in the East. With three children, we couldn't have done it without that help. Financial aid really helped our middle-class family.
>
> Parent of college sophomore

interested in paying less, you can skip this chapter. For everyone else, we hope it will be useful.

KEY CONCEPTS FOR UNDERSTANDING FINANCIAL AID

There are two major categories of financial aid: need-based aid and merit aid.

NEED-BASED AID

Colleges award need-based aid to help families cover the difference between what the college calculates they should pay and the actual cost of attending the college. Colleges use formulas that factor in current income, assets, family size, the number of children in college, and other considerations to determine what a family can pay. With need-based aid, needier students applying to a given college usually receive more aid than more affluent students who would usually be expected to pay more. Need-based aid comes in a "package": grants that do not have to be paid back, loans that do, and work-study jobs.

MERIT AID

Merit aid is different. It is essentially a tuition discount that a college offers to encourage a student to attend. Occasionally, the size of a merit award may be tied to a student's financial need, but most often merit awards are independent of need and can be awarded to any student a college would really like to have attend, using whatever criteria the college wishes to apply. Many schools award both need-based aid and merit aid, but a small number of schools, including some of the most selective, provide only need-based aid.

SOURCES OF FUNDING

Two major sources provide funding for financial aid: the federal and state governments and the colleges themselves. Outside scholarships that students apply for directly from businesses, community organizations, and foundations also provide funds, but in terms of total number of dollars awarded for financial aid, they are a very small piece of the pie.

As we will see, the differences between need-based aid and merit aid, the type of aid awarded, as well as the sources of funding can influence a student's choice of where to apply and ultimately which college to attend. But first, we need to show you how the process works.

HOW COLLEGES DETERMINE YOUR FINANCIAL NEED

Need-based aid is financial assistance awarded on the basis of a family's demonstrated need. Demonstrated need has a simple definition: it is the difference between the cost of attendance at a college (including tuition and fees, room and board, transportation, books, and personal expenses) and what a family is expected to pay for such costs (the expected family contribution, or EFC for short).

THE PRINCIPLE BEHIND NEED-BASED AID

Need-based aid is designed to reduce or eliminate financial need as a barrier to attending college. Determining what a family can afford, however, is not left up to the family, for obvious reasons. Colleges use formulas that provide an objective way of measuring how much a family can reasonably be expected to contribute to a child's education. An underlying principle is that students and parents have the primary responsibility to pay for the cost of a college education, up to their ability to do so, before receiving need-based financial aid. Need-based aid is meant to supplement, not replace, the family contribution.

> I thought we would qualify for need-based aid, but the calculations showed we didn't. It was probably just wishful thinking on my part.
>
> PARENT DISAPPOINTED BY THE RESULTS OF THE NEED ANALYSIS

FORMS AND MORE FORMS

All applicants for need-based financial aid who are US citizens or permanent residents, regardless of where they live or where they are applying, must complete the Free Application for Federal Student Aid (FAFSA). Beyond this, the required forms will depend on the colleges to which the student is applying and the student's home state. Some schools require an additional form known as the CSS PROFILE from the College Board or an institutional form that the college itself has developed. Supplementary forms may be required for particular students such as those with separated or divorced parents, those whose parents own their own business, or those who do not need to file taxes. Finally, some schools require families to submit federal tax returns. You will need to check with each school to know which forms are required and when they are due.

⊠ The Key Equation for Financial Aid

Cost of attendance (tuition and fees; room and board; books; personal expenses; travel)

– Expected family contribution

= Financial need

THE FREE APPLICATION FOR FEDERAL STUDENT AID (FAFSA)

The FAFSA is a need analysis form that all colleges use to calculate the EFC to determine eligibility for federal financial aid. It is also used to determine eligibility for most state-based aid, many private awards, and institutional-based aid at many colleges.

What Is Included in the FAFSA Formula?

The FAFSA uses the family's taxed and untaxed income and assets, with various exclusions. For example, it excludes untaxed Social Security income and does not consider the equity of the family's primary residence. In the case of separated or divorced parents, it does not consider the income and assets of the noncustodial parent, but if the custodial parent has remarried, the income and assets of the stepparent are included in the calculations. For federal student aid purposes, the custodial parent is the parent with whom the student lived the most during the 12 months before the FAFSA is filed. If time is divided equally between parents, the parent who contributed more than 50 percent of the student's support during that time is considered the custodial parent.

The FAFSA assumes a certain basic level of household expenses and asks about the size of the family, the age of the parents, and the number of household members (excluding parents) who will be enrolled at least half time during the award year in an eligible college or career school degree or certificate program. Calculation of need using the FAFSA is known as the "federal methodology."

Completing the FAFSA

The FAFSA can be found at www.fafsa.ed.gov. It can be submitted between October 1 of the year before a student plans to start college and June 30 of the year after the student starts. (For example, the 2018–2019 FAFSA can be submitted between October 1, 2017 and June 30, 2019.) It requires detailed information from the parents' and student's federal income tax returns for the calendar year two years prior to the year for which aid is being requested, known as the prior-prior year or PPY. A handy worksheet known as the FAFSA on the Web Worksheet can help families get ready for filing the FAFSA. It is available each year shortly before the October 1 launch of the FAFSA and can be found by searching for it by name online. Be sure you obtain the worksheet for the year you will be enrolling in college.

Whether or not you use the worksheet, the process for completing and filing the FAFSA is straightforward. The student and parent need to obtain separate FAFSA IDs (username and password) that serve as an electronic signature when the FAFSA is completed and filed online. This is done at www.fafsa.ed.gov. Because PPY tax returns are used to complete the FAFSA, those returns have already been filed, and most families can upload tax numbers directly into the FAFSA through the IRS Data Retrieval Tool, sometimes referred to as the DRT. When accessed through the FAFSA, the Data Retrieval Tool will pre-fill the form with relevant income data drawn from your family's tax returns for PPY. In some cases you cannot use the Data Retrieval Tool, such as when parents are separated but filed taxes jointly, when parents are married but filed taxes separately, or when you filed an amended tax return. You will then have to enter the information from your tax return manually.

You can also file the FAFSA by paper form, but it is far preferable to use the online version, which is easy to use and gives you immediate feedback about any errors you may be making in entering your data, as well as access to the Data Retrieval Tool. Confidentiality is ensured.

The Student Aid Report (SAR)

After your FAFSA is filed online and processed, you will get an e-mail with a link to your online Student Aid Report or SAR. The SAR will give your EFC based on the federal methodology. It can take two to three weeks to get your response if you submit your FAFSA by mail or do not list an e-mail address on the FAFSA, but just three to five days if you submit it online and include an e-mail address. Be sure to review your SAR carefully for any errors and correct them immediately.

Copies of your SAR are sent electronically to the campuses you designate on the form. Schools listed on the FAFSA will have access to your SAR data within a day after it is processed. Up to 10 schools can be listed at a time on the online FAFSA. After you receive your official SAR, you can return to the FAFSA, delete the original schools on your list, and add any additional schools if you have more than 10. Colleges do not have access to the school list, so you can list them in any order you wish. However, a few states require students to list an in-state public school first if they want to be considered for state aid. The FAFSA website lists these states. The student's home state receives the list of colleges on the FAFSA in order to evaluate eligibility for state aid.

COLLEGE SCHOLARSHIP SERVICE PROFILE (CSS PROFILE)

Fewer than 200 colleges, mostly private, require undergraduate financial aid applicants to complete an additional application, the College Scholarship Service PROFILE, also known as the CSS PROFILE or simply, the PROFILE. The College Board, the administrator of the SAT, also administers the PROFILE, which is more complex and detailed than the FAFSA. Colleges that use this form want to see a full portrait of the family's finances before awarding aid from institutional resources. Information about the application, a list of schools that require it, and the online form can be found at www.bigfuture.org under Paying for College. A number of foundations and other groups that award special scholarships also require the PROFILE and are included in the list.

What the PROFILE Considers

The PROFILE considers all the sources of income and assets used in the FAFSA and asks for additional information, such as the net value of the family's primary residence, amount of parental funds in the name of siblings, and amount of untaxed Social Security benefits received for all family members, excluding the student applicant. For separated or divorced parents, schools using the PROFILE usually also require the noncustodial PROFILE, which considers the income and assets of the noncustodial parent. On the other side of the ledger, the PROFILE calculations consider some of a family's expenses such as medical and dental costs and the need to save for the college costs of younger siblings.

Unlike the FAFSA, which asks the same questions of everyone, the PROFILE is customized for each student. Most of it consists of questions that are applicable for all schools, as well as supplemental questions that will vary by school. The supplement questions generally request additional financial information, such as the cash value of life insurance plans or the value of 529 College Savings Plans established for the student by someone other than their parent. A need calculation using the PROFILE is known as the "institutional methodology" and, as the term implies, can vary somewhat from college to college.

How and When to File

The PROFILE can be submitted only online. Unlike the FAFSA, which is free, students pay a fee to send their PROFILE information to colleges. Currently, the fee is $25 for the first college and $16 for each additional one, which can be added at any time. A fee waiver for up to eight colleges is available from the College Board for first-year, first-time domestic students who used a fee waiver for the SAT or who come from low-income backgrounds.

The PROFILE is available October 1 for that year's application cycle, the same date as the FAFSA. Students who apply ED or EA may need to submit the PROFILE by earlier deadlines than those applying regular decision. Submission dates vary from school to school. Like the FAFSA, the PROFILE uses PPY tax information, but it does not have access to the Data Retrieval Tool, so your family will need to enter information manually. Many colleges that require the PROFILE request that families provide copies of relevant tax returns, W-2s, 1099s, and Business/Farm supplement forms in addition to the application itself.

WHAT FORMS WILL YOU HAVE TO FILE?

You do not have to submit the FAFSA, PROFILE, and any state forms separately to each school; you simply list the colleges you want to receive the information, and the processing agency sends the forms electronically. However, you need to keep careful track of which forms your schools request because they can differ from school to school. For example, the University of Virginia requires the FAFSA, PROFILE, signed copies of student and parental federal income tax forms and W-2 forms, and an institutional form entitled "Financial Aid Application Certification Form" that requires student and parent signatures. By contrast, the University of California simply asks its aid applicants to submit the FAFSA and California residents to complete the Cal Grant Verification Form (which verifies the student's high school GPA) that the high school submits directly.

Be Sure to File on Time

If you plan to apply EA or ED, colleges will typically ask you to submit the FAFSA, PROFILE, and possibly their own institutional form on, or soon after, the admissions application deadline. Submitting your financial aid forms as early as you can is always wise. As we have seen, the FAFSA and the PROFILE are available on October 1.

Many schools have priority due dates for financial aid applications. It is critical to keep track of them. Aid can be limited for late applicants, and some schools will not award college-based funds if they receive a financial aid application after the due date. In addition, some states award aid on a first-come, first-served basis until funds run out.

The Verification Process

Verification is a process to ensure the accuracy of financial aid information submitted on the FAFSA. Verifications are conducted because of possible errors, inconsistencies, or other anomalies. You can also be selected at random.

The comments section of the SAR that you received after submitting the FAFSA will tell you if your file has been selected for verification. If so, the college where you enroll will ask you to submit a verification worksheet. If you did not use the Data Retrieval Tool to complete the FAFSA, you will be asked to do so. However, if you cannot use it because of your circumstances, the school will direct you to obtain a tax return transcript and possibly to submit signed copies of tax forms. If your file is chosen for verification, it does not mean that you have made an error. The verification process is simply a double check for possible errors.

GETTING AN ESTIMATE OF YOUR FINANCIAL NEED

Regardless of where you are in the college admissions process—years away or right in the middle of it—it is a good idea to do a quick preliminary analysis to determine how much your EFC might be.

USING A FINANCIAL AID CALCULATOR

The Department of Education has established a website, www.fafsa4caster.ed.gov, to provide you with an early estimate of your EFC as well as your eligibility for the various types of federal financial aid. It covers only federal financial aid, not other possible funds from a college. The College Board website, www.bigfuture.org, also has an easy-to-use calculator to estimate your EFC using either federal or institutional methodology. No matter which calculators you use, make sure your numbers are accurate. The calculators are only as good as the numbers you enter into them. Further on in this chapter we will look at another type of calculator, the net price calculator, which can estimate your family's out-of-pocket cost at each college you may be considering. All colleges must have a net price calculator on their website.

⊠ Differences Between the PROFILE and FAFSA Calculations of Expected Family Contribution

- The PROFILE includes the net value of the family's primary residence. Net business value is also included. The FAFSA does not include home equity of the primary residence or business value if the business is family-owned and controlled and the business has fewer than 100 full-time employees.
- PROFILE schools usually require the completion of the noncustodial PROFILE and thus include information on the income and assets of a noncustodial parent. The FAFSA does not ask for this information.
- The PROFILE collects information on private elementary and secondary school tuition, medical expenses, and so on. It allows the campus-based financial aid officer some discretion in evaluating special financial circumstances. The FAFSA does not ask for these costs, although you can write a letter explaining such costs directly to the financial aid office of the school. A financial aid officer will use professional judgment to determine whether the costs can be taken into consideration.

- Although it does not go into the calculations, the PROFILE asks the amount that parents have in retirement accounts. In addition, any funds a student has in retirement accounts must be listed and may or may not be included as a student asset. The FASFA does not ask for this information.
- The PROFILE includes additional child tax credit, earned income credit, untaxed Social Security benefits received for all family members except the student applicant, tuition and fees deduction, and the amount of foreign income exclusion. The FAFSA does not include these amounts.
- The PROFILE asks for the breakdown of the income numbers listed on the federal tax forms and will add back in any losses, such as capital loss or loss from rental property. The FAFSA simply uses the adjusted gross income.

DIFFERENCES BETWEEN FAFSA AND PROFILE CALCULATORS

Your family may be pleasantly surprised to learn that your EFC is lower than you thought it would be. Other families, however, may find that they are expected to contribute more than they had planned. In general, the need analysis formula for the institutional methodology calculates the EFC slightly more favorably than does the formula for the federal methodology. However, the PROFILE may also calculate a higher EFC than that of the FAFSA, meaning less need, because it includes income and assets specifically excluded from the FAFSA. For example, a family with substantial home equity or a noncustodial parent with significant financial resources may find that their EFC is considerably higher using the institutional methodology. A lot depends on specific family circumstances.

WHAT GOES INTO A FINANCIAL AID PACKAGE?

The financial aid award that a student typically receives from a college is made up of different kinds of assistance from federal, state, and college-based resources. Your particular combination is known as your financial aid package. Need-based financial aid packages usually have three parts: grant funds, work-study funding, and student loans. Grants and scholarships are considered gift aid because they are essentially free money, whereas work-study funding and student loans are often referred to as self-help. In addition, most schools expect the student to work during the summers, earning approximately $2,000 each summer that can be contributed toward college costs.

GRANTS

Grants are awards you don't have to repay. Some schools use the term *scholarship* rather than *grant* to refer to some need-based awards of this type, but *grant* is the common term. They are tax free when used to cover the cost of tuition, fees, books, and supplies. (Many other types of scholarships are awarded for reasons other than need; we will discuss these in the section on merit aid further on in this chapter.) Need-based grants come from three primary sources: the federal government, state governments, and college resources. In addition to the TEACH Grants Program for prospective teachers who commit to teaching in a high-need field or low-income area, currently the federal government has two major need-based grant programs open to all students regardless of field of study:

- *Pell Grants* were a maximum of $5,815 for 2016–2017. In recent years, about 90 percent of Pell Grant recipients have had family incomes below $50,000. Amounts can change annually.
- *Federal Supplemental Educational Opportunity Grants (FSEOG)* offer a maximum of $4,000 per year and are awarded to students with exceptionally high need. Pell Grant recipients have priority.

WORK STUDY

Work-study programs provide the opportunity for a student to apply for a part-time job on or near campus. Students are paid at least minimum wage, receive a paycheck every two weeks, and usually use the funds for their personal expenses. The federal government subsidizes most work-study programs.

Often the work can be related to a student's area of study or involve community service, although not all jobs meet one of these criteria. Freshmen typically work 10 to 15 hours a week during the term, a load that most can manage pretty easily.

LOANS

Loans are borrowed money that must be repaid with interest. Both students and parents can take out loans offered by the federal government. In addition, some schools offer their own loans. For a subsidized loan, the government, or college, pays the interest while the student is in school, and repayment begins after the student graduates, leaves school, or drops below half-time enrollment. The standard repayment period for a federal loan, once it begins, is 10 years. We describe several federal loan programs in the following list that are accessed through FAFSA submission. For student and parent loans, Congress sets the interest rates every July 1 for new loans in the upcoming school year. Interest rates are fixed for the life of the loan. There are also loan-forgiveness programs for federal loans that encourage students to take certain public service jobs or to teach at schools serving low-income families.

- *Subsidized federal direct loans* (to students) are awarded on the basis of financial need. For the 2016–2017 school year, the fixed interest rate is 3.76 percent. The one-time loan fee is 1.068 percent. The government pays the interest while the student is in school and for six months after graduation. The maximum award is $3,500 for a freshman, $4,500 for a sophomore, and $5,500 for a junior or senior.

- *Unsubsidized federal direct loans* (to students) are available to students independent of need, and the government does not pay the interest while the student is in school. The interest rate and loan fee is the same as for the subsidized direct loan. The student may defer payment of the principal (until after graduation, withdrawal from school, or going below half-time status), but unless the interest is paid while the student is in school, it will accrue and be added onto the principal. The total of subsidized and unsubsidized federal direct loans may not exceed $5,500 for freshmen, $6,500 for sophomores, and $7,500 for juniors or seniors.

- *PLUS Loans* (Parent Loans to Undergraduate Students) enable parents to borrow up to the total cost of education for each child, minus any student financial aid that is awarded. They are not based on demonstrated financial need. The interest rate for 2016–2017 is 6.31 percent. The one-time loan fee is 4.272 percent. The loan is unsubsidized, but payment may be deferred while the student is in school. To be eligible, parents do not need to have a high credit score, but they must not have adverse credit (for example, bankruptcy or foreclosure in the last five years).

How Is Your Package Put Together?

Grants and scholarships are clearly the most desirable source of funding, because no extra work is required and they do not need to be repaid. Most financial aid packages, however, include some form of self-help: student loans, work study, and a student summer work expectation. In comparing awards, it is important to compare the net cost to the family—the total cost of attendance minus any grant and scholarship aid received. We will discuss this more further on in the chapter.

As of this writing, about 70 colleges have adopted a "no-loan" policy in which grants replace loans in the financial aid packages of some or all of their accepted students. In many of these schools, the no-loan policy applies only to low-income students who are eligible for Pell Grants or whose families have annual incomes below a certain threshold (usually $40,000 to $60,000), and it applies only to tuition and fees, not other costs. Students at no-loan schools would still qualify for non-need-based unsubsidized federal direct loans if they submitted the FAFSA.

With these limited exceptions, loans remain an important part of most financial aid packages for undergraduate education. Even as loan burdens are attracting a lot of media attention, they are a fact of life for many. An excellent rule of thumb is that students should not graduate owing more than their anticipated first year's salary. Loans of that size can typically be paid back in 10 years or less without undue hardship.

The components of any financial aid package you receive will be listed separately, and you can accept or decline each type of aid offered. To enable you to more easily compare awards, the federal government has asked colleges to voluntarily use a standardized form to notify students about their financial aid packages. Many schools, but not all, now present their financial aid offers using the Financial Aid Shopping Sheet format. A template for the Shopping Sheet is found in Appendix C.

If a package is inadequate or less than that from another school, you can ask the financial aid office to review your case for possible adjustment. We'll talk more about what approach to use further on in this chapter.

> In general, when awarding money from programs they administer but do not fund (i.e., federal programs), colleges give priority to the neediest of the able. When awarding money from their own funds, colleges give priority to the ablest of the needy.[1]
>
> ANNA AND ROBERT LEIDER, AUTHORS OF *DON'T MISS OUT: THE AMBITIOUS STUDENT'S GUIDE TO FINANCIAL AID*

WHY NEED-BASED PACKAGES CAN DIFFER FROM COLLEGE TO COLLEGE

Your need-based aid offer may differ, sometimes sizably, even at colleges that guarantee to meet the full demonstrated need of all admitted students. Although all colleges must use the FAFSA to compute the EFC for federal financial aid, they may use the PROFILE or their own form to determine need for college-based institutional aid. Colleges have considerable flexibility in how they award their own funds.

COLLEGES THAT MEET FULL DEMONSTRATED NEED

Schools that use the PROFILE and guarantee to meet full demonstrated need may run the numbers in various ways. For example, many colleges put a cap on the amount of home equity that goes into the calculations, but the level of the cap may vary from school to school. Other schools may exclude home equity completely even though it is included on the application. Some colleges take into account the cost of a sibling in private elementary or secondary school; some make an adjustment for the cost of living in high-cost areas such as New York City or San Francisco; some exclude money received from a relative; and so on. These considerations often result in differences in the amount of awards offered by different schools, even if the cost of attendance is the same. Currently, only about 65 schools guarantee to meet the full need of all admitted students who are US citizens or permanent residents. Not surprisingly, these are among the most selective. Policies for international students, as we discuss in chapter 13, vary widely.

COLLEGES THAT DO NOT MEET FULL NEED

When a school does not meet a student's full need, a gap—or unmet need—will remain. This unmet need would have to be absorbed by the family if the student chooses to attend that school. Some schools award financial aid based on a combination of need and merit. Before these schools award college-based funds, a student must demonstrate a certain level of merit based on grades, rigor of courses taken, test scores, and so on. A student with high need and high merit might have her full need met from a combination of federal aid, state aid, and need-based aid from the college. Another student with high need may be admitted and receive only federal and state aid, because her merit standing is not strong enough in the college's applicant pool to receive need-based college aid. Other schools may award grant aid for all admitted students up to a certain percentage of their demonstrated need. Some schools award aid using a combination of the two methods. It can get complicated pretty quickly.

PROFESSIONAL JUDGMENT

Colleges have some flexibility in determining the final EFC—more so with institutional methodology than with federal methodology—based on the special circumstances of a particular family and the professional judgment of the financial aid staff members. A family can explain to a college financial aid office their nondiscretionary extenuating circumstances: the need to support a family member not living in the home, a parent's loss of job, tutoring cost for a younger sibling, and the like. Using professional judgment, a financial aid officer can decide whether to consider these circumstances. Although many schools will review such a letter before an award is made, some schools prefer to handle special circumstances through an appeals process. In the latter case, the financial aid award would be based on the numbers as submitted, and then the family would appeal.

IN SUMMARY

Colleges have different guidelines for determining financial need, and financial aid offices can exercise discretion in awarding aid. Some guarantee to meet full demonstrated need, but there may be differences from college to college in how they calculate need. The majority of colleges cannot guarantee to meet full demonstrated need and often leave a gap, or unmet need. A college that is eager to recruit a particular student may offer a higher total award or a higher percentage of grant money in the aid package, making it more desirable to the recipient.

> A number of elite privates give substantially different packages depending on how much they want you.[2]
>
> MORTON OWEN SHAPIRO, PRESIDENT OF NORTHWESTERN UNIVERSITY

Unfortunately, you can't know exactly what your award will look like, in either amount or type of aid, until you have your offer in hand. However, the net price calculators we discuss further on in this chapter can give you a ballpark preview because they are designed to take into account the financial aid policies of each individual school.

WILL YOUR NEED FOR FINANCIAL AID AFFECT YOUR CHANCES FOR ADMISSION?

Only a small number of colleges have the financial resources to admit students without regard to need and then to meet their full demonstrated need. These colleges are "need blind" in admissions and "full need" in their financial aid policies. Most of them direct all of their available financial aid, with the exception of athletic scholarships when offered, to students demonstrating financial need.

NEED-AWARE POLICIES

All colleges would like to be able to guarantee to meet full need and be need blind; that is their goal. However, most have limited financial resources. Some colleges guarantee to meet the full demonstrated need of admitted students but are need aware or need sensitive in admissions. These colleges have sufficient resources to make most, but not all, of their admissions decisions independent of financial aid considerations. Reluctantly, they consider need when making some of their admissions decisions.

> We are need aware, meaning a student's ability to pay is factored into whether or not he or she will be accepted. Some don't think it's fair, that some students might be rejected because they can't pay. But here's our perspective: once we admit you, we will find a way for you to attend.[3]
>
> ADMISSIONS DEAN EXPLAINING HOW NEED-AWARE POLICIES WORK

If you apply to a need-aware college and do not need financial aid, you may enjoy a small admissions advantage over someone with a similar record who needs substantial aid. This is especially true if you are a borderline candidate. Colleges that cannot afford to offer full support to all of their admitted students will offer the support they do have to the most compelling students in their applicant pools. But the admissions advantage associated with being able to pay the full cost of college is usually quite small—not something to count on if you have it or to fret about if you don't. Those affected by need awareness are usually only a very small portion of a school's applicants.

Colby College, Tufts University, Macalester College, and Wesleyan University are among the schools that guarantee to meet full need but, with great reluctance, are currently need aware to some extent. Policies can change, however, based on a college's financial situation. All four of these colleges had been previously fully need blind until they could no longer afford to be, reflecting changes in their own resources and the increased demand for aid.

How Can You Determine a School's Policy?

Read the information about a college's financial aid policies carefully. You can usually find this information posted on the school's website along with other background and policies related to admissions. If a college states that it meets the full need of all admitted students but doesn't state that it has a need-blind admission policy, it probably admits some percentage of its freshman class on a need-aware basis.

On the flip side, many colleges are need blind in their admissions policy but don't commit themselves to meeting the full need of those admitted. At these schools, students will often find a gap between financial aid offered and what they actually need to attend. These students have been accepted without regard to their need, but their need is not fully met. That gap has to be filled somehow if they want to attend that college. As we previously noted, families often take out large loans for this purpose, which can be unwise if the total exceeds the student's anticipated first-year salary after graduation. Another, more affordable, school may be a better choice in these cases.

HOW MERIT AID WORKS

More and more colleges, especially those seeking to build their reputations or the quality of their student body, are offering aid that is not based on need. Known as merit-based aid, these awards are often given to students in recognition of particular abilities, talents, or other criteria. Recipients may also have financial need, but need is not the basis for the award. Merit awards, as we have seen, are often referred to as scholarships. Some of the most selective colleges do not award merit aid as a matter of principle, although most colleges do award it to some extent.

> I talked to several parents who had not considered private schools because they thought the cost was prohibitive. Well, that's not always true. The most selective schools generally don't give merit aid, but many others do. Our kids applied to schools that awarded merit aid and where they were pretty high up in the applicant pool. They got a lot of merit-based aid.
>
> Mother of family not eligible for need-based aid with two children in private colleges

Why Do Schools Award Merit Aid?

Colleges have learned that a merit aid scholarship of $5,000 or $10,000 can encourage students with little or no financial need to accept an offer of admission. This kind of "tuition discounting," now common at many schools, can raise a college's yield. In addition, a large merit scholarship extended to a student with an outstanding record may result in a "catch" for the college—an academic superstar whose presence can raise standards and contribute positively to intellectual life on campus. The size of merit awards and the process and criteria for receiving them vary widely from college to college. Some schools automatically consider all applicants for merit awards, although they may set an early application deadline for those wishing to be considered. Other schools may require a supplemental application.

Some public research universities such as the University of Oklahoma, the University of Alabama, and Iowa State University, as well as some private colleges, have aggressively targeted National Merit finalists for sizable merit awards. (See chapter 6 for more information about the National Merit Scholarship Program.) These students may receive a generous scholarship from such a school if they apply and inform the National Merit Scholarship Corporation that the university is their first choice. National Merit finalists usually have stronger academic profiles than the typical enrollee at these schools and thus are seen as very desirable prospective students.

> We want kids who are good at dancing, who are good at collecting butterflies, who are good at basketball. At the point where we have the capacity to attract students with the magnetism Harvard does, we'll be happy to follow Harvard's [need-based] policies.[4]
>
> STEPHEN TRACHTENBERG, FORMER PRESIDENT OF GEORGE WASHINGTON UNIVERSITY

MAXIMIZING YOUR CHANCES OF RECEIVING MERIT AID

College-based merit aid is a bit of a wild card in the financial aid equation. If a college offers such aid, that's great, but it can be hard to predict your chances of getting it or how much you might receive. As a general rule, colleges award their most generous merit aid to the students with the strongest academic credentials in their applicant pool. You are least likely to receive merit aid at a school where you would be a borderline admit.

You can enhance your chances for merit aid by looking for schools that are generous with merit aid and where you would likely fall in the

> If money is a factor in your college search and it will impact your final choice, you should make sure to apply to colleges where you are clearly in the top third to top quarter of the applicant pool.[5]
>
> MUHLENBERG COLLEGE ADMISSIONS WEBSITE

top quartile of the applicant pool. The BigFuture website, www.bigfuture.org, shows whether a college offers merit aid and how much, and it provides fairly current information about each college's admissions profile as well. Another useful website is www.meritaid.com. It is also worth directly checking out the websites of colleges you are interested in to fully understand their practices. Occasionally, colleges require students to submit the FAFSA to be considered for merit aid, even if they would not qualify for need-based aid. This information will be posted on a school's financial aid website.

THE MERIT AID CONTROVERSY

Non-need-based financial aid is a controversial topic in higher education. The wealthiest and most selective colleges argue that all of their aid should be need based, and they see offering aid to families that do not qualify as using their finite resources to reinforce the current economic class structure at their schools. They are generous with need-based aid but do not offer any merit aid. Other colleges give scholarships to academically talented students with no financial need, while still awarding most of their aid to those with demonstrated need. This may divert money from some needy students, but it can raise the profile of a college overall. Some have claimed that by raising a school's academic reputation, merit aid leads to larger donations and more financial aid in the future. The debate over the two approaches to aid is sure to continue and in fact is intensifying as colleges compete for students with the strongest records and as the demand for need-based aid grows.

FINANCIAL AID FOR VETERANS AND THEIR FAMILIES

If you are a veteran, there are a number of financial aid programs specifically available to you and your dependents to help pay for college. Aid through these special programs is based on the length and nature of your military service and where you plan to enroll. After you read the overview provided here, we encourage you to learn more at www.vets.gov/education and by contacting your local veterans service officer. Individual campuses often have veterans affairs offices to assist potential students as well. Those without special offices have knowledgeable staff members located elsewhere on campus. A good source of general information about the college admissions process for veterans can be found through the Veterans link in the Knowledge Center at www.nacacnet.org.

Post 9/11 GI Bill

Veterans who served for at least 90 days after September 10, 2011, and were honorably discharged are eligible to receive education benefits from the Department of Veterans Affairs (VA). The program covers the entire cost of in-state tuition at public colleges and up to a national maximum amount (currently $21,085 per year) at private colleges. The program also includes the opportunity for a monthly housing allowance and an annual stipend for books and supplies. Veterans with 36 months of active service or more are eligible for full benefits; for more detail search for Post GI Bill at www.vets.gov.

The Post 9/11 GI Bill also offers eligible veterans the option to transfer some or all of their unused education benefits to their spouse and child following an approval process. Transferability requirements are fairly specific, and service members would be well advised to begin the process early. Details are available by searching for Post GI Bill Transferability at www.vets.gov.

Yellow Ribbon Program

Veterans who are entitled to the maximum benefit rate, or their designated transferees, may also be eligible for the Yellow Ribbon Program, which provides additional funding above and beyond that provided by the GI Bill, to cover tuition and fees at schools, public or private, where tuition and fees would exceed the national maximum amount. Colleges voluntarily enter into an agreement with the VA to fund charges not covered by the 9/11 GI Bill, without an additional charge to your GI Bill entitlement. These institutions choose the amount of tuition and fees that will be contributed; the VA matches that amount and issues payments directly to the institution up to the total cost of tuition and fees.

Yellow Ribbon funding can vary from college to college, and from year to year, so you should check with college financial aid offices. Detailed information about the program, with links to FAQs and a list of participating institutions, can be found by searching for Yellow Ribbon Program at www.vets.gov. Additional information in an easily searchable format can be found on the GI Bill Comparison Tool at www.vets.gov/education.

SELECTED RESERVE GI BILL

Members of the Selected Reserve, including the Army Reserve, Navy Reserve, Air Force Reserve, Marine Corps Reserve, and Coast Guard Reserve, may be eligible for education benefits; check with www.benefits.va.gov for the latest information.

DEPENDENTS EDUCATION ASSISTANCE PROGRAM

The Dependents Education Assistance program (DEA) offers financial support to eligible dependents of veterans who are permanently or totally disabled because of a service-related condition, or who died while on active duty or as a result of a condition that is service-related. Some states have programs of their own to support dependents of disabled or deceased vets who meet these criteria. California, for example, offers the College Tuition Fee Waiver for Veteran Dependents, which waives mandatory system-wide tuition and fees at any California community college, California State University, or University of California campus.

OTHER SCHOLARSHIP SOURCES

Although colleges themselves are the largest source of scholarship dollars, there are other sources as well.

STATE SCHOLARSHIPS

Although there are no federal merit scholarships for undergraduates, many states have their own scholarship programs that vary in their generosity, criteria, and flexibility. Some are need based, some are merit based, and some are based on a combination of merit and need. For example, Zell Miller scholarships in Georgia, named after a former governor, cover full tuition to Georgia's public colleges for Georgia residents who are high school valedictorians or salutatorians. Students may also qualify if they have a minimum 3.7 GPA and 1200 on the SAT or 26 on the ACT. In Florida, the Bright Futures Scholarship Program awards a fixed-dollar amount per credit hour per semester, with the amount depending on the in-state college the student attends. Florida residents who meet specified academic and volunteer service criteria are eligible. Although most state scholarships apply only to in-state institutions and sometimes to a particular campus, others are more flexible and can be applied elsewhere.

Many states that offer need-based scholarship programs use the FAFSA to determine need. A separate application may be required for merit aid awards. Check for the latest information for your state on the website of the National Association of Student Financial Aid Administrators at https://www.nasfaa.org/State_Financial_Aid_Programs.

AWARDS FROM BUSINESSES AND ORGANIZATIONS

Scholarships sponsored by organizations, foundations, and businesses are awarded to students for a variety of reasons: academic achievement, talent, writing competitions, significant community service, and overcoming of hardship. Local Rotary Clubs and Lions Clubs, for example, award scholarships to high school students in communities across the country, and some large corporations offer scholarships for their employees' children in addition to National Merit Scholarships.

These awards are typically paid directly to a college. The amounts vary greatly, from $1,000 or less to tens of thousands of dollars. Most are fairly small and are one-time awards, but even those can add up to make a difference. Although many scholarships are open to all, some scholarships are targeted to students in certain categories such as veterans, first-generation students, members of minority groups, students with a particular academic focus, or students whose parents work for particular corporations. Chances of winning a scholarship are generally higher for local scholarships because fewer students are usually competing for them than for national awards. Some of the well-known national scholarship programs that provide generous awards include the Gates Millennial Scholars Program for Pell Grant eligible students of color; the Jack Kent Cooke Foundation College Scholars Program for high-achieving students with high financial need; and the Coca Cola Scholars Program Scholarships in recognition of leadership and service.

COLLEGE PARTNERSHIP PROGRAMS

Although most of the merit money available from colleges is awarded directly by colleges to qualified students, a number of colleges partner with organizations that help identify highly qualified students meeting certain criteria for special awards. These organizations include QuestBridge, which screens low-income applicants and identifies QuestBridge Finalists who are given the opportunity to potentially match their interest in a participating college with a college that is interested in them. Successful students receive a College Match Scholarship from the college that covers the full cost of tuition, room and board, and fees. The Posse Foundation's program seeks to identify urban, typically low-income students with outstanding leadership potential who would benefit from the support of a small team of peers, or Posse, when attending college. Participating colleges select a diverse group of Posse students for their freshman class, offering a four-year, full-tuition scholarship to each member of the Posse. Golden Door Scholars is another partnership program that focuses on identifying high-performing undocumented students. Information about these organizations can be found at www.questbridge.org, www.possefoundation.org, and www.goldendoorscholars .org, respectively.

BEGIN EARLY

Because most scholarships require application forms and often essays, and sometimes by deadlines early in senior year, students should begin exploring scholarship opportunities early and not wait until spring of senior year after they have submitted all their college applications. Useful websites include www.fastweb.com, www.finaid.com, www.cappex.com, and www.zinch.com. Your high school counseling office may also be a good source of information about local as well as national scholarship opportunities.

> We encouraged our kids to apply for community-based scholarships. They are easier to get because you're only competing against other local students.
>
> PARENT OF STUDENT WHO APPLIED FOR LOCAL SCHOLARSHIPS

AWARDS CANNOT EXCEED THE COST OF ATTENDANCE

Federal law requires that financial aid not exceed the student's demonstrated financial need. Thus, if a student receives a scholarship from a business or organization in addition to a need-based package that meets the student's full demonstrated need, the college must reduce the aid package by the amount of the scholarship. This process is known as "displacement." Colleges are usually willing to substitute the scholarship, dollar for dollar, for all or part of the self-help components of the aid package rather than the gift aid component. This means that although a scholarship will not increase the total amount of your aid package or reduce your EFC, it can make your package more desirable by reducing the amount you have to borrow or work. If the college aid offer leaves a gap, or unmet need, an outside scholarship is usually first applied to the gap. Colleges vary somewhat in their treatment of outside scholarships, so you should ask a financial aid officer of each college how an outside scholarship would affect your financial aid package. Students who do not receive need-based aid may, of course, use outside scholarship awards to reduce the cost of their education without restriction.

SHOULD YOU USE A SCHOLARSHIP SEARCH SERVICE?

High school seniors and their parents often receive letters from businesses offering to help the student find or apply for outside scholarships. These letters may look very official and suggest that the student and family must participate in a special program to find out about scholarship opportunities. It is easy to see why such businesses exist. A service that promises to ferret out thousands of dollars in awards in return for a fee of a few hundred dollars may seem like a good investment. But is it?

> I'm not saying there aren't people out there who are legitimate private counselors [for aid], but we try to direct families to get help without spending unnecessary dollars.[6]
>
> DALLAS MARTIN, FORMER PRESIDENT OF THE NATIONAL ASSOCIATION OF STUDENT FINANCIAL AID ADMINISTRATORS

Financial aid experts generally agree that no family needs to pay for help finding scholarships. At best, these services provide information about funding programs that are already in the public domain. At worst, they may be shady businesses that defraud or exploit vulnerable families. The Federal Trade Commission cautions families to be aware of the following approaches that can signal a scam:

"The scholarship is guaranteed or your money back."
"You can't get this information anywhere else."
"I just need your credit card or bank account number to hold this scholarship."
"You've been selected by a 'national foundation' to receive this scholarship."
"You're a finalist"—in a contest you never entered.

FINANCIAL AID AND YOUR COLLEGE LIST

Parents and students need to talk openly and honestly about how much they, as a family, are willing to contribute to the cost of college through current income, savings, and borrowing. A college may calculate that a family can contribute a certain amount (the EFC), but the family may be either unwilling or unable to contribute that amount.

THINKING ABOUT FINANCIAL AID BEFORE YOU APPLY

Because of the many uncertainties in financial aid, it is important to have a good idea about how need is calculated at the schools you are considering applying to. Perhaps your parents are divorced, and one parent says he or she will not contribute to your college costs, yet the schools you are applying to expect a contribution from both legal parents. It is good to know information such as this as you build your college list. It is also very important to know if the schools you are applying to do not guarantee to meet full need and if a gap may likely be left.

If you are worried about your family's ability to comfortably handle the EFC, it would be wise to include at least a few colleges that you could afford and, of course, where you have a good chance of admission. Think of them as your "financial likely" colleges. These often include public colleges and universities in your home state because of relatively low in-state tuition. You should have a good selection of colleges, not only to be admitted but also for receiving financial aid. You want to have choices where the cost is workable for your family.

> It was clear early on that our kids would not qualify for need-based financial aid. So then we became pretty adept at looking through the websites to identify institutions that gave merit-based aid.
>
> PARENT OF TWO COLLEGE STUDENTS WHO RECEIVED SIGNIFICANT MERIT AID

CONSIDERING REGIONAL COMPACTS

Students interested in public universities in states other than their own should look carefully at whether their state participates in an exchange program with neighboring states that might result in a substantial discount on out-of-state tuition. Both the size and terms of the tuition break will vary, and not all schools or programs within a given school may participate. Four of the largest are the Academic Common Market in the South, the Midwestern Higher Education Compact, the New England Board of Higher Education, and the Western Undergraduate Exchange.

The Western Undergraduate Exchange (WUE), for example, is the largest of the regional compacts and includes Alaska, Arizona, California, Colorado, Hawaii, Idaho, Montana, Nevada, New Mexico, North Dakota, Oregon, South Dakota, Utah, Washington, Wyoming, and the Commonwealth of the Northern Mariana Islands. Students from these states who are eligible for WUE and who are admitted to participating programs pay tuition at 150 percent of the institution's regular rate for in-state students, rather than the regular non-resident tuition. In some cases, all admitted students are eligible for WUE. Other WUE schools have selection criteria for eligibility.

Information about regional compacts may be found the National Association of Student Financial Aid Administrators at www.nasfaa.org/State_Regional_Tuition_Exchanges.

USING THE NET PRICE CALCULATORS

A net price calculator is an online tool that will give you an estimate of your family's out-of-pocket cost, or net price, for your first year at any college you are considering. The federal government requires all colleges that award federal financial aid, which is almost all of them, to post a net price calculator on their website. Most are located on the college's main financial aid web page, but others may take some digging. You can find them all through the College Affordability and Transparency Center at www.collegecost.ed.gov.

The idea behind the calculator is simple. It starts with the sticker price for one year of school, which includes direct charges for tuition and room and board, as well as indirect costs for books and supplies, transportation, and personal expenses. After you enter financial information, and sometimes the student's GPA and test scores, into the calculator, it estimates the amount of grant and scholarship aid you are likely to receive from that college if you are admitted. The difference between the sticker price and the total amount of grant and scholarship money offered is the net cost to the family.

Calculators differ in usefulness. In general, the more detailed the information requested, the more helpful the calculator. If a school asks for GPA and test score information, that indicates that the school probably awards merit aid and that need-based aid may also be taking into consideration student grades and test scores. A school can still award merit aid, but not include GPA and test score information in its net price calculator.

A net price calculator enables you to compare the estimated out-of-pocket cost for different colleges. Of course, no calculator can tell you exactly how much grant and scholarship money you may receive, any more than a calculator can usually tell you whether you will actually be admitted to a particular college. However, a calculator can give you at least some insight into what financial aid you might be offered. Remember that special circumstances will be handled on a case-by-case basis by each school once you apply.

⊠ Net Price Calculation

Cost of attendance

− Grants and scholarships awarded

= Net price to family

The BigFuture website has a useful tool that lets you use the net price calculators of a number of different colleges using data that you enter into the system just once. Only schools that use the PROFILE are included. If you are interested in colleges that do not participate in this College Board service, you will need to enter your information into the individual school calculators.

EVALUATING AID AFTER YOU'VE BEEN ACCEPTED

Once you have your award packages in hand, comparing financial aid offers can be an important part of your decision-making process. As we noted previously, financial aid packages can vary widely, not only in the total amount of aid offered but also in the individual components. Colleges using the Financial Aid Shopping Sheet make comparing awards relatively easy. If you get offers that are not presented in this way, you can put them into that format before you begin.

IS THE COST OF ATTENDANCE REALISTIC?

Take a careful look at the total cost of attendance for each school. Is it realistic, or does it omit or underestimate some key expenses such as travel home? The Financial Aid Shopping Sheet template will show you what should be included. Because the cost of books, incidentals, and travel is a key factor in determining your financial need, an unrealistically low figure will mean that your additional expenses might not be covered by your financial aid package.

EVALUATING THE PACKAGE AND NET COST

Carefully compare the total cost of attendance and the total amount of your aid packages as well as the components. The total amount of aid is important, but so is the composition of the package. All of this is relevant for estimating the net cost to your family. You should compare the amount of gift aid offered (grants and scholarships) and the total amount of out-of-pocket costs the family must absorb. This may include the EFC, student loans, work-study, student summer contribution, and any amount of gap, or unmet need.

Two schools may offer the same amount of total aid, yet one may offer a much higher percentage of the package as grants that do not have to be repaid. From a purely financial perspective, assuming the cost of attendance is the same at the two schools, the package with a higher percentage of gift aid is more desirable. As we noted, the total cost of attendance minus grants and scholarships is the net cost to the family.

BEYOND THE FIRST YEAR

Be sure you know each college's policies on financial aid for subsequent years. You must reapply for aid each year by submitting the required forms. Even if the total aid amount is constant (assuming no change in your family's financial circumstances), will the package change? Are scholarships renewable, and if so, what does renewal require? Will subsequent packages contain a higher percentage of self-help aid? You should consider all these questions as you review your financial aid offers.

APPEALING YOUR OFFER

Students and parents often ask if they can appeal a financial aid offer. Although most colleges resist the idea of revising or "negotiating" packages, they will usually review their initial offer in light of new information.

Adjustments that reflect new circumstances or clarification of previously submitted information are the easiest ones for colleges to accommodate. Perhaps a parent's work hours have been reduced since the forms were filed, or the college did not adequately consider the expense of caring for an elderly relative. Maybe your family has high unreimbursed medical expenses. You or your parent should respectfully ask the financial aid office to review the financial aid award, making clear the basis for your request and your sincere interest in attending the college. You'll be asked to put your request in writing, and you may be asked to document your circumstances. Sending that documentation with your request can expedite the review.

You should appeal your financial aid offer diplomatically and without any hint of arrogance or entitlement. Such a review is called a "financial aid appeal," "a special circumstances review," or "professional judgment review," depending on the college.

We have been open about our willingness to review financial aid awards to compete with certain private institutions for students admitted under the regular decision plan. Unlike most institutions, the university states these principles openly to those offered first-year admission under the regular decision plan.[7]

CARNEGIE MELLON FINANCIAL AID REVIEW POLICY

WILL COLLEGES "MATCH" ANOTHER OFFER?

Most schools do not routinely increase financial aid awards simply because of better offers from other schools. As one financial aid consultant has noted, "Colleges are not car dealerships, where bluff and bluster can get you a better deal."[8] However, under certain circumstances some colleges will consider an adjustment.

A highly selective college will be more inclined to match a package offered by another highly selective college rather than a package offered by a less selective college it does not consider a competitor for students. Cornell University, for example, explicitly states that it will match a need-based financial aid award from another Ivy League school, Duke, Stanford, and MIT. Carnegie Mellon University openly invites admitted students to submit offers for potential matching—the outcome would depend on the school making the competing offer. Most schools that will consider matching, however, do it less openly, so you have to ask.

As a general rule, a school will not make merit aid adjustments based on merit offers from a less selective school. They might make an exception if you have exceptional academic qualifications or other talents relative to its overall pool of admitted students. In this case, it is better to be a big fish in a small pond rather than a small fish in a big pond. In addition, a school that offers only need-based aid will not make an adjustment based on a merit offer from any school.

> Too many parents jump quickly into negotiation mode, trying to play one school's offer against another's. If they sense you are just trying to get a better deal and you are treating it like a car, even if there's flexibility on their end, they're not likely to show it.[9]
>
> STEPHEN PEMBERTON, PRIVATE COLLEGE CONSULTANT

If you want to pursue a possible matching offer, request consideration for an adjustment respectfully in writing and provide documentation of your competing offer. It helps to indicate that the school to which you are appealing is your first choice and that you would definitely attend if the net price was comparable.

ANOTHER WORD ABOUT EARLY DECISION

In chapter 7, we noted that one of the major criticisms of ED programs is that they commit students to attend a college without giving them a chance to compare financial aid packages. Because packages can vary significantly, especially when special circumstances or merit awards are involved, ED can be a risk if you hope to maximize your financial aid offer.

Students without special circumstances (which can cause aid awards to vary), without home equity (which different schools can calculate differently), and who are applying to a school that guarantees to meet full need may apply ED with more confidence. Colleges that meet the full need of accepted students will cover the cost of tuition, room and board, and other expenses that exceeds the EFC. Those with special circumstances or those applying to schools that do not meet full need must remember that colleges vary in how they define need and how they propose to meet it. Using a college's net price calculator is especially important if you plan to apply ED and need financial aid.

You do not lose all flexibility, however, if you apply ED. You may still request that a college reconsider your ED financial aid package after admission. Colleges do sometimes make adjustments. If the package does not meet your need, you can decline the offer and continue with regular decision applications to other colleges, even though this can be emotionally painful because you have your heart set on your ED school. But you cannot hold on to your ED aid offer until April and then decide to attend if it turns out to be the best award in the end.

PLANNING AHEAD WHEN YOUR CHILD IS YOUNG

This chapter has discussed financial aid issues that families face in a student's senior year, at which time a family's income and assets are usually a given. But what if you are reading this book when your child is much younger? What can you do to prepare for the financial responsibilities of a college education? Here are some brief, important, but often overlooked points about saving for college. More detailed advice on the topic can be found on financial aid websites and in books on financial planning for college,

Whatever the age of your student, you can use an EFC estimator to determine your EFC in relation to the likely cost of college. You want to know whether you may qualify for need-based aid, given the cost of attendance at the colleges under consideration. Your approach to financial planning will differ depending on your eligibility for need-based aid. Laws and practices can change quickly, however, so be sure to seek the most current information at the time you are making your plans.

- If you determine that your EFC is less than the cost of college, you will want a "financial aid advantaged" savings plan. It may be to your advantage to save money for college in your name rather than in the student's name. Currently, federal and institutional need analysis formulas "count" parental assets at a much lower rate than student assets. Saving money in the parents' name also keeps it under parental control until it is needed. But parental income is usually taxed at a higher rate than children's income, so you have to estimate the relative pros and cons.

- If your EFC is higher than the cost of college and you pay a high tax rate, you will want to consider a "tax-advantaged" savings strategy through a 529 plan in each state. Although contributions to 529 plans are after tax, they grow tax deferred in the parent's name. When used for postsecondary-qualified educational expenses, earnings are currently tax free at the federal and state levels. In addition, some states allow income tax deductions for all or part of the contributions of the donor.

- Education IRAs (Coverdell Education Savings Accounts) are another good way for some families to save for college expenses. Contributions are nondeductible, but earnings accumulate tax free and remain tax free if they are used for qualified college costs, as well as qualified elementary and secondary educational expenses. Annual contribution limits as well as income limitations apply.

Some observers have noted that financial aid policies do not encourage families to save, because savings reduce the amount of aid for which a student is eligible. Although it is true that a small percentage of nonretirement savings (over an asset protection amount) will reduce the amount of financial aid your child is eligible for, you have no guarantee years in advance about which colleges will accept your child or what their financial aid polices will be at that time. It doesn't make sense to spend down your assets just in the hope your child may receive a generous scholarship in the future.

The more you can save toward a college education, the greater your child's future flexibility in choosing colleges and in dealing with the complexities of financial aid. In addition, it is far preferable to have savings to help pay for college costs than to depend on loans, which in the end will cost much more than paying upfront. Those who can save are helping themselves financially and, in a very real sense, investing in their children's future—one of the best long-term "investments" a parent can make.

PART 3

Tackling Your Applications

Chapter 9   Applying Well, Part I: The Application and the Essay

Chapter 10   Applying Well, Part II: Recommendations, Interviews, and Activities

Chapter 11   Making the Most of Your Special Talents

Chapter 12   Students with Special Circumstances

Chapter 13   Advice for International Students

Applying Well, Part I

The Application and the Essay

If you've read to this point in *Admission Matters,* you know it is important to do a lot of self-reflection and research before you begin applying to college. But once you have done that work and developed an appropriate list of likely, possible, and long-shot colleges, the next step is tackling the applications themselves.

You'll want your applications to distinguish you from the many other applicants with similar credentials. In this chapter and the next, we will help you do just that. We'll look at the application process overall and guide you through writing your important main essay and other supplemental essays, long and short. In chapter 10, we'll continue with other parts of your application and tell you how to get strong letters of recommendation, prepare an activities list that sets you apart, and shine in an interview. In chapter 11, we'll also have tips for athletes and for students with other special talents.

Preparing a strong college application takes work. There's no way to get around that. A typical application asks many questions, and your answers tell a lot about your academic abilities, background, talents, and interests. Less obviously, your answers also send subtle messages about your degree of interest in a college and how much time and effort you have put into thinking about yourself as a future student there. The best applications do both well.

GETTING OFF TO A GOOD START

Although the competition for admission to selective schools is greater than ever before, the actual process of filing an application has never been easier. Almost every college not only accepts but also in many cases even requires electronic submission of applications. Some even waive their application fees if you submit online. Occasionally, a document is submitted on paper and scanned into a student's electronic file, but the application submission process as well as the admissions review that follows is basically paperless.

Gone, fortunately for good, are the days when students prepared an application with a typewriter and a bottle of correction fluid. Many parents reading this may remember how hard the old-fashioned way was. It is a major advantage to be able to easily update and edit your application right up until you submit it. You can make it as complete and accurate as you want, without having to start everything over because you forgot to include something or changed your mind about how to phrase an answer.

I left my most important college application to the day before it was due. I planned to rework an essay I had written for another college, so I wasn't too worried. After spending all day Sunday putting everything together, I was ready to submit my application electronically at 9:00 p.m. Then I realized the program cut off the last seven sentences of my essay. No matter what I did, I couldn't get the word count down. My mom suggested I try the paper app—maybe it would fit in there. It did. I then spent the next two hours filling out the paper app by hand and doing cut-and-paste onto the form for my essay. It was after 11:00 p.m. when I finished. I had school the next day, but my mom mailed it for me and met the postmark deadline. It all worked out but even I agreed I cut things too close. I could have really blown it.

HABITUAL PROCRASTINATOR WHO APPLIED WHEN YOU COULD STILL SUBMIT PAPER APPS—YOU CAN'T DO THAT ANYMORE AT MOST SCHOOLS

FIGHT THE URGE TO PROCRASTINATE

Completing a college application is probably not your idea of fun. It is hard to answer all those questions and distill yourself into little boxes of 200 words or 150 characters on a form. It also takes precious time, often a scarce resource in senior year. On top of it all, just thinking about college, as exciting as it may be, can make you nervous. You wonder, "*Where will I be next year? Will I make friends? Will I be happy?*"

It is natural in this situation to put off dealing with your applications as long as possible. Our simple advice is *don't.* Do your research on colleges early and begin the actual job of applying early in your senior year or even over the summer before. Fight the urge to procrastinate. Everyone experiences it—including us, the authors of this book, as we tackled the job of preparing this revision and found it was tougher than we thought it would be. But procrastination never helps, and it can hurt if it means that you assembled your college list hastily and it does not fit your needs or that you rush to meet a deadline and do a sloppy job. Moreover, as we suggest further on in this chapter, every experienced writer believes in the power of revision. It helps to put a draft aside and return to it after a while. You need time to do that. The wise student starts early, makes a time line indicating what is needed and by when, and then just gets it done.

NEATNESS AND COMPLETENESS COUNT!

The ease of filling out an application online and submitting it electronically can lead to careless proofreading and errors. We all know that problem from our daily e-mail. We just want to hit "send" and be done with it. Resist that urge. Typos, omissions, and other errors can mar an otherwise good application. In particular, you want to avoid having your great response to the question about why you want to attend Hamilton College mention that you find the core curriculum at St. John's College exciting. Because Hamilton College has no core curriculum, the mistake is even more embarrassing. Errors of this kind, and worse, routinely happen when students use word processors to cut and paste from one application to another. Electronic applications make the process easier, but they can also make mistakes easier.

> It's always a killer when the student uses the wrong name of the college in the essay. They may have used the same essay for a different college, which can be okay, but in their attempt to personalize it they forgot to change the name of the college. We also have students who use the wrong mascot. They talk about looking forward to being a Trojan when we're the Titans![1]
>
> TONY BANKSTON, FORMER DEAN OF ADMISSIONS, ILLINOIS WESLEYAN UNIVERSITY

Mistakes can also happen when you are hastily filling out a lot of applications close to a deadline. An error-filled, incomplete application practically shouts, "I didn't take this application seriously." Why, then, should the college? So before hitting "submit," carefully proofread everything yourself and have a friend or parent proofread it as well. And then proofread it again. Sure, it's tedious, but why be sloppy when the outcome is so important to you?

FOLLOW DIRECTIONS

Be sure to read the application carefully and answer the questions that are asked, not other ones. In an effort to economize on work, you may want to recycle answers from one application to another. This is fine, as long as you make sure that the colleges are asking the same questions and, as we just noted, you are careful to remove any specific references to the first college in your answer! This is especially important in switching from an EA or ED application to a regular one, because you may have identified your first choice in your essay.

Following directions also means being aware of limits on the length of responses and the number of recommendation letters. We'll discuss how to approach these limits further on in this chapter and in chapter 10.

APPLICATION CHOICES

Depending on where you decide to apply, you may be completing not just one, but two, three, or even more different types of applications. Some schools exclusively use an application form that is unique to them. This is fairly common for public universities such as the University of Oregon, the campuses of the University of California, and the University of Minnesota, which have applications of their own. Some private schools are also exclusive users of their own application—Georgetown University and MIT are well-known examples. But more and more schools are adopting one or more application platforms used by many other schools as well. This makes it easier for students to apply to a number of schools and gives them a choice about how to do it.

THE COMMON APPLICATION

The Common Application is an application platform accepted by more than 700 public and private colleges across the country and around the world. Although most participants are private colleges, public colleges are adopting it with increasing frequency. The Ohio State University, the University of Michigan, the University of Vermont, the University of Wisconsin, and Colorado State University are examples. The number of schools using the Common App has been growing each year.

Using the Common Application can save you a lot of time. You complete a single online application—with one main essay up to a strict maximum of 650 words chosen from a list of seven prompts—regardless of the number of participating schools, with a maximum of 20, to which you apply. You also complete an "activities grid" where you can provide information on up to 10 activities, defined broadly, that you are involved in outside of the classroom. This is probably not all you will have to do, however. Many colleges that use the Common Application also require short-answer or essay-length responses to one or more college-specific questions. These supplementary questions appear on the Common App website under each individual college. Résumés, research papers, and graded assignments may be submitted through the Common Application if a college invites them. An additional information section is also available for students who wish to share details of their backgrounds that do not appear elsewhere.

The Common Application website, www.commonapp.org, contains the list of participating schools as well as the application. Essay prompts may vary somewhat over time, with the prompts for the next application cycle announced in late winter or early spring of each year. The application itself is available on August 1 each year, although students may open an account as juniors and have their log-in credentials and most parts of the Common App roll over to the following year's application. The prompts for 2017–2018 are found in Appendix B.

THE UNIVERSAL APPLICATION

The Universal College Application is another generic application that is currently accepted by about 35 colleges. Forms and member colleges can be found at www.universalcollegeapp.com. The Universal Application is similar in many ways to the Common Application so it will look familiar to you if you have a Common Application account, although it offers a single, very general essay prompt instead of a choice of five. Some colleges accept both the Common Application and the Universal Application, but most colleges on the Universal College Application list don't use the Common Application. The prompt for 2017–2018 is found in Appendix B.

THE COALITION APPLICATION

The Coalition Application is one of two new application platforms with almost 100 participating colleges, including many that we have defined as selective. Introduced for the first time for the high school graduating class of 2017, it is a work in progress that will be evolving over time. It, too, enables a student to choose from among a set of five essay prompts and it is coordinated with the Coalition Locker, a free, secure on-line storage space that enables students to keep (and potentially make available to Coalition colleges that request them) materials they believe represent them as individuals. The locker can store videos, scanned papers and school projects, résumé, college essay drafts, and other items in electronic format.

The locker is free and available to any student as early as the student wishes to set it up. A lot of the information you are asked to provide when an account is established can be imported later into the Coalition App itself when you are ready to apply to one or more schools that use the Coalition App. The locker also gives you the option of sharing individual items in the locker with your counselor, mentor, or anyone else you choose. One of the main reasons behind the creation of the Coalition Locker is to provide first-generation students and those from under-resourced schools with the tools to begin college planning earlier in their high school years. Although the locker is coordinated with the Coalition App, nothing in the locker is shared with member colleges unless you choose to submit it. The locker can also be used to store materials for other purposes, including applications to non-Coalition member colleges and scholarship programs.

Although a small number of schools are expected to use the Coalition Application exclusively, most accept the Common Application. In addition, some accept the Universal App. The list of Coalition schools, the application, and the locker can be found at www.coalition.org. The Coalition essay prompts for 2017–2018 are found in Appendix B.

THE CAPPEX APPLICATION

A second new application, the Cappex Application, was introduced for the first time for the class of 2017. About 65 colleges have signed on to use it initially, although they all accept one or more other application formats as well. Major features of the Cappex Application include a single, 600-word essay using a general prompt as well as the opportunity to share additional information in an optional section. No supplemental essays are needed, and there is no fee to submit a Cappex Application to any participating school. Information about the Cappex Application and participating schools may be found at www.cappexapplication .com. The prompt for 2017–2018 is included in Appendix B.

Does It Matter Which Application(s) You Use?

Students sometimes ask whether colleges that have more than one application form have a preference for which one you use. The simple answer is "no." You should use the form or forms that make it easiest for you to apply and that you believe help you best represent yourself in the college admissions process. Start with your list of colleges and see which applications they accept. Then take a look at the relevant application forms and their college-specific supplements. Would using one format be more advantageous for you than another, in general or for a specific school? Your choices will ultimately depend on the colleges to which you will be applying as well as your preferences. For most students, the application forms will be pretty much interchangeable, but it is worth checking just to be sure.

WRITING AN EFFECTIVE PERSONAL ESSAY

Many college application forms require an essay or personal statement. Some require more than one. In this section, we show you how to approach the essay as an opportunity for self-understanding, not just as a burdensome but mandatory assignment. Colleges differ in the emphasis they place on the essay in the admissions review, and its importance may also vary for different students because of the strength of their credentials. At many schools where your grades and scores are at the top of that college's pool, a so-so essay won't be too damaging, but at the most selective schools, it always matters, because hardly anyone is admitted by grades and tests alone.

Why Do Colleges Ask for Essays?

Colleges see the essay as a way for you to personalize your application and give it life. Along with your letters of recommendation, your

In an applicant pool with an oversupply of superbly qualified applicants, an unimpressive essay can hurt. A great essay can help tip a student into the class if he or she already looks like a good applicant. It isn't a question of an essay "changing our mind" about a candidate, as the essay is an important part of our sense of the applicant from the start.[3]

Margit Dahl, director of admissions, Yale University

essay helps admissions officers differentiate you from many others with similar records. It is a chance to share something special about yourself that will help the reader conclude that you would make a wonderful addition to the next freshman class. It can also demonstrate to a college that you can express yourself effectively and persuasively in writing—a skill that is crucial for success in college. Harry Bauld, author of a delightful book on college admissions essays, sums up the essay as follows: "It shows you at your alive and thinking best, a person worth listening to—not just for the ten minutes it takes to read your application, but for the next four years."[4]

> What exactly do admissions officers want to know when they ask you to write the college essay? No matter which question, we are asking what is really important to you, who you are, and how you arrived where you are. The whole college application process is really a self-exploration, and the essay is a way to put your personal adventure into words.[5]
>
> DELSIE PHILLIPS, FORMER DIRECTOR OF ADMISSIONS AT HAVERFORD COLLEGE

The problem with advice like this is that it is hard to follow when you get down to the individual who is you. You realize that you should be honest and open, but you are also trying to make a good impression on the reader. How can you do both? How can you avoid being stiff and impersonal, sort of like an awkward first date, as you try to make a good impression? How can you be sure you aren't making yourself too vulnerable if you admit you are not perfect? It's hard, but those are important questions to think about. In doing so, you are more likely to write a self-reflective, thoughtful, and valuable essay. Many students are so intent on being well perceived that they write bland, unengaging essays, not realizing the opportunity they are missing to have the essay really help their case for admission.

"TELL US ABOUT YOURSELF"

Although the question may not be stated so directly, most college essays are asking you a simple question—"Tell us about yourself." Colleges use the essay to get insights into who you are as a person that they might not discover from the rest of your application.

If you look at the essay prompts in Appendix B, you will see that each prompt, although phrased differently, is essentially asking you to tell your readers something about yourself that you believe is important for them to know. Many supplementary college-specific essay prompts also ask the same basic question, although more indirectly. A question asking you to write about your favorite book or a personal hero is really less about the book and hero than it is about you and why you made your choice. What you choose to write tells the reader a great deal about how you think, what your life experiences have been, and what you value.

⊠ Some "Tell Us About Yourself" College-Specific Questions

- "Caltech students have long been known for their quirky sense of humor, whether it be through planning creative pranks, building elaborate party sets, or even the year-long preparation that goes into our annual Ditch Day. Please describe an unusual way in which you have fun." (California Institute of Technology, 2016–2017)
- "There is a Quaker saying: 'Let your life speak.' Describe the environment in which you were raised—your family, home, neighborhood or community—and how it influenced the person you are today." (Tufts University, 2016–2017)
- "Tell us, in your own unique voice, something about you we cannot find elsewhere on your application. We purposefully do not prescribe any one topic for the personal statement, because we want you to share what's important to you. If you need some direction, though, a few topics you may consider include your future ambitions or goals, a significant experience that is integral to your personal identity, or a special talent or unique interests that sets you apart from your peers." (University of Oregon, 2016–2017)

WHAT SHOULD YOU WRITE ABOUT?

In writing your essay, focus on yourself, not on what you think colleges want to hear. Who are you? What makes you tick deep inside? What do you want them to know about you? Think about the qualities you want to convey and then think about how to represent those qualities in your answer to the question. Ideally, your essay should illustrate your points through personal details rather than simply state them; the old advice still holds: show—don't tell.

A Good Essay Tells a Story

Many good essays are essentially stories, based on a personal experience. Storytelling comes naturally to most of us, more easily than essay writing. The key is to make your essay lively and interesting to read. You want the reader to

> The essay topic is not usually the issue at hand. It is what an applicant does with the topic that separates an interesting and effective essay from the more typically banal essay.[6]
>
> JONATHAN STROUD, VICE PRESIDENT FOR ENROLLMENT AND COMMUNICATIONS, EARLHAM COLLEGE

think, "I would like to get to know this person." Or, "She sounds as if she would be a fun student to teach or have in a dorm or on a team."

Admissions readers like their work. Nobody does it for the money or the glory. They also like teenagers, and they are open-minded enough to realize that they come in different shapes and sizes and think differently. You can trust your reader to be interested and positive.

She is not an enemy to be tricked or a gullible target to be wowed. She may be young enough to clearly remember high school herself, or she may have teenage children of her own. Treat admissions officers as human beings, and they will respond in kind. A few colleges, including Tufts University, Johns Hopkins University, and Connecticut College share sample essays previously submitted by successful applicants to help students begin the task of writing their essays. Google "essays that worked" and the name of one or more of these colleges to find them on the web.

Look Inward for Your Essays

Standard admissions prompts are purposely very broad to encourage freethinking. But not surprisingly, certain themes appear over and over again in the essays students write. Among them are "How My Summer Trip to_____Changed My Life," "Winning [or Losing] the Race [or Game or Election]," or "The Death of My Beloved_____." These topics, and other common ones, are not necessarily bad. In fact, there are almost no bad topics, just flat or weak essays. A flat college essay tells the reader little about what makes the writer an interesting, unique person. The more common your essay topic is, the greater your burden is to write something different from all the other essays on the same topic.

When students write about a piece of literature, they tend to use something familiar, such as the Bible, Shakespeare, or *The Great Gatsby*. Or if they write about a person, they are likely to choose a grandparent or a famous person such as John F. Kennedy or Martin Luther King Jr. These choices are fine, *if* you have an original approach to the subject. But it doesn't hurt to choose something off the familiar path as long as the choice matters to you personally. It is even all right to write about a book or music that the reader might not be familiar with, as long as you explain why it matters to you. Writing about Charlemagne or an Edith Wharton novel doesn't do any good if it doesn't reflect your ideas and self.

Often a topic more unique or personal to you, no matter how ordinary it may seem, is often easier to make distinctive and interesting. Fine essays have been written on topics as simple as going fishing with a grandfather, working with young children in a summer camp, and cooking a family meal. In fact, given the tremendous volume of applications at most schools, there are few truly uncommon topics any more. Searching for one is likely to be frustrating because you can never know what someone in Spokane or Savannah is writing about. So don't worry about it.

One counselor we know challenges students who can't think of a topic to write about the time they saved someone from drowning at the beach and made the six o'clock news as a hero. Because this never happened, the students naturally look puzzled. "Look," he says, "you are a normal teenager who has led a normal life with no great tragedies, thank goodness, and no Nobel Prize at 16 either. You have to write about something in your everyday life. The solution is to look inside yourself, not out 'there,' for a topic."

> My son's girlfriend was hanging around the house bemoaning the fact that she had nothing to write about in her essay. I said, "But you like reading. You like the classics. I remember how upset you were when other kids said they didn't like *Jane Eyre*." I knew if she wrote about her love of books, her essay would show real passion.
>
> FORMER WRITING TEACHER WHO KNEW THIS WOULD BE A DISTINCTIVE ESSAY TOPIC

What to Avoid

Some topics, though, are best avoided altogether, no matter how distinctive your approach. You should almost always avoid writing about sexual experiences, rape, incest, or mental illness in your main essay. Most applications have an additional information section where you can include such information if you need it to explain an unusual change on your transcript or something else that requires explanation. We feel a little differently about controversial political and social issues such as abortion. If you

> If an applicant chooses a topic that is obscure or related to pop culture, he or she should make sure to give enough context for a reader who may not be familiar with the topic. If an applicant chooses to write about something controversial, he or she should take an educated position and be mindful to avoid what could be seen as an offensive stand.[7]
>
> ELIZABETH CHERON, ASSOCIATE DEAN OF ADMISSIONS, NORTHEASTERN UNIVERSITY

choose such a topic, be sure to present yourself as a thoughtful person, not just someone with strong convictions. You should show that you have considered opposing arguments and are not an ideologue who knows the truth and doesn't want to have a dialogue. You don't know who your readers will be, and it is foolish to write about a topic that may make a reader uncomfortable.

⊠ Essay Don'ts

- Don't write an essay that any one of a thousand other seniors could write, because they probably will.
- Avoid writing an essay that might embarrass the reader. Although you definitely must risk something personally in order to write an effective essay, the risk should not place a burden on the reader.
- Don't try to sell yourself. Rather than persuading the college that you are great, just show them who you are, what you care about, what the pivotal points in your life have been so far.
- Don't try to write an "important" essay. These can come across as more impersonal than the authors intend.
- Don't set out to write the perfect essay, the one with huge impact, the one that will blow the doors to the college open for you. Instead, give the reader a sample of yourself, a slice of the real you, a snapshot in words.
- Don't have others edit and correct it until you cannot hear your own voice anymore. Remember that the only reason this essay has for existing is to show the reader who you are.

Source: Adapted with permission from "What Not to Do and Why" by William Poirot, former college counselor, in *100 Successful College Application Essays,* New York: Penguin, 2002. Copyright © The Harvard Independent.

DO I HAVE TO COUNT EVERY WORD?

Applicants often wonder how strictly they need to adhere to a word limit. The Common Application specifies an essay of 250 to 650 words, which is about one to two and a half pages of double-spaced print. The word limit on the upper and lower ends is strictly enforced by the application, which will simply stop you when you hit the maximum. The Universal Application and Coalition Application give you a bit more flexibility and provide word-length guidelines rather than hard limits.

Whether you have hard limits or not, remember that writing clean, stylish prose is an art you can master. A 700-plus word essay can almost always be trimmed to 600 words or less and be strengthened in the process. Even if length is just a guideline, your college essay is not the place to write more than you need to. You want your readers to enjoy reading your essay and not be impatient to get to the end because of its length. Once your essay is finished, be sure to do a "print preview" before submitting to be sure everything appears the way you intend it to.

THE "WHY COLLEGE X?" ESSAY

Colleges often include a "Why College X?" question asking why their college appeals to you. Depending on the school, it may be the main essay or a supplementary one. You should respond very carefully to these questions. Colleges ask them for a reason, even if you find them annoying. They are trying to assess your motivation to attend their college as well as "fit." A good answer shows that you have carefully researched the college and thought about what you would get from it as well as contribute to it. By contrast, a vague answer, for example, "I really like your biology department" or "I want a small college" without further detail shows lack of real interest or homework.

⊠ Some "Why College X?" College-Specific Questions

- "In 500 words or fewer, please explain how Kalamazoo College's approach to education will help you explore your ideas and interests both inside and outside of the classroom." (Kalamazoo College, 2016–2017)
- "Who is the person you dream of becoming and how do you believe Syracuse University can help you achieve this?" (Syracuse University, 2016–2017)
- "Santa Clara University's strategic vision promises to educate citizens and leaders of competence, conscience, and compassion and cultivate knowledge and faith to build a more humane, just, and sustainable world. What aspect of SCU's strategic vision appeals to you? Why?" (Santa Clara University, 2016–2017)

Admissions staff members are experts on their own colleges. Don't tell them things that are obvious or just not very interesting: Boston University is in Boston, for example, and you love Boston! A good answer may never mention Boston (although it might), but it does discuss something specific about Boston University—a class or two, a program, a professor, or an activity that reveals your interests and values. You might talk about what you learned from a professor or a student you met while visiting the campus, how certain programs will help you achieve your career goals, or what features of the campus and its programs you find most exciting and why. Boston University is only the apparent subject of the short essay. You have to write about why you like the school, but even here *you* are the real subject, so your essay has to use information about the college to show your individuality.

PAY ATTENTION TO SHORT ANSWER QUESTIONS

Some colleges include a few questions to be answered in a paragraph or two or less in addition to one or two long essays. Many students focus all their effort on the long essays, leaving the shorter ones to the very end when they are rushing to meet a deadline. In fact, all are important because they give the reader insights into who you are. You might be asked to elaborate on one of your activities, discuss an academic interest, or reflect on a current issue that is important to you. Some colleges ask "Why College X" in a short answer format.

Edit and proofread your shorter answers just as you would the long essays. They can be especially challenging because you often have to be very stingy with words. But everything counts in the end, or they wouldn't ask about it, so try to give these answers some flair and personality. Even very short answers in which you are asked to list your favorite music, books, and movies reveal you.

⌘ Some College-Specific Short Questions

- "Why Lawrence? It's a short question seeking a short answer: 47 well-chosen words—give or take a few—should work." (Lawrence University, 2016–2017)
- "Virtually all of Stanford's undergraduates live on campus. Write a note to your future roommate that reveals something about you or that will help your roommate—and us—know you better." (Stanford University, 2016–2017)
- "We know that colleges ask a lot of hard questions on their applications. This one is not so hard and we promise, there is no hidden agenda—just have fun! We have all heard the saying 'laughter is the best medicine.' Recount a time when something really made you laugh." (Smith College, 2016–2017)

WHAT KIND OF HELP IS APPROPRIATE?

Colleges expect the essays that you submit with your application are your own work and they ask you to electronically sign a statement to that effect on the application. You are free, of course, to brainstorm ideas for the essays with your family, friends, teachers, and school counselor. You can also get comments on a rough draft. In fact, most professional writers go through several drafts and get reactions from others along the way. It makes good sense to write a draft, put it away for a few days, and then revisit it. William Zinsser, author of *On Writing Well*, says that there is no such thing as good writing, only good rewriting.[8]

Almost by definition, a first draft is going to be rough, so allow enough time to get feedback. Your English teacher or high school counselor can be especially helpful in making suggestions about your essays because they evaluate writing professionally and have seen many essays over the years. They also observe careful boundaries when it comes to students' writing. They know when to stop and how to let your voice stay intact.

Parents can sometimes lose sight of this and set about trying to rewrite their child's essays. Although help with brainstorming and editing is good, wholesale rewriting is not. It can even hurt more than help if it robs a student of his distinctive voice—that sense of self that admissions officers really want to hear—and signal that the parent doesn't think the child can do the job himself. In the end, your essay should be your own work and sound like you, not someone much older.

IS AN "OPTIONAL" QUESTION EVER REALLY OPTIONAL?

Occasionally an application will have a question marked "optional." Can you assume the question really *is* optional? Our advice to you is, "It depends." Sometimes colleges make it very clear that optional questions are meant to give students who would not otherwise be strong candidates for admission or who fall into certain categories an opportunity to provide additional information. At the University of Puget Sound, for example, students who choose to not submit SAT or ACT scores are asked to submit two essays that are not required of those who do submit scores. At Southern Oregon University, students who fall below the university's GPA and test score averages for admission are encouraged to submit a personal statement that others do not have to submit. If you fall into one of these categories, you should certainly submit the additional material.

But what about the "additional information" section on the Common Application or on other applications? Here the line gets a little blurry. We recommend that you ask yourself if you have important additional information that would strengthen your application that has not been included elsewhere. The additional information section is not an invitation to submit another essay just because you can, but rather a chance to provide something additional if you feel strongly that you want colleges to know about it. This could include, but not be limited to, information about special health or family challenges you have faced that may have affected your academic or extracurricular record. Or you could add more detailed information about your favorite activity if the application doesn't ask a specific question about this. These are just a few of the uses for that section. But don't feel you have to write something if you really have nothing more to add.

⋈

Let's just give a (*very* hypothetical) situation. My boss, Satya, tells me, "Jeff, we have one more spot left in the class of 2021. You can only pick one more." I come back to my office and notice I have two applicants left to read. They are identical with grades, scores and extracurricular activities, and both have glowing recommendations. One took the time to write an entertaining, engaging, and smart essay about why Tulane is the perfect fit for him, has a great major he's interested in and he loves BBQ Shrimp from Pascale Manales. The other student? Well he didn't write anything. At all. The decision for me? An easy one.[9]

JEFF SCHIFFMAN, DIRECTOR OF ADMISSION, TULANE UNIVERSITY

⋈

The last category consists of questions that attempt to get at your interest in a college. Tulane University, for example, traditionally asks applicants to "please describe why you are interested in attending Tulane University" followed by the word "optional." You could certainly submit your application without answering it, but this would not be a good idea if you were indeed seriously interested in Tulane (and why would you apply if you weren't?).

As we discuss in chapter 10, many colleges consider demonstrated interest in their review process, and a straightforward question about why a college is of interest to you is a simple way to measure it. There can also be subtler ways to get at the same point. An example is the following prompt: "Based on your knowledge of American University, what would it mean to you to call yourself an AU Eagle?" American University made this optional in its 2016–2017 application. Why take a chance that your application will not be taken seriously if you don't answer it? We see optional questions like this as essentially "required."

STEPS TO A SUCCESSFUL ESSAY

We conclude this section with some tips to help you write great essays. The Resources section at the end of this book lists some excellent books that focus exclusively on writing the college essay. We've given you a good start here, but we encourage you to consult one or more of these sources if you would like more detail about essay writing:

- Brainstorm either by yourself or with others about the personal qualities that you hope to convey in your essay. Look deep inside yourself. Who are you? Who are you becoming? What have you learned in your short life?

- Read the essay topics carefully. Which one grabs you? Which topic will best allow you to speak in your own voice and tell a story about yourself? What would you learn about yourself by writing about it?

- Show by example, don't just tell. Use vivid details when possible. You want the reader to imagine the people, places, and events in your essay as real.

- Avoid the passive voice if you can. When in doubt, cut extra words. Don't write a conclusion or moral at the end, such as, "What I learned was . . ." The essay is short enough that it should contain its moral. Make it easy and, if appropriate, fun to read.

- Set your essay aside for a couple of days and then revise it. Think carefully about who you want to ask for advice. Ask your English teacher or counselor or both to read and comment on your essay.

- Incorporate the best suggestions into another draft, accepting just the advice that works for you. Set it aside again for a couple of days, and then reread it, changing it until you are reasonably happy with it. You cannot write a perfect essay, so at some point, you have to let it go.

- Proofread your essay carefully. Then have someone else proofread it, too. Why risk mistakes that can be easily corrected?

AN IMPORTANT TO-DO LIST

It is often said that the devil is in the details. The last thing you want is for your thoughtful, carefully prepared case for admission, including a terrific essay, to be sabotaged by minor details. We offer this list to help you keep track of all those little things that can make a big difference. In chapter 10, we discuss other parts of your application besides the essay, but we suggest that you take a quick look at this list now. When you are ready to apply, review it again carefully, and then double-check it several times along the way to be sure you have covered all the bases:

- **Keep close track of all deadlines; they vary from college to college.** It is easy to forget when things are due when you have multiple applications and so much going on at school and at home. Develop a time line that will work for you and then follow it to be sure everything gets done (and sent) on time.

- **Spell your name exactly the way it appears on your passport or photo ID on all of your application materials, SAT or ACT registration, and any correspondence.** If you use your middle initial, use it every time on every form for every college-related purpose. Get into the habit of doing this right at the beginning and avoid the hassle of having three copies of every college mailing arrive at your house or recommendation letters that go astray, or the more serious problem of being denied admission to a test center because of a difference between the name on your ID and the name on your registration. If your Social Security number is required, be sure you enter it correctly each time.

- **Make sure your e-mail address reflects your maturity.** Save your funny nickname for your friends and get another address, from a reliable provider, for your college applications. Don't laugh; they do notice. And while we are on the topic of maturity, be sure that your postings on Facebook, Twitter, YouTube, or similar websites don't contain anything embarrassing or immature. Some admission officers occasionally look applicants up on social media, and you don't want them to be put off by what they may find.

- **Keep a copy of everything you send in, including online applications and other written and e-mail correspondence.** Make sure you submit all parts of the application, along with the application fee if one is required, by the indicated deadlines. Don't wait until the last minute to file; unanticipated problems can happen near the deadline. When filing electronically, check online to see that all parts of your application, including any supplements, were transmitted.

- **Give all those who are writing recommendations for you, teachers and your counselor, everything they need to submit them on time.** Check with your counseling office for its requirements and be sure to follow directions carefully, including any deadlines before your actual application deadline that your high school may impose. Arrange to pay for the transcripts if your school requires payment.

- **File your financial aid forms promptly.** The FAFSA and CSS PROFILE first become available on October 1 of your senior year. Be sure to check the specific submission deadlines for each school to which you are applying. Regardless of the deadlines, however, it is always wise to file as early as you can. Keep copies of everything you use to fill out the forms. You may need to produce them later.

- **Ask the College Board or ACT or both, if you took both tests and want to report them, to send your scores to your chosen colleges.** The College Board and the ACT will send only the scores you ask them to send. A few colleges, however, require all scores, so you need to check with each college to see what it wants. Always follow the rules. The SAT and ACT offer four free score reports if you provide the names of the colleges at the time of testing or shortly after. The only drawback to this is that the scores will be sent before you can see them, although it can save time as well as some money. Later reports can be purchased by mail, phone, or online. Allow three weeks for regular delivery of scores to be on the safe side. You can pay for rush delivery, but it is expensive and unnecessary if you plan ahead. This is your responsibility, not your high school's, even if your high school puts your scores on your transcript. Colleges consider those scores and any you self-report on your applications as unofficial. Most require official scores sent by the testing agencies.

- **Check e-mail regularly and keep all correspondence you receive from your colleges after you apply.** Some may come by regular mail, but most will come via e-mail. Read everything carefully and respond as appropriate. You will probably get a password to access the status of your application online as well as the final decision. Keep your password in a safe place and, just as important, remember where you put it.

- **Check the status of your application about three to four weeks after everything was sent.** Remember that it can take quite a while for everything to get where it needs to be, and information is not always immediately posted online. Colleges will generally contact you if something is missing. It annoys them to get anxious phone calls asking if your file is complete. You can always send something in late if it is actually missing, and it won't hurt your application.

- **Stay alert for phone messages or e-mail from alumni interviewers if your colleges offer such interviews.** Read the college material to see whether you have to formally request an interview (and by what date) or if you will be contacted automatically (and when). If you do not hear from someone in the time frame indicated, call or e-mail the admissions office. Be proactive. We'll talk more about the interview process in chapter 10.

- **By mid-January, ask your high school to send your fall semester grades to each college that requires them as part of the regular decision application process or to a school where you were admitted or deferred early.** Colleges typically require a midyear report from your high school that includes your fall grades. The midyear report also invites the counselor to note any significant additions or changes, whether good news or problems, to your academic, extracurricular, or character record.

- **If you have a new major honor or accomplishment after you apply, send a note or e-mail to the admissions office (with your name, birthdate, and ID number if one has been assigned to your application clearly indicated at the top) asking that this information be added to your file.** But only add something significant. If it makes you look as if you are trying too hard, it won't help.

We turn now, in chapter 10, to the remaining parts of your application.

CHAPTER 10

Applying Well, Part II

Recommendations, Interviews, and Activities

As we discussed in chapter 9, essays are an important way colleges learn about students beyond their grades and test scores. But many colleges consider more than your essays and obtain additional information about you in one or more of the following ways: through requiring letters of recommendation, by gathering information about honors and how you spend your time outside of class, and by requiring or recommending interviews. In this chapter, we discuss how to make the most of each of these opportunities to let colleges learn about you. Along with your essays, they are your chance to personalize the process and help you stand out from the crowd. At the end of the chapter we provide information that will be helpful to you if you plan to apply to one or more colleges outside of the United States. In chapter 11, we provide special advice for athletes and students with talents in the visual and performing arts.

GETTING GREAT LETTERS OF RECOMMENDATION

Although many schools, mostly public colleges, do not require or even accept letters of recommendation as part of the application process, the colleges that do ask for them require or recommend one or two letters from teachers. They also often require an official school report, usually prepared by a school counselor.

Along with your essay, these letters can make your application distinctive. Especially valuable in letters are anecdotes that bring a file to life and transform numbers into a real person.

Counselor and teacher letters generally serve two different but overlapping purposes. A counselor letter helps put you in the context of other students at your school—academically in terms of your grades and the rigor of your curriculum and extracurricularly in terms of your contributions to your high school community. It can also provide descriptions of special challenges you have faced and overcome, an explanation of erratic grades or other unusual aspects of your record, and an overall evaluation of you relative to your peers.

Teacher letters, by contrast, will focus on what you are like as a student in the classroom. Teachers have to be experts only in what you have achieved in their classes and related activities. In a sense, the admissions readers are working for their college's faculty members, who want to enjoy teaching you. The main point of a teacher recommendation is to give the college an idea of you as a student.

Taken together, the school report and teacher recommendations help the admissions readers develop a fuller picture of you and distinguish you from many others with similar grades and test scores.

WHICH TEACHERS SHOULD YOU ASK TO WRITE?

Although you obviously have no direct control over what your teachers will write in a letter, you can increase the chances that your teacher letters will be helpful in making your case for admission by asking the right ones.

Ask Teachers Who Have Taught You Recently

Ask teachers who have taught you recently, in 11th grade, if possible. The 10th grade is usually a bit too far back, and the 12th grade is probably too fresh, especially if you are applying EA or ED. A senior-year teacher may not have a lot to write about yet, even if you are very enthusiastic and doing well. Teachers who have taught you in more demanding courses are often good choices. They can testify to your ability to do more challenging work over a full year or semester. That is another reason not to use a 10th-grade teacher: the course work is usually less advanced.

What Fields Should They Be From?

Focus first on your teachers from your core academic subject areas: English, history, math (including computer science), science, and foreign language. Occasionally, a college will be very specific about the letters it wants to see. MIT, for example, asks students to send one letter from a math or science teacher and one from a humanities, social science, or language teacher. This is rarely mandatory elsewhere, but it would make sense to ask a math or science teacher for any college where you hope to major in one of those fields. Journalism, art, music, or drama might be very important to you, but in general you should not ask these teachers for a required teacher reference unless a college specifically asks you to do that. Otherwise consider asking that teacher to write an additional, optional letter if your schools will accept it, as many will.

Ask Teachers Who Know You Best

Students sometimes have a difficult time deciding which teachers to ask for a letter of recommendation. The most helpful letters are those written by teachers who know you well—not necessarily the teachers who gave you the highest grades—although it is nice if both are true. A well-written letter of recommendation should include specific examples of your contributions and achievements. Like a good college application essay, it should show by example rather than simply tell. A teacher who sees you as an active and thoughtful contributor to class discussions can more easily provide specific examples about you.

Which of your teachers has seen you at your best? Where did you shine? Did you write a great paper? Did you do extra work voluntarily or independent research? Help other students with their work? Add to the class energy? You don't have to have done all of this in one class, of course, but these are some things to think about when considering whom to ask.

Some schools with strong college counseling programs provide training for teachers in writing effective recommendations. Most schools, however, leave it up to teachers to do their best without guidance. Given that reality, savvy students seek out teachers who seem particularly thoughtful, know them well, and are themselves strong writers.

How Should You Approach a Teacher?

Writing letters of recommendation is part of a teacher's job, but you want your recommenders to take on the task enthusiastically. So approach your teachers early, especially if they are popular teachers who get lots of requests. In fact, it is a good idea to ask teachers at the beginning of senior year or even at the end of junior year. Asking teachers early is especially important if a teacher will not be returning in the fall. If a teacher is willing to write for you, be sure to get his or her e-mail address so that in the fall you can enable him or her to upload the recommendation to the application platform(s) you will be using. You don't have to know where you are going to apply in order to ask early; you just have to know that you will need letters. Your recommenders are not writing to a particular college but to all colleges at the same time.

Talk to your potential recommenders in person if possible, and ask them whether they feel they know you well enough to write a supportive letter of recommendation. The response you want to hear is an enthusiastic, "Sure," "Yes," or "Of course!"

If you sense any hesitation, including a time constraint because a teacher is very busy, pick up on the cue. Thank the teacher for considering your request but indicate that you'll be happy to ask someone else. A reluctant letter writer may not provide the most helpful letter, so just move on to another teacher if you can.

How Many Letters Should You Submit?

As we noted previously, most colleges that require letters of recommendation ask for one or two letters from teachers and one from a counselor. We know of two colleges—Davidson College and Dartmouth College—that also require or strongly encourage a letter from a peer.

Sometimes you can also submit an optional recommendation from a coach, employer, or someone else who knows you well in addition to the required letters. We advise sending an extra letter only if the writer is likely to share valuable information about you that might not otherwise be found in your file. This could be the drama or debate teacher you have worked with closely or someone outside the high school setting entirely who can describe another side of your personality or achievements. But don't worry if you don't have someone who fits this bill. Most successful applicants don't submit an extra letter.

If a school accepts extra letters and uses the Common App, the Coalition App, or similar applications, those letters may be submitted electronically. If an extra letter is being submitted via regular mail, be sure the writer includes your full name and birthdate, along with your ID number if one has been assigned to your application, prominently at the top of the letter so that it can be added to your file.

Resist a letter-writing campaign, however. Application readers hate "fluff"—extra stuff that clogs up a file and takes time to read through but doesn't add anything of substance in the end. The reading season is fatiguing. Don't risk annoying them. The only really helpful letters are from people who can add real substance to your file. We recommend limiting your extra letters, if you send them at all, to one. Sometimes less is actually more.

WHAT YOUR RECOMMENDERS NEED TO KNOW ABOUT YOU

Your school counselor and your teachers need relevant and useful information about you to write effective letters. You can help them gain that background. In many schools, students fill out a questionnaire that provides teachers and counselors with information about their college plans, extracurricular activities, GPA, standardized test scores, intellectual interests, hobbies, and other general background information that presents their personal strengths. Your letter writers—especially your counselor—will use this form, so be sure to complete it accurately and thoroughly. If your high school does not provide this kind of questionnaire, you can make up one of your own. The information, not the format, is the important issue.

You may want to supplement your form with specific details to help teachers refresh their classroom memory of you, because that will be the primary basis of their recommendation. Consider providing a copy of a paper or project that you were proud of and talk about anything especially memorable about your involvement in class. Tell them how much the class mattered to you. What did you learn that you didn't know before? How has it changed your perspective on your future academic plans? How have you expanded your interests based on this class? In other words, you can help your teachers help you by providing qualitative information and context for your experience in their class that they might not know about or remember. You can't tell them what to write, of course, but they will appreciate your help, and their letter will benefit from your thoughtfulness.

If you would like to see what the colleges ask your counselor and teachers, you can see representative forms in PDF format on the Universal Application website at www.universalcollegeapp.com. With the Universal App and other multi-college application formats, each person writing a letter for you prepares just one that is shared with all of your schools. Colleges generally ask for much the same information, so a teacher or counselor can usually use the same basic content for all of your recommendations, regardless of the type of application.

WHAT IF MY COUNSELOR DOESN'T KNOW ME WELL?

Colleges know that counselors in large public high schools often cannot get to know their students well, even if they try, simply because of their enormous caseloads. They see this when they visit high schools, so they don't expect detail in such letters. Nevertheless, a detailed letter can still help, so you should get to know your counselor as well as possible and you should take the task of preparing background information for her, as previously described, very seriously.

This is especially important if aspects of your record or background would benefit from explanation. For example, if your first-semester grades in your junior year suffered because of a serious illness or family problem, be sure your counselor knows. Your counselor can explain your situation only if she has this information. Or if you have a learning disability that was discovered only recently and your record shows a positive jump because you are now studying more effectively, the counselor needs to know this too, if you are comfortable having her mention this in her letter. (It is optional, but we think it is usually a good idea to disclose this kind of information. We discuss this further in chapter 12.)

THE SPECIAL CASE OF DISCIPLINARY INFRACTIONS

The school report of most college applications will ask your counselor to indicate whether you have ever been found responsible for a disciplinary violation at school from ninth grade on that resulted in serious disciplinary action. If the answer is "yes," you must disclose this information as well when you respond to a similar question on your application, even though it is obviously uncomfortable to have to do so. You must provide background information in a thoughtful, sincerely regretful way that describes what happened, demonstrates that you have learned from your mistake, and makes it clear that you will not repeat this example of poor judgment. Honesty is paramount here. The impact of such disclosures on admission will vary widely depending on the nature of the infraction, how long ago it occurred, and the college, but all colleges want students who accept responsibility for their actions. Your applications will give you ample space for an explanation.

WAIVE YOUR RIGHT TO SEE THE LETTERS

The Family Educational Rights and Privacy Act, known as FERPA, gives students the right to see their permanent college record after they enroll in a college. Applications that require letters of recommendation provide a place for you to waive your right to see any letters written on your behalf that a college may keep. You do not have a right to see a letter while you are applying, or even after you are accepted, but only after you enroll. Failing to sign the waiver could signal to your recommenders and colleges that you don't trust them. We recommend signing the waiver in all cases. Since the passage of FERPA, most colleges destroy recommendations anyway, so there is little point in reserving potential future access to them.

SHINING IN YOUR INTERVIEW

Schools vary widely in the importance placed on interviews. As we briefly discussed in chapter 2, some colleges require an interview as part of the admissions process, some make it optional but strongly recommended, and some don't offer it at all. Just how important are interviews anyway, and how should you view them?

If a college doesn't offer interviews—most public universities don't use them, for example—then obviously interviews play no role in the admissions process. Otherwise, our best advice for most students is to take advantage of an interview if offered and take it seriously. But as we will discuss subsequently, don't expect it to carry too much weight in the admissions process, if it counts at all. The only exceptions to our general advice encouraging students to interview are students who, because of severe anxiety or other reasons, cannot communicate effectively in such a setting.

THE DIFFERENCE BETWEEN INFORMATIONAL AND EVALUATIVE INTERVIEWS

Interviews fall into two main types with different purposes: informational and evaluative. Some college websites will tell you the type that is offered; if not, you should ask. Regardless of the type, interviews are also just good experience.

Inevitably you will be interviewed later in life for scholarships, graduate school, and jobs. It pays to learn the ropes now.

The Informational Interview

In informational interviews, colleges provide applicants with personalized information about their programs. The main goal of informational interviews is simply recruitment—having applicants feel the college has a human face and getting them excited about enrolling. They are always optional and are usually offered by local alums who volunteer to help their alma mater. They are sometimes offered on-site at the college as well by admissions staff members or current students who have been specially trained for the job. Informational interviews are specifically designed to help you learn more about a college and give you a chance to ask questions. Notes are rarely kept from these sessions, although the fact that you participated in one will likely become part of your file. That can show demonstrated interest, which the college may view favorably.

> While we are happy to speak with rising high school seniors during the summer, these conversations are entirely non-evaluative and play **NO** role in our admission decisions.[1]
>
> WILLIAMS COLLEGE ADMISSIONS WEBSITE

> Interviews are considered in the admission process and help the admission committee make better, more informed decisions when selecting the freshman class.[2]
>
> CARNEGIE MELLON UNIVERSITY ADMISSIONS WEBSITE

The Evaluative Interview

If an interview is evaluative, the results become part of your admissions file. Evaluative interviews may be required (though this is rare), strongly encouraged, or merely optional, depending on the college and the circumstances. Many colleges with large numbers of visitors have cut back or eliminated on-site interviews with admissions staff members or specially trained seniors because of the volume, leaving the task of conducting evaluative interviews to alumni volunteers located across the country.

You will still have ample opportunity to ask questions in an evaluative interview, even though the interviewer will have lots of questions for you as well. Come prepared with some thoughtful questions and use the opportunity to make a good impression—the questions you ask will give your interviewer additional insights into who you are.

What Are They Looking For, and How Much Will It Count?

The variability among interviewers—admissions staff members, seniors, and, especially, alumni—make it difficult for colleges to place great weight on evaluative interviews. Alums do them for fun and to give something back to the college besides money because they enjoyed their college experience. At selective colleges, alumni interviewers frequently complain that the applicants they liked most are denied admission. This simply reflects the reality that there are many more applicants who are strong than available spots and that an evaluative interview usually plays only a very small role in the final decision.

Some schools, such as Pitzer College and Wake Forest University, for example, strongly encourage interviews with an admissions representative as an important way to learn more about applicants. Each provides multiple interview formats, from on-site interviews for those living relatively close to campus, to telephone or Skype discussions, to even one-way video uploads at Pitzer. These schools are signaling that they would really like a student to interview, although it is not an official requirement.

Regardless of who is doing your interview or where it takes place, expect the experience to be positive, warm, and friendly, not an interrogation. Interviewers want you to feel comfortable and to like them. A written evaluation becomes part of a student's file after an evaluative interview. Although specifics will vary from college to college, the following categories will give you a good sense of the kind of information a college hopes to gain from an admissions interview:

- *Why is the student applying?* Is the student knowledgeable about the college and able to express why she thinks it might be a good fit for her?

- *What are the student's intellectual qualities?* Does he demonstrate curiosity, depth, creativity, or breadth of awareness? Has he challenged himself? How would he contribute to the college intellectually?

- *How has the student demonstrated commitment and personal motivation outside the*

After my interview, the interviewer said he wished he had told me from the beginning that it was only an informal conversation so that I wouldn't be as nervous. That meant he thought I was nervous. That means I rambled and did poorly. Been reading articles on how to handle college rejections the whole night yesterday.

STUDENT WHO THINKS THE INTERVIEW IS MORE IMPORTANT THAN IT REALLY IS *classroom?* Can she potentially make a positive, significant contribution to the college community outside the classroom?

- *How does the student exhibit character and personal qualities such as initiative, responsibility, resilience, and maturity?*

ARRANGING THE INTERVIEW

Colleges vary in how they set up interviews. You are always responsible for setting up interviews on-site at the college or with visiting admissions reps. You need to check college websites to see how to sign up for an on-site interview, if those are offered, as well as watch for information about opportunities to meet with a visiting rep.

Alumni interviews are different. Some schools will contact you soon after you have submitted your application to arrange an alumni interview. Others will wait for you to contact them, either before or after you have applied, by phone or through a website, depending on the school.

Some colleges have to limit the number of interviews they can offer because of the pressure of high numbers of applicants and limited on-site staff members or alumni in an area. You should research this for each college, either through the website or by calling the college admissions office. Interviews at a college are more available in the summer, but the admissions office can be very busy in August, the prime family vacation month. In some cases, interviews are available on-site as early as spring break of the junior year. Before you leap at the first chance, though, ask yourself how much you know about the college and how ready you are for an interview. If you feel unprepared, it might be better to wait for an alumni interview back home in the fall if it is offered.

Colleges typically limit interviews to one per student, so choose the kind you prefer if you have an option and must pick one.

Location and Length

Your interview may take place in a college admissions office with an admissions rep or trained student, at a hotel, at your school with a visiting rep, or in a coffee shop or other public place. Occasionally an interview will be held in the home of an alum, but this is unusual because of liability concerns.

Regardless of where your interview is held, be on time. It is okay to arrive at an admissions office early to get settled, but don't arrive early to an interview at someone's home; just be there when you are supposed to be. Expect the interview to last about 45 minutes, plus or minus 15 minutes, depending on the interviewer and how the conversation goes, unless you have been told otherwise. The first few minutes can set the tone for the rest of the interview, so go in alert and focused.

Dress

Dress neatly and look presentable—no jeans, shorts, tee shirts, sneakers, or flip-flops—but you don't need to dress up for the occasion either. If the interview is in an admissions office, it is fine for your parent to wait in the outer office for you while the interview takes place. If someone drives you to an interview at an alum's home or office, be sure he or she can take you home promptly after the interview. You don't want to have to awkwardly hang out while you wait for your ride.

> Somebody I interviewed once said he wanted to major in accounting. I said, "You know, that's not a major at Harvard." It went downhill from there.
>
> HARVARD ALUMNI INTERVIEWER

What Will You Be Asked?

In preparing for an interview, think about how you would answer the most likely questions such as those shown in the following box. You may be asked somewhat different questions, of course, but thinking about how you would answer these can boost your confidence. Don't try to memorize your answers, though, because memorized answers can come across as stiff and awkward and may not even be relevant to the specific question being asked.

Asking Your Own Questions

In addition to being ready to answer an interviewer's questions, have several questions of your own ready to go when given the opportunity (and you will always get the opportunity). It is perfectly all right to have a note card with you to remind yourself of your questions. Interviewers understand that you may be nervous. Don't ask obvious and purely factual questions, ones you could easily answer by looking at the catalog, website, or application materials, such as, "Do you have an engineering program?" or "Is there separate housing for freshmen only?" The best questions show that you have read and thought about the material provided by the college or ask the interviewer to explain how something such as the housing or advising system works. You can also ask an alumni interviewer what the high (and low) points of her own experience at the college were, how the college has changed since she graduated, and how the college changed her life. People like to talk about themselves. The more like a normal conversation, the faster the time will go.

⊠ Some Frequently Asked Interview Questions

1. What are you looking for in a college? What attracts you to this college?
2. What are your top two extracurricular activities, and why do you like them?
3. What sort of challenges have you faced in your life so far?
4. What is your favorite subject in school, and why?
5. How would you describe yourself to a stranger?
6. What is your favorite pastime?
7. How did you spend last summer, and how did you grow from it?
8. Can you name a book you have read that left a lasting impression?
9. What have you enjoyed most about high school?
10. Do you have any questions I can help answer?

After the Interview

When the interview is over, thank the interviewer for her time and ask for a card or otherwise write down her name and e-mail or postal mail address. A short thank-you note or e-mail sent after the interview is a nice gesture.

⊠ Interview Checklist

☐ Make sure you have the exact details of the interview time and location, and arrange reliable transportation. If something goes wrong and you are late, don't blame the interviewer. Just apologize for the misunderstanding or for the delay.

☐ Carefully review material about the college (online and paper) to make sure you know about its programs and special features.

- [ ] Think about your answers to possible questions, including the most important one: "Why are you interested in this college?"
- [ ] Prepare your own thoughtful questions about the college to ask your interviewer.
- [ ] Dress neatly and appropriately for the setting. Dressy clothes are not necessary but avoid jeans and shorts.
- [ ] Shake hands when you meet the interviewer, and try to maintain eye contact throughout the interview.
- [ ] Try to relax and enjoy the conversation.
- [ ] After the interview is over, thank the interviewer for taking the time to speak with you. Shake hands again, and ask the interviewer for a business card or other contact information.
- [ ] Send a short thank-you note in the next few days. A written note is nice, but e-mail is fine, too.

Above all, keep the interview in perspective. We have provided a lot of advice on the topic because students are often nervous. Just remember that the interview is a small, and certainly not the most important, part of your application.

SHOWING THAT YOU ARE INTERESTED

Some colleges try to identify who is seriously interested in them by tracking how much contact a student has had with the college—such as requesting an interview, chatting with a representative at a college fair or a high school visit, e-mailing a question to an admissions officer, or visiting campus—and then using that information when making the final decision. They see a student who has initiated contact at least once with a college as more likely to enroll than a student who has not. (In fact, an application from a student whose first contact with a college is the electronic arrival of the application is called a "stealth application.") Students who have made contact beyond their application are seen as a better bet for admission. Given hard choices among candidates with similar credentials, demonstrated interest can make the difference between an offer of acceptance or the wait list at some colleges.

Rhodes College in Memphis openly lets students know that demonstrated interest is an important part of the admissions process. Its admission FAQ page states,

Showing your interest in Rhodes is highly important to us. We look most favorably upon students who have demonstrated a significant amount of interest in the college when reviewing applications. A few ways to show your interest include a campus visit, attending a college fair, high school visit, off-campus interview, or communicating with your admission counselor. In the past, some students who have not demonstrated interest have been placed on the waitlist.[3]

> To think that when my older son applied we refrained from contacting colleges because we thought we were doing them a favor by not cluttering up their e-mail or phone lines. We won't pester them, but we won't have the same worry when our younger son applies.
>
> PARENT OF COLLEGE SOPHOMORE WITH ANOTHER CHILD IN THE ADMIS-SIONS PIPELINE

Many colleges that consider demonstrated interest are not this refreshingly candid about it. In general, it counts the least, if at all, at the super-selective colleges that already have the highest yields. These colleges have little to gain by showing preference to those who try to demonstrate interest. Rhodes College is far from unique, however, in the weight it places on demonstrated interest. It is perfectly all right to ask admissions officers if demonstrated interest plays a role in admissions decisions made on their campus.

HIGHLIGHTING WHAT YOU'VE ACCOMPLISHED

As we discussed in chapter 2, extracurricular activities, community service, family responsibilities, and work experience enable students to demonstrate their passions, initiative, leadership skills, and commitment to others. With the exception of schools that admit students primarily on the basis of grades and test scores, the application forms most colleges use ask you to list each of your activities, the grades when you participated in them, and the number of hours per week and weeks per year you spent on them. Applications typically also ask you to include any positions held, honors earned, or athletic letters awarded for each activity, as well as a very brief description of the activity. The Common Application provides room for up to 10 contributions and activities outside of the classroom, and the Universal Application and the Coalition Application allow you to list up to seven or up to five, respectively.

Colleges want to understand how you spend your time outside the classroom as well as the extent of your involvement in various activities. They want to see how engaged you are in what matters to you. Here you can showcase your talents and creativity in addition to the impact you have had and the initiative you have taken. The information is important, so be sure to give serious attention to this part of the application. You will usually have very limited space to convey all of this, so use phrases rather than complete sentences, and choose active verbs such as "led," "developed," and "helped" to describe your involvement as appropriate. Be careful with abbreviations that are not obvious—in general, spell out the name of the organizations to which you belong if you have room. Within the space provided, try to provide as much relevant information as you can.

If you are asked to put your activities in order of importance to you, do that honestly rather than try to determine what would "look better" to a college. Colleges have no preference here—they simply want to know how you prioritize your extracurricular life.

Using Technology to Provide Insights into Who You Are

Most students find that they can convey their activities and degree of involvement in the space provided on the application. Sometimes, though, students find the area too limiting in terms of space or format or both. Some new application tools can be helpful here.

ZeeMee (www.zeemee.com) is a free online tool that lets students prepare a multimedia page about themselves that highlights their extracurricular interests and academic passions through uploaded images, videos, and documents. Students can place a link to their page in their applications to any of the almost 200 participating schools. It can also be inserted into applications to other schools as well, although you shouldn't assume it will be considered by them. ZeeMee is still relatively new and totally optional, and even participating colleges are still exploring how best to use it. If you decide to prepare a ZeeMee page, we encourage you to put your best efforts first into the traditional parts of your applications before working on such a supplement.

The Coalition Locker, which we discussed in chapter 9 in the context of the Coalition Application, is another resource that students can use to provide additional material along with their application. Selected items from a student's locker can be uploaded when students apply to Coalition colleges that invite such submissions. Students can open a locker account at www.mycoalition.org. With ZeeMee and the Coalition Locker, the idea is to let students easily share information about themselves that they believe would help colleges evaluate them more fully.

THE TRIED-AND-TRUE RÉSUMÉ

Sometimes students believe that they need a simple résumé or activity sheet to supplement the brief information they provide on the application itself. Some colleges discourage this, preferring that students use only the application form, but some others will accept or even require a résumé and provide a way for you to upload one with your application. For example, the Coalition Locker can be used to store and eventually upload a résumé for member schools that accept one. You also have the option of printing out a résumé and submitting it by regular mail, along with a note asking that it be added to your application. Be sure to include your name, birthdate, and application ID number, if any, on your résumé. You can also use the "additional information" section of most applications to provide more information about activities—you have several ways to approach this.

If you do prepare a résumé, keep it short—two pages maximum. Use the extra space you will have to write a brief description of your involvement and achievements in each activity; bullet points work well and can save space. Just be sure the résumé is compact, neat, well organized, and adds to the information provided on the application itself. But although listing every debate tournament or equestrian competition you have placed in is tempting, it is overkill. Once again, less is more.

A separate résumé or activity sheet gives you the flexibility to organize your information as you want. We provide suggested categories in the next box. You can include some categories as is, combine others, and omit those that are not relevant to your situation.

⚒ Categories to Consider

Extracurricular activities (includes athletics)

Awards and honors

Hobbies and special interests

Summer activities

Work experience and internships

Community involvement

Athletes who want to play varsity sports in college as well as students with exceptional talents in the arts that they wish to have evaluated as part of the college admissions process are special cases. Although most high school athletes and student artists and performers will treat their involvement in the same way as other activities, those with exceptional talent will want to take advantage of opportunities to highlight their abilities more intensively. Chapter 11 discusses these special situations.

THE CANADIAN, BRITISH, IRISH, AND DUTCH DIFFERENCE

In chapter 4, we introduced the idea of studying abroad to obtain your undergraduate degree. If you are interested in exploring this option, it is important to know that the application process differs significantly from our description for colleges in the United States. For example, you apply by specific program to English, Welsh, and Northern Irish universities, and most universities in Holland, and are admitted specifically to that program. In Canada, Scotland, and the Irish Republic, you have the option of applying to a department (known as a Faculty) rather than a specific program within that Faculty, and you would select your specific program later. On Canadian application forms you may also designate your major as "undetermined" or "undeclared." Elsewhere, with few exceptions, "undetermined" or "undeclared" is not an option.

Admissions decisions may or may not be made by the recruiters you may have met; care is taken to keep evaluation very objective and without reference to previous personal contacts. Once you are accepted and have chosen which university to attend, the university's international office will help you apply for a student visa.

PAYING FOR COLLEGE ABROAD

Paying for college may also be different. A few programs in some countries are tuition free for everyone, but these are just a small fraction of the total; none are currently offered in the countries we are highlighting. Need-based aid from the universities themselves is rarely available for international students, although some need-based partial scholarships are available in Holland. You may use federal student loans for study at some schools outside the United States. The FAFSA website lists the schools that are eligible.

An international student can apply for merit aid, however, particularly in Canada and Holland. The Holland Scholarship, for example, is a national scholarship that is available for most programs and is usually merit based. Scholarships at Dutch university colleges may even include room and board. Merit scholarships frequently require a separate application.

The United Kingdom (UK), Ireland, Canada, and Holland all allow students to work on and off campus while at university and after graduation, but the details vary, and there are restrictions. In general, students from the US can work off campus from 10 to 20 hours a week during the term, depending on the country, and full-time during official academic holidays after meeting the requirements set in the various countries.

DEADLINE DIFFERENCES

Application deadlines vary and can be as early as October 15 for some programs. Other deadlines are quite late, even after the May 1 date by which you must reply to US colleges. The late dates can make some schools attractive options for students who get off to a late start or who want additional college options. Admissions offices are aware of the US May 1 reply date and generally notify you of your decision before that date if you apply in midwinter or before.

Worth noting is the conditional acceptance, which might require you to achieve certain scores on AP or IB exams taken near the end of your senior year or to submit your final high school transcript. British universities are often very specific about this: you might need four scores of 4 or 5 on AP tests to earn a final acceptance. The British are not known for their flexibility or openness to discussion on this topic. You would treat a conditional acceptance in the same way as a wait list—you won't know for sure if you are admitted until the college receives your final test scores and transcript. This can take until July because of the time needed to grade AP and IB exams. See chapter 14 for information about wait lists in general.

APPLYING IN CANADA

Ontario has one central application for all universities in the province, available at www.ouac.ca. Several other provinces also have developed central websites that allow applicants to start their application process to universities in those provinces: www.applyalberta.ca in Alberta, www.applybc.ca in British Columbia, and www.mynsfuture.ca in Nova Scotia. In all the other provinces, you apply directly to a specific university.

In addition to your transcript, some Canadian universities require the SAT or ACT. Some programs may require SAT Subject Tests as well. Canadian universities generally do not require essays or personal profiles as part of their application, although there are some exceptions, such as the University of British Columbia and Queen's University. Most do not require recommendation letters. Many universities ask for short essays on applications for merit scholarships. Some programs require a letter of intent addressing your interest in that program, reasons for applying, and how the program relates to your personal and professional goals; they may also request a résumé of relevant volunteer and work experience and extracurricular activities.

Be sure to check each university website for application requirements by specific program. With a few exceptions, Canadian universities generally do not seem as selective as the most selective American schools, largely because they are not yet part of the frenzy of increasing numbers of applications that we discussed in chapter 1. Your first-semester senior-year grades are the most important, and because there are generally no early application options, the university only makes a decision after they have received them. Many universities base their decision on junior- and senior-year grades.

APPLYING IN THE UNITED KINGDOM

The universities of the UK (which includes England, Wales, Scotland, and Northern Ireland) use the UCAS (Universities and Colleges Admissions Service) online application, available at www.ucas.com. A number of universities, such as St. Andrews, also accept the Common Application to attract more American students. With the UCAS, you may apply to as many as five university programs for one fee by January 15 (or submit up to four medicine, dentistry, or veterinary medicine undergraduate applications by October 15). Some art schools have a later deadline. You may not apply to both Cambridge University and Oxford University, each of which has a deadline of October 15.

Oxford and Cambridge have many separate colleges to which you must apply individually and, again, you are limited to five applications overall. Each one is as selective as the most selective American colleges. If you apply to five Oxford or Cambridge colleges and nowhere else, you risk being shut out completely from the British system. Just as we said about American schools, we advise you to apply to schools across a range of selectivity.

The Process

Oxford and Cambridge have additional complex requirements, often including separate examinations in your subject and an interview. Sometimes these are available in the United States, especially on the East Coast, or by Skype. Some programs in other universities also require an interview or other supplementary materials; as always, check the university websites. No university sees where else you have applied, and all make their decisions simultaneously and independently. You are expected to have taken AP, IB, or SAT Subject Tests relevant to your program, particularly for the English, Welsh, and Northern Irish universities.

Some universities have extended deadlines for North American students, and the UCAS has an extended deadline of June 30 for non-UK students. A word of caution: the extended deadline is useful for applications to English, Welsh, and Northern Irish universities only if you know that your program still has openings. The less specialized first-year curriculum of Scottish universities, as we discuss in the next section, may make them more accessible even in June.

What Does the UCAS Require?

The UCAS has five sections, four requesting information about you and the fifth being an essay. It also requires one school recommendation that you will be able to read online once it has been uploaded by the writer. Because you are applying to study a particular subject, a teacher most familiar with your work in that area is often the best person to write this letter.

You will make your case to all of the programs you are applying to in the same essay of roughly 500 words based on a limit of 47 lines or 4,000 characters. Space is strictly limited and there are no special questions, such as those you find on the supplements of American colleges, asking you why you are interested in a school. So all of the programs you are applying for need to be very similar. The essay should address your reasons for choosing the programs you're applying to and include all related education and experience. No more than a sixth of your essay should address other activities and interests.

The University of St. Andrews website describes how British universities evaluate the essay: "Most of the students who apply to the University will be well qualified, so decisions on who will receive offers [of admission] will often be determined by the quality of the personal statement." Further on, it states that the essay "should give the admissions officers a picture of you; someone who is interested in the subject area for which you have applied and who has the motivation and potential to do well in a university environment."[4] Unlike their American counterparts, British admissions tutors (as they are often called) focus almost exclusively on your academic preparation for the specific course of study you have chosen, with little emphasis placed on nonacademic factors unless they relate to your preparation and suitability for that program.

You must specify a subject you want to study, and, except at Scottish universities, you will be admitted for that subject and no other. So the British system is simpler and more restrictive in some ways. It is also very difficult to change majors. You must be certain you know what you want to study and that you like the academic approach of the universities to which you are applying. In Scotland, however, universities admit you to a Faculty (of Arts, of Science, and so on) that includes your subject. For most subjects, the Scottish system allows you to change the emphasis or subject of your degree during your first two years.

APPLYING IN IRELAND

With the exception of universities in Northern Ireland, which use the UCAS, American students apply directly to each Irish university. Information about Irish education, how to apply to Irish universities, and links to all undergraduate institutions may be found at Education in Ireland, www.educationireland.com, and at the Irish Universities Association, www.iua.ie.

Because they need to know whether or not international applicants are from the European Union, Irish universities require a copy of your birth certificate or the photo page in your passport. Most US applicants apply through either the Admission Office or the International Office; applicants in medicine, dentistry, or physiotherapy should apply through the Atlantic Bridge Program at www.atlanticbridge.com. Although essays are not always required, some applications provide space for a supporting statement. The more selective schools such as Trinity College Dublin, University College Dublin, and University College Cork require a personal statement and two academic recommendations as well as SAT or ACT scores. Some application forms encourage reporting extracurricular activities, work, volunteering, and any other relevant information in an additional information section. As always, check the website of each university for specific requirements.

APPLYING IN HOLLAND

Because Holland has so many English-taught undergraduate programs, we are using it as an example for studying in English in a non-English-speaking country. Like many countries that offer such programs, Holland does not have a common application procedure analogous to the UCAS. The specifics of applying to university in Holland demonstrate differences among application policies and practices.

Requirements

The basic requirement in Holland is that a student must have completed high school at a level comparable to the Dutch high school, which has a six-year track leading to further education at a research university, as well as any university college affiliated with them, and a five-year track leading to study at a university of applied sciences. The IB (International Baccalaureate) diploma is seen as an equivalent of the six-year track. If you will have a non-IB diploma, you generally must have at least four AP scores of 3 or better for it to be considered equivalent to the six-year Dutch diploma, although there are variations. The University of Leiden, for example, will take three AP scores if you have a 3.5 GPA or better. These equivalencies are common in countries that require students to pass a national exam to qualify for a high school diploma.

The Admissions Process

The Dutch admit students to programs in one of three ways, depending on the program. A degree program using an open process accepts all applicants meeting the basic qualifications. Selective programs evaluate applicants based on their qualifications, using a holistic evaluation, and accept a percentage of those students. University colleges and honours colleges at universities of applied sciences use selective admissions, as do academies of art or music. You may apply to as many as four programs using the open or selective process through Studielink at www.studielink.nl, a database with which all students must register before studying in Holland; if you apply directly to the institutions you can apply to more. The third way, the "numerus fixus" category, refers to programs with a fixed number of places, such as international business management, and you can apply to only two such programs. You can apply to only one program in medicine, dental science, or physiotherapy.

Students generally begin studies in the fall; in rare instances they may begin in the spring semester. The guidelines for each specific program will provide information about how and when to apply and when you will receive your decision. The admissions process may require one or two essays and an interview, as well as academic or professional recommendations. Students applying in the visual or performing arts will need to submit a portfolio or audition and interview.

THE INTERNATIONAL FOUNDATION YEAR

In addition to the conditional acceptance we previously described, another possible response to your application to a university in the UK, Ireland, or Holland is a conditional acceptance contingent on the successful completion of a Foundation Year or Programme. Not all universities include this path to entrance, but many do. Trinity University Dublin describes their program as "aimed at students who have the drive and ambition to attend a world-class educational institute, but cannot begin an international undergraduate degree directly. Our International Foundation Programme is a year-long programme designed to allow students to develop the skills required to succeed and excel in a competitive university environment."[5] You may apply directly to a Foundation Programme, although many of those who enroll have applied unsuccessfully to a selective university and have been advised to take this year of study to prepare for their preferred program.

YOU'VE FINISHED YOUR APPLICATIONS—WHAT'S NEXT?

Completing your applications is a major milestone in the college admissions process. Although you may still have a few things left to do (for example, checking on the status of your application and signing up for interviews), as well as submitting any scholarship applications and financial aid forms not done previously, the bulk of the work is now behind you.

If you have built your college list well, you will have at least one and probably several good choices come April. Now you can return to being a fully engaged student, keeping your grades up, and participating in meaningful extracurricular activities. But don't take it too easy. Colleges will see your final grades in June!

CHAPTER 11

Making the Most of Your Special Talents

ell before actually applying to college, student athletes, visual artists, and performers need to prepare to showcase their talents if they want them to be considered part of the admissions process. Athletes need to determine the level of their ability and decide whether to try to be recruited at colleges that offer athletic scholarships or focus on schools where they can participate in intercollegiate athletics without a scholarship. Students in the arts need to research the available options and continue to develop the skills required by the programs they are considering. Visual artists need to prepare a body of work to submit in a portfolio, and performers need to prepare for auditions. The spring or summer before junior year of high school is not too early to begin. Athletes in some sports may find recruitment starts even earlier, sometimes much earlier.

THE STUDENT ATHLETE AND ATHLETIC RECRUITMENT

As we noted in chapter 2, athletic talent can be the biggest hook of all for admission to a selective college. A very strong athlete who wants to play in college can receive a big boost from athletic ability. It might also result in an athletic scholarship if you are recruited by a school that offers them. This is the dream of many college-bound athletes. Alternatively, you may simply want to have a chance to play the sport you love, regardless of any other benefits that might come with it. The key is finding the right athletic fit; the nature and level of involvement will vary greatly from student to student.

The Structure of College Athletics

As a prospective college student athlete, you need to understand how college athletics is organized. Colleges belong to one of two main national athletic associations. The best known is the National Collegiate Athletic Association (NCAA), whose teams appear on national television and are closely watched by ardent followers all over the country. The NCAA has more than 1,100 schools sorted into three divisions. It sets very strict rules for its member colleges for how many and what kind of athletic scholarships they may offer and how they can recruit and compete. Rules vary by division and sport and frequently change. The list of NCAA membership by division and sport can be found at www.ncaa.org. The National Association of Intercollegiate Athletics (NAIA) is less well-known and has about 250 participating schools, mostly smaller colleges. Almost all NAIA schools offer athletic scholarships of some kind. The NAIA colleges and sports are listed at www.naia.org. A few popular sports are not represented in either association—men's rugby and men's rowing, for example. A third organization, the National Junior College Athletic Association (NJCAA), governs competitive athletics programs at about half of the community colleges in the United States.

NCAA Division I

Division I (D-I) in the NCAA houses the most athletically competitive programs. With the exception of the Ivy League, all offer partial or full athletic scholarships, depending on the sport. The 350 D-I schools must field teams in at least 14 sports. Some you hear of frequently, such as the University of Notre Dame, Stanford University, and the University of Alabama. Others you hear little of in a sports context, unless you happen to be a fan of the college, such as Manhattan College, Eastern Illinois University, and Seattle University.

NCAA Division II

The more than 300 Division II (D-II) schools offer some scholarships and are less competitive athletically and academically than most D-I schools. They tend to be regional universities, such as the University of Wisconsin, Parkside, and California State University, Chico, as well as private colleges, such as Pace

University in New York and Regis University in Colorado, that draw students primarily from their geographical region. The level of athletic competition at D-II schools tends to be in the middle between D-I and D-III.

NCAA Division III

Division III (D-III) schools are often more selective academically than D-II schools, though this varies greatly, and they are usually, but not always, less competitive athletically. D-III schools cannot offer athletic scholarships. D-III schools include many liberal arts colleges from Bowdoin College and Amherst College on the East Coast to Linfield College and Whitman College in the West. A small number of research universities such as Emory University, New York University, and Carnegie Mellon University also belong to D-III. D-III coaches want to win just as much as the well-publicized D-I schools do, and some D-III teams are perennial competitors in national championships in a particular sport, such as Kenyon College in swimming and Trinity College in squash. A few D-III schools have one D-I sport, such as ice hockey at Union College and Clarkson University, and they may offer scholarships in that sport. D-III is the largest NCAA division, with about 450 member schools.

WHAT A STUDENT ATHLETE SHOULD CONSIDER

First, you need to determine the level of athletic competition that is right for you given your athletic ability and commitment. In men's soccer, for example, you will find schools with teams at either the D-I, D-II, or D-III level that belong to an athletic conference governed by NCAA regulations. As we just noted, athletic competitiveness generally decreases from DI to DIII. Many schools will also have a soccer club team, not bound by NCAA rules, which plays competitively with fewer restrictions and greater access. Which one is right for you?

Get an Honest Assessment of Your Athletic Ability

If you hope to participate at the NCAA level, you need to consider the division where you fit athletically and determine if your skills will make you competitive as a recruited athlete for the schools you are interested in. It is important to make this assessment as realistically as possible. Seek honest advice from a high school or club coach who knows you well by early in your junior year or even before, depending on your sport. You can also get advice from coaches you meet at summer athletic camps.

Understand the Time Commitments

You also need to understand the time commitment to practice, team travel, and competition schedules that come with intercollegiate athletics and how that will affect your academic work at college. D-I and D-II programs demand the most time, often 30 hours per week and sometimes more in season. D-III is less demanding. A recent survey of 30,000 D-I athletes has highlighted concerns about athletic time commitments, leading college sports officials in the Ivy League and Power Five conferences to revise rules to ease somewhat the time demands on their athletes. Regardless of these changes, however, it is always important to consider the time you will have to devote to athletics, especially if your level of ability might result in your being admitted to a school that would otherwise be a big academic stretch for you. Some student athletes stop competing in their sport at college because of academic pressures and demands. Other students continue to play but their academic records suffer because of their athletic commitments. Balancing college sports and college-level academics requires significant time management skills and a strong drive to succeed at both. Be sure to learn about what would be expected of you as a team member.

I was excited to be recruited to play my sport at an Ivy League school. Before I committed, I met with the coach again, who told me that he would be asking players to commit to 6 days of long practices and games a week during our season. I didn't see how I could do that and still keep up with challenging academics. Although many people couldn't understand how I could turn down that opportunity, I realized it was my life, and I had to make the decision that was right for me and attend another college.

STUDENT ATHLETE WHO EVENTUALLY FOUND THE RIGHT FIT

Ensure Your Eligibility to Play

Both the NCAA and the NAIA require students to register with them to ensure eligibility to play at the intercollegiate level. Student athletes who plan to apply only to D-III colleges do not need to register. Sign up with the NCAA Eligibility Center at www.eligibilitycenter.org by the end of your junior year in high school if you plan to play in Division I or Division II or with the NAIA Eligibility Center at www.playnaia.org if you think you might play at a NAIA college. The registration fee in each case can be waived for eligible students; ask your school counselor if that might apply to you.

The NCAA and the NAIA require student athletes to meet specific GPA and SAT and ACT requirements to be eligible to play. The NCAA further specifies that you complete certain core courses by the time you graduate from high school. Your school should be registered with the NCAA and NAIA and have the NCAA core courses approved. Verify that your course schedule will include the required number of approved core courses before you graduate. Do this early in high school so that you can make adjustments if necessary. You can view the list of approved core courses at your high school through the NCAA Eligibility Center website.

When you visit the NCAA or NAIA website, take a moment to download their student handbooks—the *NCAA Guide for the College-Bound Student Athlete* or *NAIA Guide for the College-Bound Student Athlete*. Each contains a wealth of information about the rules governing athletic recruiting for its member colleges. You and your parents should read the guide carefully and scour the rest of the site so that you will know what to expect and what is expected of you. The guide will be a valuable resource and reference for you throughout the athletic recruiting process, our next topic. For simplicity, we will assume you are interested in NCAA schools.

What Is Recruiting All About?

College coaches are always looking for athletic talent. Sometimes that talent comes to their attention when high school students are nationally ranked in their sport, receive sports-related honors, or are seen playing at a summer camp or showcase. Coaches keep track of such students with an eye toward actively recruiting them when it comes time for college admissions. If you are an exceptionally talented athlete, often referred to as a "blue chip" athlete, coaches may find you with little effort on your part. The vast majority of college-bound student athletes, though—even the most talented—have to work to bring themselves to the attention of a coach and make the first contact, rather than wait to be discovered. They have to "self-recruit." Either way can get you a spot in a coach's recruiting database, which is the starting point for the process.

Be Proactive

Begin your college search early so that you can identify colleges that meet your academic and social needs and offer the opportunity to play your sport at the right level for you. Your high school or club coach should know of colleges that have recruited students with your athletic ability in the past. Do the research about their academic programs and life on campus in addition to their athletic program. After all, you will be a student there, not just an athlete. You have to like the school for itself, not just the coach or your future teammates. If you have identified schools on your own that would be a good academic fit, you can, for example, estimate whether your 50-meter freestyle time is fast enough to swim on their college team by looking at the team statistics. Targeted research will help you identify a good athletic fit and a good academic fit.

Reach out to college coaches at schools that interest you early in your junior year (or earlier in some cases). Cast a wide net at first; coaches expect you to do that. Many schools have

> In the simplest terms, a coach's goal for athletic recruiting is to identify, evaluate, recruit and gain commitments from potential players in order to build his/her program. Once the coach secures a firm commitment from a player, the coach then reciprocates that commitment by giving official "support" for the athlete's candidacy to the admission office.[1]
>
> *UNDERSTANDING ATHLETIC RECRUITING*

recruiting forms on their websites for prospective athletes. If a school does not have an online form, send the coach an e-mail expressing interest and include basic academic and athletic information about yourself, and explain why you believe the school would be a good fit for you. In either case, the coach will probably send you a detailed questionnaire in response, which you should complete and return immediately. Depending on the sport, athletes may also include a YouTube link with highlights of their performance in games or competitions that makes it easy for a coach to take a quick look.

If you don't hear back from a coach after a reasonable period of time, contact the coach again. They get a lot of inquiries, and some slip between the cracks. If you still don't hear back after two or three tries, though, the coach is probably not interested. Just move on past this apparent rejection and find others who want you. Of course, if you hear from a school, respond immediately. Coaches will expect to deal with *you,* not your parent. Stay in contact with the coach to provide updated information and to convey your continued interest.

Consider participating in regional summer showcases, holiday tournaments, or summer sports camps to develop your abilities and to give you access to college coaches, particularly at the schools that interest you. College coaches routinely scout championships and showcases and teach at summer camps where they can see you play. They watch your interaction with fellow players and your coaches as a predictor of how well you will fit into the college team's culture, so show yourself to be as good a team player as you are talented in your sport.

Let coaches you contacted know in advance where you will be. It is also a good idea to ask your high school or club coach to contact those coaches to discuss your ability and potential. This applies not only to those who may see you play at tournaments or in camps but also for all college coaches whose programs may interest you.

Recruitment Guidelines

Recruiting is an intricate dance with coaches looking at as many potential athletes as possible and athletes looking at as many schools as possible. Coaches have to replace graduating seniors, and students have to find the right academic fit, the right team fit, and in some cases, the right scholarship fit. Recruiting can be as different for each sport as the sports are from each other.

The NCAA sets rigid guidelines that govern the recruitment process in each sport. These rules govern when, how, and how often a coach can contact a prospective athlete. The rules are designed to ensure that eager coaches do not overwhelm young athletes, and now that the pressure of athletic recruiting has reached into sophomore year of high school in some sports and even earlier in others, this concern is heightened. You can find the guidelines that govern your sport and division at the NCAA website. Check the athletics websites of the schools you are interested in as well to investigate further the policies of those schools and their athletic conferences. By and large, the rules bind the coaches more than the students, but you should know what they are so that you will know what to expect.

At many colleges, the admissions office gives coaches a specific number of slots to fill with their highest-priority recruits. They can submit additional names, but those athletes won't get priority from the admissions office—they'll be treated like all the other applicants.

It is essential for student athletes being recruited to find out as early as possible where they rank on a coach's list. We will talk about how to do this further on in this section. Coaches have to recruit more students than they need, because they have no guarantee all will remain interested in their school and eventually enroll. In addition, a coach may not know the full potential talent pool until late in the recruiting season. A student who is high on the list at an early stage may be bumped down by more talented late arrivals. Knowing where you stand is important.

How Coaches Know You Will Be Admissible

As we noted previously, being a recruited athlete is the most powerful hook in college admissions. Ultimately, though, the admissions office makes the final decision. Colleges and coaches are under great pressure to ensure that their student athletes succeed academically and graduate with their peers. This generally prevents them from recruiting athletes who fall too far from the usual admissions standards.

> It is important to remember that this is a college admission process with an athletic component, not an athletic recruiting process that comes with the opportunity to attend college.[?]
>
> NESCAC STATEMENT ON COMMON ADMISSIONS PRACTICES

Screening for Admissibility

Regardless of the specifics of their process, all colleges have a way of determining whether a recruited athlete meets their standards for admission above and beyond NCAA or NAIA minimum eligibility standards. It is crucial for the coach to be sure that this review is done before making a commitment to you. If a coach gets ahead of the admission process and promises admission before the admissions office has reviewed your statistics, it can lead to major disappointment.

The athletics questionnaires you will fill out early in the recruiting process will ask for information about your grades and test scores to give the coach some preliminary information about the strength of your academic record. It is a good idea to do some test prep early and have some early test scores that you can report. Testing in the fall or early spring of junior year will also give you additional opportunities to retest if your scores fall on the low side for the schools that interest you.

The Academic Index

The Ivy League maintains its academic standards for athlete admissibility using a calculation known as the academic index (AI). The AI is a complex calculation that takes into account GPA and test scores and is computed for each prospective athlete. Although their admissions processes give a big boost to athletes on a coach's list, Ivy League colleges have agreed to limit just how big that boost can be. The basic premise behind the AI is that the academic credentials of recruited athletes overall and individually should not deviate too much from the credentials of their classmates.

An acceptable AI places an athlete in a group, or "band," at one of four levels, with very few places in the band with lower credentials and more places in the band with higher academic credentials. The goal is to have the bands balance out to the required AI overall. Many D-III colleges, such as those in the New England Small College Athletic Conference (NESCAC), use a similar banding process.

A young athlete at my child's private school was superb in her sport. An Ivy League coach showed intense interest and encouraged her application so forcefully that the private school's counseling staff thought it was a done deal. The girl was denied early decision. Turns out that the coach was new and inexperienced and had encouraged the girl without checking with admissions to see if she had an admissible profile. She didn't make the Ivy League grade for athletic recruits.

MOTHER OF TWO ATHLETIC RECRUITS

HOW CAN I TELL IF A COACH IS REALLY INTERESTED?

In general, the more personal the contact you get from a coach or someone in his office, the greater the degree of interest in you as a potential recruit. Initial contact may be formal—questionnaires exchanged, brochures mailed—but over time as a coach's interest in you gets more serious, the contact will become more personal. Being invited to visit campus at the school's expense is a particularly good sign. It means that the coach likes what she has seen so far and would like to get to know you better. She is willing to invest some of her limited budget to recruit you.

Official and Unofficial Visits

D-I and D-II coaches may invite athletes to campus at the school's expense for an "official visit." NCAA rules specify that schools can offer only a limited number of official visit invitations, and students may accept a maximum of five D-I invitations. D-III coaches may also offer official visits but they are uncommon. You can visit, of course, but at your own expense. D-II and D-III official visits do not count against the five-visit limit.

During a visit, you will focus on the athletic program, but you should also ask questions about academic life, go on a regular admissions tour, sit in on the information session, and visit a class if you have not already done so. You should also schedule an appointment with an admissions officer. Good coaches will help facilitate this. You are exploring the school and the team. On the athletic side, this is your opportunity to investigate policies about vacation time, training, graduation rates for athletes, and time commitments during the season and off-season.

It is also an opportunity learn about the kind of academic support that is provided through the athletics program. Many D-I and D-II schools have academic support for their athletes who practice and compete long hours each week. Not everyone needs this, of course, but it is nice to know the support is there. Athletic department advisors work with coaches to ensure that student athletes have the tools they need to succeed academically as well as athletically. Poor academic performance can restrict an athlete's eligibility to play and, of course, to graduate. Also ask about whether the demands of your sport make some majors and academic activities, such as afternoon science labs, less accessible and whether options such as study abroad and internships mesh with the sport program and schedule.

Ask the Coach Directly

Coaches like to use generalities, such as, "I will give you my full support" or "I can see you playing for us right away." These comments sound encouraging, but they may be misleading because the coach may put you near the bottom of the list despite his or her apparent enthusiasm at the time. Listen carefully to what a coach is actually saying, and try to get specific information about where you stand and what influence the coach may have with the admissions office.

Once you have a sense that a coach is seriously interested in you for his team, you should ask him directly where you stand on his list and whether he would

> Dealing with college coaches in the fall of your senior year is flattering but nerve-wracking. A coach may call and write every week, insisting that you're the 6'2" center she needs for her basketball team…but you don't know how many other 6'2" centers she has on her call list as well, and she only needs one for next year. If you delay committing, and another of those players commits, your phone will go stone cold, and you'll never know what happened.
>
> COLLEGE FRESHMAN HEAVILY RECRUITED TO PLAY WOMEN'S BASKETBALL

advocate for you with the admissions office. You should also ask if he has already shared your academic credentials with the admissions office for an early read on admissibility. As we noted, it is the coach's job to check with admissions before making a commitment to you. Some athletes are hesitant to ask a coach these questions directly, but they have heard it before, and they will respect your directness. You want honest, concrete answers.

MAKING THE COMMITMENT

At some point in the recruitment process, a coach may offer you a spot on his team. It may initially take the form of a verbal commitment, which is a verbal promise of a spot on the team and future support in admission from the coach in exchange for your verbal commitment to play for the team. Although this is a serious step, it is not ultimately binding on either the coach or you, the athlete. Verbal commitments may be made many months or even years before college applications are due, and either party may decide to cancel the understanding.

If, however, you are successful in the process in D-I or D-II in any sport and are later offered an athletics scholarship or other athletics financial aid that you wish to

> Recruiting puts some kids under tremendous pressure to apply ED. Most coaches told my daughter that the only influence they had was in the ED cycle—if she waited and applied regular decision, they could not help her. I don't know if that was the truth or just a ruse so that the coach would know which students were serious enough about the college to merit further attention.
>
> PARENT OF A HEAVILY RECRUITED ATHLETE

accept, you may be asked sign a National Letter of Intent (NLI), contractually binding you to that college for one year. The NLI binds the coach as well and guarantees your athletics-related financial support for one year. The signing date differs from sport to sport. (Information about the NLI can be found by searching for NLI at www.ncaa .org.) Neither the offer nor your signing the NLI, however, is an absolute guarantee of admission, though it would be very surprising if the coach and the admissions office were not in agreement. It does occasionally happen.

If you are not offered an athletics scholarship or other athletics aid or are being recruited at a D-III school that does not offer scholarships, the NLI will not apply. In such cases, college coaches may sometimes say that they will guarantee you a place on the list they submit to admissions if you agree to apply early decision to their school. They want to be sure that you are committed to their team. Accept the offer only if you know you want to attend that school and will be happy there. Later, you might be injured and be unable to play, your coach might leave, or your sport might be eliminated for budget reasons. In such cases you would want to be attending a college you love regardless of whether you are on the team. Placement on the coach's list may be no bargain if the school itself does not excite you. Remember that you want to be in control of your own decisions as much as possible.

IF YOU ARE NOT RECRUITED

Depending on the sport and division, a strong athlete who was not recruited may be offered a spot as a recruited walk-on who receives attention from admissions even though he is not a scholarship athlete. This can happen if a coach finds the athlete too late in the recruiting process but really wants the athlete.

And even if a coach has returning and recruited athletes, plus a few invitees, you may also be able to try out successfully as a walk-on, especially at the D-III level, once you arrive on campus. Some sports, such as rugby or rowing, may even have slots for an athletically inclined novice regardless of level.

In addition, you may enjoy playing on club or intramural teams and find the competition rewarding and the time demands much more workable. A strong athlete who can lead less talented or experienced teammates is also a gift to the community. Love of sport is not only about level of competition, as many volunteer coaches attest.

OPTIONS FOR THE STUDENT ARTIST

Whether you are a visual artist or dancer, a writer or composer, an aspiring critic or stage technician, you have much in common with other student artists if you plan to have the arts be a major focus of your studies in college. In choosing a school, you will have to decide the kind of program you want, the breadth of curriculum you would like outside your artistic field, and the general learning environment. You also face a more complex admissions process that will start earlier than that of your non-artist friends and may include an audition or portfolio to help schools evaluate your talent and artistic achievement.

Alternatively, you may simply be interested in showcasing your talent as part of the overall college application process, even though you are not planning to major in the arts in college. How can you best do this? We'll have tips specifically for you at the end of this section.

PURSUING THE ARTS AS THE FOCUS OF YOUR COLLEGE STUDIES

Students interested in majoring in the arts have a wide range of colleges and specialized conservatories and art schools to choose from, depending on the kind of educational experience they are seeking and their level of talent. Many colleges have strong arts programs that are part of their regular curriculum. At these schools students may major in music or studio art, as well as physics or French. They offer lots of options. Conservatories or art schools have the sole mission of training arts professionals at the highest level. These highly specialized schools are usually stand-alone schools, although some are part of a college that offers study in many fields other than the arts and offers dual or double degree opportunities.

Students interested in studying the arts can also choose among several types of degrees that vary in their extent of professional focus. Thinking about the type of degree you want will help you make wise choices about your other options.

Bachelor of Arts

The bachelor of arts (BA) in a college with strong arts programs will give you training in your art as well as a broad liberal arts education in which you also take courses in other academic areas. This is the degree most commonly offered by liberal arts colleges or colleges of arts and sciences within research universities. You would pick a major in your chosen arts field but also usually take a number of general education courses as well as other courses in the arts and sciences. A dance major pursuing a BA might take History of the Middle East in a class with Arabic majors or a zoology class with biology majors in addition to courses in dance. You might even choose to double major in something quite different from your art because of general interest or as a springboard to a career. Studio art majors who add a biology major may seek a career in scientific illustration, for example, or combine art with computer science and work in electronic game development.

Students pursuing a BA arts major typically take about 40 to 50 percent of their course work in the arts, leaving 50 to 60 percent for other courses. The typical BA degree in the arts places roughly equal emphasis on academic studies in the arts and studio-type or workshop-type courses.

The BA degree in the arts is not meant only for students who want to pursue careers as professional artists because the BA, regardless of a student's major, is specifically designed to give students a broad-based education that can lead to many different careers. Because their arts program is part of a larger campus, students pursuing a BA in an arts field can also take advantage of the full array of activities that are part of day-to-day life at their college, from athletics to a wide range of campus clubs and study abroad.

Bachelor of Fine Arts and the Bachelor of Music

In contrast to the BA in an arts field, the bachelor of fine arts (BFA) and the bachelor of music (BM or BMus) are initial professional degrees specifically designed to train students to be professional artists. The BFA is offered in arts areas such as dance, musical theater, creative writing, and occasionally in music. The BM, and the less common BMus, are reserved for degrees in music. The percentage of course work in the arts increases to about 70 to 75 percent in a BFA or BM program. These degrees are offered by professional schools in the arts—conservatories or art schools—and by some schools and departments within colleges and universities. Admissions offices for these programs look for solid academics, but they are primarily interested in your talent and artistic ability. Many are highly selective and admit only a small percentage of their applicants.

The levels of focus and intensity in BFA or BM programs are significantly greater than that found in BA arts programs. Opportunities to take courses in areas outside of the arts may be limited by time as well as lack of accessibility, especially at schools that are not part of a campus with a broader range of majors.

> At a traditional liberal arts school, one can also take a broad range of academic classes and choose to either double major or minor in an academic subject and as well as major in dance. Those opportunities are usually quite limited in conservatory or BFA programs.
>
> PARENT OF A DANCER REFLECTING ON AN ADVANTAGE OF A LIBERAL ARTS PROGRAM

Similarly, the opportunity for a traditional college experience outside of class may be limited, depending on the school.

Examples of free-standing conservatories and art schools that are not part of a college or university include the Juilliard School, Ringling School of Art and Design, and the California Institute of the Arts. These programs are highly focused and offer only a limited number of courses outside of the art forms represented within them, and they do not offer the array of extracurricular experiences found on a typical college campus. Other conservatories, such as those at Oberlin College, University of Rochester, and Lawrence University, combine a university or liberal arts college and a separate music conservatory on one campus, each distinct but linked to the other. These schools offer interested and energetic students the option of a dual-degree program, usually taking five years to complete, in which a student can get a BA in a field other than music and a BM in the conservatory.

Cross-registration between a college and an arts school also expands the possibilities if you seek a BA and a traditional college experience but want a more intense arts education: a student at Columbia University or Barnard College can take courses at the Juilliard School, for example, and a Mills College student can cross-register at the California College of the Arts.

> Since practically every college/university has a theater major, we found it very helpful to look at the course catalogs online. You very quickly can see what they offer—whether it's more of an overview, a very academic approach, lots of hands-on experience, or a combination of academics and training classes.
>
> TIP FROM A PARENT ABOUT HOW TO NARROW THINGS DOWN

Finding the Right Arts College for You

Begin with your teachers. Your art, dance, theater, or music teachers know your work and have seen your potential. So do those you have worked with through community theater, church choirs, or regional orchestras. Discuss whether a BA or BFA/BM makes more sense for you. Ask for suggestions about colleges and programs that offer what you want to study and that might be a good match. Offerings differ widely, even among schools of the same general category. For example, some music conservatories focus on classical music, and others focus on popular music. Still others include classical and jazz but no other contemporary forms.

If the timing and location work for you, go to one of the Performing and Visual Arts College Fairs sponsored by the National Association for College Admission

Counseling to talk with representatives from art schools, conservatories, and college arts programs around the country; ask about their programs and their special requirements. You can find the date and location of the nearest fair and the colleges that will be represented at www.nacacnet.org. National Portfolio Day is another opportunity to learn more about programs specifically in the visual arts; we will discuss it in more detail further on in this section.

It may help to participate in summer arts camps and programs, especially during the summers after sophomore and junior years. These programs help you build your skills and define yourself as an artist, and they immerse you in a community of artists much as you would be in a college arts program or a conservatory. You can see whether you really like this intensity and community feeling, and it may help you build your portfolio or prepare for auditions. In addition, your teachers will be professionals who may teach in college and conservatory programs themselves and even be involved in admissions at their home institutions. They will be a great resource to discuss your thoughts, aspirations, and choices.

If visiting colleges is important in general, visiting a conservatory, art school, or arts program is doubly so. Seeing the work produced as well as the studio facilities, performance spaces, and practice rooms is invaluable because you will be spending much of your time in those places surrounded by people producing that kind of work. Meeting the faculty and speaking with current students introduces you to the intense artistic community that will be yours for (at least) four years. Music students should also arrange for a lesson before their campus visit if possible, and dance students should arrange to participate in a class. A working visit will show the faculty members your coachability that may not be seen in an audition. Try to visit early during your junior year so that you have plenty of time to shape your college list and prepare the portfolio or audition material that will likely be an important part of your application.

AN OVERVIEW OF THE APPLICATION PROCESS

Timing and the sequence of application steps can vary widely for different art forms and different schools. Some very good BA programs admit students to an arts major without requiring a portfolio or audition. These can be

> Auditioning for a music school is all about finding the right teacher, more important than the name brand of the school. Visiting in person is a must if at all possible, and do your best to get a lesson with the teachers in your instrument.
>
> ADVICE FROM MUSIC GRADUATE

excellent options for some students. Other BA programs require a portfolio or audition, as do BFA and BM programs. In the sections that follow, we preview what your application experience will be like if a portfolio or audition is required.

Visual arts programs as well as those in creative writing and music composition tend to have later deadlines to allow for inclusion of senior work in the portfolio, although some offer an early decision option with a corresponding early deadline. If you are applying to performance programs, you may have as many as three deadlines, all prior to December 1: one for submitting a prescreening DVD, one for scheduling your audition, and one for the actual application. Some programs require that you submit your application first before submitting a portfolio or requesting an audition. Finally, if you are applying to a visual or performing arts program that is part of a college or university, you may have two different applications: one to the school itself and one to the performing arts program. It is really important to stay on top of the deadlines for each part of this complex process.

Some programs have many more applicants than available spaces, and competition can be intense. You want to put forward your best work, be it in portfolio form or in an audition, as well in other parts of your applications. You also want to have a list of schools that vary in likelihood of admission for you. But remember that schools are not looking for perfection—they are looking for talented, coachable students who are deeply committed to their art. Keeping that in mind may make the process a little less daunting.

My daughter has decided to major in dance and wants to pursue a BFA. Yikes! I am overwhelmed with the amount of time we will have to spend in the next few months getting ready for college auditions and applications.

MOM WHO REALIZES ARTS APPLICATIONS TAKE A LOT OF WORK

Portfolio and Audition Requirements

Whether you are a visual or performing artist, you need to carefully study the portfolio or audition requirements of each college, as well as any other requirements. College and program websites have detailed information about what they want you to submit as well as how to submit it. For visual artists, including those in theater design and tech, some colleges require CDs or a PowerPoint presentation or have a SlideRoom portal to which you upload your images. Performing artists may have an in-person audition but may also need to submit a prescreening audition tape first on DVD or through an online portal. Remember to read the instructions for each college carefully and follow them exactly. This is the single most important piece of advice we can give you. If you have any questions about requirements, call or e-mail the admissions office.

Résumés and Recommendations

A common requirement for all artists is the résumé. This summarizes your experience, giving the years you studied each aspect of your art, where you studied, the names of your teachers, any awards or honors you received, and any special programs or course work you undertook. Musicians, dancers, and actors would provide their repertoire; visual artists would list any exhibitions. Actors will also need a "headshot" and dancers a "head and body shot" done by a professional photographer.

You will be asked to provide a recommendation from a teacher who knows your artistic work well. When we discussed recommendations in chapter 10, we noted that colleges generally require recommendations from teachers in core academic subjects such as English, foreign language, mathematics, science, and social studies. Artists are an exception: all artists should have a solid recommendation highlighting their artistic achievements and promise. Art schools, conservatories, and most arts programs require it, and you would be at a serious disadvantage if you apply without it. So ask for a letter from an art, music, theater, or dance teacher as an extra recommendation if the application does not specifically request one. This could also include an artistic recommendation from an instructor at a camp or artistic intensive.

Your Statement of Purpose

Other common requirements involve discussing your work, whether in an interview or in an essay or artist's statement. Be prepared to address your creative process, your challenges and successes, and your vision. Talk about the artists you enjoy, the music that speaks to you, the performances that delight you, the role art plays in your life now and as you imagine your future. Martha Graham once said, "A vitality, a life force, an energy, a quickening . . . is translated through you into action, and because there is only one of you in all time, this expression is unique." Introduce your admissions readers to your uniqueness.

The "Why Us?" Question

Many arts schools and conservatories will ask a leading question wanting to know specifically what that school has to offer that is appropriate for your level of study as well as how they can help meet your future goals. This is a critical question in the application, and you need to craft a thoughtful answer.

The Visual Arts Portfolio

Requirements vary by school and may have specific and unique assignments, such as a home test or a self-portrait or selections from your sketchbook. Most colleges requiring portfolios list what kinds of work they want you to include on their website.

Assembling Your Work

Gather your work from the past two years, lay it out, and determine which pieces speak to your ability and potential. Ask your teacher to review your work with you for an objective critique. What is required beyond the work you have already done? That is your task for senior year. Overall, you need to present 10 to 20 pieces. You want to show the range of your interests and skills as well as your personal focus. If your high school does not have a strong arts program, consider taking a continuing education or summer course in portfolio development at an art school or local college at some point before your senior year.

Attending a summer or pre-college arts program the summer before 12th grade is an excellent way to not only create more portfolio-ready work but also to see whether attending an intense BFA arts program is a good fit. It is much easier to create an excellent portfolio when you have 30 to 50 or more works of art to choose from when narrowing to the final 12 to 20 portfolio images.[3]

BARRY BEACH, INDEPENDENT COLLEGE CONSULTANT AND FORMER DIRECTOR OF ADMISSIONS AT OREGON COLLEGE OF ART AND CRAFT

National Portfolio Day

At portfolio day events around the United States and Canada sponsored by the National Portfolio Day Association, you can take your work to be reviewed by any of about 50 US and Canadian art schools and programs. Participating colleges are nonprofit, regionally accredited, and nationally accredited through the National Association of Schools of Art and Design.

Because of large crowds, come early and decide in advance which colleges to seek out first to increase the likelihood that they will indeed be able to speak with you before the end of the day. The schedule and list of art schools can be found at www .portfolioday.net. In addition, most colleges of art provide a portfolio review when you visit their campus if you have scheduled it in advance. This can be an excellent way to get feedback from colleges to which you are most interested in applying.

Documenting Your Portfolio

When you have assembled your portfolio, you need to photograph it. You can have this done professionally or do it yourself. Photograph each piece separately using a neutral background and good lighting (some say that outdoor light is best). The piece should fill the camera frame, and three-dimensional work should be photographed from several angles using lighting that helps define edges or textures. While uploading your files, assign each image a number, identified with your name, the title (if any) of the work, the date it was done, its medium, and its dimensions. If you send slides, be sure that the colleges to which you are applying will accept them. Label them and send a separate typed description sheet of the portfolio along with it. Be sure to keep master copies of everything that you send.

Notes for Abroad: United Kingdom

If you are applying to a British college of art and design, you need to prepare a very different portfolio. Most of these art schools are interested mainly in process: they want applicants to present their creative ideas from inception through development and encourage students to submit their most recent work even if it is unfinished. They value the interview in particular because they can talk with you about your creative process and artistic goals. These schools also emphasize including your sketchbook to show your exploration of ideas, techniques, and media.

FOR FILMMAKERS, WRITERS, AND THEATER TECH AND DESIGN

Required materials for filmmaking programs vary widely, from only visual information to only written information. Although most film programs at colleges of art want a visual portfolio, film programs at liberal arts colleges or universities often review writing samples only. Application requirements can range from photographs or a short film clip, to a full film with script or storyboard (or both), to just a script. There is usually a 10- to 20-minute time limit for film but sometimes as little as 5 minutes.

Samples of screenwriting or other creative writing should be about 10 pages, but many BA and BFA programs in creative writing do not require portfolios or do so only during a student's freshman or sophomore year in college. Students interested in theater tech and scene or costume design typically will need to submit a portfolio of their work for freshman admission.

The Performing Arts Audition

Auditions are a critical part of the application process for actors, singers, dancers, and musicians. Scheduling and preparing for auditions starts early. Auditions can be scheduled as early as October and most commonly take place in January and February of your senior year, either on campus or in major cities around the country.

Plan Your Schedule

First, consider how many auditions you can do in a day; we advise limiting yourself to one, with the possible exception of acting because theater auditions are usually relatively short. Music auditions sometimes involve sight-reading or music theory tests, as well as specific prepared (and often memorized) performance pieces. Dance auditions may involve dancing in class groups as well as solo. Before you start to schedule, check the college websites for precise information on the audition. Consider your energy as well as time; auditions can be draining.

Scheduling is like assembling a puzzle: you start with one piece, and arrange other pieces around it, sometimes rearranging until it all fits. Some colleges do not schedule an audition until they have received your application, and others may want to prescreen you from a DVD or recording uploaded onto a website or a dedicated portal. Make a spreadsheet with deadlines and requirements. If you must schedule two auditions in one day, be sure to get a time frame from the first college so you have enough time to get to the next one. The earlier you can plan and arrange your audition schedule, the better. You should be able to get all the information you need by late summer or early September, if not earlier, with very specific guidelines for your instrument, monologue and song selection, or dance techniques.

Theater Auditions

Over two dozen colleges offer centralized theater auditions during the first half of February through Unified Auditions in New York, Chicago, Las Vegas, and Los Angeles, allowing students to travel to one location and audition several times over the course of a day or two. For musical theater, a single audition may last most of the day. Participating schools, locations, and dates may be found at www.unifiedauditions.com. Some colleges that are not a formal part of the Unified Auditions use the same locations and schedule, and other colleges usually offer audition slots around the country on specific dates as well as on their own campuses. At an audition you may be asked to modify your monologue performance in different ways. An audition also usually includes some discussion with the evaluators about the craft of acting and your own experience. They want to see how teachable you are. At some colleges, the audition can involve callbacks either at the unified auditions or on the campus.

My son auditioned at fourteen schools and applied to two non-audition schools. We had very large pieces of white butcher paper taped to his bedroom walls—one was a matrix of all the schools, spaces for scores/transcripts, recommendations sent, audition scheduled, etc. This helped us see at a glance what was left to do at any given time. We kind of turned his bedroom into a "war room," which sometimes it felt like the process was.

THEATER MOM

Music Auditions

Music auditions usually include a general information session, ear-training, and music fundamentals or theory exams, and about 20 minutes of actual performance following a warm-up. They may take place on the school's campus or at locations around the country. Some schools allow an off-campus audition if the student lives more than a few hundred miles away. Both on-campus and off-campus auditions may be videotaped for further faculty member review. When colleges require a prescreening process, they review recordings submitted on DVDs or uploaded to a portal before scheduling an audition, and many require at least a partial application. Early audition options at some schools enable you to stretch out the audition scheduling and build audition experience before January and February when most schools hold their auditions.

Dance Auditions

Dancers usually participate in two different technique classes and present a short solo, either a repertory piece or original choreography, and also interview with faculty members. Because you will be dancing, expect a dress requirement. You might be asked to dance *en pointe,* so don't hang up your toe shoes prematurely. If you submit a DVD instead of auditioning live, requirements are clear and specific, and they usually cover a range of ballet and modern. You may also be asked to include an oral statement about your goals in dance.

SHOWCASING YOUR ARTISTIC TALENTS AS PART OF A GENERAL APPLICATION

What if you are not interested in applying to an arts program but want to bring your artistic ability to the attention of an admissions committee so that it will be part of the review of your application? As we discussed in chapter 2, colleges seek to build a freshman class with students who will contribute in many different ways, including through their artistic activity. One way to make admissions committees aware of your talent, of course, is to include your participation in the arts in the activities section of the Common Application and other applications. However, students with a deep commitment to the arts as well as notable talent can do more to ensure that colleges consider their talent in the admissions process.

How and What Should You Submit?

Colleges using the Common Application may give students the opportunity to submit arts-related material through a SlideRoom portal integrated with the Common App. Others colleges, those that use the Common App as well as those that don't, may have their own forms and process for submission that may or may not involve SlideRoom. Procedures vary by college, so you have to check websites carefully to see how each one handles submissions for your specific art form— dance, music, theater, or visual arts.

Unlike conservatories and art schools that clearly specify what an audition or portfolio must include, many colleges do not provide detailed information about what to include in your supplemental submission. As you assemble your art or plan your audition for taping, your teachers will be your best resource. Most arts teachers have seen many students through the process. Admissions offices may also provide you with further guidance. Another helpful resource is the information on portfolios and auditions provided on the websites of conservatories and arts schools.

How Is Your Arts Submission Reviewed?

After your arts submission is received by the admissions office, they will generally send it to the relevant academic or artistic department for review. There may be an earlier deadline to compensate for the extra processing time. The admissions office will then receive a professional assessment of your supplementary material from its own faculty members. When the evaluation comes back to the admissions office, it is entered into your file and is considered part of the overall application.

If the evaluation indicates exceptional ability in a given area, your talent may serve as a significant admissions hook, especially if it is highly desirable to the college. If the evaluation of your work isn't particularly strong—if, for example, you are just good, not great, at the piano—it won't hurt you because you cannot be faulted for trying, but it probably won't help either. A small number of schools discourage the submission of supplements unless the student's level of talent is very high; these colleges include this advice in their submission instructions.

If you have any questions about how to submit evidence of your talent, call or e-mail the admissions office. The website will often give you the name of a specific contact person for arts-related questions. The earlier you do this the better, because it often takes significant time to prepare your portfolio or audition materials.

Finally, if a college does not provide a way for you to submit supplementary arts-related materials, consider writing about your interests and achievements elsewhere in the application in addition to listing them among your extracurricular activities. The "additional information" section of most applications is a good place for this. If you have a great deal of information to share, consider putting it in an arts résumé format containing details about teachers, workshops attended, performance or exhibits, and so on. Because the arts are an important part of your life, conveying that will give a college a fuller sense of who you are and what you will contribute to the campus.

CHAPTER 12

Students with Special Circumstances

Students with disabilities, homeschoolers, and those planning to transfer each have special considerations in their college search and selection process. If you fall into one or more of these categories, key information in this chapter will help answer the many questions you no doubt have.

STUDENTS WITH DISABILITIES

Do you receive or have you been offered accommodations in high school such as extended time on tests, extra help keeping on top of assignments, large-type books because of a vision problem, or the option to leave class for brief periods of time without needing permission because of a medical condition? If so, you are far from alone. About 10 percent of students who plan to enroll full-time in colleges and universities in the United States meet the federal definition of *disabled*, making them eligible for various types of accommodations from their high schools. You are probably familiar with the terms *504* and *IEP* if you belong to this group.

WHAT IS THE DEFINITION OF DISABILITY?

The federal government considers you to have a disability if you have a medical or psychological condition that substantially limits a major life activity such as walking, eating, concentrating, learning, and so forth. Some disabilities, such as those that affect mobility or vision, are usually fairly obvious. Others, such as learning disabilities, attention deficit hyperactivity disorder (ADHD), autism spectrum disorder, psychological disabilities, and some medical conditions, are not. They are considered hidden disabilities. All, however, qualify you for certain legal protections if the condition impairs a major life activity.

When students with a federally defined disability prepare to apply to college, the first question they (or their parents) often ask is whether the disability should play a role in the decision about where to apply. Following soon after is the question of whether the disability should be disclosed to colleges at all before the student is accepted. Then, if the answer to the second question is yes, the next question is how to do this in the most positive way. The answer to all of these questions, as is often the case, is, "It depends." There is no one-size-fits-all answer because students have widely differing disabilities and accommodations. This section is designed to help you figure out the answers that work for you, including how to request appropriate accommodations on the SAT or ACT if needed. As we discuss further on, you will need up-to-date documentation regarding the nature and extent of the disability to obtain accommodations on the SAT or ACT as well as to obtain accommodations once in college.

THE MOST COMMON DISABILITIES

The most common diagnoses that allow accommodations in high school are learning disabilities—a broad, umbrella-type category that includes such things as dyslexia, processing speed problems, and dysgraphia—and ADHD. To simplify the discussion, we focus here on accommodations for these disabilities, although much of this can be adapted easily for students with physical disabilities that affect mobility, vision, or hearing, as well as for students with psychiatric disorders and other medical conditions.

Before we discuss the specifics of college selection and application, we first want to share some background information to help you better understand the differences in the federal laws that apply when you are in high school and the laws that apply once you enroll in college. The differences are important because the services offered by a particular college may differ, sometimes greatly, from what you have come to count on.

WHAT LAWS APPLY IN HIGH SCHOOL

Two main laws define and protect the educational rights of high school students with disabilities.

The Individuals with Disabilities Education Act

The Individuals with Disabilities Education Act (IDEA) is a federal law designed to help students from preschool through high school whose disabilities require special education services. Depending on the disability, the help provided can be extra time on tests, tutoring, more frequent breaks, testing in a quieter environment, orally administered exams, or other kinds of assistance, in addition to special classes or modifications to the regular curriculum. The law requires that the appropriate services for each eligible high school student be provided free of charge and that they be documented in an Individual Education Plan (IEP) or other intervention plan. Coordination with the student's public school district may be needed for students who attend a private high school or who are home-schooled if district funding is needed to support the services.

The IDEA is an education law designed to promote student success in K–12. Students with a disability who can nevertheless function adequately in a regular classroom without any additional educational support would generally not qualify for services under IDEA because they have demonstrated that they can be successful without them.

Section 504

A second route to help for students with disabilities is Section 504. Section 504 is part of the Rehabilitation Act of 1973 that prohibits discrimination against a student whose "physical or mental disability substantially limits one or more major life functions such as . . . seeing, breathing, learning, and walking." The law entitles students to appropriate accommodations for access to educational programs and activities. Unlike students covered by IDEA, students do not have to be eligible for special education services to be covered under Section 504. Accommodations under Section 504 may include access to medication during the school day, use of a school elevator, and extra time on tests for students with a specific reading disability.

DIFFERENT LAWS APPLY IN COLLEGE

The benefits of IDEA end when a student graduates from high school. Replacing it is the Americans with Disabilities Act, or ADA, a far-reaching law that applies to institutions of higher education and businesses.

The Americans with Disabilities Act

The ADA requires colleges and universities to provide students with reasonable accommodations to ensure that they are not being discriminated against because of a disability. It seeks to ensure that qualified students with disabilities can have equal access and opportunity for participation. The IDEA promotes student success; the goal of ADA is to level the playing field. Whereas the IDEA is an education law dealing with entitlement programs, the regulations of the ADA are civil rights protections, just like Section 504.

Student Success Versus Student Access

This difference in approach between promoting student *success* and ensuring student *access* is very important to understand, particularly for students with learning disabilities or ADHD. Some colleges provide the basic access services mandated by the ADA, and others go beyond—in some cases, well beyond—the minimal requirements. Each student needs to determine what he or she needs to be successful and then seek out colleges that can provide the appropriate level of support in addition to the many other qualities that make a school appealing.

Some Important Questions to Ask Yourself

Students who have received accommodations in high school for learning disabilities, ADHD, or any other disability, whether in conjunction with special education services or not, should continue the honest self-assessment begun in chapter 4. Along with your family, you should ask yourself additional questions to help you understand the role your disability and accompanying accommodations play in your education. The greater the role or impact of the disability, the more important it will be to find schools that will meet your needs as they relate to the disability. *The K&W Guide to College Programs and Services for Students with Learning Differences* is a valuable resource that provides an extensive list of questions for a self-assessment that applies to all students with a diagnosed disability of any kind.[1] These are some of the most important ones to ask:

- What is the nature of my disability, and when was it first diagnosed? When were my last diagnostic tests given?
- What is my level of performance in high school?

- Am I enrolled in college-prep courses, modified courses, special education courses, or a combination?

- What accommodations have been approved for me, and which ones do I use and need?

- What are my academic strengths and weaknesses?

- What are my long-term goals, and are they realistic?

With answers to these questions in hand, you and your family will be better able to evaluate colleges and the disability services they offer. Colleges will be interested in this information if you choose to share it with them.

> My son was diagnosed with ADHD his senior year in high school. Because he was very smart and his dad and I helped keep him organized and on track, we did not consider ADHD assistance when he picked a college. That was a big mistake.
>
> MOM OF SON WHO EXPERIENCED DIFFICULTY BUT EVENTUALLY GOT THE HELP HE NEEDED

CATEGORIES OF DISABILITIES SUPPORT

Colleges and universities vary widely in the nature and extent of the support they provide students with disabilities, but each can be placed in one of three broad categories. Knowledge of these categories will help you find colleges that best meet your needs.

Tier One or Basic Support

Most colleges provide what is often referred to as "basic support," or Tier One support. Basic support meets the federal mandate that requires reasonable accommodations for students with disabilities who provide the appropriate documentation of those disabilities. They are sometimes called "limited" or "self-directed programs."

Each college must have a staff member responsible for ensuring that appropriate accommodations are provided for students who submit adequate documentation. Tier One support provides accommodations such as extended time on tests, large-print materials, and access to text-to-speech software. At a Tier One school, the disabilities service office generally provides a student needing extended time on exams with copies of a letter to give to each teacher explaining the need for such accommodations and asking that they be provided. The student is responsible for answering any questions a teacher might have and in general for self-advocating in the process, with the support of the disabilities service office. There would likely be no monitoring of the student's academic progress by staff members trained in disabilities issues, nor is it likely that trained staff members would be available to provide additional disabilities-related support if needed, although there are exceptions. The advising, support, and tutoring services provided would be similar for all students on the campus.

Many students find that the minimal level of disability support provided at Tier One is all that they need to be successful in college. It generally works quite well for students who have strong self-advocacy and time management skills and have performed well in high school, as many hard-working students have.

Tier Two or Coordinated Services

Tier Two support goes beyond the minimum required by law and provides specialized services beyond basic accommodations to students who submit adequate documentation of their disability. Another common term for Tier Two support is "coordinated services." In addition to basic accommodations, Tier Two support can include special tutoring at no cost to the student, special skills classes, and remedial classes when needed.

A Tier Two support college typically has at least one certified learning disabilities specialist on staff to help students develop strategies to meet their individual needs. Tier Two programs typically require students to request services proactively, and monitoring of student progress, if provided, would be modest. Coordinated services work well for students with a solid high school record but who might need help effectively managing their time as well as in requesting accommodations. Students are often surprised by the greater challenges of college work; having support in place early is important.

Tier Three or Structured Programs

The highest level of disability support is known as Tier Three, or "structured programs." These offer the most comprehensive set of services designed to support students with learning disabilities or ADHD. They are also sometimes called "proactive programs."

These programs have staff members with specialized training in learning disabilities and related areas and offer an extensive array of services, such as diagnostic services, special counseling and advising, special courses and tutoring, and a wide array of specialized aids including text-to-speech or speech-to-text software and note takers. Staff members monitor the progress of each student and recommend changes to the program as needed, although the extent of the monitoring will vary from program to program and will likely be less than the student had in high school.

Tier Three schools often charge an additional fee for these special programs over and above regular tuition, and students typically have to submit a separate application to the program beyond the application for general admission to the school. One of the best-known programs in this category is the SALT program at the University of Arizona, with about 600 students participating out of an undergraduate body of about 33,000. Each participant is assigned a learning specialist who meets with the student weekly on matters ranging from self-advocacy to time management, as well as help from tutors on assignments and subject matter areas. Landmark College in Putney, Vermont, is another example. A college exclusively for students with ADHD, learning disabilities, and high-functioning autism spectrum disorder, it offers four-year and two-year degrees.

Structured programs can work well for students who have relied heavily on accommodations in high school and are unlikely to succeed without more extensive support that may include assistance in effectively managing their time. Close monitoring of student progress can be very important to head off problems before they become overwhelming. Structured programs are also very helpful for students with weaker self-advocacy skills.

CHOOSING COLLEGES THAT MEET YOUR NEEDS

I encourage all students to "own the process" and be in the driver's seat. These decisions should be your dreams as long as you have done your "homework." Keep your family on your team, your priorities in order, and enjoy the journey.[2]

MARYBETH KRAVETS, COAUTHOR OF
THE K&W GUIDE

An excellent resource to begin your search with once you have determined the kind of disabilities support that will meet your needs is *The K&W Guide* that we previously mentioned. It gives detailed information about support for students with learning disabilities or ADHD at over 350 colleges and universities, ranging from well-known four-year universities to community colleges. College websites also provide information about the disability services and programs that may be offered for students with learning disabilities or ADHD and other disabilities. A good place to start is a search for "disability services." Colleges that offer a wide range of services and programs generally make information about them readily available on their website, although you may have to explore a bit to find its location. Some additional sources of help are located in the Resources section of *Admission Matters*.

Once you have narrowed your list of schools, visiting them can give you valuable information. Make an appointment to visit the disability services office and talk to the person in charge. Those offices typically work independently of the admissions office so you need not worry that your visit will be associated with your future application unless you choose to mention it in the application. It is also a good idea to ask about what kinds of documentation the office will require if you enroll and wish to access services. Tier Three programs ask for recent documentation as part of your formal application to the program. Colleges offering Tier One and Tier Two levels of support ask you to submit documentation after you are admitted. Knowing the requirements in advance of enrollment will help you be prepared.

SHOULD I DISCLOSE MY DISABILITY ON MY APPLICATION?

Families often wonder whether a student should disclose a disability on a college application. The decision is almost always a personal one, because colleges cannot ask about disabilities or needed accommodations on the application. The only exceptions, of course, are those programs specifically designed for students with such disabilities. Structured programs such as SALT typically require students to submit two applications—one to the college and the other to the structured program itself. In these cases, the disability is an important part of the application, and disclosure is a given.

But what about disclosing in general? Sometimes students feel that their need for accommodations may disadvantage them relative to other applicants or that they don't want their disability to be highlighted on their application when they are considered for admission. The choice about whether to disclose is really up to you. It can actually help to disclose your disability if any of the following situations applies to you:

- Your grades (or your test scores) are lower because of the disability.
- Your disability was identified later in high school, and your grades have improved significantly since.

- Your disability has affected the classes you took in high school; for example, you have not taken a foreign language, or you regularly take study skills courses that most other students do not take.

- Your disability has affected the nature and extent of your involvement in activities outside the classroom.

Disclosing will help admissions officers put your application into context and answer the questions that would naturally arise in their minds when reading your file: "Why did her grades go up so much in junior year?" "Why are his test scores so low relative to his academic performance?" It is generally better to provide the answer yourself rather than have admissions officers guess the reasons. Colleges cannot by law discriminate against you in the admissions process because of your disability, and learning disabilities and ADHD are now so common and so commonly disclosed that admissions officers are very familiar with them. In fact, disclosing can actually help you if you have shown the personal qualities, such as determined hard work, self-advocacy, and insight, that colleges want to see in general and in particular for students with learning disabilities. The additional information section of the Common Application and other college applications is a good place for this information.

A special case has to do with certain medical and psychiatric disorders because they frequently affect a student's academic record and other aspects of high school life. Sometimes disclosure of a medical condition, whether physical or psychiatric, is unavoidable because of facts on the transcript, such as a medical withdrawal. In such a case, you should stress the extent of your recovery and your confidence in taking on college life. Again, insight, maturity, and thoughtfulness in providing this information on your application will go a long way. You want to minimize the thought that you are a risk. We caution against disclosing too much detail, because it is not really necessary at this point.

> Because the A.D.A. is outcome neutral, we are not looking to maximize a student's performance so that they can do the best they can. We are looking to provide equal access.[3]
>
> SUSAN MICHAELSON, DIRECTOR OF TEST ACCOMMODATIONS, ACT

STANDARDIZED TESTING— ACCOMMODATIONS AND MORE

Students with diagnosed disabilities of all types that warrant accommodations may seek them from the College Board (for the PSAT, SAT,

SAT Subject Tests, and Advanced Placement Tests) and from the ACT (for the ACT).

The most frequently requested accommodation is extra time, usually time and a half, but accommodations can also include frequent breaks, a separate testing site, testing over multiple days, large-print materials, use of a computer for the essay, and others. Some accommodations are offered at the regular test site, but other types may require in-school testing at another time. The College Board and ACT do not flag or annotate test scores obtained with accommodations, so colleges cannot tell whether you had any.

Families seeking test accommodations should work through the student's counselor to obtain them. The counselor or another person designated by the school will submit the request for accommodations, along with supporting documentation as needed, through the online systems for the College Board or the ACT. The College Board or ACT can approve accommodations, deny them, or request additional information before making a decision. The College Board has recently overhauled its process so that the majority of students who are approved for and use testing accommodations through a formal plan at their high school will have those same accommodations automatically approved for all College Board tests, including SAT Subject Tests and AP tests.

> I encounter students who come into class the first day with a note from student services and a detailed plan for helping them in class (everything from note takers and/or tape recorders to extra time on exams). Aiding these students is a breeze.
>
> COLLEGE TEACHER COMMENTING ON THE VALUE OF ADVANCE PLANNING

The process of requesting accommodations needs to start early. Accommodations should be approved and in place at least a week before a test date to ensure that there will be time for the appropriate arrangements to be made.

Information about the process for obtaining accommodations on tests administered by the College Board may be found by searching the College Board website at www.collegeboard.com for "Accommodations for Test Takers with Disabilities" and the ACT website at www.act.org for "Services for Examinees with Disabilities." These websites will also provide information for families who are unable to work through a school to obtain accommodations and who need to follow a different process.

After You Have Been Accepted

Whether or not you have disclosed your disability on your application, once you are accepted, we encourage you to contact the disabilities services office if you have not already done so to find out what documentation is required to be eligible for accommodations.

The process varies from school to school, so get this information as soon as you can. In general, most schools require testing done within the past three years, and any IQ test must use the adult version (as opposed to the version for children). For many students, this will likely mean retesting at their own expense if they do not have the appropriate test results available. Sometimes, though, your family may be able to arrange for the testing through your high school if you would otherwise be retested in 10th or 11th grade. Schools often administer the adult version of the IQ test if requested and if the student was on schedule to be tested. Advance planning can potentially save worry, time, and a lot of money.

TIPS FOR HOMESCHOOLERS

Over the past 25 years, homeschooling has become an increasingly popular option for American families. Homeschoolers are very difficult to count, but the National Home Education Research Institute estimates that over two million students are homeschooled in the United States. If you are reading this section, you are probably one of them.

Families homeschool for many reasons. The most often cited are concerns about school environment, a desire to provide religious or moral instruction, and dissatisfaction with the academic program available in other schools (including a wish to provide a more challenging curriculum). Athletes competing and training nationally and internationally, artists performing around the globe, and students with serious health issues are also among the homeschooled. Whatever the reason or reasons, although you and your family have chosen homeschooling for high school, like most homeschoolers you probably see a traditional college education as your goal.

Colleges Welcome Homeschoolers

The good news is that most colleges welcome homeschoolers. Many have considerable experience evaluating the credentials of homeschooled students, and some have developed formal admissions guidelines and policies for homeschoolers.

You will find that colleges generally evaluate homeschoolers based on the same criteria as other students—grades, rigor of curriculum, testing, activities, essays, interviews, and recommendations.

As you approach the college application process, we advise you to try to emulate the approach and research of a regular high school applicant as much as possible. Everything we have said in *Admission Matters* about self-inquiry, visiting colleges, writing essays, preparing for standardized tests, and deciding on a balanced list of colleges applies to homeschoolers as much as to regular students. On several points, however, the experience of homeschoolers does diverge significantly, and you need to take special care so that you will have the strongest possible applications.

In the remainder of this section, we will briefly consider each of these points. Additional insights into the process at specific schools may be found on college websites by searching for "homeschool applicants" or "homeschool guidelines." If you can't find the information you need, contact the admissions office and ask. Getting this information early will give you the time you need to prepare for the admissions process.

> Hamilton welcomes applications from home schoolers. Home schoolers have been part of our community for many years, and we recognize the particular assets they bring to college life: initiative, independence, and a penchant for learning creatively.[4]
>
> HAMILTON COLLEGE ADMISSIONS WEBSITE

Grades and Transcripts

Most colleges, and certainly all selective ones, will want you to have taken a broad array of courses in high school. This will usually include laboratory science and a language other than English. Although colleges may grant you some flexibility because you followed your passion for ornithology for a year but didn't take a basic biology course or read Greek and Celtic mythology without a regular English class, you want to avoid looking unbalanced. College is the time to specialize. Even if your homeschool curriculum is unusual, you have to think about meeting colleges halfway and ensure that your curriculum meets basic requirements.

Colleges want to see grades, but they mean something only in a comparative context. Even in a regular high school, all As don't help much if half the class gets all As. Similarly, if you are the only one in the class and your parents are your teachers and give you all As, it is hard for a college admissions officer to use that information to compare you to other applicants, even other homeschoolers. It can help if you supplement your homeschooling with some regular courses from a high school, community college, or quality online program—anything that allows the college to evaluate your record relative to other applicants. Special cases are students who have used the full high school diploma curriculum and teacher support of a distance learning school such as Laurel Springs School or the Oak Meadow School. Those students will find that the organization itself provides a transcript and recommendations much like a regular high school. The same is true of public virtual schools and academies.

Test Scores

Standardized testing is often more important for homeschoolers than it is for traditional applicants because colleges have greater difficulty in evaluating your grades. Even many test-optional colleges will require or strongly recommend that you report SAT or ACT scores to help them evaluate your preparation for college. Similarly, SAT Subject Tests and Advanced Placement (AP) tests can help a selective college evaluate the rigor and your mastery of your curriculum. Good scores on several SAT Subject Tests can strengthen your application, and many colleges recommend that homeschoolers take them, even if they are not recommended or required for traditional applicants. If you want to take AP exams, you need to contact a local high school several months in advance to register for them because they are offered only in high schools each May; registration is through a school.

A recommendation should come from someone who really knows the student well. It is not about the title of the writer, but about the applicant as a student and as a person. It is about really filling a gap in information and anticipating questions an admissions officer will have—about engagement and thinking aloud with others, about comfort with other people and with instructors, about the ability to self-advocate and to follow curiosities and see things through.[5]

BRUCE POCH, EXECUTIVE DIRECTOR OF COLLEGE COUNSELING AT CHADWICK SCHOOL AND FORMER DEAN OF ADMISSIONS, POMONA COLLEGE

Recommendations

Is your mother your "school counselor" as well as your teacher? Can she write an objective recommendation letter on your behalf that will be persuasive to a college admissions officer? Some colleges will want such a letter. Beyond this, anything you can do to supplement your file with recommendations from others not related to you who have taught you will help as well. Here, courses taken at a high school or community college, or even from a private tutor, can be especially valuable because you may be able to ask an instructor to write a recommendation for you. Claremont McKenna College also requires an extracurricular recommendation for homeschoolers, preferably written by a nonfamily member who knows you in the context of your larger community: a coach, employer, or clergy member, for example. They want to assess your social skills beyond your academic credentials. Consider adding such a letter even when it is not explicitly required.

Activities

Participation in activities is important for all high school students, and especially so for the homeschooled. Precisely what you choose to do is not important, but it is good to show energy, commitment over time, and social experience that demonstrates you get along well with your peers. Because you generally won't have access to clubs and activities at your local high school, seek out opportunities in your community. If you are a musician, take private lessons and participate in a local orchestra or choir. Athletic club teams can bring together students from different schools, and those interested in drama can participate in community theatre. Scouting and religious organizations provide excellent opportunities. Community service activities are also ideal for homeschoolers, because a flexible schedule can be very helpful. Opportunities abound.

Interviews

Although we think it is a good idea for all students to take advantage of an interview with an admissions officer or alumni interviewer, we strongly recommend that homeschooled students have an interview if one is available.

> I asked them to write me recommendation letters about how I function as a leader and as a member of a community. Because when you ask for recommendation letters as a homeschooler you have to think about what admissions officers take for granted from a public school student that they wouldn't take for granted from a homeschooler.
>
> HOMESCHOOLED STUDENT NOW ATTENDING COLLEGE

In fact, some colleges require that homeschoolers interview as part of the application process. An interview gives you an opportunity to talk about your experience as a homeschooler, discuss your aspirations, and display your social and communication skills firsthand. The interview tips we provide in chapter 10 will be helpful to you.

Highlighting the Homeschool Experience

Parents: Keep good records of your child's education from ninth grade on, including what textbooks you used, what books your child read for English, and what special projects she worked on. Special projects are an advantage for homeschoolers, who can demonstrate more easily than regular high school students that they can pursue projects on their own and take responsibility for their own education. Colleges like this ability, but they want details. Having this information readily at hand will help your child when it comes time for her to fill out her application.

Students: Explaining why you and your family chose to homeschool, how you went about it, what you accomplished, and how you feel about it now will all be important elements of your application. Homeschooled students often use the additional information section on an application to provide this kind of detailed information. Homeschooling can take very different forms for different students. The individual student must frame the picture of his home school experience for admissions officers.

IN SUMMARY—WHY YOU SHOULD START EARLY

We cannot stress too strongly that you need to be proactive much earlier than regular high school students in finding out what specific colleges will want from you in terms of required course work, testing, recommendations, and the like. Most colleges want to see an explanation of the reasons for homeschooling, how you approached it, and a comprehensive overview of your curriculum, including descriptions of the courses taken and the books used in those courses. Each college is likely to be different, however, in terms of what it asks for specifically. A call to discuss requirements with an admissions officer at each college you are interested in is a good idea if information on the web is incomplete or unclear. As a homeschooler, you will probably not have access to the resources found in a high school counseling office, so the process of applying to college may be more challenging. The extra work, though, will be well worth the effort.

MAKING A CHANGE: HOW TO SUCCESSFULLY TRANSFER COLLEGES

The largest number of students who transfer colleges have enrolled in a community college with the idea of completing the requirements for transfer to a four-year college in two years. Others enroll immediately after high school in a four-year college that accepted them, while also intending right from the beginning to transfer as soon as possible to a school they prefer more. Still others find that their first school turns out not to be such a good fit after all.

Sometimes students want to transfer for very tangible reasons. Perhaps the cost of tuition, fees, and living expenses turns out to be too great a burden despite some financial aid, or family circumstances may force you to move closer to home. Maybe you have developed an interest in an area of study not offered by your current school, or you have found the academic demands of the school to be too great (or not challenging enough).

Other reasons are less tangible. You might find that you are lost in the big university you thought would be exciting with a big stadium full of devoted fans on six Saturdays in the fall. In hindsight, you realize you would be more comfortable at a smaller school. Alternatively, you may find that the small school you loved at the outset now feels too small or too isolated geographically, and you want a bigger school. Maybe you find the student climate (or the actual climate!) uncomfortable at your current school. Or you might feel homesick and just want to be closer to home.

Much of what you have already read in this book applies to transfer students because the process is very similar to the freshman process but with some twists. In this section, we discuss the similarities and differences to help you decide whether transferring makes sense for you. If you conclude the answer is yes, we'll advise you how to move forward.

SOME TRANSFER BASICS

Many colleges like to admit transfer students because they are generally a bit older, are more mature, and bring a seriousness of purpose with them when they enroll. Transfer students have also been put to the test by their previous college, so a college does not have to predict whether a student will do well in college because transfer students have an actual college track record that they can evaluate. Transfer students also help colleges fill gaps in their enrollment from students dropping out, stopping out, or transferring themselves.

Here are some important points about transferring to keep in mind:

- Colleges vary greatly in how many transfer students they admit. Some of the most selective colleges are even more selective for transfer admission because they have so few open spots to accept these students.
- Students generally transfer at the end of either their first or second year. Most schools want a student to be enrolled for at least two years of credit in order to award a bachelor's degree from that school.
- State universities often have articulation agreements with community colleges in the state to ease the transfer process for students. Students who meet grade point average requirements in a set of general education and preparation for major courses may be guaranteed admission.
- Colleges vary in how much weight they place on standardized tests and your high school record in the transfer admissions process. That weight may depend on whether you transfer after one or two years. The later you transfer, the less weight they will carry. In most cases when a student will be transferring as a junior, they might not matter at all. If your high school record and test scores were modest, be sure to check with the college where you are thinking of transferring to see what they will ask for. If they will look at your high school record and testing, remember that although you can't change your high school record, you can improve your test scores.
- Applications are generally due by February 1 or March 1, although some may be earlier or later.
- Decisions are generally made later than for freshman admission. Students can be notified as early as the end of April, but generally by June 1.
- Colleges vary widely in how much financial aid (need-based and scholarship) is available for transfer students. You need to ask.

Is Transferring Right for You?

The decision to transfer from one four-year college to another is complex. Most decisions made to transfer after two years tend to be well founded. By that point, students have a good idea of what their current school does and does not offer, as well as the advantages and disadvantages of transferring. Assuming a student has a clear, realistic view of the options, submitting transfer applications can make good sense.

More problematic are decisions to transfer after one year, which means that students may have decided to transfer in their first semester of college, in other words, not long after they have enrolled. Because applications are due in late winter or early spring, you generally need to begin the process early in the second semester. Is that really enough time to know if a college is a good fit for you? Previously in the book, we discussed how there are no perfect colleges but that there are plenty of colleges where a student will be perfectly happy. Have you looked beyond any immediate problem, such as an incompatible roommate or a couple of teachers you may not be too excited about? Have you joined clubs or gotten involved in activities that interest you? If you find some of your classmates in freshman classes unengaged, have you gone to a professor to see if you can get involved in research? (Yes, freshmen can do research. Professors like them because they will be around a long time.) If you are having academic difficulties, have you sought help from the academic support services center or your teachers or teaching assistants?

If you are considering transferring after one year for these or any other reason, we encourage you to talk to others about it. A good place to start is the advisor you were likely assigned when you started school. Some schools assign an academic advisor as well as a peer advisor, a junior or senior specially trained to help first-year students. Talk to one or both or to the dean of students or someone in that office. Talk to your parents. The problem may resolve itself with a bit of time.

> When I applied to college, I was wait-listed or denied at my top schools. So I went to Big State U. determined to transfer ASAP. But I didn't transfer. I found that the honors programs, opportunities to know professors, and the undergrad research made what I thought was going to be my "back-up school" my dream institution.
>
> STUDENT WHO HAD PLANNED TO TRANSFER BUT DECIDED NOT TO

One student we know went back to talk to his high school counselor after one semester at college. The college was too small, he said; there was just one party each weekend—always the same party, it seemed. The counselor volunteered to help with the transfer process if he wanted to pursue it, but he never heard from the student again until the end of his junior year. The student said he was now very happy at his college. When the counselor asked what, in retrospect, had been wrong freshman year, the student replied, "I was a freshman."

How Does the Application Process Differ for Transfers?

Many colleges use the same application for transfer students that they use for freshman admission, with some modifications. We will use the Common Application as an example to illustrate how the transfer process differs from the one you went through as a freshman—the same principles apply to most other applications as well.

> I've been rejected everywhere I applied as a transfer. Granted, I did apply to schools with low admit rates and knew that I was probably going to be rejected.
>
> STUDENT WHO ENGAGED IN WISHFUL THINKING AND NEEDED A BETTER LIST

Your Grades in College Courses

Although your high school grades and curriculum were likely the most important factors in your admission to college as a freshman, your college academic record will now be the most important factor in transfer admission. Staying engaged academically, even if you are disillusioned with the program where you are enrolled, is very important. You will be asked to report your current college courses or those you have taken during the current academic year, as well as submit a transcript from each college you may have attended.

Certainly many schools will review your high school transcript and test scores, especially if you are transferring after just one year in college, but your college record will receive more careful scrutiny. One college we know counts the high school record as roughly two-thirds of your academic record if you are a first-year transfer and only one-third if you are a second-year applicant. Some colleges publish the minimum college GPA a student must have to be considered for admission as a transfer. Meeting the minimum, however, may not be enough, especially if a college receives many more transfer applicants than it has room for and the intended major you stated on your application is very popular. Admissions officers also know that some colleges grade more strictly than others, just as high schools do.

Colleges with open admissions or lenient admissions policies are good options for transfer applicants who find their current academic environment too demanding and whose college grades have suffered as a result. Selective colleges, by contrast, want to see evidence of strong academic performance.

Your Reasons for Wanting to Transfer

The second difference between the Common Application for freshmen and transfers is a required prompt for your personal essay. You will be asked to address your reasons for transferring and the objectives you hope to achieve. The strongest transfer applicants have a compelling, mature reason for wanting to transfer.

The answer is easy, of course, if you are completing a two-year degree: you need to transfer to receive a bachelor's degree. If you are already enrolled in a four-year college, perhaps you cannot pursue a newly discovered academic interest at your current school because no major is offered or the school has few small seminar-style classes or not enough opportunities for undergraduate student research. Maybe the sport or other activity you wanted to pursue has been discontinued or is under-supported. Lots of compelling reasons can prompt a transfer application.

When I was in high school applying to colleges, I selected schools based on their location, what I thought their academic programs were like, and their social reputation (in that order). I thought location was more important than anything. When I transferred, I still considered all of these factors, but location was at the end of the list. I was much more focused, much more mature in my thinking, and I knew what I wanted out of my academic experience.

HAPPY TRANSFER STUDENT

Staying Engaged

The third difference between the freshman and transfer application is the time period for which you will be asked about your activities. Instead of grades 9, 10, 11, and 12, you will be asked to list extracurricular and work experiences for grades 11 and 12, as well as freshman, sophomore, and junior years of college, if applicable. Quite reasonably, colleges are more interested in how much you have contributed at your current college and how that may have supported your academic interests than what you did in your high school years.

This means that even if you enter as a freshman intent on transferring at the first opportunity, you should still get involved in the life of your school as soon as you can. This may even lead to a change of heart about transferring. Through that community service project or club sport, you may find your niche. But even if that doesn't happen, that activity will strengthen your transfer application. Colleges want transfer students who will be engaged, contributing members of the campus community, and the best predictor of future engagement is your most recent level of activity.

Activity itself is usually enough. College freshmen and sophomores rarely hold the leadership positions, such as editor of the school paper, president of the student body, and captain of a sports team, that they may have held in high school. At a large state university, it may be harder to get involved significantly at the outset. Your transfer colleges will understand this, so don't force yourself to be active simply because you want to transfer. Just get involved in something you like.

"Why Are You Interested in Our College?"

Many schools that accept the Common Application for transfers also require a supplement with questions that often focus on the student's area of academic interest as well as on the by-now-familiar question, "Why are you interested in our college?" Sometimes you will find these two combined into one big question: "How will our college help you achieve your academic goals?" Notice the word *academic*.

Here, as in the freshman application, you should explain as specifically as possible why a particular college would be a great fit. Especially at schools with very low transfer admit rates, generic answers about "outstanding reputation" or "wonderful facilities" will not help you. Schools want to know that the few transfer spots they have will go to the students who will most benefit from them. A thoughtful, insightful response to the "how" or "why" question can help make the case that you are such a student. So you need to do some research on the college and the courses offered in your major of interest. Who are the leading professors in your prospective field? What courses do you find attractive? What intellectual problems interest you?

Letters You Will Need

Public universities that accept community college students or other transfer students after two years generally do not require letters of recommendation to support the transfer application. In fact, if your community college has an articulation agreement with the college you are interested in, your transfer process will be simple, smooth, and predictable. Even without an articulation agreement, you still probably won't need any letters of recommendation.

If you are applying to transfer to private colleges, however, you may need one or perhaps two letters from college instructors, one from a college dean or other official, and perhaps even a secondary school report from your high school. Each college sets its own requirements regarding the forms and letters it wants to see for a transfer application, so you have to check with each school to be sure that you submit what each one asks for.

If your college classes are large and you don't feel you know any instructors well enough to ask for a letter, consider asking a teaching assistant in a discussion section. It is much better to get a detailed letter from someone who knows your work well than a perfunctory letter from a distinguished faculty member who doesn't know you at all. You don't want your letter to say, in effect, "I don't know Joe Smith, even though he received an A in my large lecture class."

Many schools also designate a specific person to write the official "school letter" that many colleges require. Be sure to find out how this is done at your current college by asking early at the student advising office. Again, this varies at different schools and is often done by the registrar or office of student services, so we can't tell you specifically where to go to get this information, but it should be easy to find. Don't feel bad about asking a teacher for a recommendation to transfer. You are not criticizing the faculty member's teaching; you just want to move on. You are not the first to want to transfer, so most faculty members will gladly help you. Providing your professor with a résumé is often very helpful and demonstrates organized and thoughtful planning.

TRANSFER ADVISING, VISITS, AND INTERVIEWS

College visits can help you decide if a particular school is right for you as a transfer student, just as they did for high school students. Colleges that accept large numbers of transfer students may even have special information sessions for transfer students. We encourage you to attend these if you can, because you may pick up tips that will be helpful for your applications. Many larger colleges also have dedicated transfer advisors whose job is to answer questions from prospective transfer students and assist them.

In addition, some schools offer on-site interviews for potential transfer students as well. They can be especially helpful for students who have had a major gap in their education as a result of military service or other reasons. A transfer interview generally focuses on your reasons for wanting to transfer and how you have grown since you first applied to college. Although you will no doubt be asked about your experience at your current school, avoid criticizing it too strongly. Focus instead on what you have learned from the experience and how you will benefit from the opportunities at your new college.

Admissions issues aside, it will also be useful for you to know how many of your college credits will transfer with you to your new college. If you are transferring to a college that has an articulation agreement with your community college, most if not all of your credits will transfer. In all other cases, a course-by-course review is necessary. Private colleges may do this kind of unofficial review for you before you apply, but you have to ask. The designated transfer admissions officer or the transfer advisor or counselor is the place to start.

CHAPTER 13

Advice for International Students

If you are reading this chapter, you are probably one of the many high school students born and educated outside the United States who are not US citizens or permanent residents and who plan to apply to American colleges and universities as freshmen each year. Now more than ever before, schools in the United States welcome applications from international students and value the important contributions they will make to their new academic communities.

Although the information in the rest of this book applies to you as much as to American students, international students need additional information to be successful applicants. You need to understand why the American admissions process is so different from that of other countries and how that affects your application, what additional information international applicants need to provide to colleges, and how American admissions offices respond to applications from international students.

This chapter builds on the information in previous chapters to provide more specific detail and emphasis on issues that pertain to you. Not all of this information applies to all countries equally. We cover some important background information first and then consider specific details for your application. At the end of the chapter, we will discuss briefly other special circumstances, such as undocumented students and foreign nationals educated in the United States.

> Education in the United States is not centralized nationally as it is in many countries, so it's important to note that admission requirements will vary greatly from one university to another.[1]
>
> STACEY KOSTELL, VICE PRESIDENT FOR ENROLLMENT MANAGEMENT, UNIVERSITY OF VERMONT

THE ADVANTAGES AND DISADVANTAGES OF BEING AN INTERNATIONAL APPLICANT

International students bring new perspectives and experiences to campus life and are therefore highly sought after by colleges that want to provide a more global educational culture for their American students. Colleges know that students learn from their peers as well as from their professors, and international students greatly enrich the diversity of the educational experience, inside and outside the classroom. Colleges also have financial incentives to increase their population of international students. A growing number of families from around the world are willing to pay the full cost of an American education at a time when many American families are finding it difficult to do so. The rise in international applicants and enrollments has been a real bonus for American colleges, especially large state universities, who see this expanding market as an opportunity to balance their budgets with full-pay students from overseas and to increase global awareness on their campuses at the same time.

However, some countries, including China, Korea, and India, send many more students to the United States than other nations, so these students may be competing with their compatriots for a limited number of places at some universities. In addition, if an international student has significant financial need, few colleges can provide all of the necessary financial support because international students cannot receive US government financial aid. Further on in this chapter, we will discuss ways to approach the college selection and application process that may help you deal with these challenges if they apply to you.

WHAT ARE COLLEGES LOOKING FOR?

In many countries, university admission is by national exams or university entrance exams, with little else required. As you have realized by now from reading chapter 2, the American admissions process is more complex. It varies from college to college, or from state to state for public universities, and involves much more than exams.

ENGAGEMENT BEYOND THE CLASSROOM

Unlike most universities in other countries, American colleges and universities see themselves as communities. More than institutions with just classes and labs and libraries, they have orchestras, sports teams, debating societies, theaters, newspapers, and some unusual activities that might surprise you. All of this is meant to enrich your educational and social growth. Students learn structured competition through participating in or supporting college athletic teams, and they are enriched by student-produced arts performances whether they actively contribute or just observe. Student organizations provide opportunities for leadership, and community service helps off-campus organizations and serves the local population. The variety and level of activity of an American college community are themselves an education.

These factors affect the application process. The admissions office goes beyond determining your academic readiness to identify how you will contribute to the whole college community. By asking for recommendations from teachers, they want to know how you learn, not just that you have done well. This is a big adjustment for some international students whose school systems emphasize grades above all else. Furthermore, by asking for personal statements or essays, the college wants to evaluate you as a unique individual who will participate not only in classes but also in residence halls and in campus activities.

> Since colleges and universities seek international students who will contribute both inside and outside the classroom, applicants should definitely highlight in their admission applications what they will bring to the campus academically, culturally, and socially.[2]
>
> JAMES MONTOYA, COLLEGE BOARD CHIEF OF MEMBERSHIP, GOVERNANCE, AND GLOBAL HIGHER EDUCATION

INTERNATIONAL STATUS AS A HOOK

In chapter 2, we described the hooks that help a student stand out in the applicant pool. International status can be one of those hooks, especially for students who come from a country or part of the world that is not well represented in the student body. Some countries send large numbers of their students to the United States for a college education, as we previously noted, and colleges can choose among those applicants. But just as a student from Wyoming is a rarity in the Northeast United States and a rural Alabaman unusual in California, so a qualified English speaker from countries that rarely send students to a given college may be sought after as a major addition to the diversity of the student body. To get a sense of geographical diversity at various schools, look for recent class profiles on college websites.

For most international students, one factor that can distinguish them from their peers in their home country, as well as from most American applicants, is

> When applying to schools in the United States, don't try to "Americanize" your application by focusing on your trip to the United States or even your participation in out-of-class activities prevalent in the United States. It won't help differentiate you and may make your candidacy less appealing.[3]
>
> SETH ALLEN, VICE PRESIDENT AND DEAN OF ADMISSIONS AND FINANCIAL AID, POMONA COLLEGE

their political or cultural awareness of their country and its place in the world. Your task is to make your national identity appealing and distinctive.

HOW WILL YOUR APPLICATION BE REVIEWED?

Just as admissions officers read applications from different parts of the United States where they visit high schools and give presentations, a college with a large number of international applicants may divide up the applications to allow officers to develop specialized knowledge of certain countries or areas. Many colleges now send their admissions officers to different parts of the world to recruit students, visit schools, and keep current with education abroad.

There is a knack to reading files from Singapore, India, France, Brazil, or China, so the admissions officer for each country must have special expertise about the different educational systems. These applications are much more different from each other than New York applications are from Florida's or Oregon's. If they need additional information to evaluate an application from an unfamiliar part of the world, these officers can and do consult with colleagues at other universities and with members of their own faculty.

For the most part, international admissions reflects the same pattern of factors that is used in evaluating applications from the United States. Colleges use the same factors: grades and rigor of course work, standardized tests, the student's writing, extracurricular activities, recommendations, and special talents, including music and athletics. Yet as an international student, you are also evaluated through an international lens.

Is there a standard national curriculum in your home country so that all students take essentially the same courses? What are grading practices and standards? Does your school (or the country in general) put little emphasis on extracurricular activities, or are these carried out away from schools, as, for example, in private sports clubs? Is community service an unusual endeavor? Does your school have an idea of what American colleges want to see in a recommendation? (The French, for example, notoriously stint in giving praise. An admissions officer will know this and factor it in.) Of course, some international students attend American-style or international high schools abroad with Advanced Placement (AP) and International Baccalaureate (IB) curricula that are familiar to admissions officers. Their teachers and counselors write American-style detailed and personal recommendations.

WHERE SHOULD YOU APPLY?

As we described in chapter 4, the United States has various kinds of colleges that you may not be familiar with. In particular, the concept of a liberal arts education—breadth of study across the humanities, arts, social sciences, and sciences and mathematics, as well as specialization in a major—is almost uniquely American. It is the main educational philosophy in American undergraduate education, even more so than pre-professional training in fields such as engineering, architecture, or business, although these are popular, too.

Offered at research universities as well as at liberal arts colleges, a liberal arts curriculum enriches your intellectual experience by prompting you to consider issues from the viewpoint of various disciplines. It may surprise you that most American undergraduates begin college without having decided on a major field of study. Not only is that acceptable but also it encourages students to explore fields unavailable to them in high school before they commit to a major field of study. Many secondary school systems in other countries encourage and even require students to specialize in high school. So you may already have a clear idea of your interests and a background in the sciences or economics, for example. That is okay. Admission officers expect that from many countries and you will not be hurt by having a clear sense of direction. But indicating that you are also open to other subjects may help you.

> As an international student, what most attracted me to my liberal arts college was the incredible diversity and smaller size of its student body. The great sense of community made me feel at home, and having helpful and compassionate faculty made my college experience better than I ever could have expected.
>
> INTERNATIONAL STUDENT REFLECTING ON HER EXPERIENCE IN THE UNITED STATES

International students and parents often think that the college a student attends must be known and respected in their home country, which sometimes leads them to apply only to the best-known and extremely selective colleges or colleges whose name includes a state or city they know. In some countries, lists circulate of the 10 or so universities recommended for a wide variety of majors. Given the difficulty of researching institutions in a foreign country in another language, families struggling to distinguish among hundreds of American institutions take these lists seriously. These lists are not reliable or sufficient sources of information, but they do succeed in funneling students into a few colleges and thereby increase the level of selectivity for those students. We suggest you consider some alternative approaches that we describe in the following sections.

START AT YOUR COUNSELING OFFICE, WHICH MAY BE ONLINE

If your school has counselors, teachers, or administrators knowledgeable about American college education, you have an excellent resource to help you. But if not, the Internet offers abundant support. Begin with the BigFuture website, www.bigfuture.org. Also visit www.educationusa.state.gov, the website of EducationUSA, a global network of more than 400 advising centers supported by the Bureau of Educational and Cultural Affairs at the US Department of State. It offers a wide range of helpful information as well as the location of advising centers in each country. EducationUSA centers also host college fairs in different parts of the world, where admissions representatives from various colleges come to meet students. If you attend such a fair, bring a translated transcript, test scores, and a résumé of your extracurricular activities to share with college representatives.

If college fairs do not come to your city and arranging to visit American campuses is not realistic, the Internet can provide good substitutes. You can visit a virtual college fair, as described in chapter 5, designed specifically for international students at www.collegeweeklive.com. You can find virtual campus tours on many campus websites and also at www.youniversitytv.com and www.campustours.com.

Read the Catalog

An often overlooked but very helpful source of information is the college catalog, available on almost every college's website. Look for general information about the educational philosophy of the college, also called its "mission," as well as specific information about graduation requirements, the requirements for completing any majors you might be interested in, course offerings, and so on. It is probably easier to find admissions information on the admissions page of the college website. Admissions offices welcome contact from prospective students, so you shouldn't hesitate to e-mail questions about anything not covered elsewhere.

Check the Basics

As you research colleges, be sure that each college you are interested in is accredited, meaning that the American educational community has certified its academic quality. Most well-known schools are indeed accredited, but if you find a school that is unfamiliar, you can check its accreditation status through the US Department of Education at www.ope.ed.gov/accreditation/. To be sure that a college has been approved by the US Student and Exchange Visitor Program, check with its database, SEVIS (Student and Exchange Visitor Information System), at https://studyinthestates.dhs.gov/school-search. You can also use a SEVIS site to navigate obtaining an appropriate visa, www.ice.gov/sevis/students. The National Association for College Admission Counseling, www.nacacnet.org, has a link to helpful information on student visas on the International page of its Knowledge Center.

Some Thoughts on Agents and Consultants

Some American colleges hire agents overseas to recruit international students. Although these agents may help with the application process, their allegiance may be divided between helping you and recruiting for those specific colleges because they are usually paid by the colleges and your family. If you are working with an agent, you should ask whether the agent also recruits for any universities. Because commercial recruitment agents representing specific universities do not ensure unbiased information about the full range of American higher education opportunities, EducationUSA centers do not partner with them. The use of agents is very controversial in the United States and is the subject of heated discussion in the admissions profession.

Be careful—some educational placement agencies may claim that they can guarantee college acceptance, the I-20 (certificate of eligibility for a student visa), or a student visa. They can do no such thing. Only colleges grant acceptances, only colleges issue the I-20 form, and only the US State Department can issue a student visa. The National Association for College Admission Counseling has published a guide for students entitled *Trusted Sources: Seeking Advice on Applying to Universities in Another Country* that explains these issues. You can find it through the International page at the NACAC website.

Independent educational consultants, if available in your country, are another resource and are not paid by colleges. Some consultants based in the United States work effectively with students overseas through e-mail and Skype, despite the time differences. Some also travel overseas just as admissions officers do. A good consultant should help you and your family to consider the full range of educational possibilities, should make no promises of admission, and should serve as a guide as you prepare your applications, but not write the applications for you. Do your own research to assure yourself that you have explored widely

> EducationUSA advisers refrain from partnering with any recruitment agent who receives compensation in the form of a per-student commission from an institution in which a student enrolls following recruitment by the agent. Agents receiving compensation under such an arrangement cannot be expected to give priority to a student's need to explore the full range of options provided by the diversity of U.S. higher education.[5]
>
> EDUCATIONUSA POLICIES

and have all the facts you need, and be sure to take responsibility for your own applications.

THE ROLE OF STANDARDIZED TESTS

Standardized testing plays a lesser role in American college admissions than it does in most other countries, but it can be an important factor in admissions to any college that requires SAT or ACT scores. Sometimes students can take this to mean that they should devote every school vacation to studying for the SAT or ACT, but, in fact, colleges would prefer to see you spend part of the summer either doing an unpaid internship to explore career choices or volunteering in the community.

A few selective colleges require students to send all of their test scores if they have taken a test more than once. Most allow students to choose the test scores they wish to submit, and still others don't require students to take these tests at all. A word of caution on test-optional colleges: some of them require standardized test scores for merit scholarships, others for certain programs only, and some for all international students. We always recommend that you check with each college. Chapter 6 describes how these tests are used.

Which Test Should You Take?

The SAT and ACT are not available everywhere and at all times. At this writing, students in mainland China who do not attend authorized international schools must take the SAT elsewhere, and usually take it in Hong Kong. The March SAT is not available anywhere outside the United States, for example. The ACT website advises, "Before choosing your test date, view available test dates and centers by country. If there are no test centers in your country scheduled for any test date and there is not a center in another country within reasonable traveling distance, check the requirements for Arranged Testing."[6] So after you discover which tests you must take, find out where and when you can take them. It is good to plan far ahead.

If both tests are available, compare them carefully and decide which one would work best for you. If neither test is offered in your country, colleges that require testing will find it more difficult to evaluate your application but may consider it nonetheless. It is best to take one of the tests if at all possible. Even if a college is test optional, international students should submit their scores because scores from these tests provide a familiar benchmark for admissions officers.

An Important Caution

Recently, unscrupulous organizations in some parts of the world have facilitated cheating on these tests: "While the vast majority of test-takers are honest, a small number of individuals—and a growing number of adults and organized fraud rings—are unfortunately seeking to undermine the system for their own financial gain and jeopardizing the hard work of honest test-takers," notes Kenton Pauls, director of Higher Education Partnerships at ACT.[7] When testing companies detect this kind of activity, they will invalidate scores of compromised tests—even in rare instances invalidating all scores from testing centers where widespread cheating has been detected. If you prepare for the ACT or SAT with a tutor or test-prep company, make sure that they follow the ethical guidelines expected by the testing companies.

TESTS TO SHOW PROFICIENCY IN ENGLISH

Colleges want to be sure that students can do challenging academic work in English. Some may admit students who are less proficient in English but then require them to first complete an English transition program, or bridge program, in which the students must improve their English skills before being admitted to the college's regular academic program.

Colleges determine an applicant's level of English fluency in a number of ways, many of which apply to American students as well: the quality of writing on the application, grades in English courses, a recommendation from an English teacher if provided, living in an English-speaking country, and, of course, standardized tests such as the SAT, ACT, AP, IB, and state exams in other countries if they are in English. Colleges vary widely in how much importance they place on any one of these factors. Colleges also rely on special tests of English language proficiency for international students.

THE TOEFL

The best-known test is the TOEFL (Test of English as a Foreign Language), a four-hour exam developed by the Educational Testing Service (ETS) and given almost exclusively over the Internet at ETS-authorized test centers around the world. It is also available in mainland China, where the SAT is not. It frequently appears with the acronym iBT (Internet-based test; the paper-based test, or PBT, is being phased out and is offered only in areas where testing via the Internet is not available).

The reading and listening sections of the test are scored electronically. The speaking responses are scored by human raters and the writing responses are scored by human raters in combination with ETS's automated scoring system. The TOEFL is scored on a scale from 0 to 120 points overall, with each section worth up to 30 points; the score is valid for up to two years. A score of 80 or higher or even 100 or higher is required for admission to some selective colleges. The international section of a college admissions website should provide minimum TOEFL scores. If it doesn't, that's a good question for the admissions office. Check to see how the minimum is specified: by total score only or by total with minimum subscores.

THE IELTS ALTERNATIVE

A similar test, the IELTS (International English Language Testing System), was developed at Cambridge University in England and has made considerable headway among US colleges. It is most popular in India and Pakistan, where many students apply to British universities as well as American ones. Scored on a 1 to 9 scale, the test takes two hours and 45 minutes, with a speaking component conducted by a live examiner. The IELTS test is primarily paper-based. Detailed information about how the IELTS is scored may be found at www.ielts.org. You are usually required to achieve a minimum score, as with the TOEFL.

THE CHOICE MAY BE YOURS

Many US colleges accept either one, but you need to check with a particular college to be sure. The Educational Testing Service has a tool for comparing a TOEFL and an IELTS score on its website, www.ets.org. Both tests have taken on increased importance because of concern about widespread fraud in the writing of applications from overseas.

EXEMPTIONS FROM TAKING THE TOEFL OR IELTS

> TOEFL and IELTS results help admission staff determine whether a candidate's level of English language proficiency will be a barrier to their academic progress as an enrolled student. It is in the candidate's best interests to take one of these tests to eliminate any question about whether their proficiency is high enough to ensure academic success.[8]
>
> MICHAEL STEIDEL, DIRECTOR OF ADMISSION, CARNEGIE MELLON UNIVERSITY

If you are an international student who has studied in the United States for three or more years and have nearly native-speaker fluency, you may not need to take the TOEFL or IELTS. The same is true of international students who have studied at an American or English-speaking international school. Nevertheless, you should verify this with each college; some selective colleges require very high Evidence-Based Reading and Writing scores on the SAT to waive the test requirement for an international student.

You may want to provide TOEFL or IELTS scores anyway to enhance your application. The Reading and Writing sections of the SAT and Reading and

English sections of the ACT are designed for native English speakers, whereas the TOEFL and IELTS are designed for students who speak English as a second (or third or fourth . . .) language and therefore can highlight your English skills more positively. Many selective colleges recommend taking a language proficiency exam for this reason, because it gives them more detailed information about your English ability. In some cases, a strong score can compensate for weaker standardized test scores in a college's admissions deliberations. In any case, "it's value added to an application," according to one admissions officer from a highly selective college. International students who have studied in English for high school might also consider taking an SAT Subject Test in their own language, if available, to demonstrate literacy skills in their native tongue.

GETTING THE APPLICATION COMPLETED

Applying to colleges in the United States can be a complex process that may differ greatly from what you would experience when applying to colleges in your home country.

DEADLINES

Be aware that the American application process begins many months earlier than it does in most other countries. Standardized tests should be taken before your final year of secondary school, so you have time to repeat a test if needed. The application forms themselves may often be completed as early as August 1 of the year before you plan to begin college and are usually due at some point between October 15 to March 15 of your senior year; the exact deadline varies from college to college. The same deadlines generally apply to all students, international or not, but some colleges may have restrictions for international applicants. Always check the websites of the individual colleges for the most accurate information.

TRANSCRIPTS AND OFFICIAL DOCUMENTS

Most colleges require an official transcript of your course work and grades at the time you apply, sent directly from each high school you have attended beginning with ninth grade. You may also need to provide a photocopy of your current valid passport. Other required or recommended documents may include diplomas, school certificates, and results of national examinations. If not in English, these may need to be sent along with a notarized or certified translation, occasionally accompanied by an evaluation of the education credentials by an approved service that specializes in converting foreign educational information into US equivalencies.

College websites generally describe their requirements and recommendations and designate approved service companies so that you will know how to proceed. You do not need to send copies of awards or certificates of honors unless these are asked for. Those just expand your file with unnecessary material. Always follow the instructions.

Just as with American students, admissions offices scrutinize the transcript to assess the level of difficulty of your courses and how you have performed in each class. Your English grades will be very important, because as an international student, you need to show definitively that you are ready to do college work in English. To ensure accuracy, colleges can hire experts to verify the authenticity of foreign transcripts and credentials.

An offer of admission, whether for an international student or an American student, is always conditional on successfully completing senior year. The high school is required to send a transcript with all final grades and the date of graduation before a student can enroll. If the final grades are lower than those submitted with the application, the college could respond with anything from a harsh letter to academic probation to cancelling the student's acceptance. For many international students accustomed to admission by test, this is shocking—almost unbelievable. Believe it.

EXTRA FORMS FOR INTERNATIONAL STUDENTS

International students need to submit more forms than do their American counterparts, as well as more information generally. If you are studying in a non-American school system, you will need to make sure that your school describes its curriculum and grading system in English. If your transcript is being sent by an approved translation and evaluation service, this information should be included. A school official will usually be asked to provide some additional information about you, such as predicted scores on secondary leaving examinations, if offered. Testing requirements may be more extensive, as we have just discussed. Some colleges also require international applicants to submit statements of financial support, which we discuss further on in this chapter.

Essays and Statements

Each applicant is unique, and it is that singular person whom the college wants to hear, in his or her own voice. In fact, the application essay or essays are often called the "personal statement" for just this reason. As an international student, you should be confident in sharing your unique perspectives. Each country is interesting, and each citizen of that country should have something interesting to say about it. Each country has a culture, a history, a literature, and some relationship with the United States, hostile or friendly. Every student can find something to write about that will bring that culture to the fore in the application.

> This is your chance to write about your interests, long-term goals, and strengths—one of the most important aspects of your application.[9]
>
> EducationUSA Website

This is not essential, of course. An international student can write about sports just as an American can, but an Indian student writing about cricket, a Spanish student writing about soccer (football), or a Japanese student discussing baseball can express something cultural in addition to his or her love of the sport. Global warming may be global, but it is different in Bangladesh and Russia than in the American heartland. It is the quality of the essay that matters most, not the subject alone; your own ideas and experience should always be central.

When Help Is Not Appropriate

American teachers and admission officers assume that all writing submitted is the student's own original work. Admissions officers are experts at detecting the touch of writers who are several years (or decades) older than 18. They may also have access to the essay portion of the SAT and ACT to compare the timed writing there with the more polished application prose. Essays crafted with too much outside help have been an issue for years, from applicants everywhere.

We understand that in some cultures, especially those where admission to university is determined solely or mainly by examinations, application essay writing can be routinely outsourced to hired hands and is acceptable behavior within that culture. Each culture defines acceptable behavior in its own way, but a student entering a different culture is moving to different academic assumptions and protocols, as well as different modes of courtesy and behavior. This begins with the application process itself.

The American admissions process demands that the student be the sole author of the application. This is an important discussion to have with any agent or counselor who may be working with you. Any suspicion that someone other than the student applicant has created any part of the application may result in a dismissal of the application.

SENDING THE APPLICATION AND SUPPORTING DOCUMENTS

It is wise to submit applications over the Internet to ensure timely arrival. In fact, many applications, including the Common Application, are online only. Even if a school accepts a paper application, it may waive application fees if it is submitted online. Check the admissions page of each college website for specific information. If you must mail your application or any other documentation, be sure to keep copies of everything and, if at all possible, arrange for confirmation of delivery. Many colleges require that you set up an account on their website so you can check the status of your application, know what materials have been received, and even read your admissions decision at the end of the process.

RECOMMENDATIONS

Most colleges require a school report, a general recommendation letter by a school counselor or administrator, and require or recommend one or two teacher recommendations. In many countries, this is unheard of. Many international students report that the administrator or teacher they approached has asked the student to write the recommendation for the school official's signature. This may be tempting, but do not write such a letter yourself. Provide the administrator and teachers with a list of your courses and grades, your other activities, and a description of the purpose of the recommendation. The Massachusetts Institute of Technology provides a good and very specific "Guide to Writing Recommendations for MIT" that would apply to any college requiring them, noting that "letters of recommendation hold substantial weight in our admissions decisions. A well-written letter for an outstanding applicant can highlight impressive characteristics beyond his/her own self-advocacy."[10]

To make this process even more challenging, the letters must be written in English or accompanied by a translation and sent directly to the colleges or uploaded to the Common Application or other online application site. You will also be asked to "waive your FERPA right," which is the right granted by US

> Both guidance counselor and teacher evaluations are most helpful when they are specific and storied. They should provide us with the information and impressions we cannot glean from the rest of the application. Try to give a complete sketch of the student and the context of his/her accomplishments. Support your conclusions with facts and anecdotes whenever possible.[11]
>
> "GUIDE TO WRITING RECOMMENDATIONS FOR MIT"

law to read your application file once you enroll at your college. No matter how tempting it might feel to see what your file contains (if, indeed, the college has kept it), we strongly urge you to waive this right so that your letter writers have the power of unfettered honesty. It also shows the college that you trust your recommenders.

INTERVIEWS

Not all colleges offer interviews. When an interview is available, by all means accept the opportunity. It may be conducted in person by an admissions officer or a graduate of the college or by Skype or telephone. Interviews may be useful in assessing your proficiency in English, but they also involve getting to know you better. We discuss interviews in more detail in chapter 10.

PAYING FOR YOUR EDUCATION

For most international students, the opportunity for an American undergraduate education depends on having the financial resources to afford the tuition, living expenses, and other costs. Only a handful of American universities practice need-blind admission for international students and meet full demonstrated need as well. (We defined these terms and others important to understanding financial aid in chapter 8.)

Why? The reason is very simple and entirely based on economics. The US government provides financial support for college for American citizens with significant financial need, even if the amount of that aid may not meet their full need. But US federal student aid is not available to international students. Aside from their families, the only source of financial assistance most international students have is their future American college, although some countries provide scholarships for their very best students.

COLLEGES THAT OFFER AID TO INTERNATIONAL STUDENTS

Many colleges offer substantial, if partial, financial aid to international students. Some colleges are even able to meet the full financial need of those students whom they admit. A comprehensive spreadsheet of nearly 400 US colleges and universities detailing their financial aid policies for international students can be found under Resources at www.educateabroad.com or www.personalcollegeadmissions.com. The spreadsheet is prepared annually by two experienced independent educational consultants, Jeff Levy of California and Jennie Kent of Bogota, Columbia, and is currently the only resource of its kind available.

> Some colleges offer aggressive scholarship programs for international students. Others have very limited aid for internationals. Some offer merit aid to international students. Others are need-based only. It can vary widely from campus to campus, so check the financial aid and international student sections of college websites for specific information about each college in which you have serious interest.[12]
>
> CHRIS HOOKER HARING, DEAN OF ADMISSION AND FINANCIAL AID, MUHLENBERG COLLEGE

APPLY WIDELY

Don't be put off from applying to a school just because it cannot meet your full demonstrated need. Every college would like to do so, but they just don't have the financial resources. But they still have financial aid available, and only the students who apply for it will get it. If you limit yourself to schools that meet full need, you will miss out on other opportunities. A student who needs aid must apply widely and consider colleges that are less well-known in their home country but that have a record of providing financial aid to international students.

As usual, the Internet is a good place to start. In addition to the spreadsheet we already noted, several other websites can also help. Be sure to check for the degree program you are interested in:

- NAFSA, www.nafsa.org
- EduPass, www.edupass.org
- International Student Network, www.internationalstudent.com
- EducationUSA, www.educationusa.state.gov/find-financial-aid
- Funding for US Study, www.fundingusstudy.org/

Be careful not to succumb to offers from unscrupulous agencies promising scholarships: they are easily identified because they ask you for money first. Real scholarship agencies are free of cost to applying students.

Forms and More Forms

Students seeking financial aid from a college may be able to use the College Board's form, "International Student Application for Financial Aid," but they may also need to complete a college-specific form. Sometimes international applicants for financial aid are also asked to use the same forms as domestic applicants: the Free Application for Federal Student Aid (FAFSA) or the CSS PROFILE or both. As always, check with each college for its policy.

Most important, either when they apply or on accepting an offer of admission, all international students need to provide proof that they have the financial resources to attend the college. In order to obtain the document that allows you to apply for a student visa for study in the United States (the I-20), you and your family must submit evidence that you can pay for the full cost of your first year of study minus any financial aid you will receive. The financial support needs to be sufficient to cover tuition, books and supplies, room and board, health insurance, travel, and daily essentials. Each college will help you determine the proper amounts.

One commonly used form is the Certification of Finances. You may be sent this form by the colleges that accepted you. You can find samples on the Internet by searching for "Certification of Finances." Some colleges use alternative forms as well, such as the Affidavit of Financial Support. You will need bank account records and records of other assets to fill out the forms. Colleges may also request original documents.

Some Additional Points About Finances

Several caveats and qualifications are appropriate at this point. First, on the plus side, some colleges include Canadian and Mexican students in their American need-blind admissions policy as a kind of good neighbor relationship with these strategic American allies. This can help you if you are from either one of these countries. On the minus side, some schools have very little or no money for international transfer students, and at some you cannot apply early decision if you need aid because those colleges want to evaluate all international applicants together in the regular admissions round. Schools can change policy at any time.

Enterprising students sometimes hope to work while attending college and thereby earn enough to pay the costs of their education. Because of the stipulations of the student visa, international students have very limited employment options in the United States, none of which can provide enough income to fully fund a college education or significantly supplement partial financial aid. We caution you against planning to pay for your education in this way.

SPECIAL CIRCUMSTANCES

Undocumented students, international students attending high school in the United States, and American students attending high school abroad all have special circumstances to consider when applying to college.

UNDOCUMENTED STUDENTS

Although not formally considered international students, undocumented students raised and educated in the United States face special challenges when pursuing higher education. Although they can attend college, they are not eligible for federal financial aid and may not be eligible for state aid, although private colleges can use their own funds for these students. The situation is in flux.

Policies Differ from State to State

In 2001, legislation, sometimes called the "DREAM Act," was first proposed in Congress to offer undocumented students a path to citizenship. It has not yet been passed, although a 2012 program, DACA (Deferred Action for Childhood Arrivals), partially addresses the issue; details can be found at www.ice.gov/daca. In-state status at public colleges and universities varies from state to state. In California, the California DREAM Act passed in 2011 allows children of undocumented immigrants who graduate from California high schools to receive state financial aid; since then at least 20 states have passed similar laws that provide various benefits for undocumented students, such as in-state tuition or eligibility for state financial aid. However, Alabama, Georgia, and South Carolina currently prohibit undocumented students from attending some or all public universities in those states.

To help undocumented students find the information they need, the Department of Education has published a resource guide entitled *Supporting Undocumented Youth*. You can find it by entering the title into the search bar at www.ed.gov. Other sources of helpful information include http://getmetocollege .org, which has a section on college policies for undocumented students located under the Funding for College tab, and *College Advising Guide for Undocumented Students* at www.iacac.org/undocumented. Typing "undocumented" into the search window on the college admissions home page of specific colleges often leads to useful information as well. For advice on applying for or renewing DACA status, check the National Immigration Law Center website at www.nilc.org.

Because of DACA, you may have a Social Security number; if not, you will need to fill out college applications without it. Do not invent one, and be assured that the FERPA law protects the privacy of the information contained in your application and financial aid forms. Even if information about your citizenship or immigration status is requested, you do not need to provide it, and you should not do so unless you have DACA status. Sometimes online forms make it difficult to leave some items blank; if so, print out the form if possible or obtain a paper application, fill it out by hand, make a copy, and mail it in.

Begin Early and Do Your Research

Because undocumented students need to investigate the implications of their legal situation at every college, you need to begin your search early and seek help from teachers, counselors, community organizations, and older students who have traveled this road before you. The FinAid website at www.finaid.org provides excellent initial information on financial aid and state support for undocumented students. Put "undocumented" in the search box at this site to go directly to this information. Another useful site is the blog at https:// mydocumentedlife.org, with information about educational opportunities, scholarships, and more.

The Mexican American Legal Defense Education Fund publishes a Scholarship Resource Guide in English and Spanish at www.maldef.org; many of the scholarships listed do not ask about immigration status or require a valid

Social Security number. Another resource is the Congressional Hispanic Caucus Institute, which publishes a bilingual *Guide to Applying for Financial Aid & Scholarships* and a list of URLs where you can find more information about financial aid. Enter the title of the guide into the search bar at www.chci .org to access these resources.

Who Counts as an International Student?

As noted, universities define an international student as someone who is neither a citizen nor a documented permanent resident of the United States. International students may have had their entire education in the United States and may speak excellent English, but they are still international students. Similarly, an American citizen may live abroad, even since birth, may have dual citizenship, and may be educated in another country's school system but is officially considered an American student for purposes of admission and financial aid. What are the implications of these special situations for college admissions?

An international student educated in the United States would apply just as an American would, but with the addition of forms providing proof of financial support. TOEFL or IELTS scores could be helpful if your SAT or ACT Reading, English, or Writing scores are low. A Subject Test in your first language, if available, would support your academic skills in your native language.

As an American citizen educated overseas, you might need to describe the local educational system if you are studying in a local school or a non-American international school. You might confront some of the challenges we described previously about getting teacher recommendations and a school report. If your SAT or ACT verbal scores are at the low end of a college's midrange of scores, taking the TOEFL or IELTS might be recommended even though English is your first language. Your application will usually be read in the context of your international experience.

In either case, your international experience is of great interest to an admissions office and may boost your chance of admission if you can effectively articulate the value of having lived in two or more cultures. An international student living and educated in the United States can bring a unique perspective to that experience as can an American student living and educated abroad. We urge you to display that perspective in an application essay.

THE BIGGER PICTURE

International students have been attending American colleges and universities for a long time, but their number has almost doubled over the last ten years, with a greater percentage coming as undergraduates. The number of Chinese students alone has more than doubled over the last five years.

As a potential international student, you will soon belong to a large community of young people from all over the world who have left the cultural and academic norms they have grown up with to explore new cultures. We hope the information provided in this chapter will make your transition to education in the United States a little smoother.

PART 4

Bringing the Process to a Close

Chapter 14   Making *Your* Decision After the Colleges Make Theirs

Chapter 15   What Matters Most: Advice to Parents and Students

Making *Your* Decision After the Colleges Make Theirs

Up to this point, *Admission Matters* has focused on choosing colleges and preparing strong applications. We now want to shift to the end of the process and discuss how to approach the choices you and your family will have to make once you receive the colleges' decisions.

For students applying ED or EA, closure may come quickly. Colleges usually notify students mid-December (or mid-February for ED II options offered by some colleges). Many colleges with rolling admissions, most often public universities such as the University of Pittsburgh, Indiana University, and the University of Minnesota, also generally provide fast turnaround in just a few weeks or less. But students applying regular decision (including those deferred from an early round) may not get all their decisions until the middle or end of March. The Ivy League colleges are usually among the last to announce their decisions, observing a common notification date in late March.

> Getting in doesn't mean life's doors are now open to you without effort and drive. Being rejected doesn't mean your dreams are suddenly and forever dashed. Sure, celebrate or mourn a bit, but then realize that the truly important stuff—the love of family, the support of close friends, the desire to learn and explore—really hasn't changed at all.
>
> PARENT REFLECTING ON THE NOTIFICATION PROCESS

HOW WILL YOU BE NOTIFIED?

Whether you applied early or during the regular round, hope and anxiety naturally rise as the notification date nears. Most colleges notify students electronically, either through e-mail or via a website, to speed up the process and reduce uncertainty about when decisions will be available, because regular mail can be unpredictable. Colleges that post their decisions online typically announce the precise date and time when they can be accessed. At the appointed hour, thousands and sometimes tens of thousands of students across the country sit tensely in front of their computers checking for the outcome.

THE SPECIAL CASE OF EARLY DECISION

The wait for an early answer is often an emotionally intense time. Because students have made a major investment in a college as their "top choice," a lot seems to be riding on the outcome. A happy outcome elates students and families. An unfavorable outcome, however, can be severely disappointing, even if everyone knew in their hearts that it was a long shot.

Students can easily get caught up in their own feelings and forget that their friends are dealing with their own concerns over the admissions process. We encourage everyone to save overt bursts of emotion, whether shrieks of joy or tears of disappointment, for a private setting. Some high schools discourage students from using on-site computers or cell phones to access admissions results for just this reason.

⊠

I applied early action to Harvard. That's where my sister goes, but I didn't get in. The decision came on Wednesday, and I was pretty upset for a couple of days. By Friday, I was OK. Then the weekend came, and I just kind of forgot about it. Just because I didn't get into Harvard doesn't mean that there's anything wrong with me. It also helped that my sister had been rejected by Princeton and Yale. That showed me how random things could be. The other thing that really helped was that those who did get in did not run around screaming, "Oh, I got in early. My life is great!" That would have made it much worse for those of us who didn't get good news. Everyone was really respectful of everyone else. A lot of terrific kids got rejected or deferred. It was like "Join the club." We shared the pain.

HIGH SCHOOL SENIOR

⊠

We also urge parents to respect their children's privacy for decisions received at home. Some students may want family members present. Faced with possible disappointment, however, some prefer to be alone to absorb the decision. Parents should take their cue from their child and be there, literally or figuratively, to support him or her regardless of the outcome. If the news is disappointing, parents should avoid adding to their child's burden with displays of anguish or anger. This applies not only for the early admissions round but also for the regular decision notifications that come later.

ACCEPTED!

If your early application is binding, your acceptance brings your college search to an early, happy conclusion. If your notification does not include financial aid information, it will follow shortly, and if the offer adequately covers your need, you are expected to submit your intent-to-enroll form and deposit by the deadline indicated, usually within a few weeks. You must also withdraw all other submitted applications. Other than some unforeseeable family catastrophe, unmet financial need is the only legitimate grounds for not attending a college that has admitted you under binding ED.

FINANCIAL AID AND EARLY DECISION

If your financial aid package provides less money than you will need to attend, contact the financial aid office immediately to explain the situation in detail and respectfully request a review of your financial aid package. They may be able to work something out. Remember, though, that the difference between what a college believes a family needs and what the family feels it needs (sometimes known as "felt need") may not be totally reconcilable. The family, however, makes the final decision about whether the ED financial aid package is sufficient to allow the student to attend.

Financial aid issues aside, colleges primarily rely on an honor system to enforce the binding agreement, because they cannot legally force you to attend against your will. School counselors also do what they can to enforce the rules. Some selective colleges share their ED acceptance lists as a way to police compliance with the binding policy. If your name were to show up on two ED admit lists, you would be in trouble with both schools, and both could withdraw their acceptance. Students who are not released from their binding commitment and choose not to enroll at their ED college may also find some other doors closed to them. The vast majority of students admitted ED, however, never even remotely think of not attending their chosen college. If they do, the buyer's remorse usually passes quickly.

THE EARLY ACTION ACCEPTANCE

An EA acceptance can also bring your college search to a happy ending. But under the terms of EA, you have until May 1 to formally accept your offer. If your EA school is clearly your first choice, it is courteous (although certainly not mandatory) to withdraw other applications from the regular decision process and not submit any new ones (especially if financial aid is not an issue). The reason is simple: the more applications in the college pipeline, the lower the percentage of applicants a college can accept. If you know for sure where you will be going the following fall, share your good fortune by giving your fellow students (locally and nationally) a better chance for a regular decision admission at a college they would like to attend.

But an EA acceptance need not end your college search. You may be interested in other colleges as well and want more time to make a decision. You may also want to see what all your other financial aid packages look like when you receive other acceptances in the spring. In that case, you'll have to wait until you receive your regular round decisions. You can do so, however, knowing that you already have an acceptance from a school you would happily attend.

DENIED OR DEFERRED

Not all early applications end happily. As more and more students seek the advantage of applying early, colleges have to deny or defer more of them to leave room for regular round admits.

If you are denied, your application will not be considered further by that college. This can be a tough decision to receive right around the holidays, but it is important to accept it and move forward confidently. If you have taken the advice we gave you about applying early in chapter 7, you have other applications submitted or ready to go. This is also a good time to reassess your college list one more time: consider trimming some of the long shots and perhaps adding another possible or likely school to balance it out.

If you are deferred, a college is saying that it is not yet ready to make a final decision on your application. This, too, is disappointing news to receive at holiday time. As a deferred student, your application will remain active and be automatically reconsidered again along with regular decision applicants—you do not need to reapply. You may be admitted in the end, but you also may not be, depending on the number of students deferred and the strength of the regular decision pool. Statistically the odds are usually about the same as if you had applied in the regular round to begin with. Schools defer students for many reasons: to see fall semester grades, to get a better sense of the applicant pool from your high school or area, or because they consciously hold back from admitting too many in the early round. The admissions office may tell you how many students have been deferred. If they don't volunteer that information, you can often get it by calling and asking.

WHAT YOU CAN DO IF YOU ARE DEFERRED

It is natural to continue to hope and to ask, "What can I do to increase my chances of admission after being deferred?" We suggest starting with another question. If you applied ED, is this really still your first choice? You have been released from your binding commitment to enroll if you are admitted later. You can play the field again. Sometimes there is a sense of relief that comes with this realization. You might still want to be admitted, but you no longer have a laser focus on just one school.

> I applied ED to my first choice school and I was devastated when I was deferred and not admitted. I then did all the things you are supposed to do to increase your chances of admission in the spring. It turned out that by the time I received my acceptance in March, that school was no longer my top choice. I decided to go elsewhere and couldn't be happier. Funny how these things sometimes work out.
>
> COLLEGE SOPHOMORE WHO DISCOVERED THAT "FIRST CHOICE" CAN CHANGE

UPDATE YOUR APPLICATION

Our best advice to you as a deferred student is to determine how to update your application to make your case for admission stronger. You can't resubmit your application, but you can add to it. A good place to start is with a letter or e-mail reaffirming your strong interest in the college. Some schools provide deferred students with a form that asks for updated information on grades, any testing that was not reported with your early application, activities, and achievements. If the college does not provide such a form, include this information in your letter.

Follow closely any directions the college may give you. If the college indicates that it welcomes additional submissions, think about whether you would like to send in a graded paper or project or even an additional essay. Don't send this kind of material, however, unless a school specifically invites it. It won't help if they don't ask for it, and you run the risk of irritating your readers.

Other Things to Consider

If you haven't visited and the school considers demonstrated interest in its decisions, consider visiting if possible as long as the college does not advise against it. If your scores are low, but you are otherwise a strong applicant, consider retesting in February if you are prepared to take or retake the ACT. The next SAT date in March will be too late for consideration. We suggest calling first, however, to find out if scores would arrive in time and be considered.

Finally, finishing the fall semester with a strong record is essential. During the regular cycle, unlike the early review, colleges will see your fall semester grades, and strong grades can help you. In fact, maybe that is why you were deferred: they want to see your first semester grades.

WHEN IT IS YOUR TURN TO DECIDE IN THE SPRING

Mid-December, as intense as it may be, is just a dress rehearsal for the spring when the regular round results start arriving. This time, many more students are waiting for responses from even more schools—and everything is drawn out over a longer period. But now, after waiting several months to hear their decisions from colleges, students and families once again can make their own decisions.

Choices Can Be Tough to Make

The process of making a final decision to attend a college will vary, from student to student and from family to family. A lot depends not only on personality and decision-making style but also on the specific choices. A student admitted to his top-choice school with sufficient financial aid or no need for aid probably has a pretty easy decision to make.

Other students may have several desirable choices, with financial aid sometimes weighing heavily in the final decision. Because many highly selective colleges offer only need-based aid or very little merit aid, some less selective colleges can compete for strong students by offering generous merit aid packages. It can be hard to turn down a good school that offers significant merit aid in favor of one, no matter how attractive and prestigious, that would cost your family much more. Many students who do not qualify for need-based aid find merit aid attractive in the end.

> I've asked people ahead of me in school, "How did you choose?" They all said, "I walked on campus, and I just knew." Well, I need something more concrete. I don't ever just know about anything. I don't have gut instincts on major life decisions.
>
> SENIOR APPROACHING DECISION TIME

REVISIT YOUR PRIORITIES

Sometimes students facing a difficult decision find it helpful to make a list of pros and cons for each college. We suggest revisiting the priorities that emerged when you completed the questionnaire at the end of chapter 4. Thinking through what is really important to you is critical, now more than ever before. Your priorities may have changed over the past few months. Now that you know your choices, prestige may play a less important role because the high-prestige schools turned you down. Or you may have a better idea of the major you want to pursue because a senior-year course has changed your academic direction. Or you may be more willing to go farther from home, or, conversely, you may feel less need to do this. All of these are valid factors to consider.

You may, however, prefer to bypass lists and go with gut instinct. Both approaches can work, and in fact, elements of both may work best of all.

MAKE A DECISION BY MAY 1

All colleges ask that students declare their intentions, one way or the other, by May 1, the widely observed candidate reply date. It is courteous to respond as soon as you have made your decision—not only to the college you plan to attend but also to the others you are turning down.

All colleges admit more students than they have room for because they know some will go elsewhere. As we'll see in a following section, your decision not to attend a college may open up a spot for a student on the wait list. The earlier a college can determine it has space, the sooner it can send the happy news to someone else.

> What I did was flip a coin, and wherever it landed, I tried to decide how I felt about that. Every time it landed on College X, I got a gut feeling that I wasn't going to feel comfortable on that campus.
>
> SENIOR WHO DECIDED TO ATTEND COLLEGE Y

DEALING WITH DISAPPOINTMENT

Although many students look forward to choosing a college in April, others are disappointed. If you are admitted to only one or two likely colleges and denied or wait-listed by the others, you may not be excited by any of the choices. It isn't fun to be rejected by a school you were enthusiastic about. When several say no, it is even harder. Remember, though, what we emphasized in chapter 3: many factors in the college admissions process are beyond your control and have no bearing on you as a person. Realizing how uncertain the outcome can be at some colleges can make it easier to accept each outcome gracefully.

> My parents knew I was nervous, so they sat me down and said, "Look, you've done everything you can do." But when the rejections came in, I still felt like every mistake I'd made in the last four years of high school was coming back to haunt me.
>
> HIGH SCHOOL SENIOR

Even students with several acceptances may feel uncomfortable as they second-guess their original choices. Now that they are real options, suddenly none of the colleges looks that good, and some students wonder whether they should have "aimed higher."

I really wanted to have that happy acceptance thing, when I would jump up and down and call my mom to tell her the great news. I missed that. But I learned that if you don't get in where you want to go, it's not the end of the world. I'm not a religious person, so when people say everything happens for a reason, I'm like, "Yeah, well." But I think in this case, everything did happen for a reason. I'm really happy here.

COLLEGE FRESHMAN ATTENDING ONE OF HER LIKELY SCHOOLS

REMIND YOURSELF THAT THERE ARE NO PERFECT COLLEGES

These reactions are normal, but it is important to move beyond them. Dwelling on the negative, as well as what-ifs, makes it harder to embrace the opportunities you do have. All colleges, no matter how highly rated or well regarded, have faults.

And all colleges, even the most humble by most measures, have strong points. If you have done your research carefully at the outset, your choice will be a good one no matter what you choose. In fact, the college itself does not make the crucial difference in your future contentment; rather, it is your degree of commitment to your own education. The choice is your first step of that commitment.

One young woman we know was denied by all colleges except her one likely. Although disappointed, she took a positive approach. Ten weeks into her freshman year, she enthusiastically reported how happy she was with her college, even though she had had no choice. She loved her classes, her new friends, and the college itself. Each year many thousands of students have similarly happy endings after a disappointing March.

THE TRANSFER OPTION

Remember also that choosing a college is not an irrevocable act. Students can and do transfer after freshman or sophomore year. Some students transfer from their first-choice schools, even an ED school, and some from their likelies, as well as everything in between. Doing well in the final semester of high school and during your freshman year will boost your transfer odds, although some colleges may be as selective for transfer students as they are for freshmen (or even more so). Choosing a college as a springboard to transferring to another one is a recipe for being an unhappy freshman. Instead, find the good points of your college and vow to make the best of it. If it doesn't work out, then you can consider transferring, but first give your college an honest try. We discuss the transfer process at greater length in chapter 12.

SPRING ADMITS

Inundated with more good applicants than they can accept, some colleges have found a creative solution so they can admit more students each year: they offer a group of students the option to enroll as freshmen starting in the spring semester rather than in the fall. Colleges knows that some students will not return for spring semester. Students withdraw because of health, adjustment, financial problems, or poor academic performance; others go to study abroad, and a few seniors usually graduate early. The spots they open up create space for students willing to start midyear.

Middlebury College and the University of California, Berkeley are two schools that have offered spring admission for many years. Middlebury calls their spring arrivals "Febs" for the month of February, when the spring semester starts. The University of Southern California, Brandeis University, and Wheaton College (Massachusetts), as well as a growing number of other colleges, have spring starts as well. Colleges offering spring admission encourage students to use the fall semester productively, either through course work at another college or other enriching activities. A few schools offer their spring admits a first semester overseas: for example, Skidmore College in London, Colby College in Dijon, France, and Northeastern University in several countries.

The disadvantage of a midyear start is obvious: you don't experience the first exciting semester of college life with your new classmates. On the plus side, though, after just a few months you will join them at a school you want to attend.

> The scary thing is that no one in our family, adult or child, has the slightest clue which school would be best. They all have pros and cons. Sometimes I think it might be a relief to get rejections from all but one to avoid having to make these incredibly difficult decisions.
>
> A PARENT AT DECISION TIME

You usually don't apply for spring admission. If a school cannot accept you for the fall but expects to have room in the spring, it will tell you in your admissions letter. This is different from the midyear admissions process that some public universities and a small number of private colleges use. In these cases, students apply specifically for a midyear start and have a different application time line.

TAKING ANOTHER LOOK

Most colleges host special admit days or weekends in April before the May 1 Common Reply Date. Even if you have visited a college before, going to an admit program can be fun and a good way to get a feel for the campus. It can be especially useful, of course, if you have not visited previously.

Finally, the pressure is off, and you can enjoy being courted with tours, receptions, panels, and faculty lectures. Everyone realizes that the campus is at its best on this special day or weekend, but you'll still get to know the campus better because you can meet so many students, including your potential classmates.

Usually students must pay the cost of travel to admit programs. In some cases, though, a campus may be particularly eager to recruit a student and will offer to help with travel expenses up to a certain dollar limit. This applies most often to students who are underrepresented minorities and those from low-income families. If you are not offered financial assistance but find that the cost of travel is a hardship, consider asking the admissions office to help with your travel costs. They may say no because of budget limitations, but it doesn't hurt to ask.

Admit programs, especially when you stay overnight, give you a good chance to talk to current students about what the college is really like, as well as get a sense of who might be joining you in the freshman class. It is worth rereading the section on college visits in chapter 5 to refresh your memory of what to look for. Some colleges also encourage parents to attend and even offer special programs for them (although no housing), and all colleges welcome them regardless of whether formal events are provided. It's fine to accompany your child to an admit weekend; just be sure you give him or her lots of space.

> I want to look at the academics and which college really fits my academic goals the most. Visiting becomes more important. Getting a feel for the people that go there. Making sure that they're compatible. Do I want to live in New Jersey? In Southern California? How much of a stretch do I want from my current lifestyle?
>
> SENIOR TRYING TO MAKE A DECISION BETWEEN TWO VERY DIFFERENT COLLEGES

REVISITING FINANCIAL AID

If your financial aid offers are disappointing, reread the section on how to request reconsideration near the end of chapter 8. Once you have all your acceptance and financial aid offers, you may want to make your top-choice college aware of any offer that is significantly larger than theirs if the differences in the aid packages may affect your final choice. Also be sure to tell them of any changes in your financial situation that might make you eligible for more aid. They can sometimes make adjustments even without such new information as the result of a second careful look, but these cases are less common, and this might happen only for the applicants the college is most eager to enroll. Courteously requesting a financial aid review to see whether anything more can be done is appropriate and smart. Be prepared, of course, for a negative answer.

As we noted in chapter 8, however, don't expect a college that offers only need-based aid to adjust its package to offset a merit scholarship at another college. At the same time, don't let a "no" discourage you from continuing to consider the college as an option if you are excited about it and it is within financial reach, even with a less-than-ideal aid package.

HOW WAIT LISTS WORK

Most colleges hold a group of students in reserve—on a wait list—after admissions decisions have been made in the spring. These are applicants who were not admitted outright but who came close. The colleges tell them that they will be reconsidered for admission if they accept their wait-list spot and space becomes available later in the spring. What should you make of a letter that essentially puts you in limbo?

On the basis of experience, each college calculates an estimated yield on its offers of admission. Then the college waits—usually, but not always—until after the May 1 reply deadline to see whether the freshman class is full. If the yield is lower than anticipated—that is, fewer students accept their offer of admission than predicted—the college offers admission to students on the wait list. The process is very similar to the way airlines fill their planes. They often overbook a plane, because they know some passengers will not show up. If empty seats remain near departure time, those seats can be filled by standbys who know that they may or may not get a seat but have been patiently waiting.

The analogy with the airline standby process ends at this point. Although airline standby lists are ordered so passengers can assess their chances of getting a seat, wait lists are usually unranked. Openings are not filled from the list in any prearranged order. They don't order the wait list because they don't know who will stay on it—ordering it in advance would be a lot of extra and possibly unnecessary work—and they don't know the final composition of the freshman class by gender, geography, or major interest, for example. They want to retain the flexibility to balance the class using the wait list. So as openings occur, a college may examine its whole freshman class and use the wait list to fill any gaps. A student who came closest to admission during the regular round will not necessarily be chosen from the list because he or she doesn't fit the college's need at this time.

I was put on the wait list. "After long and careful consideration, the admission committee has decided to place your name on the waiting list ... I congratulate you on your fine record of accomplishments which deserve a much more fitting recognition than I can provide right now. I hope you will remain interested in our college and that you will choose to hold a place on our waiting list." An accompanying attachment stated that about a thousand students were placed on the wait list, that about 300 to 400 were expected to remain on it, and that over a 10-year period, on average fewer than 30 students were admitted from the wait list. At least they were upfront about how tough it would be.

WAIT-LISTED STUDENT

⋈

WHO GOES ON THE WAIT LIST?

Over the last few years, wait lists have gotten longer as colleges find predicting yield more difficult. Colleges always put far more students on the wait list than they expect to be able to admit, however. This reflects, for the most part, the increasing number of highly qualified candidates who apply to an increasing number of selective institutions. A wait-list decision can mean that a candidate was fully qualified to attend and would indeed have been admitted if only there were room. This is the most common reason. It can also be a gentle way for a college to say no to a weaker candidate it finds difficult to deny outright for other reasons, such as a legacy applicant. In addition, as we saw in chapter 1, some colleges will wait-list exceptionally qualified candidates if they think the student might accept an offer elsewhere.

Because of a combination of all or some of these factors, many wait lists are as big as or bigger than the entire freshman class. The "Principles of Good Practice" of the National Association for College Admission Counseling say that each college should tell you how many applicants have been placed on the wait list for your year and for each of several previous

I didn't like being wait-listed. It felt like a consolation prize. Why would they wait-list so many people when clearly they're letting in very few? It seemed so pointless.

SENIOR WHO WAS WAIT-LISTED BY
HARVARD UNIVERSITY AND DECLINED
TO REMAIN ON THE LIST

years, along with the number on the wait list eventually offered admission. If you don't receive this with your wait-list notification, be sure to ask for it.

The number admitted from a wait list can vary greatly, from zero to low single digits to several dozen or more. It all depends on the accuracy of a college's prediction of its yield in the first place. The importance of predicting yield is one reason colleges like ED so much and why some colleges consider demonstrated interest in making their admissions decisions. Both policies give them a better advance idea of their yield.

> Essentially, the wait-list exists to accommodate for demographics that were not met in the initial round of admission offers. If you have the right number of deposits from the West coast, you go to your wait-list for more East coast students. If you have enough Chemistry majors, you may be going to the wait-list for Business students.[1]
>
> RICHARD CLARK, DIRECTOR OF UNDER-GRADUATE ADMISSIONS, GEORGIA TECH

The domino or trickle-down effect from wait lists can be disruptive to colleges. As students are admitted from the wait list at College A, other schools that those students had accepted now have empty spots that they in turn fill from their wait lists. And so on down an invisible ladder. A college with a full class on May 1 may have space on May 15 after losing some students to other colleges. The sequence can take a while to work out, sometimes well into June or even later.

YOU ARE WAIT-LISTED—NOW WHAT?

What should you do if you are offered a place on a college's wait list? No single answer fits everyone. Don't fall into the trap of automatically thinking that the college that didn't take you at first is automatically better than any that accepted you. It was just a different admissions process. Usually, depending on the school, fewer than half of those placed on a wait list opt to remain. If your other college choices are more attractive to you, why remain on the wait list? Sometimes you just need closure, rather than the emotional limbo of staying on a wait list, even if it means knowing that you will definitely be attending a college lower on your list. You know yourself best: be sure to weigh the wait-list option carefully before deciding what to do.

But if the wait-list college still appeals to you, you may decide to accept the offer, even knowing that your chances for being accepted later are low. You should also inquire about a college's policy regarding financial aid for wait-list admits. In some cases, aid is not available for wait-listed students. You have to ask.

If you decide to remain on a wait list, be sure to send your intent-to-register form by May 1, along with your deposit, to your preferred college from among your acceptance options. This is essential because you don't know if you will be admitted to a wait-list school. Given the uncertainties, you need to have plan B firmly in place for the fall.

I encourage families to treat a wait list offer a little bit like a lottery ticket—if it comes through and you win, everything's great, but you don't plan on it.[2]

MONICA INZER, DEAN OF ADMISSION AND FINANCIAL AID, HAMILTON COLLEGE

A To-Do List for Waitlisted Students

- Return the reply postcard or send an electronic reply indicating you want to remain active on the wait list. It is okay to remain on more than one wait list.
- Write a letter or e-mail to the dean of admissions or the admissions officer who works with your region saying that you are still very eager to attend. Include any significant new information since you last wrote: grades, awards, and so forth. If it is your clear first choice, say so upfront, and promise to enroll if admitted. But, ethically, you cannot say this to more than one college.
- Ask your counselor to contact the admissions office of private or out-of-state public universities to convey your enthusiasm and his or her support for you.
- Consider sending an additional recommendation from a teacher or another person who knows you well. But don't overdo it so that it looks like a campaign.
- Carefully select a school from those that have admitted you, and send in your deposit.
- Recognize that most students placed on the wait list at many colleges, especially selective ones, are ultimately not admitted. Once you have taken the outlined steps, put the wait list out of your mind and focus on the college you will probably attend in the fall. By the time you are admitted from a wait list, you might be very happy with your May 1 choice and want to stick with it. Telling a college where you were wait-listed that it is your first choice is not binding like ED.

REEMPHASIZE YOUR INTEREST

If you decide to remain on one or more wait lists, be sure to follow each college's instructions about responding. A letter from you expressing your continued interest, why you see the college as such a good fit, and reporting any new accomplishments will be the most important step. If a college is your first choice and you would accept admission from the wait list if offered, say so. You can accept a spot on the wait list of more than one college, but of course only one can be your "first choice" at this point. The others can be "top choices."

It is also wise to discuss your continued interest in the colleges with your high school counselor. Tell your counselor whether a college is your first choice, particularly if it is a private college or out-of-state public university. Your counselor may be able to help your cause by contacting that college and conveying support for you as well as your enthusiasm for the college. But again, movement from the wait list, especially at the most selective colleges, can be a long shot at best. It is hard to know. Don't let hope of admission, which could even come well into the summer, spoil your excitement about college.

WHEN AND HOW WILL YOU HEAR?

As we noted, colleges generally do little with the wait list until they have a good idea of their yield after May 1. Mid-May through early June is thus the busiest time for wait-list notifications, although some colleges may begin drawing from the wait list earlier if they see that enrollment is falling behind their expectations. Because of competition for good students, colleges know that some of their wait-listed students are likely to be wait-listed at other comparable colleges. So they may even start to take students from the wait list before May 1 to get a head start on their rivals, with more admitted later when their yield is clearer.

Wait-listed students who are accepted are usually notified first by phone, followed by written confirmation. You may be given two weeks or sometimes a much shorter deadline for reply. If you tell the caller you are no longer interested (and that is okay even if you agreed to stay on the wait list a month earlier), the college will move on to another wait-listed student and repeat the process. Sometimes a college will call your high school counselor to see if you are still interested. They want 100 percent yield on wait-list offers and try to nail these down in advance. It can all happen very quickly and without warning. Public universities generally notify students accepted from a wait list via e-mail rather than by phone. Be sure to continue to regularly check your in-box—you don't want to miss an important message.

I was waitlisted by a UC campus but thought it was unlikely I would be accepted. I deposited at another school and moved on. I was never good at checking my e-mail and I figured I no longer had to since I knew where I was going to college in the fall. When my mom learned I wasn't checking my e-mail regularly, she asked if she could do it for me. I figured, yeah, whatever. The first day she looked she found an old message from the UC campus informing me that I had been admitted from the wait list and that I need to notify them if I was interested—by the very day she checked my mail! That was a close call.

STUDENT NOW HAPPILY ENROLLED AT A UC CAMPUS

Many colleges have very little activity from the wait list after Memorial Day. Other colleges may keep an active wait list into the summer. Most selective colleges officially close their wait lists by the end of June and inform students who have not been accepted.

If you subsequently decide to join a college that accepts you from the wait list, you will need to send a deposit to that college. You will forfeit the deposit you made to your plan B school, but it may be worth it if you end up where you really wanted to go. Some deposits are quite large, even as much as $1,000, to encourage you to stick with your first school.

> Colleges are looking for a 100 percent yield from any students they take off the wait list, so they are going to be looking for commitment. The key is for students to demonstrate as much honest interest as they can and say that if offered admission, they will definitely enroll. They are the students the admissions office will most likely look at first.
>
> EXPERIENCED HIGH SCHOOL COUNSELOR

DEPOSIT ETHICS

Students are expected to send a deposit to hold a spot at only one college by May 1 and any time thereafter. Holding more than one spot, known as double depositing, deprives others of the potential opportunity to move from a wait list. Double depositing is unethical, and if either college finds out, you can lose your place at both colleges. It is tempting, we know, to think you can buy some time to consider your choices a little longer, but resist that temptation.

If you are on a wait list and later accept admission, you'll have to inform the first college you accepted of your change in plans as quickly as possible. A phone call usually isn't enough—they will want something in writing. Your letter doesn't have to be long; a simple note informing the college of your new plans is sufficient. This happens all the time, so don't be bashful or embarrassed about your change in plans.

It is important to notify the college quickly. The place you release may then generate an opening for another student on that school's wait list unless the school is oversubscribed, continuing the cascading effect.

SHOULD YOU CONSIDER A GAP YEAR?

> Gap years, done well, challenge a student to step outside her comfort zone, re-evaluate assumptions about herself and the world around her.[3]
>
> JOSEPH O'SHEA, PRESIDENT OF THE BOARD OF DIRECTORS OF THE AMERICAN GAP ASSOCIATION

Most students who have finished the college admissions process in good spirits are eager to put it all behind them and look forward to college life in the fall. But maybe you are different.

Perhaps you've sent in your deposit to a great college, but are starting to feel that you need an extended break from school. Foreign travel to strengthen your language skills, full-time volunteer work for a meaningful cause, or work in a field for which you have passion are all attractive ways to spend a year before you start college.

Or maybe the college admissions process didn't work out as well as you had hoped, and you can't get really excited about any of your options. Rather than settle for a college that you truly feel doesn't suit you, you may want to use the next year to strengthen your record in various ways and reapply to college.

> I am not suggesting the gap year as a viable alternative to a great safety school, but if your heart isn't in it, maybe you should take time to rethink where you want to be (and how you want to get there) rather than attending a college you aren't excited about simply because they accepted you.
>
> STUDENT WHO DECIDED TO TAKE A GAP YEAR

Maybe you didn't apply to college at all, knowing that you needed a stronger record before you would be a successful applicant. Now you need to figure out how best to do that.

All of these are great reasons to consider a gap year. Colleges know that students who take a gap year usually arrive on campus with greater maturity and interesting experiences to share with their classmates, so a gap year can be a win-win affair—great for the student and great for the college.

GAP YEAR AFTER YOU HAVE BEEN ADMITTED

Although most colleges will happily review a student's request to take a gap year before enrolling, a few colleges, most notably Harvard, actively encourage recently admitted students to consider one. For over 20 years, the Harvard letter of admission has included a paragraph suggesting that students consider taking a gap year, noting that Harvard wants them to avoid arriving on campus burned out from an intense high school experience. Of course, Harvard (and any other college) would be in trouble if large numbers of students took them up on the offer, but about 50 to 70 do each year out of its freshman class of about 1,700. Other schools report a similar proportion of students choosing a gap year.

Typically, students must submit a formal request for a gap year that outlines how they plan to spend their time. Most schools are very flexible but want to see that you are going to use your time productively: being a coach potato won't impress them, and enrolling full-time in a degree-granting program at another college is usually not allowed, though a college course here or there should be fine. That still leaves a lot of wonderful options. You should also be aware that some schools do not routinely approve gap year requests or may do so only on a very limited basis. If a gap year is important to you, inquire about the policy at the school you are planning to attend well before you submit your deposit.

For nearly two generations we have encouraged students to consider deferring entrance for a year. Many students have done so, finding their varied experiences extremely rewarding and their subsequent college careers greatly enriched. If you would like to defer, please inform us of your intention at the response website to register your deferral.

FROM THE HARVARD UNIVERSITY ACCEPTANCE LETTER FOR THE CLASS OF 2020

You will also usually be expected to submit your deposit to secure your place in the freshman class entering the following year, as well as sign a pledge that you will not apply to other colleges during your gap year. If you end up changing your mind part way into your year, you should notify the college that granted the gap year of your change in intentions.

TAKING A GAP YEAR WITH A PLAN TO APPLY FOR THE FOLLOWING YEAR

If you plan to take a gap year without making a commitment to attend a specific college the following fall, you just have to decide to do it. No college has to give you permission. It is just as important, though, to have a good plan in place to help you strengthen your record for future college admission.

Consider the following pragmatic advantages of a gap year:

- If you are not satisfied with your SAT or ACT results, you can retake the tests to raise your scores. You may have more time for preparation and be more familiar with the tests.

- If you had a good senior year, you may now have stronger options for recommendations, because your 12th-grade teachers will have known you for a full academic year.

- If you took Advanced Placement or International Baccalaureate courses in your senior year and did well, those test scores, along with your senior-year grades, will be part of your record.

- Your gap year activities may make you a more interesting or distinctive candidate for admission and give you a great topic for your college essay, even if you have just a few months of experience before submitting your applications.

- A successful gap year can help address any academic, personal, or extracurricular weaknesses in your record and enable you to demonstrate your maturity and readiness for college.

The Post-Graduate Year Option

A small number of students seek to gain these advantages through a formal post-graduate (PG) year at a private high school, most commonly located in the Northeast. Some programs are available as boarding only, which means that you would have to live on campus, whereas others are day programs. Athletes who want to improve their academic record while continuing to play their sport at the high school level often choose a PG year. The full array of extracurricular activities, courses, test prep, and college counseling is available in such programs. Tuition can be expensive, however, rivaling the cost at some colleges. Many PG programs fill up early, but others may still have room right before school begins in the fall.

The Self-Directed Gap Year

Most students seeking to apply to college the following year choose a self-directed gap year. Through careful time management (always an important skill), students can prepare for standardized tests if needed, enroll in community college classes if they need to demonstrate that they can do college-level work, or engage in a meaningful gap year experience similar to that of students already admitted to their dream college. Be careful, though, about the number of credits you take at a community college if you decide to go that route. Some colleges limit the number of credits you can complete elsewhere if you want to apply as a freshman as opposed to a transfer student, so it is wise to check the policies of each school you are considering. The Resources section at the end of *Admission Matters* includes references with ideas about ways to spend your gap year.

Things to Do to Ensure a Smooth Gap Year

Regardless of the form of your gap year, be it PG or self-directed, we strongly recommend that you talk with your high school counselor and teachers whom you would like to write recommendations on your behalf and let them know your plans as soon as possible. Then stay in touch with them. They won't need to do anything right away, but you don't want them to be surprised when you ask them to write letters for you in the fall. And when you are ready to ask for their letters, we suggest you write each of them a note updating them on your gap year activities.

You will also need to do careful research into colleges that will be a good fit for you across the range of selectivity. Unless you are doing a PG year, you probably won't have easy access to a high school counselor, so you will have to do more on your own. You will be fine using the many online tools available as well as carefully rereading this book. An independent counselor may also be helpful if you feel you need additional personalized advice.

A WORD ABOUT SENIORITIS

Senioritis typically strikes seniors in March or April after they receive their college acceptances, sometimes earlier. For those accepted early, it may hit in mid-December, but for most others it attacks in mid-April. (Being wait-listed may retard it.) Teachers know to expect senioritis, but they dread it nonetheless. Students start performing significantly below their pre-infection levels: they turn in homework late and take tests without preparing. High school no longer seems to matter very much because the big hurdle is over.

> We know there are plenty of distractions in your senior year, from college visits, open houses, and even the burgeoning excitement of graduation. It is important to keep in mind how you finish will matter—it really does. Grades and *graduating* are still important. College admissions officers want to make sure the students they admitted are ready to arrive in the fall and hit the ground running.[4]
>
> JOSEPH GORE, ASSISTANT DIRECTOR OF ADMISSIONS, UNIVERSITY OF MICHIGAN

We encourage you to avoid falling victim to this disease. We'll review several reasons—perhaps one or more will resonate with you. First, colleges stated clearly in their acceptance letter that your performance for the remainder of the year should remain at its prior level. It is easy to ignore that cautionary paragraph at the bottom in the moment of joy of being accepted, but colleges mean what they say. The last official part of your college application process is having your final transcript sent to your chosen college at the end of the school year. Colleges review these in the summer to identify any marked drop from previous performance or even changes in the courses you said you were going to take in the spring.

If your grades have dropped dramatically, colleges will send letters of varying degrees of harshness expressing their dismay and possibly asking for an explanation and quickly. A serious decline may result in a more strongly worded letter threatening that your admission is in jeopardy. Colleges reserve the right to put conditions on your enrollment (requiring summer school classes, for example) or even to rescind your admission entirely if your performance deteriorated drastically or if you dropped demanding courses without good reason. True, the drop in grades has to be pretty striking and without mitigating conditions for an offer of admission to be withdrawn, but a college can and will do this in serious cases. All of this is foreseeable. Frustrated counselors compare these students to trains running down a track out of control. Their warnings are frequently ignored. Why risk everything that you have worked so hard for?

Your high school record will be with you forever. Although your high school grades may not matter much once you enter college, you may want to transfer to a different college later. A weak record in the second half of senior year will not help your case. Finally, and maybe most important, continuing your best effort shows respect for your parents, your teachers, your counselors, and especially yourself. Show your appreciation and maturity by continuing to be a good student. Almost everyone will cut you a little slack—just don't abuse it.

CELEBRATE AND ENJOY!

With your college choice now behind you, you can enjoy the remaining weeks of high school. You can look forward to the senior prom, graduation, and, increasingly common, an alcohol-free all-night party or trip for the entire senior class. Make the most of this time to cement the bonds with your classmates, knowing that you will soon launch on your next major life adventure.

CHAPTER 15

What Matters Most

Advice to Parents and Students

We wrote *Admission Matters* to help families navigate the increasingly complex and sometimes daunting college admissions process. We wanted to show you how the role of the student and the role of the parent are complementary yet different and provide you with the information and practical advice you need to work together to achieve a good outcome.

In this final chapter, we offer some parting thoughts that summarize and capture the heart of what this book is about. It is easy to get caught up in the whirlwind and lose perspective, but this chapter will remind you what matters most. The chapter is divided into two parts. The first part is for parents; the second part is for students. As with the rest of the book, we hope you will read not only the part intended for you but the other part as well.

SOME PARTING THOUGHTS FOR PARENTS

WHAT YOUR CHILD WILL REMEMBER LONG AFTER THE COLLEGE ADMISSIONS PROCESS IS OVER IS HOW YOU SUPPORTED HIM OR HER.

He or she will be your child for the rest of your lives. This year is a small portion of your overall time as parent and child. Keep that in mind as you think of imposing your own ideas or detaching completely from the process. Above all, don't do anything that might impinge on your future relationship. Whatever seems so important at this moment really isn't so crucial in the long run.

It can be hard to accept that your almost-grown child has ideas and preferences that differ significantly from your own. This is especially true when it comes to college choice because so much seems to be at stake. Your child may want to experience a different part of the country; you may want your child to be close to home (or vice versa). You may feel an education at a liberal arts college is best; your child may be looking forward to the excitement of a large research university (or the reverse). The list goes on and on. The bottom line is that although your child should respect your views and may ultimately embrace them, the final choices—where to apply, how to prepare the application, and where to go after acceptance—should be the student's.

Ideally, you want to be able to look back after the final college choice is made and know that your emotional and practical support for your child contributed to a successful outcome. It may take your child a while to appreciate your good intentions and acknowledge your contribution. That too is part of being a parent, and you should be used to it by now.

THE PARENT'S ROLE IS TO SUPPORT, ADVISE, AND LISTEN, EXCEPT WHEN IT COMES TO MONEY.

You can support your child in the college admissions process in many ways: sharing your own thoughts and experiences; encouraging research into colleges, including visits when feasible; and providing useful feedback and organizational support. But you need to realize that your child must own this process. It is the student, not the parent, who is applying to and ultimately attending college.

It is critical, however, that you be upfront about financial considerations. As we discussed in chapter 8, colleges use complex formulas to determine the expected family contribution, the amount they believe a family should be able to pay to help support their child's education. This is rarely the amount that parents are eager to pay. Doing some early calculations and being frank about what you are prepared to contribute financially to your child's education is imperative to avoid misunderstanding and disappointment later on. This is not as easy as it sounds. Most parents keep their family finances and discussions of big expenses to themselves. This may have to change now. Most teenagers, we have found, are realistic and understanding if you treat them as intelligent adults. If you trust them, they will respond.

THIS IS NOT THE TIME TO LIVE VICARIOUSLY THROUGH YOUR CHILD, HOWEVER TEMPTING THAT MAY BE. TRY NOT TO USE COLLEGE ADMISSIONS TO VALIDATE YOUR PARENTING SKILLS.

Most parents of high school seniors are forty years old or older. Participating in the process with their child enables them to reexperience, or perhaps experience for the first time, a uniquely American rite of passage. However, if you catch yourself saying, "We're applying to college," or "We got a 1400 on the SAT," you may be overly involved. Even the most confident children may fear they will disappoint a parent if they do not get into their parent's alma mater or dream college(s) or if they do less "well" than a superstar older sibling. Wise parents try not to inadvertently contribute to that fear by their words or actions. At the end of the year, a parent recently told a counselor that the family "was resigned to settling for College C" after the child was not admitted to two super-selective schools. Although the child had four other choices that most students would have been thrilled about, the outcome was a letdown for them. How could the child not think that she had disappointed her parent? The good news is that she is enjoying College C very much anyway. Things have a way of working out.

Parents sometimes lapse into the misguided belief that all of their parenting efforts over the past 18 years will be held up to scrutiny during the admissions process. The parents of a student accepted by one or more prestigious colleges have "done a good job," and parents of students who apply to less prestigious institutions or who are denied by brand-name colleges didn't do their job quite as well. Don't fall into this trap. Parents who do can end up directly or indirectly putting their teen under great pressure and promoting values that are at best superficial and at worst actually harmful. What we said previously in *Admission Matters* really is true—there are no perfect colleges, but a given student will be perfectly happy and thrive at many colleges, academically and socially. A wise parent learns to be upbeat when the news is disappointing and modest when the news is good.

REMEMBER THAT AT MANY FIRST-RATE INSTITUTIONS WITH REASONABLE ACCEPTANCE RATES, YOUR CHILD CAN GET A FINE EDUCATION AND BE HAPPY.

Most people know surprisingly little about the amazing array of institutions of higher education in the United States. One counselor challenges audiences to see if they collectively can name more than 300 colleges. If they come up short, they have to pay him. If they go over 300, he has to pay them. Nobody takes him up on the challenge. Try it for fun. See how many you can come up with without a guidebook. Most parents can name some local colleges, probably some Ivy League schools and a few peers, and some schools whose football games are televised nationally, but that's about it.

As part of the college admissions process, you can support your child by learning about colleges you may not be familiar with and helping her realize that a successful college experience is the result of a good fit between her and a college—and that many good fits are possible. Many wonderful colleges accept a much higher percentage of their applicants than the minority considered very selective. By all measures, these colleges offer an education that is every bit as good as and maybe even better than some highly selective, brand-name institutions. Helping your child explore options and supporting his or her choices can be immensely rewarding.

HELP YOUR CHILD WITH ORGANIZATIONAL MATTERS, AND BE A GOOD SOUNDING BOARD AND EDITOR DURING THE APPLICATION PROCESS— BUT DON'T DO THE WORK FOR YOUR CHILD.

The process of applying to college can be intimidating. There are forms galore, short and long essays to be written, score reports and transcripts to request, and lots more, all by looming deadlines. When asked what they would do differently if they had a chance to start over, many high school seniors say that they would have started the whole process earlier and procrastinated less. Procrastination is a normal human reaction in face of an unappealing task, say, writing a will or paying taxes. But it is just a bad habit, not a sin. And it can be foreseen. With your greater adult experience, you can encourage your child to get started early and keep track of what he has done and what he still needs to do. Some teens resent this, of course; they have always been able to complete their work by deadlines, so they are convinced they can do the same now. The problem, though, is that college applications are probably much more complex than any task they have undertaken before, and more hangs in the balance. College deadlines are also more stringent and inflexible than those usually imposed in high school.

Students should be encouraged to organize their materials and set deadlines for themselves. If your child decides to apply EA or ED, he or she will probably have to get everything together by November 1 or November 15—a very early date indeed, especially if he or she starts preparing them on October 1. What kind of help can you provide? Proofreading of applications and help with essay ideas and constructive criticism can be very helpful (just be aware that your efforts may not be enthusiastically welcomed!). Resist the urge at all costs to rewrite the application yourself, however, even if your child seems willing or even eager for you to do that. Admissions readers get pretty good at telling an authentic student voice from one that has been significantly doctored by an adult.

You can also assist with organizational matters if you have those skills and your child welcomes the help. You can register your child for the SAT or ACT, for example; it's your credit card, after all. It is fine for you to download maps from Google for the college trip, as long as you don't pick the colleges, too. Make the organizational tasks easier and less time-consuming for your child, so he or she can devote energies to the hard parts. Of course, some teens enjoy these organizational tasks because they're easy to do and yield a sense of progress. Offer to help, and let your child decide.

MODEL ETHICAL BEHAVIOR AND INTEGRITY.

Children learn by observing others, and the most powerful role models are parents. The college admissions process is a major opportunity for parents to model ethical behavior and integrity for their children. Use it accordingly.

The pressure to do everything possible to ensure "success" in college admissions is powerful, even if it means compromising integrity along the way. Don't yield to this temptation. Don't offer inappropriate help with the application itself ("editing" an essay to the point of essentially writing it yourself, for example), and don't permit your child to seek it elsewhere (paying someone to write the essay). Similarly, discourage any tendency toward exaggeration of activities or accomplishments. Admissions officers look for consistency between what students have written about themselves and what teachers and counselors say about them. Why take a risk by embellishing too much?

But getting caught in a fabrication is the least of the reasons to encourage honesty in the application process. Our society has too many people who believe shaving the truth is not only okay but also the smart thing to do. Young adults need to know that their integrity is their most precious asset. Parents can reinforce that lesson through their actions and advice.

Everyone wants to be accepted for his or her own efforts and for who he or she really is. Allow that for your children. You don't want them to arrive freshman week and think, "I'm not the person who was on my application. This school wouldn't want the real me."

ACCOMPANY YOUR CHILD ON COLLEGE VISITS, BUT STAY IN THE BACKGROUND.

As we have said before, probably the best way for a student to get the feel for a college is to visit it. When possible, encourage your child to visit a number of campuses, perhaps in conjunction with vacation, and go along if you can. Going first to some nearby colleges of different sizes can help give your child an idea of the kind of college she might be interested in. When it comes time to look seriously at colleges, you can help schedule tours and encourage your child to have an interview if one is available. But remember that the visits are for your child's benefit. Encourage, but let your child make the final call about whether to visit a given campus.

HELP YOUR CHILD MAKE REALISTIC CHOICES.

A major theme of this book is that admission to selective colleges can be quite unpredictable. Your child can have a wonderful record yet be denied at a given college, whereas a classmate with a weaker record is accepted. You never learn why, but in the end, it doesn't matter. If you understand the difficulty and uncertainty of selective college admissions, you can help your child consider a good range of colleges. This means you have to control your own vicarious ambitions as much as possible.

If your child wants a super-selective college and would be a competitive applicant, he or she should certainly apply. But your child should understand that admission to colleges that select less than 20 percent of their applicants is a long shot for almost everyone simply because of the numbers. After the final decisions arrive, support your child by sharing the disappointment at the denials and the joy over the acceptances. Model poise over the former and humility for the latter. All parents know that if the worst thing that ever happens to their children in life is being denied from a college at the age of 18, then they will have a long and happy life. If your family carefully made the list at the outset, your child should be happy with the outcome regardless of the particular decisions.

BE SUPPORTIVE AS YOUR CHILD MAKES HIS OR HER FINAL CHOICE.

When the decisions arrive, your child may be elated or disappointed or somewhere in between. Give him or her space to sort it out and make the final decision. Offer your perspective when appropriate, but remember that within the boundaries of financial constraints and family responsibilities, the choice is your child's, not yours.

REJOICE WITH YOUR CHILD.

Regardless of the outcome, express your love, and let your son or daughter know how proud you are of the young adult he or she has become. Savor the moment!

SOME PARTING THOUGHTS FOR STUDENTS

PARENTS WANT THE BEST FOR YOU AND WANT TO HELP. LET THEM, WITHIN BOUNDARIES.

Although parents differ widely in their knowledge, abilities, and resources, almost all want to help a college-bound student however they can. Be gracious and communicate with your parents so that they can help appropriately. The trick is to define boundaries for what is helpful, what is intrusive, and what is counterproductive. Each family is different, so you'll have to work this out together with help from this book.

Parents can sometimes make great suggestions about colleges to consider. They can also be congenial traveling companions on college trips. And they can sometimes be good editors, proofreaders, and clerical assistants, depending on their skills, as you prepare your applications. The more you both know about the college admissions process, the easier it will be to agree on what form their help should take. Encourage them to partner with you. If they see you taking charge maturely, they will likely feel less need to be constantly on your case.

RECOGNIZE THAT LAUNCHING A CHILD TO ADULTHOOD IS EMOTIONALLY DIFFICULT FOR MANY PARENTS—HELP THEM GET THROUGH IT.

Sending a child off to college is bittersweet for many parents. They share your delight at your prospects for a wonderful future, but at the same time they inevitably feel a sense of loss. The child they have loved and nurtured for 18 years is now a young adult, ready to leave home for a new life in which they will play a much less prominent role. Try, even briefly, to put yourself in your parents' place. Something as simple as an occasional heartfelt "thank you" in response to help that they offered can make all the difference to a parent struggling, sometimes unconsciously, with a changing role.

Share something about the high school scene with your parents. Most know surprisingly little about the pressures at school, and they do not participate in the discussions about college that go on between you and your friends or with your counselor. If you help your parents understand your everyday environment, they will appreciate why your experience of the college admissions process may be very different from theirs.

THE MOST IMPORTANT PART OF THE COLLEGE ADMISSIONS PROCESS IS CHOOSING SCHOOLS THAT YOU THINK WILL BE A GOOD MATCH. BE HONEST WITH YOURSELF ABOUT YOUR INTERESTS, PREFERENCES, STRENGTHS, AND WEAKNESSES AS YOU CONSIDER COLLEGES.

A recurring theme throughout *Admission Matters* is that a successful college experience is all about fit—finding a college that is a good match for you. The most important and probably hardest part of the process is self-assessment—an honest self-evaluation of your interests, preferences, strengths, and weaknesses. The next toughest part is doing the necessary research to find colleges that you like based on your self-assessment. Part of that match includes a determination of the likelihood of acceptance. You want to be sure to have a range of colleges on your list so that you are more likely to have a good outcome.

MAKE ALL YOUR CHOICES FIRST CHOICES.

You should be sure that you will be happy to attend any of the colleges to which you apply, whether they are likelies or long shots or somewhere in between. Because you cannot predict the response from possible or long-shot colleges, having several first choices, including at least one that is a likely (and also a financial likely), virtually guarantees a happy result. The multiple first choices rule applies even if you apply early decision, because it might not work out.

DON'T PROCRASTINATE.

When high school seniors are asked what they would do differently if they could relive their college application experience, the most common response is, "I would start earlier and not procrastinate." Procrastination is a normal reaction to a stressful process. But it really does make things worse. Leaving applications to the last minute invariably means rushed decisions, careless mistakes, and potentially missed opportunities, not to mention needless stress. Establish a reasonable time frame for your efforts, setting deadlines for yourself along the way. Setting and meeting deadlines will also reduce stress on your parents. Do this for them, as well as for yourself.

GET AND STAY ORGANIZED, KEEP EVERYTHING TOGETHER, AND MAKE COPIES OF EVERYTHING YOU SEND IN.

The college application process is complicated. Brochures and college view books may arrive by the dozen early on, and e-mails may flood your in-box. Later, applications have to be completed, recommendations and transcripts requested, and financial aid forms filed. Adding to the complexity are the colleges' different requirements and deadlines. Staying on top of it all, as well as your normal school and social routine, is a real but important challenge. A simple, old-fashioned filing system in a cardboard box is all that you need, along with a record of each school's requirements and deadlines that you can check off as you meet them. Online methods of organization are great, too, as long as you back up your computer regularly. Be sure to keep a copy of everything you send in, even online applications. Colleges rarely lose materials, but you don't want to take any chances. Starting over when you thought you were done is no fun.

TALK TO YOUR FRIENDS, BUT REMEMBER THAT EACH PERSON IS DIFFERENT.

Peers can be wonderful sources of information and support. For example, a friend may return from a trip excited about the colleges he saw and open your eyes to new possibilities. But a good choice for one person, even a good friend, may not be a good choice for you. When someone offers an opinion of a college, whether good or bad, try to find out what's behind it. Get to the facts, then see how those facts fit with your own needs. And respect the choices of others. A likely college for one person may be a possible or even a long shot for another.

ENJOY YOUR SENIOR YEAR. COLLEGE APPLICATIONS ARE IMPORTANT (THAT'S WHY YOU ARE READING THIS BOOK), BUT THEY SHOULD NOT BE ALLOWED TO TAKE OVER YOUR LIFE.

College admissions can easily become the focus of your senior year. There is so much to do, and so much seems to be at stake. But the senior year in high school should also be special in other ways—sharing adventures with old and new friends, enjoying a fleeting year of being top banana, and beginning to enjoy the freedoms of young adulthood. Balance is key. A wise student takes the college application process seriously but keeps it in perspective with everything else. If you approach things calmly, rationally, and in a timely way, you can end the year with fine college choices and wonderful personal memories.

END THE COLLEGE ADMISSIONS PROCESS ON A HIGH NOTE.

When the final decisions from colleges come in, you get to decide. Do so carefully. Your choice may or may not be the one you hoped or thought you would make when you began the process, but if you have followed our advice, it will be a good choice. Celebrate with your family and friends, and begin to plan for your new life as a college student (but remember you still have to successfully complete your senior year).

Thank your teachers and counselors again for writing letters for you and tell them where you got in and didn't. Visit them to say "hi" when you return home over winter break during freshman year, or send them e-mails if you can't see them in person. They will appreciate it.

Above all, thank your parents for all they have done and still do for you, and tell them that you love them. Do this along the way, of course, but especially when the process is over. You are going to college!

Appendix A
College Research Worksheet

(Make copies of this form and complete one for each college you are seriously considering.)

Name of school _____ Location _____

Admissions phone and e-mail _____ Campus website____ _____

Testing Requirements (circle all that apply)

Required: SAT   ACT   Essay   SAT Subject _____

Recommended: SAT   ACT   Essay   SAT Subject _____

Optional: SAT   ACT   Essay   SAT Subject _____

Freshman Class Profile

GPA: % in the top 10% of class _____ % in the top 20% of class _____

       % in the top 50% of class _____

applications _____% admitted _____

early applications _____% admitted _____% of class filled early _____

SAT: mid-50% math _____ mid-50% Evidence-Based Reading and Writing (EBRW) _____

ACT: mid-50% composite _____

Total # undergraduates _____   Total # students on campus _____

Academic Profile

Circle one: Research university   Liberal arts college   Other _____

Majors of interest to you: _____

_____

(continued)

Academic Profile *continued*

Curriculum requirements (general education, senior thesis, etc.): _____

_____

Special programs of interest (honors program, arrangements with other colleges, etc.):

_____

_____

Overall impression of academic pace and rigor: _____

_____

Other: _____

_____

Campus Life

Campus housing: Guaranteed for ____ years

Details (process for assignment, housing options, % living on campus): _____

_____

_____

Characteristics of student body (single sex, geographic and ethnic diversity, liberal/
conservative, etc.): _____

_____

_____

Social life and activities (% in sororities and fraternities, intramural and club sports,
recreational facilities, clubs of special interest, etc.): _____

_____

_____

_____

Other: _____

_____

Special Interests

Intercollegiate athletics: Your sport: _____ NCAA division or NAIA: _____

Coach's name and contact info: _____

Arts, Music, or Special Academic Focus

Area: _____   Contact: _____

Area: _____   Contact: _____

Other: _____

_____

Financial Aid Policies

Circle all that apply: Guarantees to meet full demonstrated need   Offers merit aid

Need-blind admissions   Need-based aid only

Financial aid deadlines: FAFSA _____   CSS PROFILE _____   Other(s) _____

Application Process

Circle all that apply: College-specific form   Pre-application

Common Application   Common Application Supplement   Other application form

Application deadlines: Early Action _____   Early Decision _____

Regular _____   Rolling _____   Fee _____

Interview: Required   optional   not offered

Details: _____

_____

Other notes: _____

_____

Appendix B
Essay Prompts, 2017–2018

COMMON APPLICATION

Choose one prompt and write an essay of no more than 650 words.

- Some students have a background, identity, interest, or talent that is so meaningful they believe their application would be incomplete without it. If this sounds like you, then please share your story.

- The lessons we take from obstacles we encounter can be fundamental to later success. Recount a time when you faced a challenge, setback, or failure. How did it affect you, and what did you learn from the experience?

- Reflect on a time when you questioned or challenged a belief or idea. What prompted your thinking? What was the outcome?

- Describe a problem you've solved or a problem you'd like to solve. It can be an intellectual challenge, a research query, an ethical dilemma—anything that is of personal importance, no matter the scale. Explain its significance to you and what steps you took or could be taken to identify a solution.

- Discuss an accomplishment, event, or realization that sparked a period of personal growth and a new understanding of yourself or others.

- Describe a topic, idea, or concept you find so engaging that it makes you lose all track of time. Why does it captivate you? What or who do you turn to when you want to learn more?

- Share an essay on any topic of your choice. It can be one you've already written, one that responds to a different prompt, or one of your own design.

UNIVERSAL APPLICATION

Write an essay (650 words or fewer) that demonstrates your ability to develop and communicate your thoughts. Some ideas include: a person you admire; a life changing experience; or your viewpoint on a particular current event.

COALITION APPLICATION

Choose one prompt, with a strong recommendation that your essay be no longer than 500–550 words:

- Tell a story from your life, describing an experience that either demonstrates your character or helped to shape it.
- Describe a time when you made a meaningful contribution to others in which the greater good was your focus. Discuss the challenges and rewards of making your contribution.
- Has there been a time when you've had a long-cherished or accepted belief challenged? How did you respond? How did the challenge affect your beliefs?
- What is the hardest part of being a teenager now? What's the best part? What advice would you give a younger sibling or friend (assuming they would listen to you)?
- Submit an essay on a topic of your choice.

CAPPEX APPLICATION

One required essay, 600 words or fewer:

Tell us a story about yourself that is key to understanding who you are. This could be a moment you changed, grew or made a difference.

Appendix C
Financial Aid Shopping Sheet

University of the United States (UUS)
Student Name, Identifier

⬇ Download

Costs in the 2017–18 year

Estimated Cost of Attendance		**$ X,XXX** / yr
Tuition and fees	$ X,XXX	
Housing and meals	X,XXX	
Books and supplies	X,XXX	
Transportation	X,XXX	
Other education costs	X,XXX	

Grants and scholarships to pay for college

Total Grants and Scholarships ("Gift" Aid; no repayment needed)		**$X,XXX** / yr
Grants and scholarships from your school	$ X,XXX	
Federal Pell Grant	X,XXX	
Grants from your state	X,XXX	
Other scholarships you can use	X,XXX	

What will you pay for college

Net Costs
(Cost of attendance minus total grants and scholarships)   **$X,XXX** / yr

Options to pay net costs

Work options

Work-Study (Federal, state, or institutional) .... $ X,XXX

Loan Options*

Federal Perkins Loan	$ X,XXX
Federal Direct Subsidized Loan	X,XXX
Federal Direct Unsubsidized Loan	X,XXX

*Recommended amounts shown here. You may be eligible for a different amount. Contact your financial aid office.

Other options

Family Contribution   **$X,XXX** / yr
(As calculated by the institution using information reported on the FAFSA or to your institution.)

- Payment plan offered by the institution
- Parent or Graduate PLUS Loans
- American Opportunity Tax Credit *
- Military and/or National Service benefits
- Non-Federal private education loan

*Parents or students may qualify to receive up to $2,500 by claiming the American Opportunity Tax Credit on their tax return during the following calendar year.

Customized information from UUS

Graduation Rate
Percentage of full-time students who graduate within 6 years

XX.X%

Low	Medium	High

Repayment Rate
Percentage of borrowers entering into repayment within 3 years of leaving school

XX.X%

X.X% National Average

This Institution

Median Borrowing
Students who borrow at UUS typically take out $X,XXX in Federal loans for their undergraduate study. The Federal loan payment over 10 years for this amount is approximately $X,XXX per month. Your borrowing may be different.

$

Repaying your loans
To learn about loan repayment choices and work out your Federal Loan monthly payment, go to:
http://studentaid.ed.gov/repay-loans/understand/plans

For more information and next steps:
University of the United States (UUS)
Financial Aid Office
123 Main Street
Anytown, ST 12345
Telephone: (123) 456-7890
E-mail: financialaid@uus.edu

Glossary

Cost of Attendance (COA): The total amount (not including grants and scholarships) that it will cost you to go to school during the 2017–18 school year. COA includes tuition and fees; housing and meals; and allowances for books, supplies, transportation, loan fees, and dependent care. It also includes miscellaneous and personal expenses, such as an allowance for the rental or purchase of a personal computer; costs related to a disability; and reasonable costs for eligible study-abroad programs. For students attending less than half-time, the COA includes tuition and fees; an allowance for books, supplies, and transportation; and dependent care expenses.

Total Grants and Scholarships: Student aid funds that do not have to be repaid. Grants are often need-based, while scholarships are usually merit-based. Occasionally you might have to pay back part or all of a grant if, for example, you withdraw from school before finishing a semester.

Net Costs: An estimate of the actual costs that you or your family will need to pay during the 2017–18 school year to cover education expenses at a particular school. Net costs are determined by taking the institution's cost of attendance and subtracting your grants and scholarships.

Work-Study: A federal student aid program that provides part-time employment while you are enrolled in school to help pay your education expenses.

Loans: Borrowed money that must be repaid with interest. Loans from the federal government typically have a lower interest rate than loans from private lenders. Federal loans, listed from most advantageous to least advantageous, are called Federal Perkins Loans, Direct Subsidized Loans, Direct Unsubsidized Loans, and Direct PLUS Loans. You can find more information about federal loans at StudentAid.gov.

Family Contribution (also referred to as Expected Family Contribution): A number used by a school to calculate how much financial aid you are eligible to receive, if any. It's based on the financial information you provided in your Free Application for Federal Student Aid (FAFSA). It's not the amount of money your family will have to pay for college, nor is it the amount of federal student aid you will receive. The family contribution is reported to you on your Student Aid Report, also known as the SAR.

Graduation Rate: The graduation rate after 150% of normal program completion time has elapsed. For schools that award predominately bachelor's (four-year) degrees, this is after six years, and for students seeking an associate's (two-year) degree, this is after three years. For students seeking a certificate, the length of time depends on the certificate sought, for example, for a one-year certificate, after 18 months. These rates are only for full-time students enrolled for the first time.

Repayment Rate: The share of students who have repaid at least $1 of the principal balance on their federal loans within 3 years of leaving school.

Median Borrowing: The median federal debt of undergraduate borrowers who completed. This figure includes only federal loans; it excludes private student loans and parent PLUS loans.

Customized information from UUS

Appendix D
Cost of Attendance Worksheet

Name of college   _____ _____ _____ _____

Tuition and fees   _____ _____ _____ _____

Room and board   _____ _____ _____ _____

Books and supplies   _____ _____ _____ _____

Personal expenses   _____ _____ _____ _____

Travel   _____ _____ _____ _____

Total   _____ _____ _____ _____

College Preparation Time Line

This college preparation time line covers key points in the college preparation process. The specifics will vary depending on you and the counseling program at your high school. Use this time line as a preview of what is to come and as a general guide, but be sure to supplement and refine it with information provided by your counseling office and the colleges where you will be applying. Recruited athletes, visual and performing artists, and students with disabilities who wish to obtain testing accommodations will have additional tasks to include in their time line.

In preparing the time line, we have assumed that you will begin thinking seriously about college admissions by your junior year. If, like many students, you wait until senior year, we have a special senior-year fall semester time line designed especially for you. You'll find it at the end of the time line.

FRESHMAN YEAR

Although you do not need to focus on the college application process during freshman year, the following steps are good preparation for success in general:

- Take challenging courses in academic solids: English, foreign language, mathematics, science, and social studies.
- Study hard.

- Seek help from your teachers early if you experience academic difficulties. Do so every year, not just freshman year.
- Explore extracurricular activities inside and outside school to find those that interest and excite you.
- Read as much as you can.
- Plan summer activities that will enrich you in some way: summer school, work experience, family travel, and so forth. Don't be a couch potato. But don't worry about whether these activities will make you look good to a college.
- At the end of the year, begin a permanent record of your extracurricular and volunteer activities, academic honors and awards, and so on.

SOPHOMORE YEAR

In your sophomore year, continue taking challenging courses and developing your extracurricular interests and talents. It is also a time when a number of students take on part-time jobs. Families may begin thinking about college in more concrete terms. Some high schools begin a formal program of college orientation in the sophomore year, but most do not.

All Year
- Study hard in a challenging curriculum.
- Continue your involvement in extracurricular activities; look for opportunities to assume leadership roles.
- Consider volunteer activities.
- If you work part-time, be sure you keep on top of your academics.
- Save samples of your best papers and work in the arts (if applicable) for potential later use.

Fall
- Consider taking the PSAT or PreACT (or both) for practice, if they are offered to sophomores through your high school. The PreACT may be given in winter or spring.

Winter

- PSAT results arrive in December. After reading the information that comes with your scores, consider meeting with your counselor to discuss steps you might take to address your weaker areas. None of these scores actually counts for anything, so don't worry about them.

- Plan a challenging program of classes for your junior year.

- Begin to make plans for enriching summer activities (for example, paid or volunteer work, classes, travel).

- Register at school for May Advanced Placement tests if appropriate.

Spring

- If your family will be traveling over spring break, consider including a visit to one or two colleges that may interest you.

- Consult your counselor and register for SAT Subject Tests if appropriate. This may apply to students taking advanced math, science, or foreign language courses if they are interested in the small group of colleges that require or recommend them.

- Update your record of extracurricular activities, awards, and so on that you began at the end of freshman year.

Summer

- Reap the benefits of your earlier planning for a productive summer. Continue to read.

- Some students who are interested in qualifying for the National Merit Scholarship Program may wish to do some preparation for the PSAT that they will take in October.

JUNIOR YEAR

Junior year typically marks the start of the college selection process. Junior year grades play an especially important role in college admission, so a focus on academics is very important. By junior year, most students have identified the extracurricular areas in which they have the greatest talent and passion, although new interests can develop.

All Year

- Study hard in a challenging curriculum.

- Continue involvement in extracurricular and volunteer activities and seek leadership roles as appropriate.

- If you work part-time during the school year, make sure to continue a strong focus on your academics.

- Continue to save samples of your best papers and work in the arts (if appropriate) for potential later use.

- Students interested in athletics at the Division I and Division II levels should talk to their coaches and review eligibility requirements on the NCAA website, www.ncaa.org.

Fall

- Buy or borrow a copy of a "big book" college guide such as the Princeton Review *Best Colleges* or *Fiske Guide to Colleges.* It will be a useful resource over the next 18 months.

- Take the PSAT in October.

- Study hard in your classes. If you experience academic difficulty, seek help early.

- Complete the "Determining Your Priorities" questionnaire at the end of chapter 4 to help you decide what to look for in a college.

- Many colleges send representatives to high schools in the fall. If your school allows juniors to participate, consider attending sessions that interest you.

- If you want to be a varsity athlete in college, contact the coaches at the schools that interest you if they have not already contacted you.

Winter

- PSAT results arrive. After reading your score report, talk to your counselor about steps you can take to improve your performance on the upcoming SAT or ACT as appropriate.

- Learn the differences between the ACT and SAT and decide which one(s) you will take. Register for winter or spring SAT or ACT tests or both. February or April is a good month for a first ACT, March or May for a first SAT.

- Late fall or winter is a good time to prepare (using a book, software, courses, or tutor) for standardized tests.

- If you have not already met with your counselor to begin discussing college selection, do so now.

- Explore search engines such as BigFuture and College Navigator.

- Register at your school for May Advanced Placement tests if appropriate.

- Choose challenging courses for your senior year.

- Make plans for an enriching summer. Once again, consider travel, course work, volunteer or paid employment, workshops, or clinics that match your interests.

- If your applications will require a portfolio or audition tape, get started on it now.

Spring

- Continue to develop your college list, ideally in consultation with your counselor.
- Start a filing system to help you keep all your college materials organized.
- Consider using the spring break to visit colleges.
- Register for and take spring SAT Subject Tests as appropriate, depending on the requirements or recommendations of the colleges that interest you. Register to take or retake the SAT or ACT as appropriate.
- Request materials from colleges that interest you.
- Attend a nearby college fair if possible.
- Consider visiting colleges over the summer, and plan these visits early.
- Continue to meet with your counselor as you develop your short list.
- Update your record of extracurricular activities, awards, and so forth.

Summer

- Reap the benefits of your planning for an enriching summer experience, whether it involves work, travel, study, or other activity.

- Visit colleges as appropriate to help refine your college list.
- Consider getting a head start on the college application process by brainstorming about or actually drafting a personal essay.

SENIOR YEAR

The senior year is the busiest in the college selection process. Students who choose to apply early need to have a completed application ready to go by November 1 or 15. In general, students should have their college list settled by mid-November so that they can submit their rolling admissions and regular decision applications by the deadlines without being rushed.

All Year

- Study hard in a challenging curriculum. Colleges will receive your fall grades if you apply regular decision, and they may ask for quarter grades if you apply ED or EA.
- Part-time work is often a part of senior year. Again, be sure to maintain your academic focus.
- Continue your extracurricular and volunteer activities and leadership roles.

Fall

- Visit additional colleges if time and circumstances permit. Arrange overnights and on-campus interviews when feasible and available.
- Meet with college representatives who are visiting your high school, and attend a fall college fair and college nights to get more information.
- Use net price calculators to get estimates of out-of-pocket costs at different colleges.
- Finalize your college list in consultation with your counselor. Decide if an early application is right for you.
- Be sure to make note of all deadlines for each of the colleges on your list.
- Register and take fall SAT or ACT tests if necessary. Be aware of early deadlines if you want a fall test score to be part of your application.

- Ask teachers for letters of recommendation at least one month before the first letter is due, preferably earlier.

- Finalize your essays, having carefully edited them with the benefit of appropriate input from teachers and counselors.

- Submit applications by the required deadlines, proofreading carefully and double-checking that all parts are complete.

- Arrange to have standardized test scores and high school transcripts sent to colleges by their deadlines.

- Have alumni interviews as appropriate.

- If applying early, receive your decision by December 15. If admitted, congratulations! If not, move on. If you haven't yet submitted your regular decision applications, do so right now. Consider an ED II application, if appropriate, to another school that is very high on your list.

- If you will be applying for financial aid, alert your parents that the FAFSA and CSS PROFILE may be filed as early as October 1, using PPY data. File early. Start your outside scholarship search as well.

Winter

- If deferred when applying early, express in writing your continued interest in attending.

- Submit any remaining applications and scholarship forms.

- For deferred and regular applications, send significant new information regarding accomplishments and awards, if any, to colleges.

- Ask your counselor to send a midyear report to colleges.

- Have alumni interviews as appropriate.

- Keep focused on your academic work.

Spring

- Decisions may arrive as early as February or as late as early April.

- Attend admitted student programs in April, if possible, to learn more about the colleges that have admitted you.

- Carefully consider and compare your financial aid packages and consider requesting a review if a package is not adequate for your needs. Do this earlier if awards are available earlier.

- Make your final decision about where you want to go, and submit your deposit by May 1. Notify the other schools that admitted you that you will not be attending.

- If you are wait-listed, decide whether to remain on the wait list. Be sure to make a deposit by May 1 at a school where you were accepted. If you decide to remain on a wait list, follow any instructions from the college. Write to the admissions office conveying your enthusiasm as well as any new information. Ask your counselor to do the same, if the school is a private college or out-of-state public university.

- Enjoy the remainder of your senior year!

WHAT IF YOU ARE BEGINNING YOUR SEARCH IN SENIOR YEAR?

A lot of students put off serious thinking about college until the fall of their senior year. Maybe you are one of them. Although we don't recommend that approach, don't worry—you can make up for lost time if you use your time wisely. By January of your senior year, you'll be in sync with your classmates who started their college search much earlier. The following special fall senior year time line will help you get going:

- Use the college search engines at BigFuture and College Navigator to develop a list of colleges that meet your criteria.

- Make sure you have already taken (or are registered to take) the SAT or ACT and SAT Subject Tests if they are likely to be recommended or required by the colleges where you may be applying. If you can't take certain tests in time, you will need to focus on the many test-optional colleges or the vast majority that do not require Subject Tests.

- Read chapters 4 and 5 of this book carefully, and fill out the "Determining Your Priorities" questionnaire to help you identify your preferences. Meet with your counselor as soon as possible to discuss colleges that will meet your needs.

- Talk to friends, family members, and classmates about colleges they may recommend.

- Do careful research on the colleges that emerge from your data-gathering efforts. Study college websites.

- Watch for visits by college representatives, evening programs, and nearby college fairs. Use them to gather additional information.

- Visit colleges on your list if you can, taking advantage of high school vacations. But don't worry—you can still visit in the spring after you are accepted and before you must make a decision.

- A good application takes time to prepare, especially if it requires a special essay or other custom responses.

- Make sure that your college list has an appropriate range of colleges: likely, possible, and long shot. Check back with your counselor before you finalize it.

- Ask one or two teachers whether they would be willing to write a letter of recommendation on your behalf if your schools require such letters. Talk to them as early as you can in the fall semester once you know that your probable colleges require or recommend such letters. Tell them that you will give background information about yourself once you have your final college list and application forms. Give them at least three to four weeks to write their letters.

- Be aware that EA and ED applications are generally due by November 1 or November 15. You may not have enough time to do a careful job of selecting a college and preparing a strong application by that date. If you are rushed, don't apply early. Some colleges have a second early decision due date in mid-December or early January. This works better for late starters.

- Make sure you know all of the deadlines (applications, financial aid, test scores) for your schools. Complete financial aid forms ASAP. Be sure to have your SAT or ACT scores sent to colleges on your list.

- Use the Common Application or other multi-campus application forms whenever possible to save time and effort, and apply online if given a choice.

- Prepare your applications carefully and thoughtfully, and proofread everything well. Have someone else help you proofread as well.

Resources

This section includes sources of additional information on selected topics covered in *Admission Matters*. We've chosen web resources, some apps, and a few books that we find helpful, although there are many more we could have included. Additional resources can be found in the text of *Admission Matters* in the appropriate chapters. Please check our website at www.admissionmatters.com for updates, changes, and new additions.

GENERAL ADMISSIONS INFORMATION

Web

www.bigfuture.org: College Board site includes information about all aspects of college search and selection, as well as test preparation and registration.

www.nacacnet.org: Site of the National Association for College Admission Counseling. The Knowledge Center tab contains links to good information on a wide range of topics.

www.princetonreview.com: Free information about the college admissions process, including test preparation.

www.fairtest.org: Lists almost 900 schools that admit a substantial number of students without regard to SAT or ACT scores.

www.campustours.com: Links to virtual campus tours and videos at hundreds of campuses.

http://nsse.indiana.edu: Students and Parents tab links to "Pocket Guide to Choosing a College: Questions to Ask on Your College Visits" based on the National Survey of Student Engagement. Mobile version available.

Book

Where You Go Is Not Who You'll Be: An Antidote to the College Admissions Mania by Frank Bruni (New York: Hachette Book Group, 2015): Broadens the view of what makes a good college experience.

REFERENCE GUIDES TO COLLEGES

See the BigFuture and Princeton Review sites in the previous section. Each contains detailed profiles of individual colleges as well as a search feature that identifies colleges meeting criteria entered by the user.

Web

www.collegecost.ed.gov: College Affordability and Transparency Center that includes a link to College Navigator, a database allowing college search by location, program, and degree offerings. Also links to other resources including net price calculators of all colleges.

www.usnews.com/education: Free limited access to the *U.S. News* database used to generate college rankings. Although we do not favor use of these rankings, the data used to generate them can be helpful.

Books

College Handbook by the College Board: Updated annually. Contains profiles of all 3,900 four-year and two-year colleges in the United States.

Book of Majors by the College Board. Updated annually. In-depth descriptions of 200 popular majors as well as listings of over 1,200 majors offered at more than 3,800 colleges.

The College Finder by Steven Antonoff (Westford, MA: Wintergreen Orchard House, 2016): Lists of recommended programs by major, sport, and other categories.

Mobile Apps

CollegeGo—The College Board. iOS and Android app for college planning.
Schoold—Vested Finance. iOS and Android app for college search and scholarship match.

NARRATIVE AND EVALUATIVE GUIDES TO COLLEGES

Web

www.ctcl.org: Lots of good information about college selection.
https://colleges.niche.com: Student-generated evaluations of colleges.

Books

Colleges That Change Lives: 40 Schools That Will Change the Way You Think About Colleges by Loren Pope and Hilary Masell Oswald (New York: Penguin Books, 2012): Descriptions of 40 lesser-known but excellent liberal arts colleges.
Fiske Guide to Colleges by Edward Fiske (Naperville, IL: Sourcebooks): Updated annually. Contains profiles and personal descriptions of more than 300 popular colleges and universities.

Insider Accounts

These are best viewed as a window into the admissions process at highly selective institutions rather than as a how-to guide to gain admission to them.

The Gatekeepers: Inside the Admissions Process of a Premier College by Jacques Steinberg (New York: Penguin, 2003): Describes the author's experience observing an admissions cycle at Wesleyan University.
Creating a Class: College Admissions and the Education of Elites by Mitchell Stevens (Cambridge, MA: Harvard University Press, 2009): The author's experience observing the admissions process at Hamilton College.

SPECIAL FOCUS GUIDES

www.ajcunet.edu: Site sponsored by Jesuit colleges. See also www.accunet.org: Site dedicated to Catholic higher education in general.

www.hillel.org: Site of Hillel, the Foundation for Jewish Campus Life.

www.womenscolleges.org: Official site of the Women's Colleges Coalition.

www.blackexcel.org: The College Help Network for African American students.

http://carla.umn.edu: The Center for Advanced Research on Language Acquisition lets you search for course offerings in less commonly taught languages at colleges and universities.

TEST PREPARATION

Web

www.bigfuture.org: Information for College Board tests and registration for SAT and SAT Subject Tests.

www.khanacademy.org: Provides free online personalized practice for the PSAT and SAT.

www.ACT.org: Information, preparation, and registration for the ACT.

www.ets.org: Information, preparation, and registration for the TOEFL (Test of English as a Foreign Language).

www.ielts.org: Information and preparation for the IELTS (International English Language Testing System).

Books

The Official SAT Study Guide, 2016 Edition by the College Board (Princeton, NJ: College Board, 2015).

The Official ACT Prep Guide (San Francisco, CA: Jossey-Bass, 2017).

Mobile Apps

Daily Practice for the New SAT—The College Board. iOS and Android app.

ACT Prep Online—ACT, Inc. iOS and Android app coordinated with ACT Online Prep (fee).

ESSAY WRITING

On Writing the College Application Essay, 25th Anniversary Edition: The Key to Acceptance at the College of Your Choice by Henry Bauld (New York: Collins Reference, 2012): A former Ivy League admissions officer provides tough and funny advice on coming up with the best essay possible.

The College Application Essay, 6th Edition by Sarah Myers McGinty (Princeton, NJ: College Board, 2015): Excellent advice on writing effective essays.

ADVICE FOR ARTISTS

Web

www.portfolioday.net: Site of the National Portfolio Day Association, a group of accredited arts colleges and university art departments that are members of the National Association of Schools of Art and Design.

Book

I GOT IN! The Ultimate College Audition Guide for Acting and Musical Theatre, 2015 Edition by Mary Anna Dennard (Mary Anna Dennard, Inc., 2015): How to prepare for the highly competitive college audition process.

ADVICE FOR ATHLETES

Web

www.ncaa.org: Website of the National Collegiate Athletic Association.

www.naia.org: Website of the National Association of Intercollegiate Athletics.

Books

The Student Athlete's Guide to Getting Recruited: How to Win Scholarships, Attract Colleges and Excel as an Athlete by Stewart Brown (Belmont, CA: Supercollege, 2016): Guidance on choosing an NCAA division, recruiting, and so on.

Understanding Athletic Recruiting: A Comprehensive Guide for the High School Student-Athlete, 2nd Edition by Jeffrey Durso-Finley and Lewis Stivall (CollegeRecruitingResource@gmail.com, 2014): A 150-page handbook covering all aspects of the college athletic recruiting process.

SPECIAL CIRCUMSTANCES

Web

https://ldaamerica.org: Site of Learning Disabilities Association of America with wide range of information about learning disabilities; for college-specific information, search for "college."

www.nacacnet.org: Click on Undocumented Students through the Knowledge Center: Information on DACA and many links to articles and websites about college admission and financial aid for undocumented students.

www.nilc.org/issues/daca/: Site of the National Immigration Law Center. Provides information for students concerned about immigration status.

Books

I'm First! Guide to College—2017 (Strive for College, http://store.ImFirst.org): Guidebook for first-generation college students.

K&W Guide to Colleges for Students with Learning Differences, 13th Edition by Marybeth Kravets and Imy Wax (New York: Random House, 2016): Profiles the services for learning disabled students at over 350 colleges.

Life After High School by Susan Yellin and Christina Cacioppo Bertsch (Philadelphia, PA: Jessica Kingsley Publishers, 2010): Advice and support for students with disabilities and their families.

And What About College? How Homeschooling Leads to Admissions to the Best Colleges and Universities by Cafi Cohen (New York: Holt Associates, 2000): Resource for homeschooled students about the college search and application process.

FINANCIAL AID

Books

Scholarship Handbook by the College Board. Updated annually. Information on private, federal, and state funding sources of financial aid.

Getting Financial Aid by the College Board. Updated annually. Advice on all aspects of the financial aid process.

Secrets to Winning a Scholarship by Mark Kantrowitz (CreateSpace Independent Publishing Platform, 2011): Advice on finding and applying for private scholarships.

Web

www.bigfuture.org: Click on Pay for College for information on the FAFSA, CSS PROFILE, net price calculators, and expected family contribution calculators.

www.fafsa.ed.gov: Federal site for FAFSA (Free Application for Federal Student Aid). Also http://studentaid.ed.gov for additional information.

www.fastweb.com: Scholarship search.

www.scholarships.com: Scholarship search.

www.finaid.org: General site with lots of information about all aspects of financial aid.

www.newgibill.org: Provides tools to calculate post-9/11 GI Bill benefits and compare college costs after benefits are considered.

https://mydocumentedlife.org/2016/09/12/scholarships-open-to-undocumented-students/: Up-to-date scholarship information with deadlines.

INTERNATIONAL STUDENTS

Web

www.nafsa.org/About_Us/About_International_Education/For_Students/: Site of the Association of International Educators with pages for US students studying abroad and international students studying in the United States, including financial aid.

www.edupass.org: Provides information on every topic about studying and living in the United States.

www.educateabroad.co (click on Resources): Data on nearly 400 US colleges and universities detailing financial aid policies for international students.

Books

International Student Handbook by the College Board. Updated annually. Information on 3,200 colleges, including TOEFL requirements, financial aid, housing availability, and other services.

Learn in the United States: The International Student's Guide for Applying to American Colleges by Ryan Byrne and Gayle Byrne (Kindle, 2011) (electronic version only): The total international student application process from exploring the US educational system to securing a visa.

GAP YEAR

www.americangap.org: Site of the American Gap Association; lists accredited programs and provides information on travel, financial aid, and so on.

http://usagapyearfairs.org: Lists upcoming gap year fairs (click on Browse Programs for a full list).

STUDYING IN CANADA, THE UNITED KINGDOM, IRELAND, AND HOLLAND

www.aucc.ca: The official website of the Association of Universities and Colleges of Canada, in English and French.

www.ucas.ac.uk: The basic guide and application site for universities in the United Kingdom.

www.theguardian.com/education/universityguide: Authoritative online guide to all universities and programs of study in the United Kingdom.

http://unistats.direct.gov.uk: The official website for comparing UK higher education data on programs and outcomes at all UK universities.

www.iua.ie: Website of the Irish Universities Association, with links to the seven major Irish universities.

www.studyinholland.nl: The official starting point for information about studying in Holland.

Guide to International University Admission by the National Association for College Admission Counseling. Access through the International link in the Knowledge Center at www.nacacnet.org.

Notes

INTRODUCTION

1. F. Bruni, *Where You Go Is Not Who You Will Be: An Antidote to College Admissions Mania* (New York: Grand Central Publishing, 2016).

CHAPTER ONE

1. M. Shaevitz, "Why Is College Admissions Such a Mess?" *Huffington Post,* March 29, 2016, www.huffingtonpost.com/marjorie-hansen-shaevitz/why-is-college-admissions_b_9535524.html.
2. N. Anderson, "Applied to Stanford or Harvard? You Probably Didn't Get In. Admit Rates Drop, Again," *Washington Post,* April 1, 2016, www.washingtonpost.com/news/grade-point/wp/2016/04/01/applied-to-stanford-or-harvard-you-probably-didnt-get-in-admit-rates-drop-again/.
3. S. Rosenberg, "New SAT Brings New Challenges, Same Old Pressure," *Boston Globe,* March 4, 2016, www.bostonglobe.com/2016/03/04/new-sat-brings old-familiar-pressures/xaPF5Wbqzqlsx5zuMWrsSK/story.html.
4. R. Perez-Pena, "Best, Brightest and Rejected: Elite Colleges Turn Away Up to 95%." *New York Times,* April 8, 2014, www.nytimes.com/2014/04/09/us/led-by-stanfords-5-top-colleges-acceptance-rates-hit-new-lows.html.
5. V. Strauss, "How College Admissions Has Turned into Something Akin to 'The Hunger Games,'" *Washington Post,* March 28, 2016, www.washingtonpost.com/news/answer-sheet/wp/2016/03/28/how-college-admissions-has turned-into-something-akin-to-the-hunger-games/.
6. L. Colarusso, "Why Colleges Aggressively Recruit Applicants Just to Turn Them Down," *PBS News Hour,* January 12, 2015, www.pbs.org/newshour/updates/colleges-ratchet-recruiting-applicants-just-turn/.

7. A. Wong, "The Absurdity of College Admissions," *The Atlantic,* March 28, 2016, www.theatlantic.com/education/archive/2016/03/where-admissions-went-wrong/475575/.

8. P. Bransberger and D. Michelau, *Knocking at the College Door: Projections of High School Graduates* (Boulder, CO: Western Interstate Commission for Higher Education, 2016).

9. B. Mayher, *The College Admissions Mystique* (New York: Farrar, Straus and Giroux, 1998), 28.

10. G. Casper, letter to James Fallows, editor of *U.S. News and World Report,* September 23, 1996, www.stanford.edu/dept/pres-provost/president/speeches/961206gcfallows.html.

11. Graduation rate performance measures the difference between a school's six-year graduation rate for a given class and the predicted rate based on characteristics of the students as entering freshmen and the school's expenditures on them.

12. L. Bollinger, "Debate over the SAT Masks Trends in College Admissions," *Chronicle of Higher Education,* July 12, 2002, B11.

13. M. Fitts, cited in M. Strecker, "Tulane Surges to No. 41 in Latest 'U.S. News' Ranking," Tulane Undergraduate Admission web page, September 9, 2015, http://admission.tulane.edu/livecontent/news/298-tulane-surges-to-no-41-in-latest-us-news-ranking.php.

14. R. Toor, *College Confidential: An Insider's Account of the Elite College Selection Process* (New York: St. Martin's Press, 2001), 2.

15. G. Goldsmith, cited in G. Golden, "Glass Floor: Colleges Reject Top Applicants Accepting Only Students Likely to Enroll," *Wall Street Journal,* May 29, 2002, www.wsj.com/articles/SB991083160294634500.

16. S. Dale and A. Krueger, "Estimating the Payoff to Attending a More Selective College: An Application of Selection on Observables and Unobservables," *Quarterly Journal of Economics* 117, 2002, 1491–1528.

17. A. Krueger, cited in D. Leonhardt, "Revisiting the Value of Elite Colleges," *New York Times,* February 21, 2011, http://economix.blogs.nytimes.com/2011/02/21/revisiting-the-value-of-elite-colleges/.

18. D. Davenport, "How Not to Judge a College," Scripps Howard News Service, September 9, 2003.

19. S. Lewis, cited in A. Kucsynski, "Best List for Colleges by *U.S. News* Is Under Fire," *New York Times,* August 20, 2001, C1, www.nytimes.com/2001/08/20/business/the-media-business-best-list-for-colleges-by-us-news-is-under-fire.html.

CHAPTER TWO

1. G. W. Pierson, "Historical Statistics of the College and University, 1701–1976," 1983, www.yale.edu/oir/pierson_original.htm.

2. Trinity University, Selection Criteria, September 27, 2016, https://new.trinity.edu/admissions-aid/applying-trinity/selection-criteria.

3. D. Hawkins, cited in A. B. White, "Under Pressure," *Arlington Magazine*, September–October 2014, www.arlingtonmagazine.com/September-October-2014/Under-Pressure/index.php?cparticle=1&siarticle=0#artanc.

4. David Erdmann, personal communication, January 2004.

5. W. Black, cited in C. Capuzzi Simon, "The Test-Optional Surge," *New York Times*, October 28, 2015, www.nytimes.com/2015/11/01/education/edlife/the-test-optional-surge.html.

6. D. Gould, cited in R. Shea and D. Marcus, "Make Yourself a Winner," in *America's Best Colleges* (Washington, DC: *U.S. News and World Report*, 2001).

7. S. McMillen, "In Admission, How Do You Separate the Wheat from the Wheat?" *Chronicle of Higher Education*, June 27, 2003, B13, www.chronicle.com/article/In-Admissions-How-Do-You/10607.

8. F. Hargadon, "Advice from the Inside," in Harvard Independent Staff (eds.), *100 Successful College Application Essays* (New York: New American Library, 2002), 6.

9. S. McGinty, "Issues of Access," *NACAC Journal* 177, Fall 2002, 27–30.

10. P. Marthers, "Admissions Messages vs. Admissions Realities," in L. Thacker (ed.), *College Unranked: Affirming Educational Values in College Admissions* (Portland, OR: Education Conservancy, 2004), 79.

11. C. Deacon, cited in E. Craig, "GU Defends Use of Legacy Admissions," *Hoya*, April 16, 2004, 1.

12. T. Parker, cited in M. Klein, "Bill Aims to Increase All College Opportunities," *Amherst Student*, November 12, 2003, 1.

13. D. Golden, *The Price of Admission: How America's Ruling Class Buys Its Way into Elite Colleges—and Who Gets Left Outside the Gates* (New York: Crown Publishers, 2006).

14. W. Bowen and S. Levin, *Reclaiming the Game: College Sports and Educational Values* (Princeton, NJ: Princeton University Press, 2003).

15. J. Bagnoli, cited in S. Bushman, "College Receives Record Applications for 2020," *The Scarlet and Black*, April 8, 2016, www.thesandb.com/news/college-receives-record-applications-for-2020.html/comment-page-1.

CHAPTER THREE

1. The descriptions of the Wesleyan admissions review process are drawn from J. Steinberg, *The Gatekeepers: Inside the Admissions Process of an Elite College* (New York: Penguin, 2003). Updated and confirmed as current as of 2016–2017 through personal communication with Nancy Hargrave Meislahn, Dean of Admission and Financial Aid.
2. J. Merrow, transcript of "Inside College Admissions," broadcast on KVIE, November 15, 2000.
3. Shawn Abbott, personal communication, January 2004.
4. A. Wright, personal communication, October 2016.
5. M. Rubinoff, personal communication, November 2012.
6. M. Jones, "Parents Get Too Aggressive on Admissions," *USA Today*, January 6, 2003, 13A, http://usatoday30.usatoday.com/news/opinion/editorials/2003-01-05-jones_x.htm.

CHAPTER FOUR

1. Michael Tamada, personal communication, April 2004.
2. Noel-Levitz, "Academic Advising Highly Important to Students," www.ruffalonl.com/documents/shared/Papers_and_Research/2009/AcademicAdvisingHighlyImportant09.pdf.

CHAPTER FIVE

1. *The Best 381 Colleges* (New York: Princeton Review, 2016); E. Fiske, *Fiske Guide to Colleges* (Naperville, IL: Sourcebooks, 2016).
2. J. Greenberg, personal communication, October 2012.

CHAPTER SIX

1. D. Coleman, cited in T. Balf, "The Story Behind the SAT Overhaul," *New York Times*, March 6, 2014, www.nytimes.com/2014/03/09/magazine/the-story-behind-the-sat-overhaul.html.
2. J. Applerouth, personal communication, August 2016.

CHAPTER SEVEN

1. Duke University admissions website, Early and Regular Decision, September 27, 2016, http://admissions.duke.edu/application/timeline.

2. University of Pennsylvania admissions website, Early Decision and Regular Decision, September 27, 2016, www.admissions.upenn.edu/apply/freshman-admission/early-and-regular-decision.

3. E. Furda, cited in C. Simon, "Likely Letters Aim to Recruit Top Students," *The Daily Pennsylvanian,* March 2, 1015, www.thedp.com/article/2015/03/likely-letters-aim-to-recruit-top-applicants.

CHAPTER EIGHT

1. A. Leider and R. Leider, *Don't Miss Out: The Ambitious Student's Guide to Financial Aid* (Alexandria, VA: Octameron, 2000), 42.

2. M. O. Shapiro, cited in J. Russell, "Top Applicants Bargaining for More Aid from Colleges," *Boston Globe,* June 12, 2002, A1.

3. Union College admissions website, Need Blind vs. Need Aware, September 27, 2016, www.union.edu/admissions/school-counselor/resources/needblind-needaware/.

4. S. Trachenberg, cited in M. Bombardieri, "Needy Students Miss Out," *Boston Globe,* April 25, 2004, A1.

5. Muhlenberg College admissions website, The Real Deal on Financial Aid, September 27, 2016, www.muhlenberg.edu/main/admissions/therealdealonfinancialaid/.

6. D. Martin, cited in S. Teicher, "Not Enough Financial Aid? Seek Counseling," *Christian Science Monitor,* April 26, 2004, 13.

7. Carnegie Mellon University admissions website, Financial Aid Principles and Practices, September 27, 2016, https://admission.enrollment.cmu.edu/pages/financial-aid.

8. M. Kantrowitz, cited in D. Douglas-Gabriel, "How to Negotiate a Better Financial Aid Package," *Washington Post,* April 2, 2015, www.washingtonpost.com/news/get-there/wp/2015/04/02/how-to-negotiate-a-better-financial-aid-package/.

9. S. Pemberton, cited in Teicher, "Not Enough Financial Aid?"

CHAPTER NINE

1. T. Bankston, personal communication, July 2016.

2. S. Hallenbeck, former dean of admission at Hood College, personal communication, January 2004. She reported that the student was admitted after giving everyone a good chuckle.

3. M. Dahl, personal communication, July 2016.

4. H. Bauld, *On Writing the College Application Essay* (New York: Collins Reference, 2012), xviii.

5. D. Phillips, "The Question of the Essay," in G. Georges and C. Georges, *100 Successful College Application Essays* (New York: New American Library, 2002), 12.

6. J. Stroud, personal communication, July 2016.

7. E. Cheron, personal communication, July 2016.

8. W. Zinsser, *On Writing Well* (New York: HarperCollins, 2006).

9. J. Shiffman, Tulane University admissions blog, The Optional Statement, September 27, 2016, http://tuadmissionjeff.blogspot.com/2013/09/the-optional-statment.html?view=flipcard.

CHAPTER TEN

1. Williams College admissions website, Apply, September 27, 2016, http://admission.williams.edu/apply/.

2. Carnegie Mellon University admissions website, Admission Interviews, September 27, 2016, https://admission.enrollment.cmu.edu/pages/admission-interviews.

3. Rhodes College admissions website, Frequently Asked Questions, September 27, 2016, https://apply.rhodes.edu/admission/27069.asp.

4. University of St. Andrews admissions website, How to Apply for Undergraduate Study, October 8, 2016, www.st-andrews.ac.uk/admissions/ug/apply/.

5. Trinity University Dublin admissions website, International Foundation Programme, September 30, 2016, www.tcd.ie/study/FoundationProgramme/overview.php.

CHAPTER ELEVEN

1. J. Durso-Finley and L. Stival, *Understanding Athletic Recruiting: A Comprehensive Guide for the High School Student-Athlete* (2014), 37.

2. NESCAC Statement on Common Admissions Practices, September 27, 2016, http://athletics.bates.edu/nescac-statement.

3. B. Beach, personal communication, November 2012.

CHAPTER TWELVE

1. M. Kravets and I. Wax, *The K&W Guide to College Programs and Services for Students with Learning Differences*, 13th ed. (New York: Princeton Review, 2016).

2. M. Kravets, personal communication, October 2012.

3. S. Michaelson, in A. Moore, "Accommodations Angst," *New York Times,* November 4, 2010.

4. Hamilton College admissions website, Home Schooled Students, October 13, 2016, www.hamilton.edu/admission/apply/homeschool.

5. B. Poch, personal communication, July 2016.

CHAPTER THIRTEEN

1. A. S. Kostell, *U.S. News Education Blog,* September 14, 2011, www.usnews.com/education/blogs/college-admissions-experts/2011/09/14/what-are-some-tips-for-international-students-applying-to-us-colleges.

2. J. Montoya, *U.S. News Education Blog,* September 14, 2011.

3. S. Allen, "Tips on American College Admissions Essays, from a Veteran Dean, India Ink Blog," *New York Times,* January 11, 2012, http://india.blogs.nytimes.com/2012/01/11/choice-blog-admissions-essay/#more-15231.

4. EducationUSA, "Your Steps to USA Study," July 2, 2016, https://educationusa.state.gov/your-5-steps-us-study/research-your-options.

5. EducationUSA, "EducationUSA Policies," July 2, 2016, https://educationusa.state.gov/educationusa-policies.

6. ACT, "Questions About Registering to Test Outside of the United States," July 5, 2016, www.act.org/content/act/en/products-and-services/the-act/questions-about-registering-for-the-act-test-international.html.

7. K. Pauls, personal communication, July 2016.

8. M. Steidel, personal communication, November 2012.

9. EducationUSA, "Your Steps to USA Study," October 8, 2016, https://educationusa.state.gov/your-5-steps-us-study/complete-your-application/undergraduate.

10. MIT admissions website, "A Guide to Writing Evaluations for MIT," September 30, 2016, http://mitadmissions.org/apply/prepare/writingrecs.

11. Ibid.

12. C. Hooker Haring, *U.S. News Education Blog,* January 4, 2012, www.usnews.com/education/blogs/college-admissions-experts/2012/01/04/what-financial-aid-is-available-for-international-students.

CHAPTER FOURTEEN

1. R. Clark, Georgia Tech admissions blog, The Wait List Sucks, March 14, 2016, http://pwp.gatech.edu/admission-blog/2016/03/14/the-wait-list-sucks-part-1-of-3/.

2. M. Inzer, cited in A. Kaminer, "On a College Waiting List? Sending Cookies Isn't Going to Help," *New York Times*, May 11, 2013, www.nytimes.com/2013/05/12/education/on-the-waiting-list-some-college-applicants-try-a-little-dazzle.html.

3. J. O'Shea, cited in M. Miller, "What Is a Gap Year? Why More High School Seniors—Including Malia Obama—Are Hitting Pause Before College," *Vogue,* June 7, 2016, www.vogue.com/13443593/gap-years-malia-obama-how-to/.

4. J. Gore, University of Michigan admissions blog, Shaking Off Senioritis, January 15, 2015, http://admissions.umich.edu/explore-visit/blog/suffering-senioritis-time-shake-it.

About the Authors

Sally P. Springer, associate chancellor emerita at the University of California, Davis, is a psychologist with more than 30 years of experience in higher education as a professor and university administrator on both the East and West coasts. She is the coauthor of *Left Brain, Right Brain,* published by W. H. Freeman, which was honored by the American Psychological Foundation for contributing to the public's understanding of psychology. It has been translated into seven languages and appeared in five editions. Her second book, *How to Succeed in College,* published by Crisp, is a guide for college freshmen. She received her bachelor's degree summa cum laude from Brooklyn College of the City of New York, where she was a commuter student before venturing cross-country to Stanford University for her doctoral and postdoctoral work in psychology. She has been a volunteer admissions reader for the UC Davis campus and is a member of the National Association for College Admission Counseling and the Western Association for College Admission Counseling. She is a professional member of the Independent Educational Consultants Association and has served on its Committee on Education and Training. She is currently a member of the Advisory Committee for the Independent Educational Consultant certificate program at UC Irvine. She has personally taken the college admissions journey twice, with her son and her daughter.

Jon Reider is the director of college counseling at San Francisco University High School, an independent 9–12 high school. Before that, he served as an admissions officer at Stanford University for 15 years, rising to the post of senior associate director of admissions. He has two degrees in history, including a doctorate from Stanford, where he cofounded and taught in the Structured Liberal Education program, a freshman humanities course, for which he won the university's Gores award for outstanding teaching. Previously, he was a Marshall Scholar at the University of Sussex in England and taught sociology at the University of Tennessee at Chattanooga. He has also taught in the College Counseling Certificate Program at the University of California, Berkeley and has taught "Admissions 101" for Stanford's Continuing Studies Program. He is a nationally known speaker and essayist in the admissions profession and is widely cited in the media for his candid opinions and willingness to speak hard truths. He is a member of the National Association for College Admission Counseling and has served as the chair of its Committee on Current Trends and Future Issues.

Joyce Vining Morgan was a classroom teacher before becoming a college counselor. She earned her PhD in Slavic Languages and Literatures at Yale University and taught Russian language and literature at public and private universities, established a Russian language program for grades 7–12 in a public school in New Hampshire, and also taught Russian and English at private high schools. She was New Hampshire's Teacher of the Year in 1994. She also initiated and advised exchanges with schools in Russia, Crimea, Kazakhstan, and France and was the advisor of the first refugee Bosnian students to attend a US high school. When she began working as a college counselor at The Putney School in Vermont, she brought this breadth of experience with her. She also won awards for her teaching of Russian and for her work as a counselor. An active member of the New England and the National Associations for College Admission Counseling and an associate member of the International Association for College Admission Counseling, she has served on several regional and national committees including the NACAC Ad-Hoc Committee on Standardized Testing; most recently she served on the NEACAC Ad-Hoc Committee on Resources for Counselors Advising International Students. She served as vice president of the New England Association for College Admission Counseling, and in 2016 wrote the history of its first 50 years. Currently an independent educational consultant, a certified educational planner, and a member of the Independent Educational Consultants Association, she advises students and mentors new college counselors.

Index

Abbott, Shawn, 53

Academic advising: college–student fit and issue of, 92–94; importance of support services and, 92–93; pre-professional, 93–94

Academic index (AI), 250

Academic programs: bachelor of arts (BA), 254–255, 262; bachelor of fine arts (BFA) and bachelor of music (BM or BMus), 255–256, 262; filmmaking, 261–262; liberal arts colleges, 68; research universities, 70–71. *See also* Majors

Academic record: evaluated using a numerical rating, 49–50; as heart of a college application, 23; putting the GPA in context of your, 26–28; school report on, 28; transcripts of your, 27–28, 227–278, 300–301, 334–335. *See also* Grades (GPA)

Acceptance decisions: admit programs to take another look before, 322–323; dealing with disappointment when making your, 320–321; making tough choices for your, 318–319; making your ED (early decision), 316; remembering the transfer option when making your, 321; revising financial aid before making, 323–324; revisiting your priorities before making your, 319; for spring admits, 321–322.
See also Admissions decisions

Accommodations: Section 504 on, 268; for standardized testing, 146–147, 267, 274–276

Accreditation status, 295

ACT. *See* SAT/ACT

ADHD (attention deficit hyperactivity disorder): disclosing on application, 273–274; federal government definition of, 266; student success versus student access, 269; Tier One, Tier Two, Tier Three school support services for, 270–272

Admissions: Common Application used for, 6; comparing ED and overall class of 2020, 154; examples of changes in, 21–22; factors driving competitiveness of, 3–7; financial need-aware vs. need blind policies on, 179–180, 306; rolling, 162–163; selectivity of, 7–9, 56–57

Admissions decisions: the academic record criteria, 23–28; contacting disabilities services after receiving, 276; deferrals, 160, 218, 316–318; denials, 52–54, 160, 316–317; difficult choices required for the, 53–54; engagement beyond the classroom criteria, 23, 29–33; evaluating aid after you've been accepted, 190–193; extracurricular activities and other accomplishments criteria, 30–31, 97, 232–235; "holistic" process and, 47–48; hooks and institutional priorities factors of, 24, 36–42; likely letters and early notification, 161–162; personal qualities criteria, 24, 33–36, 49–50, 219–232; process of the, 45–61; spring admits, 321–322; standardized tests criteria, 24, 28–29; strategies for

Admissions decisions (*Continued*)
dealing with disappointment, 320–321;
summarizing the factors determining the,
42–44; tentative, 51–52; unpredictability of
the, 20–21; *See also* Acceptance decisions;
Student applicants

Admissions officers: ambassador and
gatekeeper roles of, 46–47; how they help
build the applicant pool, 46; what they look
for in letters of recommendation, 33, 279,
303–304; who are the, 45–46

Admissions process: the admissions officers
involved in, 45–47; "holistic," 47–48; how
college access programs can help you in,
58–59; how the application is evaluated,
49–50; how the final decision is made,
52–54; at the most selective colleges, 56–57;
the parental role during the, 60–61; reading
the application and file, 48–49; role of your
high school counselor in the, 57; tentative
decisions made during, 50–52; UCLA
example of the, 54–55; what happens to
your submitted application, 47–50

Admissions rates: factors that affect, 14–15;
how they contribute to college frenzy,
14–16; ways colleges can increase their
yield, 15–16

Admit programs, 322–323

Advanced Placement (AP) courses: academic
record inclusion of, 24–25; "Be reasonable
and stay sane" approach to taking, 25–26;
importance of both course load and grades
in, 25; required by English, Welsh, and
Northern Irish universities, 238; school
profile on, 27

Affirmative action admissions, 40

Affordability. *See* Finances

Agnes Scott College, 78

Air Force Academy, 76

Alcohol use, 87

Allen, Seth, 292

American University (AU), 215

Americans with Disabilities Act
(ADA), 268–269

Amherst College, 68, 92, 154, 244

Appealing financial aid package, 192

Applerouth, Jed, 138

Applicant pool: the competitiveness of the, 53;
parents' lack of understanding of the, 53;
personalized "search" letters used to build
college, 109–110. *See also* Student
applicants

Application choices: Cappex Application,
204–205; Coalition Application, 204, 210,
232; Common Application, 6, 202–203,
210, 214, 232, 264, 285, 303; Universal
College Application, 203, 210, 224, 232;
what should determine your, 205

Application preparation: fighting the urge to
procrastinate, 162–163, 200–201, 344;
follow directions, 202; neatness, proofing,
and completeness, 201–202; for student
artists, 257–261; tips for getting off to a
good start, 200–202; to-do list and timeline
for your, 216–218. *See also* The essay

Applications: the academic record as the heart
of your, 23; build your college list for
sending your, 101–126; Canadian, British,
Irish, and Dutch universities, 235–241;
evaluating the, 49–50, 52; getting them in
early vs. procrastinating your, 162–163,
200–201, 344; priority deadlines for,
162–163, 216; reading the submitted,
48–49; what happens to your submitted,
47–50; what to do after you've submitted
your, 241; whether to disclose disability on
your, 273–274. *See also* EA (early action)
applications; ED (early decision)
applications

Arizona State University, 73, 146

Artists. *See* Student artists

Asbury College (Kentucky), 75

Aspire (ACT-related test for younger
students), 137

Athletic recruitment: admissibility and
academic index (AI) required for, 249–250;
issues for the student athlete to consider,
244–246; making the commitment,
252–253; signs of coach interest in,
250–252; structure of college athletics
impacting, 243–244; understanding the
process of, 246–249; what if you are not
recruited, 253. *See also* National Collegiate
Athletic Association

Atlantic Bridge Program (international applicants), 239
Auditions: performing arts, 262–264; student artist preparation for, 258–259
Autism spectrum disorder, 266–267

Babson College, 74
Baccalaureate colleges, 74–75
Bankston, Tony, 201
Barnard College, 69, 78, 256
Bauld, Harry, 206
Beach, Barry, 260
Bentley College, 76
BigFuture website: information on college majors and careers on, 88–89; international student resources on, 294; to narrow down your college list, 110–111; net price calculators available on, 190; as tool to build college list, 103–104
Black, William, 29
Bagnoli, Joe, 40
Bollinger, Lee, 13
Boston College, 77, 157
Boston University, 211–212
Bowdoin College, 154, 244
Bowen, William, 39
Brandeis University, 77, 322
Brigham Young University, 77
Bright Futures Scholarship Program (Florida), 184
Brown University, 92
Bucknell University, 36, 67, 69, 73

California College of the Arts, 256
California Institute of Technology, 207
California Institute of the Arts, 75, 256
California State University, Chico, 243
California State University system, 134, 184
Caltech, 48, 72
Cambridge University (UK), 237–238
Campus safety: Cleary Report on crime statistics and, 86; college–student fit and issue of, 85–86
Campus size and community feel: college website as way to explore the, 112; college–student fit and issue of, 84–85; intellectual atmosphere, 86–87; liberal arts colleges, 69;

outside of class time, 87; research universities, 72; social life, 86
Campus social life: college–student fit and, 86; recreational time and activities, 87. See also Athletics and activities; Extracurricular activities
Canadian universities: applying for, 236–237; SAT, ACT, and SAT Subject Tests required by, 237; study abroad at, 79
Cappex Application, 204–205
Career planning, 87–94
Carnegie Mellon University, 193, 244
Carroll College (Montana), 75
Casper, Gerhard, 11
Catalogs (or college bulletins), 112–113, 295
Catholic colleges, 77
CBOs (community-based organizations) college access programs, 58
Certification of Finances (international student applicants), 306
Cheron, Elizabeth, 209
Claremont Colleges consortium, 68, 78
Claremont McKenna College, 68, 78, 279
Clark, Richard, 326
Clarkson University, 244
Class rank, 26–27
Clery Report, 86
Clinton, Hillary, 78
Coaches: how to assess real interest by, 250–252; NCAA recruitment guidelines followed by, 248–249; screening for student admissibility and academic index (AI), 249–250; understanding the recruiting process by, 246–248
Coalition Application: Coalition Locker, 204, 233; description of the, 204; essay word-length guidelines by the, 210; highlighting what you've accomplished on the, 232
Coca Cola Scholars Program Scholarships, 185
Colby College, 41, 179
Coleman, David, 128
Colgate University, 73
College access programs, 58–59
College Affordability and Transparency Center website, 104, 189
College fairs: virtual, 106–107; getting the most out of, 105–106

College Greenlight, 58
College lists: college search tools used to build, 103–105; financial considerations, 125–126, 188–190; how to begin building your, 101–103; how to narrow down your, 110–113,113–118, 121–123; length of, 123–124; meeting college representatives to build your, 105–109; selectivity and your, 119–121
College Navigator, 104
College partnership programs, 185–186
College priorities: college–student fit and issue of institutional mission and, 66; influence on college admissions decisions by, 24, 36–42
College programs abroad: in Canada, 79, 236–237; deadline differences, 236; Dutch example of English-taught programs in non-English-speaking country, 81–82; Foundation Year or Programme (UK, Ireland, or Holland) requirement, 241; language differences, 80; overview of, 78–79; paying for, 235–236; tuition, 79, 80, 81–82; understanding the differences among countries, 235; in the United Kingdom and Ireland, 79–81
College Scholarship Service Profile (CSS PROFILE), 166, 169–171
College search tools: 103–105
College Summit, 58
College visits: the "bench test" to end your, 114; how parents can help your, 117–118; narrowing down your college list through the, 113–118; parent accompany but stay back during, 341; transfer student applicants and, 287; YouniversityTV for virtual, 118
College Week Live (virtual college fair), 106–107
Colleges: admission decisions influenced by priorities of the, 50–51; admissions rates of, 8–9, 14–16; checking accreditation status of, 295; elite, 7–9, 11–14, 16–18; Ivy League, 8, 10–11, 39; need blind, need-aware, and full need policies of, 165, 179–180, 306; priorities and institutional mission of, 24, 36–42, 66; rankings of, 5–6, 8, 10–14; receiving personalized "search"

letter from, 109–110; test-optional, 148–149; watching out for similar names or names that may mislead you, 73; websites of individual, 111–113. *See also* Selective colleges
Colleges with special affiliations: Historically Black Colleges and Universities (HBCUs), 77; religious affiliations, 77; women's colleges, 77–78
College–student fit factors: campus size, 84–85; the intangibles to consider, 85–87; location, weather and culture, 65–66, 83–84
CollegeXpress, 105
Colorado School of Mines, 76
Colorado State University, 203
Columbia University, 78, 256
Common Application: "additional information" section of the, 214, 232; description of the, 202–203; essay word limit, 210; increasing use of, 6; international student applicants using, 304; SlideRoom portal for artist applications, 264; for transfer student applicants, 285
Common Data Set, 122
Community colleges: college–student fit at, 66–67; students transferring from, 281–288
Community service: admission decision influence of, 31; highlighting your accomplishments in, 232–235
Connecticut College, 208
Cooper Union (New York), 76
Cornell University, 161, 193
Costs. *See* Finances
Counseling and health services, 94
Counselors. *See* High school counselors; Independent college counselors
Coverdell Education Savings Accounts (Education IRAs), 195
Creighton University, 74
CSS PROFILE: deadline for, 217; description of the, 166–167, 169–170; differences in aid calculations of FAFSA and, 172–173; for international students, 306; net price calculators on schools using, 190; submitting the, 170–171

DACA (Deferred Action for Childhood Arrivals) program, 307, 308

Dahl, Margit, 205
Dale, Stacey, 17–18
Dance auditions, 263–264
Dartmouth College, 52
Davenport, David, 18
Davidson College, 77
Deacon, Charles, 37
Decisions. *See* Admissions decisions
Deferral decisions: handling ED (early
     decision), 160, 316–317; send fall semester
     grades to college that has sent, 218; what to
     do if you receive a, 317–318
Degrees. See Academic programs
Demonstrated interest: how to show your,
     231–232; increasing college yield by
     considering, 16; by wait-listed
     students, 327, 329
Denial decisions: handling ED (early
     decision), 160, 316–317; high school
     senior's remarks upon hearing the, 54; how
     the final decision is made, 52–53. *See also*
     Admission decisions
Dependents Education Assistance program
     (DEA), 184
Deposit ethics, 329–330
Development admits, 38
Disabilities: disclosing on application,
     273–274; federal government definition of,
     266–267; laws relevant to, 268–270; support
     for, 270–272. *See also* Students with
     disabilities
Disciplinary violations in high
     school, 224–225
"Displacement" financial aid rule, 186–187
Diversity: admissions decisions based on,
     40–41; college–student fit and issue of, 65;
     "fly-in programs," 40
DREAM Act proposed legislation, 307
Drexel University, 93
DRT (IRS Data Retrieval Tool), 168, 171
Dual-degree programs, 90–91
Duke University, 41, 108, 193
Dutch university system: applying for the,
     240–241; Foundation Year or Programme
     requirement of, 241; study abroad at
     the, 81–82
Dysgraphia, 267
Dyslexia, 267

EA (early action) applications: comparing
     different options for, 157; CSS PROFILE
     submission deadline for, 170; differences
     between ED (early decision) and, 146;
     follow the directions for, 202; honoring
     your commitment to, 157; making the
     decision for, 158–159; restrictions that may
     be placed on, 156–157. *See also*
     Applications
Eastern Illinois University, 243
ED (early decision) applications: advantages
     and disadvantages of, 151–156; class of
     2020 admission rates by percentage, 154;
     comparing different options for, 157; CSS
     PROFILE submission deadline for, 170;
     differences between EA (early action) and,
     156; ED I and ED II rounds of, 160–161;
     financial aid issue related to, 193–194;
     handling denial or deferral decisions, 160,
     316–317; have Plan B in place, 160;
     honoring your commitment to, 157;
     increasing college yield by accepting more,
     15–16; likely letters and early notification,
     161–162; making the decision for,
     158–159; overview of early acceptance programs,
     150–151; your college list used to select,
     124. *See also* Applications
ED (early decision) notifications: emotions of
     waiting and receiving, 314–315; financial
     aid issues, 193–194, 315–316; handling
     denied or deferred, 160, 316–317; how you
     will receive, 314; student acceptance of
     positive, 316; what to do once you've
     received the, 315
Education IRAs (Coverdell Education Savings
     Accounts), 195
Educational Opportunity Program (EOP)
     [University of California], 93
Educational quality: admission to graduate
     school and undergraduate, 18; belief that
     college rankings indicate, 13; characteris-
     tics of student, not college, as key to, 17–18;
     "I'll make more money if I graduate from
     elite college" myth, 16–17. *See also* Prestige
Educational Talent Search, 58
EducationUSA website, 294, 295, 296, 302
EFC (expected family contribution): college
     flexibility in determining the final, 178;

description of the, 172; evaluating the financial aid package and, 191; planning ahead when your child is young, 194–195; thinking about options for handling the, 188

Elite colleges: admissions selectivity of, 7–9; association between college selectivity and, 17; future income tied to characteristics of student and not, 17–18; myth of "I'll make more money if I graduate from," 16–18; ranking of, 11–14

Elizabethtown College (Pennsylvania), 75

Elon University, 74

Emory University, 244

Engagement beyond the classroom: community service and service to others, 31, 232–235; extracurricular activities, 30–31, 97, 232–235; follow your interests as best approach to, 32–33; increasing influence on admission decision by, 29–30; involvement in research, internships, and special programs, 32; tips on highlight what you've accomplished, 232–235; work experience, 31–32, 232–235.

English proficiency tests, 298–300, 309

Erasmus Programme (UK and Ireland), 80

Erdmann, David, 28

The essay: admissions decisions importance of, 34; getting inappropriate help on your, 213, 302–303; how colleges use, 34–35; how much they count in admissions decisions, 35; international student application, 302–303; SAT and ACT optional add-on, 131, 134, 139; transfer students and the Common Application, 285; why colleges ask for a written, 205–206; writing an effective personal, 205–215. *See also* Application preparation

Essay writing process: adhering to word limits, 210–211; for answering the "Tell us about yourself" question, 206–207; answering the "Why College X?" question, 211–212; importance of the "optional" questions, 213–215; look inward for a topic, 208–209; pay attention to short answer questions, 212; recommended steps to take for your, 215; show–don't tell advice for, 207; tell a story, 207–208; what is and is not appropriate help, 213; what topics to avoid and essay don'ts, 209–210

Expected Family Contribution. *See* EFC (expected family contribution)

Ethical behaviors: deposit ethics, 329–330; honesty on standardized tests, 297–298; parents modeling integrity and, 340–341; write your own essay and applications, 213, 302–303

Extracurricular activities: admission decision influence of, 30–31; homeschoolers and, 279; international student applicants, 290–291; tips for highlighting your high school, 232–235; transfer student applicants and, 285–286. *See also* Campus social life

FAFSA. *See* Free Application for Federal Student Aid (FAFSA)

Family Educational Rights and Privacy Act (FERPA), 225, 304, 308

Federal Supplemental Educational Opportunity Grants (FSEOG), 174

Finances: College Affordability and Transparency Center site on, 104; college programs abroad, 79, 80, 81–82; College Scorecard to compare affordability and, 104; financial aid to help cover, 125; international student applicants, 304–307; "net price calculators" for calculating, 125, 172, 189–190; paying for college abroad, 235–236; planning ahead when your child is young for, 194–195; tuition, 79, 80, 81–82, 104, 167, 180–181, 184, 189

Financial aid: calculating your, 167, 172–173, 189–190; "displacement" rule of, 186–187; Financial Aid Shopping Sheet for, 176; full need policies, 179, 180; international students and offers of, 305; key concepts for understanding, 165–166; need blind, need-aware, and full need, 165, 179–180, 185, 306; questions to ask colleges about, 188; revisiting before making acceptance decision, 323–324; two major types of, 164; for veterans and their families, 182–184; your college list and considerations of,

125–126, 188–190. *See also* Scholarships/ merit aid awards; Tuition

Financial aid calculation: CSS PROFILE's "institutional methodology" for, 170; differences between PROFILE and FAFSA, 172–173; EFC,172, 178, 188, 191, 194–195; FAFSA "federal methodology" formula for, 167–168; flexibility of colleges in determining the final, 178; IRS Data Retrieval Tool (DRT) for, 168, 171; the key equation for, 167

Financial aid package: appealing your offer, 192; ask if colleges will "match" another's offer of, 192–193; college differences in need-based, 177–178; components of the, 173–174; ED (early decision), 193–194, 315–316; evaluating after you've been accepted, 190–193; grants, 174, 176; how it is put together, 176; loans, 174–175, 176; understand what goes into the, 173–174; work study, 174

First-generation students: academic advising and support services to, 93; colleges interested in identifying, 41

Fit: be honest with yourself when choosing schools for, 343; for colleges with special affiliations, 76–78; for community colleges, 66–67; deciding which kind of college will provide your, 82–87; determining your priorities worksheet, 94–98; for earning your degree abroad, in English, 78–82; help your child make realistic choices for a good, 342; how to begin finding the, 63–64; how to get the advice and help you need to find your, 92–94; importance of predicting the, 62; for liberal arts colleges, 67–69; majors, careers, and curriculum issues of the, 87–92; for master's universities and baccalaureate colleges, 73–75; for research universities, 70–73; some questions to ask yourself to find the, 64–66; for specialized programs, 75–76. *See also* Student applicants

529 College Savings Plans, 170

Florida's Bright Futures Scholarship Program, 184

Foundation Year or Programme (UK, Ireland, or Holland), 241

Free Application for Federal Student Aid (FAFSA): deadlines for, 171, 217; description, federal methodology, and completion of the, 166–168; differences in calculating aid by PROFILE and, 172–173; for international students, 306; required for state need-based scholarship programs, 185; sometimes required for merit aid application, 182; verification process for, 171

FSEOG (Federal Supplemental Educational Opportunity Grants), 174

Furda, Eric, 162

Gap year: considering a, 330–332; post-graduate (PG) year option, 332–333; recommendations for a smooth, 333; self-directed, 333; taking it after you have been admitted, 331–332; taking one with plan to apply the following year, 332–333

Gates Millennial Scholars Program, 185

General education requirements, 91–92. *See also* Majors

Georgetown University, 48, 77, 108, 202

Georgia's Zell Miller scholarships, 184

Get Me To College website, 40

GI Bill: the Post 9/11, 183; Selective Reserve, 184

Golden, Daniel, 38

Golden Door Scholars program, 186

Gore, Joseph, 334

Grades (GPA): caution against senioritis and declining, 334–335; class rank and, 26–27; college recalculation of your, 25; homeschooler transcripts and, 277–278; importance of both course load and, 25; putting grades in context, 26–28; school profile included with transcript of, 27–28; transfer applications and college course, 284. *See also* Academic record; Transcripts

Graham, Martha, 259

Greenberg, Joseph, 115

Hamilton College, 92, 201

Hampshire College, 68

Hargadon, Fred, 35

Haring, Chris Hooker, 305

Harvard University: 4, 43, 108, 157

Harvey Mudd College, 67, 68, 78

Haverford College, 77

Hawkins, David, 26

Health and counseling services, 94

Hendrix College, 69, 162

High Point University (North Carolina), 75

High school counselors: building your college list role of, 101–103; college admissions process role of your, 57; letters of recommendation from, 224, 303–304; special case of disciplinary infractions and role of, 224–225.

Higher Education Consultants Association (HECA), 60

Hispanic students: admissions decisions for underrepresented, 40; college selectivity and future income of, 17–18

Historically Black Colleges and Universities (HBCUs), 77

"Holistic" admissions process, 47–48

Holland universities: applying to, 240–241; Foundation Year or Programme requirement of, 241; study abroad at the, 81–82

Homeschoolers: activities participation by, 279; colleges welcome, 276–277; grades and transcripts of, 277–278; interviews of, 279–280; keep records and highlight the homeschool experience, 280; letters of recommendations for, 278–279

Honors programs (research universities), 73

Hooks (tags): considering the fairness of, 42; description of admissions, 36; development admits, 38; diversity, 40–41; international status as a, 291–292; legacy status, 21–22, 36–38; recruited athletes, 38–39; special talents, 41–42

Howard University, 77

IELTS (International English Language Testing System), 299–300, 309

Ifill, Gwen, 78

Independent college counselors, 59–60

Indiana University: 115, 162

Individuals with Disabilities Education Act (IDEA), 268

International Baccalaureate (IB) program: description of, 24; required by Oxford and Cambridge universities, 238; school profile on, 27

International student applicants: advantages and disadvantages of being an, 290; application tips, 300–304; college search tools available to, 294, 305–306; English proficiency tests for, 298–300, 309; financial issues, 304–307; getting the application completed, 300–304; growing community of, 310; how colleges define, 309; how your application will be reviewed, 292–293; interviews of, 304; agents and consultants, 295–296; standardized tests and, 296–298; strategies for deciding where to apply, 293–296; student visas for, 295, 296; undocumented, 307–309; what colleges are looking for in, 290–292

Internships, 32

Interviews: alumni interviewers conducting the, 218; arranging the, 228–231; frequently asked questions, 229–230; homeschoolers, 279–280; informational versus evaluative, 225–226; international student applicants, 304; as misunderstood part of college admissions process, 35–36; tips for shining in your, 225–231; transfer student applicants, 287

Inzer, Monica, 327

Iowa State University, 146, 181

Ireland universities: applying for, 239–240; Foundation Year or Programme requirement of, 241; studying abroad at UK and, 79–81;

IRS Data Retrieval Tool (DRT), 168, 171

Ivy League colleges: academic index (AI) required for athlete admissibility, 250; the "admissions advantage" for athletes at, 39; description and origins of term, 10; matching financial aid offers offered by other, 193; now synonymous with prestige and academic reputation, 11

Jack Kent Cooke Foundation College Scholars
    Program, 185
Jacksonville State University (Alabama), 74
Johns Hopkins University: 72, 154, 208
Jones, Marilee, 60–61
Juilliard School, 75, 76, 256

The K & W Guide to College Programs and
    Services for Students with Learning
    Differences, 269, 272
Kalamazoo College, 211
Kent, Jennie, 305
Kenyon College, 244
Kostell, Stacey, 289
Kravets, Marybeth, 272
Krueger, Alan, 17–18

Lafayette College, 67
Landmark College, 272
Lawrence University, 212, 256
Learning disabilities: common types of, 267;
    disclosing on application, 273–274; federal
    government definition of, 266; special
    accommodations for standardized testing
    due to, 146–147, 267, 274–275; student
    success versus student access, 269;
    submitted documentation of, 147; Tier
    One, Tier Two, Tier Three school support
    services for, 270–272
Legacy status: boost provided by, 36–37;
    controversy over admissions based on,
    37–38. *See also* Parents
Leider, Anna and Robert, 176
Letters of recommendation: waive your FERPA
    right to see the, 225, 304; get them in on
    time, 217; get to know your teachers prior to
    asking for, 34; homeschoolers and, 278–279;
    how many letters should you submit,
    222–223; international student applicants,
    303–304; student artists, 259; tips for getting
    great, 219–225; transfer student applicants,
    286–287; what admissions officers look for
    in, 33; wide variation in usefulness of, 33–34
Levin, Sarah, 39
Levy, Jeff, 305
Lewis and Clark College, 108
Lewis, Stephen, 19

Liberal arts colleges: academic programs of, 68;
    campus size and community feel of, 69; the
    college–student fit at, 67–69
Likely letters/early notification,
    161–162
Linfield College, 244
Loans: description of, 174–175; different types
    of, 175; "no-loan" policy on grants
    replacing, 176
Location: college–student fit and issue of,
    65–66, 83–84
Macalester College, 69, 179
Majors: college–student fit issue of, 87–91;
    different paths to the same career, 90;
    dual-degree programs, 90–91; relationship
    between career and, 88–89; selecting, 88;
    student artists pursuing the arts, 254–257;
    3/2 programs, 89–90; United Kingdom
    and Ireland universities, 80. *See also*
    Academic programs; General education
    requirements
Manhattan College, 243
Marthers, Paul, 36
Martin, Dallas, 187
Maryville University, 162
Master's universities, 73–74, 75
Matching financial aid packages,
    192–193
Mayher, Bill, 7
Medical conditions, 267
Merit aid awards. *See* Scholarships/merit
    aid awards
Merrow, John, 52
Mexican American Legal Defense
    Education Fund, 308
Miami University (Ohio), 73
Michigan State University, 162
Middlebury College, 144, 154, 322
Mills College, 256
Millsaps College, 144
MIT, 147, 193, 202
Montoya, James, 291
Morehead State University (Kentucky), 74
Morehouse College, 77
Mt. Holyoke College, 68, 78
"Multicultural fly-in programs," 40
Music auditions, 263

NAFSA website, 305
National Association for College Admission Counseling (NACAC) website: college fairs listed on, 106; colleges still seeking applicants posted on, 6; Performing and Visual Arts College Fairs sponsored by, 256–257; "Principles of Good Practice" on wait lists by, 325–326; student visas information on, 295
National Association of Intercollegiate Athletics (NAIA), 74, 75, 243, 245–246, 249
National Association of Student Financial Aid Administrators, 189
National Collegiate Athletic Association (NCAA): Divisions I, II, and III, 69, 243–244, 245, 249, 250, 251, 252, 253; master's universities as typically Division II, 74; "official visit" rules of, 251; recruitment guidelines by, 248–249
National Hispanic Recognition Program, 146
National Immigration Law Center, 308
National Junior College Athletic Association (NJCAA), 243
National Letter of Intent (NLI), 252–253
National Merit Scholarship, 145–146, 181
National Portfolio Day Association, 26
Naviance: scattergrams on college data created through, 122; SuperMatch college search engine using, 102, 104
Need-aware policies, 179–180
Need-based aid: description of, 165; differences between colleges offering, 177–178; FAFSA required for state scholarship programs, 185; financial aid package for, 173–176; forms to file for, 170–171; getting an estimate of your, 172–173; how colleges determine your, 166–170; loans as, 175; need-aware vs. need blind admission policies, 179–180, 306; principle behind, 166
Need blind admissions: colleges with policies on, 179, 180; international Canadian and Mexican students included in, 306
Net price calculators, 125, 172, 189–190
The Netherlands university system: applying for the, 240–241; Foundation Year or Programme requirement of, 241; study abroad at the, 81–82
New England Conservatory, 75
New England Small College Athletic Conference (NESCAC), 250
New York University, 144, 244
"No-loan" policy, 176
Northeastern University, 41, 93–94, 322
Northwestern University, 154

Oberlin College, 256
Occupational Outlook Handbook (online resource), 104
Ohio State University, 203
Optional add-on essay (SAT/ACT), 131, 134, 139
Organization scholarship awards, 185
O'Shea, Joseph, 330
Out-of-pocket cost. *See* Net price calculators
Oxford University (UK), 237–238

Pace University, 243–244
Parents: advice for, 336–342; college admissions process and appropriate role of, 60, 61; and child's essay, 213; financial aid information required from, 168, 170, 171; financial planning when your child is young, 194–195; helping with college visit, 117–118; over-involvement, 60–61; respecting your child's privacy, 315; a word about standardized tests to, 149. *See also* Legacy status
Parker, Thomas, 38
Pauls, Kenton, 297
Pell Grants, 174, 176, 185
Pemberton, Stephen, 193
Pennsylvania State University, 73
Performing and Visual Arts College Fairs, 256–257
Performing arts audition, 262–264
Personal qualities: admission decision influence of, 33–36; the admission essay to assess, 34–35; evaluated using a numerical rating, 49–50; interviews of applicants to assess, 35–36, 225–232; letters of recom-

mendations to assess, 33–34, 219–225, 279. *See also* Special talents

Phillips, Delsie, 206

Physical environment. *See* Campus size and community feel

Pitzer College, 41, 68, 227

PLUS loans (Parent Loans to Undergraduate Students), 175

Poch, Bruce, 278

Poirot, William, 210

Ponoma College, 68

Portfolios: for applying to British schools, 261; documenting your, 261; National Portfolio Day Association sponsoring portfolio day events, 260–261; résumés and recommendations, 259; visual arts, 260

Posse Foundation, 186

Post 9/11 GI Bill, 183

Post-graduate (PG) year, 332–333

PPY (prior-prior year), 168, 170

Pre-professional advising, 93–94

PreSAT/PreACT: checking the box for receiving information from colleges on, 109; how they fit into the application process, 137

Prestige: belief that college rankings indicate, 13; college–student fit and issue of, 65. *See also* Educational quality

Princeton University, 36, 157

Prior-prior year (PPY), 168, 170

Priority deadlines (rolling admissions), 163

Private high schools: decreasing use of class rank by, 26–27; letters of recommendation from public versus, 33–34

Procrastinating application, 162–163, 200–201, 344

PROFILE. *See* CSS PROFILE

Programs abroad. *See* College programs abroad

Providence College, 74

PSAT (PSAT-NMSQT): checking the box for receiving information from colleges on, 109; how they fit into the application process, 137; National Merit Scholarship semifinalists based on score of, 145–146; special accommodations for, 274

QuestBridge, 185–186

Race-sensitive admissions, 40

Rankings: belief in "quality" or "prestige" association with, 13; concerns about, 13–14; interest focused on small group of, 10–11; Ivy League, 8, 10–11; ranking of, 11–14; reasons behind popularity of, 14; social media investment by, 5–6; United Kingdom universities, 81; *U.S. News and World Report's*, 11–13, 14

Recruited athletes: the admissions advantage of, 39; admissions decisions on, 38–39; definition of a, 39

Reed College, 108

Regional compacts, 189

Regis University, 244

Religious affiliation colleges, 77

Research activities (student applicants), 32

Research universities: academic programs of, 70–71; athletics and activities of, 72; campus size and community feel of, 72; college–student fit at, 70–73; Division I teams of, 72; honors programs of, 73; the role of research at, 71–72

Residence halls: alcohol- and substance-free, 87; college–student fit and, 85

Résumés (student artist), 259

Rhode Island School of Design, 75

Rhodes College, 69, 231–232

Ringling School of Art and Design, 256

Rolling admissions, 162–163

Rollins College, 28, 74

Rose-Hulman Institute of Technology (Indiana), 76

Rubinoff, Matt, 58

St. John's College, 201

St. Olaf College, 77

Saint Louis University, 162

Saint Mary's College (California), 74

SALT program (University of Arizona), 272, 273

San Francisco State University, 74

San Jose State University, 74

Santa Clara University, 211

SAR (Student Aid Report), 169

SAT Subject Tests: homeschoolers, 278; overview of the, 147–148; required for international colleges, 237, 238; special accommodations for standardized, 146–147, 267, 268, 274–275

SAT/ACT tests: admissions decision role of, 28–29; all about the scores and superscoring, 132–136, 143, 144–145, 278; checking the box for receiving information from colleges on, 109; comparison of the SAT and ACT, 129–134; concerns over the test prep industry, 29; concordance table to compare scores of SAT and ACT, 138; deciding whether to take the SAT or ACT, 138–139; essay optional add-on of, 131, 134, 139; how much they count in the application, 134–136; international student applicants and, 296–298; National Merit Scholarship and, 145–146; origins and evolution of, 127–128; practice tests for, 138; Question-and-Answer Service for copy of your, 143; required by colleges abroad, 237, 239–240; school profile on distributions of, 27–28; special accommodations for, 146–147, 267, 274–275; submitting scores to colleges, 217; test fees, 142, 143; test-optional schools and, 148–149; test prep for, 29, 139–142, 297–298; a word to parents about, 149. *See also* Standardized tests

Savings plans/programs: Education IRAs (Coverdell Education Savings Accounts), 195; "financial aid advantaged," 194–195; "Tax-advantaged" savings strategy (529 state plan), 195

Sawyer, Diane, 78

Schiffman, Jeff, 214

Scholarship search service, 187

Scholarships/merit aid awards: apply early for, 186; awards cannot exceed cost of attendance, 186–187; from businesses and organizations, 185; college partnership programs, 185–186; community-based, 186; controversy over, 182; description of, 165, 180; evaluating aid after you've been accepted, 190–193; FAFSA sometime required for applying for, 182; grants, 174, 185; maximizing your changes of receiving, 181–182; National Hispanic Recognition Program, 146; National Merit Scholarship, 145–146, 181; state scholarships, 184–185; thinking early about applying for, 188; using a scholarship search service, 187; Veteran financial aid programs and, 182–184. *See also* Financial aid; Tuition

School profile, 27–28

School report, 28

Scripps College, 68, 78

Seattle University, 243

Selective colleges: admissions process at the most, 56–57; association between income and, 17; of colleges by admissions rates for class of 2020, 8–9; definition of, 7, 9; importance of fit to, 18–19; understanding what it is all about, 7; your college list and consideration of, 119–121. *See also* Colleges

Selective Reserve GI Bill, 184

Self-directed gap year, 333

Senioritis, 334–335

SEVIS (Student and Exchange Visitor Information System), 295

Shapiro, Morton Owen, 178

Skidmore College, 67

SlideRoom portal (Common App), 264

Smith College, 68, 78, 212

Social changes, 5

Social life. *See* Campus social life

Sophia University (Japan), 78

Southern Oregon University, 213

Special circumstances: homeschoolers, 276–280; students with disabilities, 146–147, 266–276; transferring from community colleges, 281–288; undocumented student applicants, 307–309

Special interests and hobbies, 234

Special talents: admissions decisions preference of, 41–42; filmmakers, writers, and theater tech and design, 261–265; student artists, 253–261; student athlete and athletic recruitment, 242–253. *See also* Accomplishments; Personal qualities

Specialized colleges, 75–76

Spelman College, 77

Spring admits, 321–322

Standardized tests: admissions decision role of, 28–29; all about scores and superscoring, 132–136, 143, 144–145, 278; CAT (computer adaptive testing) used for, 129; cheating on, 297–298; checking the box for receiving information from colleges on, 109; concerns over the test prep industry, 29; concordance table to compare, 138; deciding which test to take, 138–139; how much do they count?, 134–136; international student applicants and, 296–298; National Merit Scholarship and, 145–146; overview of the, 127–134; the PSAT, PSAT10, PreACT, Aspire, 109, 137, 145–146, 274; required by some Canadian universities, 237; scattergrams to help interpret college data on, 122–123; school profile on distributions of, 27–28; to show proficiency in English, 298–300; special accommodations for, 146–147, 267, 274–275; submitting scores to colleges, 217; test-optional schools and, 148–149; test prep for, 29, 139–142, 297–298; a word to parents about, 149. *See also* SAT/ACT testing

Stanford University: 36, 108, 157,193, 212, 243

State scholarships, 184–185

Statement of purpose (student artists), 259

Steidel, Michael, 299

Stephens College, 78

Stetson University, 162

Stony Brook University, 162

Strive for College, 58–59

Stroud, Jonathan, 208

Student Aid Report (SAR), 169

Student applicants: acceptance decision by, 316, 318–324; building your college list of where to apply, 101–126; colleges sponsoring regional events for parents and, 108; demonstrated interest by, 16, 231–232, 327, 329; deposit ethics for, 329–330; e-mail address that reflects maturity of, 216; educational quality determined by characteristics of, 17–18; explaining high school disciplinary violations, 224–225; first-generation, 41, 93; getting applications in early vs. procrastination by, 162–163, 200–201, 344; homeschoolers, 276–280; international, 289–310; parting thoughts for, 342–345; receiving personalized "search" letter from colleges, 109–110; remarks by one on her denial, 54; senioritis, 334–335; social media postings by, 216; students with disabilities, 146–147, 266–276; taking a gap year, 330–333; transferring from community colleges, 281–288; undocumented, 307–309; wait listed, 16, 324–329. *See also* Admissions decisions; Applicant pool; Fit

Student artist applications: assembling your work, 260; evaluation of your, 265; portfolios and auditions, 258–261; process of the, 257–258; résumés and recommendations, 259; showcasing your artistic talents as part of, 264–265; statement of purpose, 259; visual arts portfolio, 260; the "Why us?" question, 260

Student artists: application process for the, 257–261; filmmakers, writers, and theater tech and design, 261–264; multiple options for the, 253–254; portfolios and auditions, 258–261; pursuing the arts as major, 254–257; showcasing your artistic talents, 264–265

Student athletes: the academic index (AI) and, 250; admissibility of, 249–250; athletic recruitment of, 246–249; how to assess real interest by a coach, 250–252; if you are not recruited, 253; issues to consider for the, 244–246; National Letter of Intent (NLI) and making the commitment, 252–253; options available to, 242–243; structure of college athletics and, 243–244; time commitments of, 245

Student support services: academic advising, 92–94; advance planning by inquiring

SAT/ACT tests (*Continued*)
about, 94; advance planning to finding out about, 94; categories of disabilities support and, 270–272; health and counseling, 94; *The K & W Guide to College Programs and Services for Students with Learning Differences* (Kravets), 269, 272; pre-professional, 93–94

Student visas, 295, 296

Students with disabilities: blind (or visually impaired students), 146–147; categories of disabilities support for, 270–272; choosing colleges that meet your needs, 272–273; contacting disabilities services office after acceptance, 276; definition of disability, 266–267; laws that apply in college, 268–270; laws that apply to high school, 267–268; the most common disabilities, 267; standardized testing accommodations, 146–147, 267, 274–275; whether to disclose disability on application, 273–274.

Subsidized federal direct loans, 175

Summer activities, 234

SuperMatch college search engine (Naviance), 102, 104

Superscoring SAT/ACT, 144–145

Swarthmore College, 77

Syracuse University, 211

Tags. *See* Hooks (tags)

TEACH Grants Program, 174

Test-optional schools, 148–149

Test prep: different forms available for, 140–141; how does it work?, 139–140; industry grown around, 29; what is covered in, 141–142

Test scores: comparing SAT and ACT, 132–134; concordance table to compare SAT or ACT, 138; homeschoolers and, 278; how much do they count?, 134–135; middle 50 percent of, 135; percentile and likelihood of admission and, 135–136; superscoring SAT/ACT, 144–145; TOEFL (Test of English as a Foreign Language), 298–299

Testing accommodations: Section 504 on, 268; standardized tests, 146–147, 267, 274–275

Texas A&M University in College Station, 72

Theater auditions, 262–263

TOEFL (Test of English as a Foreign Language), 298–300, 309

Toor, Rachel, 15

Trachtenberg, Stephen, 181

Transcripts: college review of final, 334–335; homeschooler, 277–278; international student applications, 300–301; school profile included with, 27–28. *See also* Grades (GPA)

Transfer student applicants: advising, visits, and interviews of, 287–288; assessing if transferring is right for you, 282–283; Common Application and essay for, 285; extracurricular activities of, 285–286; how the application process differs for, 284–287; letters you will need, 286–287; reasons to transfer colleges, 281

Trinity College (Hartford), 69, 73, 244

Trinity University (Dublin), 239, 241

Trinity University (Texas), 24

TRIO programs, 58

Tufts University, 41, 179, 207, 208

Tuition: College Affordability and Transparency Center site on costs of, 104; college programs abroad, 79, 80, 81–82; College Scorecard to compare affordability and, 104; financial aid calculation consideration of, 167; regional compacts for reducing, 189. *See also* Financial aid; Scholarships/merit aid awards

Underrepresented student applicants, 40

Undocumented student applicants, 307–309

Unified Auditions, 262–263

Union College, 67, 244

United Kingdom universities: Foundation Year or Programme requirement of, 241; preparing art portfolios for, 261; studying abroad at, 79–81; UCAS (Universities and Colleges Admissions Service) online application for, 237–239

Universal College Application: description and when to use the, 203, 210; essay word-length guidelines by the, 210; highlighting what you've accomplished on the, 232; what they ask teachers writing letters of recommendation, 224

University College Cork (Ireland), 239

University College Dublin (Ireland), 239

University of Alabama, 181, 243

University of Arizona's SALT program, 272, 273

University of California, Berkeley: 4, 3

University of California, Davis, 70

University of California, Los Angeles, 54–55, 73

University of California system, 41, 54–55, 93, 144, 171, 184, 202

University of Chicago, 4

University of Georgia, 144

University of Leiden (The Netherlands), 240

University of Massachusetts at Amherst, 68

University of Miami (Miami), 73

University of Michigan: 37, 73, 203

University of Minnesota, 202

University of New Mexico, 146

University of North Carolina at Chapel Hill, 41

University of Notre Dame: 77, 157, 243

University of Oklahoma, 146, 181

University of Oregon, 202, 207

University of Pennsylvania: 36, 108

University of Puget Sound, 108, 213

University of Richmond, 69, 73

University of Rochester, 256

University of St. Andrews (UK), 238–239

University of Southern California, 322

University of Texas, Austin: 41, 73

University of Vermont, 203

University of Virginia: 37, 41, 171

University of Wisconsin, 203

University of Wisconsin, Parkside, 243

Unsubsidized federal direct loans, 175

Upward Bound, 58

U.S. News and World Report college rankings: formula used to come up with the, 12–13; origins and description since 1983, 11; used by students and parents, 14

US Student and Exchange Visitor Program, 295

Utrecht University (Holland), 78

Veteran financial aid programs: Dependents Education Assistance program (DEA), 184; overview of, 182–183; Post 9/11 GI Bill, 183; Selective Reserve GI Bill, 184; Yellow Ribbon Program, 183

Villanova University, 74

Virtual college fair (College Week Live), 106–107

Visits. See College visits

Visual arts portfolio, 260

Wait lists: how they work, 324–325; what to do when you are on a, 326–327; when and how will you hear if accepted, 328–329

Wake Forest University, 227

Wellesley College, 48, 78

Wesleyan College (Georgia), 73

Wesleyan College (Texas), 73

Wesleyan University (Connecticut): 48–50, 69, 77, 92, 179

Wheaton College (Massachusetts), 322

Whitman College, 108, 244

Willamette University, 108

Williams College, 154

Women's colleges, 77–78

Work experience: admission decision influence of, 31–32; highlighting what you've accomplished, 232–235

Work study programs, 174

Wright, Ann, 56

Yale University: 21–22, 54, 157

Yellow Ribbon Program, 183

Yield, 15–16, 231–232

YouniversityTV, 118

ZeeMee (online multimedia tool), 233

Zell Miller scholarships (Georgia), 184

Zinsser, William, 213